Trust and Confidence in Government and Public Services

Trust and confidence are topical issues. Pundits claim that citizens trust governments and public services increasingly less—identifying a powerful new erosion of confidence that, in the United States, goes back at least to Watergate in the 1970s. Recently, media exposure in the United Kingdom about MP expenses has been extensive, and a court case ruled in favour of publishing expense claims and against exempting MPs from the scrutiny which all citizens are subject to under 'freedom of information'. As a result, revelations about everything from property speculation to bespoke duck pond houses have fuelled public outcry, and survey evidence shows that citizens increasingly distrust the government with public resources.

This book gathers together arguments and evidence to answer questions such as: What is trust? Can trust be boosted through regulation? What role does leadership play in rebuilding trust? How do trust and confidence affect public services? The chapters in this collection explore these questions across several countries and different sectors of public-service provision: health, education, social services, the police, and the third sector. The contributions offer empirical evidence about how the issues of trust and confidence differ across countries and sectors, and develop ideas about how trust and confidence in government and public services may adjust in the information age.

Sue Llewellyn is professor of accountability and management control and director of the Herbert Simon Institute at Manchester Business School, University of Manchester, UK.

Stephen Brookes is a senior fellow in public policy and management at Manchester Business School, University of Manchester, UK. He is editor (with K. Grint) of *The New Public Leadership Challenge* (2010).

Ann Mahon is a senior lecturer in health and public sector management at Manchester Business School, University of Manchester, UK. She is editor (with K. Walshe and N. Chambers) of *A Reader in Health Policy and Management* (2009).

Routledge Critical Studies in Public Management

Edited by Stephen Osborne

The study and practice of public management has undergone profound changes across the world. Over the last quarter century, we have seen

- increasing criticism of public administration as the over-arching framework for the provision of public services,
- the rise (and critical appraisal) of the 'New Public Management' as an emergent paradigm for the provision of public services,
- the transformation of the 'public sector' into the cross-sectoral provision of public services, and
- the growth of the governance of inter-organizational relationships as an essential element in the provision of public services

In reality these trends have not so much replaced each other as elided or co-existed together—the public policy process has not gone away as a legitimate topic of study, intra-organizational management continues to be essential to the efficient provision of public services, whist the governance of inter-organizational and inter-sectoral relationships is now essential to the effective provision of these services.

Further, whilst the study of public management has been enriched by contribution of a range of insights from the 'mainstream' management literature it has also contributed to this literature in such areas as networks and inter-organizational collaboration, innovation and stakeholder theory.

This series is dedicated to presenting and critiquing this important body of theory and empirical study. It will publish books that both explore and evaluate the emergent and developing nature of public administration, management and governance (in theory and practice) and examine the relationship with and contribution to the over-arching disciplines of management and organizational sociology.

Books in the series will be of interest to academics and researchers in this field, students undertaking advanced studies of it as part of their undergraduate or postgraduate degree and reflective policy makers and practitioners.

Trust and Confidence in Government and Public Services

Edited by Sue Llewellyn, Stephen Brookes and Ann Mahon

Routledge
Taylor & Francis Group

NEW YORK AND LONDON

First published 2013
by Routledge
711 Third Avenue, New York, NY 10017

Simultaneously published in the UK
by Routledge
2 Park Square, Milton Park, Abingdon, Oxon OX14 4RN

*Routledge is an imprint of the Taylor & Francis Group,
an informa business*

Library of Congress Cataloging-in-Publication Data

Trust and confidence in government and public services / edited by Sue
    Llewellyn, Stephen Brookes and Ann Mahon.
        pages cm. — (Routledge critical studies in public management ; 12)
    Includes bibliographical references and index.
    1. Public administration—United States—Public opinion.   2. Trust—
United States.   I. Llewellyn, Sue.   II. Brookes, Stephen, 1955–
III. Mahon, Ann.
    JK421.T87 2013
    320.97301'9—dc23
    2012040274

ISBN: 978-0-415-89619-1 (hbk)
ISBN: 978-0-203-54834-9 (ebk)

Typeset in Sabon
by Apex CoVantage, LLC

Contents

PART III
Trust and Citizens' Confidence in Public Services

PART IV
Conclusion

Acknowledgements

We thank all the presenters and participants at the workshop 'Has trust in government and confidence in public services been eroded?' run by the Herbert Simon Institute for Public Policy and Management at the University of Manchester in October 2009. The quality of the discussion and people's enthusiasm to take the debate further encouraged us to embark on this edited volume. Many of the presenters are also contributors but more joined us along the way. We thank our contributors for adding to the international dimensions of the debate, taking us into diverse areas of public service delivery and providing a nuanced discussion on the complexity of the trust and confidence issues. We also thank Sarah Campbell for her patience over the editing of the volume and, lastly, Chris Wood for his excellent support throughout the process of bringing the book to fruition.

Sue Llewellyn, Stephen Brookes, and Ann Mahon
November 2012

1 Introduction

Trust and Confidence in Government and Public Services

Sue Llewellyn, Stephen Brookes and Ann Mahon

CONTRIBUTIONS AND AIMS OF THE BOOK

This book evolved from a workshop entitled 'Has trust in government and confidence in public services been eroded?' which was hosted in October 2009 by the Herbert Simon Institute for Public Policy and Management at Manchester Business School, University of Manchester. Many contributors to this volume were participants at this workshop, where there was intense debate on many complex issues. In this book we garner arguments and evidence to address some of these contentious issues, such as: What is trust? Is trust different from confidence? Does trust depend on shared values and confidence in performance? Does it make sense to speak about trusting institutions (such as governments) or can we only trust people we know? Does public trust matter for the business of government and the delivery of public services—for example, does declining trust correlate with loss of democratic values and/or tax avoidance? Does transparency (e.g. the provision of information and public inquiries) about the performance of governments and public services increase trust and confidence? Can trust be augmented through regulation? Is trust emergent in networks? What role does leadership and management play in building trust?

ARGUMENTS AND EVIDENCE ON TRUST AND CONFIDENCE

Trust and confidence are topical issues. On the basis of evidence of declining trust in several advanced democracies (Canada, Sweden, the United Kingdom [UK] and the United States [US]), Hardin (2006) questions whether we are now living in an 'age of distrust'. O'Neill (2002, p. 9) speaks of an apparent 'crisis of trust' to the extent that '"loss of trust" has become a cliché of our times.' Many claim that citizens now trust governments and public services much less, identifying a powerful erosion of confidence and credibility that, for example, in the US, goes back to the Vietnam war in the 1960s and Watergate in the early 1970s (see, for example, Hardin, 2006, p. 5; Putnam, 1995a, 1995b, 2000; Lynn, this volume). Nye, Zelikow and

King (1997, p. 1) report that back in 1964, three-quarters of Americans trusted the federal government to do the right thing most of the time: thirty years later only one-quarter did. Currently, pollsters in the UK report the following: only 16% of the population trust politicians (Ipsos MORI, 2008); 77% of the population do not trust politicians to tell the truth (ComRes, 2012a); 68% of the public think that most Members of Parliament (MPs) make a lot of money out of using public office improperly (Ipsos MORI, 2009). Over governmental control and competence, only 18% of the public trust the government to regulate the banks (Dispatches, 2012) and over two-thirds of people do not trust the government's handling of the National Health Service [NHS] (ComRes, 2012b). Government is less trusted than other institutions. Ipsos MORI (2008) compared trust across seven prominent UK organizations/collectives: the British Broadcasting Corporation [BBC]; big British companies; the Church of England; the government; the military; media in general; and the NHS. The government was least trusted, with the BBC commanding most trust, closely followed by the NHS. Aside from statistics such as these and other evidence on trust and confidence, this volume adds to the conceptual background on both.

The chapters in this book, as befit their specific questions, adopt somewhat varying definitions of trust, but an overarching theme is citizens' expectations that government (and public officials) will be honest and competent, even without scrutiny. One starting point in understanding trust, therefore, is to suggest that it is most easily established within the context of shared values on honesty and competence along with knowledge gained through experience (Barber, 1983; Coleman, 1988; Gillespie and Mann, 2004; Jones and George, 1998). Such a perspective signals more difficulty in creating trust in institutions and public officials than building trust between individuals who know each other. However, a counter argument is that the public realize that institutions locate individuals in roles that have certain fixed practices and codes of conduct to try to ensure ethical behaviour (Bottery, 2003, p. 249). Within organizations, behaviour and relationships are, at least in part, driven by institutionalized role expectations. Invoking trust as an aspect of social capital within social organization enables trust between individuals and individuals' trust in institutions to be built on the same foundations. For example, Portes (1998) states that Pierre Bourdieu was the first to define social capital as 'the aggregate of actual or potential resources which are linked to the possession of a durable network of more or less institutionalized relationships of mutual acquaintance or recognition' (Bourdieu, 1985, p. 248). Such a perspective views social capital not just as an individual asset but as inherent in all forms of social organization. Putnam (1993, p. 167) sees social capital as 'features of social organization, such as trust, norms and networks.' In consequence, where individuals perceive that an institution, such as government, or a public service, such as healthcare, has social capital, in that it embeds their values, reflects their norms and meets their expectations, trust can form. Although individuals' direct experience may be limited and intimate knowledge is lacking, the public can and do trust some institutions. For example, the polls (referred to above) show high levels of trust in two UK institutions: the BBC and the NHS. But in the absence of intimate knowledge, such trust may only be sustained through continued positive feedback on institutional integrity in the media. When the institutional integrity of an institution is challenged by the media, levels of trust are likely to decrease unless swift actions are taken to restore trust and rebuild confidence. At the time of writing trust in the BBC is undergoing unprecedented challenge from politicians, the media and the public. The long-term impact of the 'Jimmy Savile scandal' and the management of the 'Newsnight Investigation' on the historically high levels of trust remains to be seen.

Giddens (2002, p. 13) comments on how, in relation to government, the media increasingly structure and filter the dialogue between politicians and citizens, requiring politicians to respond to media stories on a daily basis. This media scrutiny may be most intense for politicians but applies to other institutions, also. For example, although public trust in the UK NHS is still high, it is no longer 'Britain's only immaculate institution' (Klein, 1995, p. 229). There is evidence that less trust in the NHS may be linked to the changing public perception of doctors (Eve and Hodgkin, 1997). Edwards, Kornacki and Silversin (2002) report that doctors, themselves, perceive a loss of public trust which they link to much more media hostility towards the medical profession. The public now seem to have a more instrumental view of all the professions (Broadbent, Dietrich and Roberts, 1997; O'Neill, 2002, pp. 43–59; Mahon, this volume).

Although this book is about public trust, we should mention, briefly, that 'trust' is experienced by individuals and, therefore, has a psychological dimension. Jones and George (1998) suggest that an individual's propensity to trust is driven by their values, attitudes, moods and emotions. Rotter (1980) studied the characteristics of trusting individuals, he found that those who trust other people are more likely to be trustworthy themselves and that trust is psychologically rewarding. 'Trusters don't need immediate reciprocity: their faith in others rests on an optimistic world view and a sense of personal control that gives them a psychological cushion against occasional bad experiences' (Uslaner and Badescu, 2002, p. 31). Such perspectives imply that any decline in public (or collective) trust in government and/or public services may have a negative impact on any individual's propensity to trust which, in turn, damages their psychological well-being.

If there is a meaningful distinction between public trust and confidence, public confidence may be more linked to indications of good performance, whilst trust is more driven by perceptions of public integrity and shared values (Hardin, 2006, p. 69). So paradoxically, although trust and confidence are clearly interwoven, it may be possible to maintain value-based trust in a relatively low-performing institution or have confidence in the performance of a less-than-principled public service. For government, economic performance appears to be the main confidence issue (see Lynn, this volume). The declining trust in government charted by Nye, Zelikow and King (1997, p. 6) was accompanied by judgements that government was 'wasteful and inefficient' (81% of respondents) and 'spent too much money on the wrong things' (79% of respondents). For public services, personal experience and media exposure drive confidence judgements (see Gunter and Hall, this volume). Having said this, if the concept of trust shifts to that of 'trustworthiness', the latter seems to reflect judgements over both integrity and motivation *and* confidence over performance (cf. Hardin, 2006, p. 36; O'Neill, 2002, pp. 8–14). So, for example, the 68% of the UK public who think that most MPs make a lot of money out of using public office improperly are questioning trustworthiness from the point of view of integrity and motivation. At the same time, the 'trustworthiness judgements' of the 82% of the UK population who do not trust the government to regulate the banks are more focused on competence than integrity and motivation.

Despite the arguments and evidence, already discussed, on a general global decline in trust, judgements over trustworthiness still vary considerably between different countries. The World Values Survey (2005–2008) includes a question which asks respondents to choose between 'Most people can be trusted' and 'You need to be very careful when you are dealing with people.' Over 57 countries, only 26% felt that 'Most people can be trusted.' But there was considerable variation: 68% of Swedes 'trusted' as compared to only 4% in Trinidad and Tobago, 5% in Turkey and 9% in Brazil. The US and UK occupied intermediate positions, with 39% and 30% 'trusting', respectively. Unsurprisingly, such national variation in the propensity for 'generalized trust in others' has been linked to issues of legitimacy, for example, the absence of corruption and high to above average levels of economic equality (Uslaner, 2008, p. 215). Nordic countries have the most trusting citizens, the least corruption and the least economic inequality, whereas countries with the highest levels of corruption and the lowest perceptions of government legitimacy (e.g. Brazil, the Philippines and Turkey) have the least trusting citizens and high levels of economic inequality (Rothstein and Uslaner, 2005).

It has been argued that social trust in other people forms as a consequence of a reasonable level of economic equality between citizens and a belief that national government policy enables legitimate equality of opportunity (Rothstein and Uslaner, 2005; see also Manning and Guerrero, this volume).

Although evidence from the World Values Survey (2005–2008) shows considerable national variation over 'trusting others', it does support a worldwide general decline in confidence in government and, hence, perceived government legitimacy. Even in a 'trusting' nation like Sweden, when asked about confidence in government, 58% of respondents had 'not very much' or 'none at all'. Although, unsurprisingly, confidence in government was lowest in countries such as Peru and Poland (89% and 82%, respectively, had 'not very much' or 'none at all'), even in an economically prosperous country such as Germany, 77% of citizens said they had 'not very much' or 'none at all' confidence in government. In contrast, other public institutions and public services tended to fare rather better than government. When asked about confidence in the police, the percentage of respondents who replied 'A great deal' or 'Quite a lot' was 78% in Sweden, 74% in Germany and 47% in Poland but only 16% in Peru. When asked about confidence in the armed forces, the percentage of respondents who replied 'A great deal' or 'Quite a lot' was 47% in Sweden, 50% in Germany, 67% in Poland and 23% in Peru. On confidence in the third sector (defined as charitable and humanitarian organizations), there was less variability: the percentage of respondents who replied 'A great deal' or 'Quite a lot' was 66% in Sweden, 65% in Germany, 66% in Poland and 43% in Peru.

Although, generally, trust in government and public services is viewed positively as it encourages cooperation and civic participation, citizens' distrust is clearly sometimes justified and appropriate. Institutional corruption also works through trust, although this is 'particularized trust' between 'in-groups', political elites or others in positions of power (Uslaner, 2000). Clearly, it would be wrong for citizens to trust corrupt political elites or public officials; such a situation would only increase levels of corruption. Moreover, corrupt elites pass corrupt practices on; they create the conditions within which corruption grows more widely throughout society (Uslaner, 2004). But knowledge is required to form a view on corruption. Trust or distrust in people or institutions will be mistaken if the information about them is wrong (Hardin, 2006, p. 18). In the absence of citizens' personal experience with most politicians, government officials and public services, the contemporary importance of the media in providing knowledge to enable the public to form views has been mentioned above. But the media are not the only conduit. Networks are significant organizational forms in the complex and diverse societies most citizens now inhabit; networks can also convey knowledge (see Klijn and Eshuis, this volume). Networks form between individuals, but networks can also bring institutions together. One section of this book is concerned with trust between public institutions, for example, between the government and the third sector, where informal network contacts prevail. Generalized trust can emerge in networks as knowledge is gained through reciprocal interaction based on some degree of trust. This point emphasizes that trust is both an input and an output. Trust invites trust and reciprocity; trust can be a 'virtuous spiral', but placing trust can be risky—vulnerability and even misfortune and deceit can result (O'Neill, 2002, p. 25). This is why there is always a question mark over whether to trust others and why we chose the question of trust and confidence in government and public services as the central focus for this book.

STRUCTURE OF THE BOOK

We explore questions on trust and confidence from an international perspective, across several public institutions (the BBC, the military, local government and the third sector) and for different sectors of public service provision, including education, health, social services and the police. The book has introductory and concluding chapters by the editors and three main parts: 'Understanding trust and confidence'; 'Trust in government and major public institutions'; and 'Trust and citizens' confidence in public services'.

Part I: Understanding Trust and Confidence

This section addresses some fundamental issues. Does public trust matter to governments? What are the correlates of high/low trust in government? Does information on the performance of public services increase public trust? How does trust emerge in networks? Can trust within public-service networks be actively managed?

In chapter two, Laurence Lynn explores the question of whether public trust matters to government. Specifically how does public trust and confidence impact on the governing of the US? For anti-statist and individualistic Americans, low levels of trust in government may be somewhat inevitable. Over and above this, do we know the correlates of low trust? Lynn reports evidence for several: the performance of the national economy; socio-cultural indicators (e.g. rising crime, infant mortality and divorce rates); citizens' evaluations of political actors and institutions; incivility in public discourse; and civic participation. Does low trust have political consequences? Whereas, over fifty years, there is no clear narrative concerning trust and US election results, Lynn argues that citizens' trust is necessary for political leaders to secure citizens' compliance without state-based force, make binding decisions and commit resources to attain societal goals. This seems borne out by the experience of the current US president, Barack Obama. Obama was warned that low trust in government would limit his freedom to pursue bold initiatives but he appeared to judge that this would be outweighed by high trust in him, backed by his personal popularity and capital. In the event, it seems that Obama was wrong. He failed to push through a major healthcare initiative, along with a financial rescue plan. Commentators judged they had no real chance of enactment while the economic downturn dominated the political landscape. On the basis of such evidence, Lynn concludes that for the US's complex democracy, you can trust in trust but you can't count on it!

In chapter three, Christopher Pollitt and Naomi Chambers argue against the claim that performance information on public services will increase public trust. They declare that this simple equation (better performance information = higher public trust) is multiply mistaken. The argument is not concerned with government but with specific public services, such as the health service, schools and the police. They draw on evidence from the developed liberal democratic states of north-west Europe and North America. The logic is that the circumstances under which performance information *could* increase public trust are rare; i.e. the information would have to reach citizens, command their attention, be understood, be trusted and report performances that exceed the citizens' expectations. It is often thought that trust increases with knowledge, indeed cognitive 'knowledge-based trust' has been distinguished from 'identification-based trust' where the latter is emotional and stems from shared values. Pollitt and Chambers argue that 'knowledge-based trust' is best seen as 'confidence', whereas 'true trust' goes beyond any immediate information. Indeed, if trust is defined as citizens' expectations that public services will be honest and competent, *even without scrutiny*, the provision of performance information appears to be a low-trust alternative to trust. Pollitt and Chambers end by emphasizing that although performance measurement probably does *not* promote public trust, it is important in helping managers and professionals focus on critical performance dimensions and may, sometimes, be necessary to hold people to account.

In chapter four, Erik Hans Klijn and Jasper Eshuis point out that, contemporarily, many complex public-service issues are addressed within networks of actors. These groups have their own histories, cultures and strategies. These are, sometimes, at variance. Mutuality, coordination and network management are important to ensure effective communication and to avoid misunderstandings or even conflict. As the professional groups are autonomous, and some have more power than others, some network actors can still act opportunistically in pursuit of their own strategies. In consequence, effective service delivery in networks is difficult. Trust can, therefore, improve the performance of networks. Klijn and Eshuis argue that trust is not automatically present in networks. Trust cannot be 'stored' and then deployed when needed. Rather, trust in networks is active trust; it needs to be actively developed and nurtured. They argue that the development and maintenance of trust within networks is a managerial challenge. Managerial activities that facilitate the emergence of trust in networks include: implementing agreements over which processes to use, searching for goal congruency, creating new organizational forms which transcend professional boundaries and creating incentives for cooperation.

Many of the fundamental issues raised in Part I are explored further in later chapters. The issues of whether trust matters and whether performance information increases trust are explored in the context of the future projects of UK local government by Greasley. On the basis of data from Colombia, Manning and Guerrero argue that local government can capitalize on trust to implement reforms. The chapter by Dudau and Kominis in Part III looks at an empirical example of trust in networks: children's services are a network of social workers, the police, health professionals, teachers, educationalists and youth offending officers.

Part II: Trust in Government and Major Public Institutions

Along with exploring trust in government, Part II also addresses public trust in three major public institutions: the BBC, the military and the third sector. The issue of trust between institutions (the BBC and the government, the military and the government and the public and the third sector) is also discussed.

In chapter five, Stephen Greasley addresses two questions: first, how does a public decide whether its government is trustworthy, and, second, how do government actions influence the public's perceptions of government trustworthiness? He explores these questions through data on the relationship between information on local government performance and citizens' perceptions of government trustworthiness. His focus is on the 'political-citizen' rather than the 'client-citizen' who has experienced specific public services. He contends that it would be foolish to trust on the basis of no information about reliability, and yet the supply of detailed and comprehensive information on government motives and competences may entirely eradicate any need for political trust! A way around this seeming paradox is to recognize that a government record of good performance in specific areas may enable citizens to trust their government to embark on new projects into the future. In relation to local government, citizens now inhabit a richer information environment that is more easily understood than it was in the past. Data show that there is a positive and fairly substantial relationship between measures of local government performance and its perceived trustworthiness. Greasley concludes that local governments should be formulating strategies for performance dissemination to attract the attention of a somewhat disinterested public!

In chapter six, Nick Manning at the World Bank and Alejandro Guerrero at the Inter-American Development Bank address the question of whether local politicians' knowledge of the drivers of trust drives their reforms. Manning and Guerrero argue that trust matters to politicians because it reduces transaction costs between governments and citizens, facilitates tax collection and compliance with other regulations and, if general trust in government extends to incumbent politicians, provides the political capital necessary for policy reform. They are sceptical about cross-country meta-narratives on trust, arguing that local data can tell a clearer story. Citizens are likely to be more familiar with local organizations and officials and better able to assess their trustworthiness based on direct and, sometimes, frequent interaction with them. The municipality of Medellin, in Colombia, has been one of the world's most violent, crime-ridden, drug cartel–controlled cities; the state had, generally, retreated. More recently, the rule of law has been reinstated, the drug cartels almost defeated and murder rates much reduced. The municipality now guarantees almost universal access to relatively high-quality basic public services (energy, water and sewage and gas), with subsidies for the less affluent. The mayor is seen as leading these improvements. Manning and Guerrero conclude that at the local level rapid turnaround can happen when political leaders spot signals that initial, visible improvements in service delivery are associated with increases in trust and compliance with tax collection and then capitalize on trust and revenues to implement further reforms.

In chapter seven, Greg Dyke and Nick Clifford argue that, contemporarily, people form views and negotiate their lives largely through media information. In consequence, if that information misleads and people become aware of this, trust and confidence in the media is lost. More important, the public's sense of what's happening and what's important may come adrift. The chapter focuses on an issue that has come to epitomize the power dynamic between the media—specifically, the British Broadcasting Corporation [BBC]—and the government in securing the trust and confidence of the British public: the question of weapons of mass destruction in Iraq. The chapter reports that the British prime minister at the time, Tony Blair, whilst admitting that weapons of mass destruction did not exist in Iraq, characterizes his assertion that they did as an 'error'. He comments, 'but in today's environment, it [an error] doesn't have that sensational, outrage-provoking "wow" factor of scandal' (Blair, 2010, p. 463). Hence an error is made into a deception. His point is that the media sensationalize events to secure the public's attention. Whilst this may sometimes be true, it may also be true that governments sometimes mislead the public. A prime function of a free press is to uncover deception. The chapter then discusses the challenges faced by the BBC and how it might meet them—specifically, the impact of new technology that generates both huge amounts of information and ever-widening channels and platforms through which to broadcast it. Following unanticipated and unprecedented challenges to trust in the BBC, referred to earlier in this introduction, the chapter ends with a postscript outlining recent events and speculating on their impact on the institution.

In chapter eight, Mike Dunn examines the tripartite trust relationship between the government, the armed forces and the nation, as embedded in the 'Military Covenant'. The essentials of this covenant are that the nation respects and owes gratitude to the armed forces for keeping them safe, the armed forces are committed to the government which sustains them, and the government explains and justifies the use of armed force to the nation, as members of the armed forces are bound by the Official Secrets Act not to communicate directly with the public. However, in the wake of some unpopular wars (e.g. Iraq and Afghanistan) public confidence in military strategy is shaky. Whilst, at the same time, national reverence for military personnel, as expressed in homecoming parades for military units returning from deployment and repatriation ceremonies for soldiers killed in action, has been described by at least one powerful commentator as 'excessive'. Moreover, the relationship between the armed forces and the government is ambiguous. Whilst the political reality is usually that the armed forces are an instrument of government policy, the chiefs of the armed forces see themselves as officers of the Crown with an independent sense of what is in the national interest. The chapter concludes that the military covenant is the outcome of encounters and negotiations within a transient network of powerful actors, where trust, and hence cooperation, has waxed and waned over time.

In chapter nine, Alex Murdock explores trust at the interface between the third and public sectors. There has been growth in third sector service provision, against the background of an increasingly contract-based mode of engagement with the public sector. He argues that each sector has a distinct perspective on the other that is not shared across the divide. The public sector views third sector provision through the lens of public value, equity and choice in provision. Some of the larger third sector organizations see contractual relations with the public sector as an opportunity, but others, especially those with a campaigning or advocacy role, worry that independence may be threatened and organizational values eroded. The modus operandi of the two sectors differs. The third sector is characterized by extensive informal contacts which build trust, whereas the public sector is governed through rules and accountability. The different landscape of the third sector fosters innovations that may not fit or flourish in the public sector context. Murdock uses the example of Emmaus Communities. Individuals who join these communities agree to give up all income-related state benefits to become 'companions' who receive accommodation whilst working as part of a community with common goals and values. Murdock ends by noting that the public trust third sector organizations far more than they trust government. As trust is the basis for cooperation, this indicates greater potential for organizations, such as Emmaus, in engaging disadvantaged or marginalized individuals in common pursuits that encourage social inclusion.

Looking across the contributions, a common theme in this section is how trust builds social capital which can enable institutions to reform or embark on future projects. One perspective on the conflict between the UK government and the BBC is over 'who has more social capital with the public'. The ambiguous relationship between the government and the military, where the latter sometimes lays claim to an independent sense of the national interest, can also be cast in social capital terms. Evidence shows that the third sector enjoys greater social capital than the government, which, in turn, indicates that the third sector may be able to accomplish more.

Part III: Trust and Citizens' Confidence in Public Services

Part III turns to the issue of trust between the client-citizen and public services. Traditionally, clients' trust has underpinned professional autonomy and decision-making, but this is changing. In health, for example, the public are renegotiating their relationship with clinicians. Many patients may wish to 'trust less' and assume more active roles in their own care. The balance between trust and government control is a theme taken up with regard to both education and children's services. In education more control is evident, whereas in children's services the government trusts the professionals more. Trust is a basis for cooperation. Co-production is a feature of all public services but is of special relevance to the police. Community policing only works if the community trust the police sufficiently to engage with them in addressing crime and disorder.

In chapter ten, Ann Mahon considers the nature of trust in healthcare relationships. Various drivers are influencing a transition from unquestioning and deferential trust in doctors by patients and other stakeholders towards more active and negotiated relationships. Using the social ecology model, these relationships are explored at the interpersonal level, at the organizational and institutional level and at the macro level where social, political and cultural contexts are impacting on trust. The evidence suggests that there are lower levels of trust in healthcare systems and institutions than in individual practitioners, with levels of trust being lower for managers than for clinicians. Although published work has focused more on doctor–patient relationships, trust between clinicians and managers is vital for effective engagement in management systems intended to protect patients. Mahon considers the ways in which trust is important in healthcare relationships, both intrinsically as a core defining characteristic of the relationships between doctors and nurses, for example, and instrumentally in its impact on health outcomes and patient satisfaction. Trusting relationships in healthcare can also contribute to generating wider social value. Finally, Mahon notes that it is important to remember that trust can be misplaced.

In chapter eleven, Helen Gunter and Dave Hall explore the issue of public trust in education, focusing on teachers and their work. They maintain that the media have positioned teachers as a 'not to be trusted' profession, that the argument has been made that teachers have lost public confidence by working in their own interests and so the government has legislated for more transparency and accountability for the conduct and outcomes of professional teaching practice. Gunter and Hall are critical of more accountability and transparency. They think such monitoring devices do not and cannot safeguard against deception and may be counterproductive in the education context. Based on three case studies, they argue that deception operates in several ways. First, staff consultation is a facade as school leadership is restricted to a few. Second, rhetoric on improvement in teaching and learning is used to implement greater head teacher control. Third, consensus amongst teaching staff is manufactured through excluding those whose views differ. Gunter and Hall conclude that intelligent accountability, rather than fantasies about control, is required; this is possible only if teachers are trusted to work in the public interest.

In chapter twelve, Adina Dudau and Georgios Kominis explore the relationship between trust and control as modes of governance for the delivery of public services; they argue that the balance between the two is determined by the level of policy uncertainty. Their research focuses on children's services, where, in the UK, there is a thirty-year history of adverse events which place both government and professionals under intense scrutiny. The professionals who deliver policy outcomes for children and young people are diverse: social workers, the police, health professionals, teachers, educationalists and newer groups, such as youth offending officers. This diversity gives rise to communication difficulties, particularly when the professionals come from very different knowledge bases (e.g. social services and health). What works in keeping children and young people safe from harm is uncertain, and this vulnerable population is at high risk. Trust is evident where professionals can exercise considerable autonomy within the framework of general regulatory control. Dudau and Kominis find that in this high-profile social policy area, after waves of regulatory challenges to their professional autonomy, the government is currently moving away from mechanistic control and trusting professionals to an unprecedented degree. The creation of Local Safeguarding Children's Boards, to ensure that diverse professional groups co-operate, is a key element in this.

In chapter thirteen, Stephen Brookes and Peter Fahy (chief constable of Greater Manchester Police) address the question of whether the public value of policing can be determined by the levels of trust and confidence expressed by the community in the police. Government policy now encourages community-based policing; this clearly depends upon the trust and cooperation of the community. Brookes and Fahy say that public value is not about delivering what the public most value but what adds most value to the public sphere. Collaborations in tackling social problems with other partner organizations, such as the local authority, health authority and community groups, add to public value. When members of the public encounter the police, their trust is based on judgments about the fairness of procedures in the context of the police's state-backed authority. The community express more trust in individual officers than they did in the wider institutional collective: 'the police'. Brookes and Fahy conclude that local policing is more important to the public, and they have more trust and confidence in local officers to deal with local incidents. Regional and national police may tackle more serious crime and disorder, but this is less immediate to the public and, concomitantly, their trust and confidence in these more remote institutions is less.

Throughout this volume, contributors return to two broad themes: first, how much does trust *matter* for the responsibilities of governing and the delivery of public services; and, second, what is the *basis* for trust and confidence in government and public services? The distinctive responses on these issues from our learned contributors make for a rich and informative volume.

REFERENCES

Barber, B. (1983) *The Logic and Limits of Trust*. New Brunswick, NJ: Rutgers University Press.

Blair, T. (2010) *A Journey: My Political Life*. London: Random House.

Bottery, M. (2003) The Management and Mismanagement of Trust. *Educational Management and Administration*, 31(3), pp. 245–261.

Bourdieu, P. (1985) The Forms of Capital. In: Richardson, J. G., ed. *Handbook of Theory and Research for the Sociology of Education*. New York: Greenwood, pp. 241–258.

Broadbent, J., Dietrich, M. and Roberts, J., eds. (1997) *The End of the Professions? The Restructuring of Professional Work*. London: Routledge.

Coleman, J. S. (1988) Social Capital in the Creation of Human Capital. *American Journal of Sociology*, 94, pp. 95–120.

ComRes (2012a) *ITV News Poll*, 2 July. Available at: http://www.comres.co.uk/poll/694/itv-news-index.htm.

ComRes (2012b) *Radio 5 Live Poll*, 21 February. Available at: http://www.comres. co.uk/poll/616/victoria-derbyshire-bbc-radio-5-live-nhs-poll.htm.

Dispatches—Can You Trust Your Bank? (2012) Television, Channel 4. 23 July.

Edwards, N., Kornacki, M. J. and Silversin, J. (2002) Unhappy Doctors: What Are the Causes and What Can Be Done? *British Medical Journal*, 345, pp. 835–838.

Eve, R. and Hodgkin, P. (1997) Professionalism and Medicine. In: Broadbent, J., Dietrich, M. and Roberts, J., eds. *The End of the Professions? The Restructuring of Professional Work*. London: Routledge, pp. 69–84.

Giddens, A. (2002) *Where Now for New Labour?* Cambridge: Polity Press.

Gillespie, N. A. and Mann, L. (2004) Transformational Leadership and Shared Values: The Building Blocks of Trust. *Journal of Managerial Psychology*, 19(6), pp. 588–607.

Hardin, R. (2006) *Trust*. Cambridge: Polity Press.

Ipsos MORI (2008) *BBC Survey on Trust Issues*, 22 January. Available at: http://www.ipsos-mori.com/Assets/Docs/Archive/Polls/bbc.pdf.

——— (2009) *Expenses Poll for the BBC*, 2 June. Available at: http://www.ipsos-mori.com/researchpublications/researcharchive/2349/Ipsos-MORI-Expenses-Poll-for-the-BBC.aspx.

Jones, G. R. and George, J. M. (1998) The Experience and Evolution of Trust: Implications for Cooperation and Teamwork. *Academy of Management Review*, 23(30), pp. 531–546.

Klein, R. (1995) *The New Politics of the NHS*. 3rd ed. London: Longman.

Nye J. S., Jr., Zelikow, P. D. and King, D. C. (1997) *Why People Don't Trust Government*. Cambridge, MA: Harvard University Press.

O'Neill, O. (2002) *A Question of Trust: The BBC Reith Lectures*. Cambridge: Cambridge University Press.

Portes, A. (1998) Social Capital: Its Origins and Applications in Modern Sociology. *Annual Review of Sociology*, 24, pp. 1–24.

Putnam, R. D. (1993) *Making Democracy Work: Civic Traditions in Modern Italy*. Princeton, NJ: Princeton University Press.

——— (1995a) Bowling Alone: America's Declining Social Capital. *Journal of Democracy*, 6, pp. 65–78.

——— (1995b) Tuning In, Tuning Out: The Strange Disappearance of Social Capital in America. *PS: Political Science and Politics*, 28(4), pp. 664–683.

——— (2000) *Bowling Alone: The Collapse and Revival of American Community*. New York: Simon and Schuster.

Rothstein, B. and Uslaner, E. M. (2005) All for One: Equality, Corruption and Social Trust. *World Politics*, 58(1), pp. 41–72.

Rotter, J. B. (1980) Interpersonal Trust, Trustworthiness and Gullibility. *American Psychologist*, 35, pp. 1–7.

Uslaner, E. M. (2000) Producing and Consuming Trust. *Political Science Quarterly*, 115(4), pp. 569–590.

——— (2004) Trust and Corruption. In: Lambsdorff, J. G., Taube, M. and Schramm, M., eds. *The New Institutional Economics of Corruption*. London: Routledge, pp. 76–92.

——— (2008) *Corruption, Inequality and the Rule of Law: The Bulging Pocket Makes the Easy Life*. New York: Cambridge University Press.

Uslaner, E. M. and Badescu, G. (2002) Honesty, Trust and Legal Norms in the Transition to Democracy: Why Bo Rothstein Is Better Able to Explain Sweden Than Romania. In: Kornai, J., Rothstein, B. and Rose-Ackerman, S., eds. *Creating Social Trust in Post-Socialist Transition*. Basingstoke: Palgrave Macmillan, pp. 31–52.

World Values Survey (2005–2008) Available at: http://www.wvsevsdb.com/wvs/WVSAnalizeStudy.jsp.

Part I

Understanding Trust and Confidence

2 How Do Trust and Confidence Affect the Governing of America?

Laurence E. Lynn, Jr.

In April 2010, the Pew Research Center for the People and the Press[1] reported 'a perfect storm of conditions associated with distrust of American government—a dismal economy, an unhappy public, bitter partisan-based backlash and epic discontent with Congress and elected officials,' including the once-adulated Barack Obama (Pew, 2010, p. 1). As a consequence, said the report, only 22% of those polled 'trusted the government in Washington almost always or most of the time'; this result was 'among the lowest measures in half a century' (p. 2).[2] Six months later, the November 2010 midterm elections overturned results of the two previous nation-wide elections: the disaffected electorate inflicted sweeping electoral defeats on President Obama's Democratic Party at all levels of government. The prospect of a one-term presidency suddenly became thinkable.

These developments suggest a 'tidy' theory of trust in government: levels reflect several related public attitudes, such as how survey respondents view their own economic prospects, ideology, perceived government performance and attitudes towards elected officials. Low trust has political consequences. The Pew analysis anticipated, accurately, that widespread anti-incumbent sentiment was almost certain to favour Republicans in the forthcoming midterm elections. But trust is both effect and cause. Distrust is bound to redirect the nation's public policy agenda towards the perceived sources of that distrust: in this case, jobs, debt, big government, 'government' healthcare and unpopular 'wars of government choice' in Iraq, Afghanistan and Libya.

While not wrong, this theory oversimplifies a complex reality about which scholars and survey research experts often disagree. According to Hetherington (1998, p. 791), 'scholars have profitably defined political trust as a basic evaluative orientation towards the government founded on how well the government is operating according to people's normative expectations.' But fifty years of comparable data on public trust in American government (Pew, 2010) reveal no obvious story concerning trust and election results. Beginning in the late 1960s, Americans' trust in government spiralled downward during the administrations of Lyndon Johnson, Richard Nixon and Jimmy Carter, reaching lows of less than 35% at the time of

Ronald Reagan's election. Even the personally popular Reagan could not inspire trust. Trust in Reagan never reached 50% of Americans polled and trust sank to nearly 25% despite the also-popular Bill Clinton's prosperous economy. George W. Bush briefly rallied more than half the country to trust their government following the September 2001 terrorist attacks, but even the dramatic and feted election of Obama could not arrest the continuing decline in trust thereafter.

This steep decline in trust attracted the lively interest of political scientists and other social scientists. Public opinion polling organizations were also enthralled by the issue.[3] Keele (2007, p. 242) summarizes the literature as demonstrating that 'various aspects of government performance are important to perceptions of trust.' He notes, however, that some investigators have suggested that a decline in social capital (discussed further below)—as measured by civic participation and trusting attitudes towards others—also may be a factor explaining why, since its post-war highs, trust in government has declined to and remained at low levels.

Conceptualizations of trust in government that have emerged from academic research cast it in a nuanced, even controversial, light (Hetherington, 2006). 'We set up institutions that were designed to cut down on people imposing their will on ordinary folks,' says Hetherington (quoted by Shapiro, 2010). 'Given those circumstances, it's not surprising that we've had a legacy of distrust or mistrust of government ever since the beginning.' The significance of the steep post-1966 decline in trust is its complex association with wars in Vietnam and Iraq and with episodes of fraud, waste and abuse. Distrust has also been exacerbated by the growing ideological conflict between the Democratic Party and the increasingly conservative Republican Party. As discussed further below, partisans tend to distrust governments they do not control. Thus, with the Senate and House controlled by different parties, citizens distrust not only 'government' but both houses of Congress as well.

This chapter addresses two issues related to Americans' trust in government: (1) the extent to which citizens trust political institutions, such as legislatures, elected executives, political parties and specific policies, programmes and agencies, and (2) the ways in which levels of trust affect, for good or for ill, the political behaviour of citizens and political institutions and, therefore, political outcomes. Trust will first be considered as a theoretical cause of numerous social behaviours that have political implications. A discussion of definition and measurement follows. As the chapter title suggests, there are many measures and indicators related to trust or distrust—including dissatisfaction and discontent with, and disapproval of, governance, political and social leaders, institutions, public policies and economic and social circumstances. These indicators and measures will be considered in relation to the concept of trust in order to identify its causes and correlates. Finally, the chapter addresses how and to what extent trust in government influences governing outcomes in context of American electoral politics, in particular, the dramatic midterm elections of 2010.

THEORY-BASED ANALYSIS OF TRUST

As a concept, trust reflects the perceived reliability, competence, legitimacy, or honesty of an individual, organization or institution. A breach of trust, then, is a perceived failure by the object of trust to live up to or to fulfil expectations to which it has been assumed to be unconditionally committed. In the absence of trust, parties to a relationship will take steps to protect themselves against possible breaches of trust. These steps include the avoidance or withdrawal altogether from unreliable or potentially harmful relationships. The following discussion is concerned primarily with theories that attempt to explain actors' behaviour and its consequences conditioned on the strength of trust among them.

Trust in Government

In academic literature on trust in government, trust tends to be conceptualized as a correlate or cause of a wide variety of social behaviours that have significant direct or indirect consequences for political outcomes, such as effective and stable governance. The question postulated to be of interest to politicians is how trust is formed and sustained and, therefore, how (indeed, if) precipitate declines in trust in government can be intentionally increased by political actions and decisions.

Although the issue of political trust and its consequences is inherently interdisciplinary, different disciplines and fields of scholarship have their own preoccupations.

- **Political scientists** are concerned with the nature, reasons for and political significance of public trust in institutions, such as governments, politicians, the judiciary, the media, the professions and the military (Keele, 2007). They are concerned as well with the political consequences of trust and the lack of it. Trust, or its absence, is translated into political outcomes via various institutional, structural and behavioural mechanisms, including civic participation, contributing to campaigns and voting
- **Political economists** tend to view trust based on assumptions of rational behaviour and formal reasoning. Trust may reduce the costs of economic transactions, including those between the public and the government. Secured by appropriate institutional design, trust may enable the maintenance of equilibrium and stability in repeated interactions
- **Public administration** scholarship is drawn towards instrumental issues, often in organizational contexts, such as the interrelationships among trust; the measurement and management of organizational performance; the nature, extent and quality of democratic participation; and the trustworthiness of administrators and their agents
- In **law**, trust tends to be viewed as the basis for the social acceptance and legitimacy of the rule of law and of lawfully constituted governing institutions. A major role of legal institutions is to foster and sustain that trust

- **Sociologists** study the role of social trust in establishing and sustaining social cohesion, solidarity and social capital, the institutions of civil society and the functioning of post-modern/post-industrial societies. Relatedly, **psychologists** view trust as an element in human development, in interpersonal relationships and in social influence relationships as well as in the predictability of such relationships

No single discipline addresses all questions associated with trust in government, however. Therefore, the discussion that follows is organized in terms of these questions and draws on discipline-based scholarship as appropriate.

What Do We Mean by Trust?

In a 1998 Russell Sage Foundation publication, *Trust and Governance*, editors Braithwaite and Levi organized conference presentations by scholars from diverse perspectives and fields to discuss the status of research on trust in government.

Multiple disciplinary perspectives produce a wide variety of arguments.

- Braithwaite, a psychologist, argues, for example, that, partly influenced by institutions, people switch between rational and communal understandings of their relationships to government; this switching is the phenomenon to be explained
- Hardin, a rational choice political scientist, argues that citizens cannot rationally trust government because they lack the information to judge the trustworthiness of complex agencies. Thus, they cannot determine if such agencies are governed by the incentive compatibility that is essential to rational expectations of trustworthy performance in the absence of transparency
- Based on an empirical analysis of federal, state and local governments, Jennings, also a political scientist, associates trust with performance
- Bianco, an economist, explains why elected officials may not always vote according to the interests of their constituents: a wish to be trustworthy motivates them to vote their best judgement, a more transparent indication of their future conduct than interest-based voting and a potential source of moral credit
- Blackburn, a philosopher, believes that the social desirability of being trusting and trustworthy motivates trusting and trustworthy behaviour by citizens and officials alike

In a review of the volume, Di Maggio (1999, p. 732), a sociologist, observes that:

> Most of these [authors] identify two kinds of trust: 'rational', 'exchange', or 'instrumental' trust ('I trust you because I believe it is in your interest

not to betray me') based in effective sanctions and mutuality of interest, and 'communal', 'familial', or 'social' trust ('I trust you because I believe you will not betray me even if it is in your interest to do so'), based in intimacy, emotion and shared identity.[4]

Most believe, Di Maggio says, that (a) trust is good for politics because it enables agreement on the provision of public goods and (b) institutions promote both public and governmental trustworthiness.

How Does Trust Affect Political Outcomes?

According to a broad consensus, trust matters to political outcomes. In a typical view, Chanley, Rudolph and Rahn (2000, p. 240) contend that 'citizen trust in government is necessary for political leaders to make binding decisions, commit resources to attain societal goals and secure citizen compliance without coercion.' Lack of public trust may undermine the legitimacy of an administration or of governing institutions more generally. The authors cite empirical research findings that 'distrustful voters are more likely to support non-incumbent and third-party candidates and are more likely to express support for devolution of decision making from federal to state governments on issues such as crime, welfare and the environment' (p. 240). In a similar vein Yang and Holzer (2006, p. 114) state, 'Without trust, citizens are less likely to pay taxes and invest in the work of government.' Ulbig (2008, p. 526) comments, 'Political trust has long been viewed as bedrock for successful democracy.'

According to Keele (2005, p. 884), 'trust creates a climate in which elected officials are able to enact policy and avoid stalemate and gridlock.' He distinguishes, however, between the basis of trust for partisan voters and for independent or floating voters. 'Partisans trust government more when their party controls the government . . . [whereas] Independents care little for which party controls the government,' instead valuing actual performance (2005, p. 884).[5] Similarly, Anderson and Lo Tempio (2002, p. 335) find that 'political trust is highest among voters who voted either for both the presidential and congressional winners or the presidential winner and congressional losers; trust is lowest among those who voted for both the presidential and congressional losers or congressional winners and the presidential loser.'

Hetherington (1998, p. 803) concludes that 'higher levels of trust are of great benefit to both elected officials and political institutions. More trust translates into warmer feelings for both, which in turn provides leaders more leeway to govern effectively and institutions a larger store of support regardless of the performance of those running the government.' According to Cook and Gronke (2005, p. 799), 'a presumption among political scientists [suggests] that low levels of trust in government and confidence in institutions represent at least the potential for a crisis in governability if not democracy in the United States.'

Yet, Shapiro (2010) says, 'Look at the IRS statistics on whether people are cheating on their taxes: that hasn't changed. Look at filling out census forms: that hasn't declined significantly. So Americans may actually have more confidence in government institutions than they are willing to admit to pollsters.' (The question of what standard survey responses on trust in government actually predict is discussed further below.)

What Determines Public Trust in Government?

Summarizing the research literature on determinants of trust in government, Chanley, Rudolph and Rahn (2000, p. 240) caution that 'declining trust in government is a complex phenomenon with multiple potential causes.' They identify three clusters of factors as contributing to (as causes of) the previously discussed decline of trust in American government: the performance of the national economy; rising crime, infant mortality and divorce rates and other socio-cultural indicators; and citizens' evaluations of political actors and institutions.

A different question is how short-term shifts in trust and cognate variables such as approval, satisfaction and confidence affect governing. Evidence suggests that the performance of the economy is important in the short run, as well as the longer term (Keele, 2007). Chanley, Rudolph and Rahn (2000) note, however, that there is some evidence that trust relationships between citizens and elected officials at the federal level are reciprocal. Citizens' trust causes government's trustworthiness and is a result of trustworthy performances by government. With similar implications, Hetherington (1998, pp. 803–804) concludes that 'in addition to the economy, improved perceptions of government effectiveness and higher levels of congressional approval can effect substantial changes trust in government.' A study by Mutz and Reeves (2005), moreover, suggests that incivility in public discourse—not disagreement but the ways in which disagreement is expressed—can reduce public trust in government.

These sources suggest that, whereas evidence supports some propositions concerning causes of trust and distrust, comprehensive explanations of various types of perceptual measures and the terms in which evaluations are expressed are lacking. Survey responses to 'Do you expect government to do the right thing?', 'Do you believe the country is moving in the right direction?', 'Do you approve of how the president is doing his job?' and 'Are you satisfied with government?' are conditioned by partisan and sectarian affiliation among other factors. These responses and affiliations are likely to be interrelated in complex ways and vary with short-term changes in political environments.

How Is Trust Related to Government Performance?

In recent years, the 'performance movement' (Radin, 2006) has gained momentum in the United States and elsewhere. Research has been concerned with exploring the interrelationship between government performance and trust in government. Of such efforts, Keele (2005, p. 242) declares:

> Trust is a reflection of government performance. The performance of Congress and the president and how well they manage the economy, control crime and avoid scandal are a large part of what causes the public to trust or distrust the government. So one thing we might say that we know about trust is that various aspects of government performance are important to perceptions of trust.

Keele puts forward a 'simple', individual-level theory: 'the link between trust and government performance,' he says, 'is grounded on basic concepts of democratic representation and accountability.' Citizens delegate the power to act in their name to elected officials with the expectation that these officials 'will produce good policy, peace and sound economic stewardship' (p. 243). Performance-based trust at a macro level will take time to emerge, however, and may be confounded by errors of perception concerning the quality of government performance.

A logical next step is to strengthen the accuracy of perceptions through better performance measurement and management. Yang and Holzer (2006, p. 114) argue that 'performance measurement can serve as a more effective link between performance and trust if current measurement practice is improved to embrace such factors as government-wide evaluation, institutional arrangements, citizen involvement and communication strategies.'

A number of factors weaken the performance–trust relationship. These include the failure of both public managers and legislators to make use of performance information; the tendency of one-size-fits-all performance mandates to be customized or selectively implemented at operating levels; the difficulty of ascribing the causes of performance improvements to specific policies and managerial strategies and actions; the tendency to divert resources towards measured factors and away from unmeasured ones, thereby producing 'performance paradoxes', that is, negative correlations between specific performance measures and actual agency performance, the lack of relevant data, and political disagreements over the goals and objectives of policies and programmes.

Yang and Holzer acknowledge that evidence supporting the performance–trust relationship claim is weak. They lay the blame for this weakness on the fact that existing performance measures do not capture those aspects of performance that matter to citizens. Tolbert and Mossberg (2006, p. 354) found, for example, that 'e-government can increase process-based trust by improving interactions with citizens and perceptions of responsiveness.' Civic engagement, in contrast, has no detectable effect on government performance across states. Rice (2001, pp. 782–783) similarly found no relationship between membership of groups such as fraternal organizations and civic groups and perceived local government performance across communities in the state of Iowa.

What Is the Relationship between Civic Participation and Trust?

The challenges of democracy in pluralist societies are twofold. First, citizens do not always know what is in their, or society's, best interests, making preference aggregation misleading. Second, citizens disagree about what is in society's best interests, making consensus difficult to achieve. This is true whether the issue is going to war or siting a public incinerator. Confronting and attempting to resolve disagreements and conflicts are what politics is about, and systems of electoral representation are the primary institutions for collective action in modern societies. Debates over whether representative institutions exclude or disempower too many citizens are ongoing in democratic theory, in political science and public administration, and in political forums. The protagonists include advocates for strong, centralized governments, capitalist societies in which government is limited to providing public goods (defence, law enforcement) and decentralized, debureaucratized governments that rely for policy guidance on civic participation and direct forms of democracy.

Does Participation Increase Trust?

Assessing the virtues and defects of 'participation' is a staple of research on political behaviour. Participation refers to non-republican mechanisms and institutionalized arrangements for giving citizens, affected stakeholders such as taxpayers and programme beneficiaries, administrators and service providers, among others, opportunities to influence policy and administrative decisions. Facilitating participation is widely believed to have a positive effect on the level of satisfaction with, approval of and confidence and trust in government. Participation shortens the distance between government and governed and makes experts and bureaucrats more accountable to citizens. Mechanisms include surveys and focus groups, e-government, contracting out, collaboration through networks and partnerships, negotiated rule- and policy-making and deliberative and decision-making forums.

A large body of systematic empirical research informs efforts to 'test' the claims of those who believe that participation has intrinsic merits, such as inclusiveness and egalitarian outcomes. For example:

- Based on her empirical research, Ulbig (2008, p. 523) argues that 'giving people a voice in politics is not a universal remedy for ailing democracy.' She finds that 'feelings of policy satisfaction and political trust are increased only when respondents believe citizens had both increased voice and [actual] influence.' Indeed, she says (2008, p. 524), 'voice without influence can be more detrimental than no voice at all'
- Markham, Johnson and Bonjean (1999, p. 176) conducted a study of how well participatory community service organizations meet community needs. They concluded, 'From a broader policy standpoint, our findings question the ability of community service organizations

to identify and respond to community needs.' A survey of research on neighbourhood-representing organizations (Cnaan, 1991, p. 629) found 'a low level of both participatory and representative democracy' in such organizations

- Research on alternative dispute resolution processes in German environmental policy-making concluded that discourse involving knowledge disputes must occur earlier and at more senior levels of administration than at the 'end-of-pipe' citizen level, where discourse founders (Keller and Poferl, 2000)
- Winners and losers in political contests express different levels of satisfaction with democratic institutions. Winners prefer majoritarian government; losers prefer consensual processes (Anderson and Guillory, 1997). This finding guarantees political contests over institutional forms that threaten stability
- In a study of the formation of integrated health-services networks, Nolan and Zuvekas (2001) found that, paradoxically, the emergence of trust among collaborators, often thought to be a substitute for hierarchy, may be a reason why hierarchical mechanisms necessary for efficiency can function well. The existence of hierarchical coordination may obscure the extent of formal and informal collaborative relationships and agreements

In short, there is nothing straightforward about the effects of participation on trust in government. The pathologies of national deliberative and decision processes—using agents to represent one's interests, failing to reveal preferences, failure to cooperate, manipulation of the terms of and participants in debate, indifference to monitoring one's agents, ignorance of relevant information, ideological resistance to factual claims, ignoring low-priority issues—flourish at every level of society when collective action is required. Civic participation is not a panacea for distrust of government.

Does Trust Increase Participation?

Nearly concurrent with the decline in trust in government which began in the late 1960s is the decline in voter turnout in American presidential elections. Linking these trends makes sense: voting is more a matter of civic responsibility than it is the desire to affect electoral outcomes, and distrust is plausibly linked to a lack of civic responsibility. But voter turnout began increasing in 2000 in America and trust did not. Moreover, scholars have adduced other explanations for voter turnout, including lifestyle changes associated, for example, with changes in information and communication technology, work behaviour and electoral strategies.

Issues also arise concerning the influence of trust in political institutions to forms of civic participation and engagement, including voting. One study, a five-country study of civic participation of young people, found, for example, that 'civic knowledge is a predictor of the expectation of voting (and obtaining information about candidates), but it is not related to the expectation of civic participation in the community (through volunteering or collecting for charity). Service learning experiences show small positive effects on expectations of voting and larger effects on expectations of civic participation in the community (especially in the United States)' (Torney-Purta et al., 2004, p. 2). These kinds of issues are more fully explored by scholars concerned with the relationship between social capital and trust.

How Does Trust Relate to Social Capital?

Sociologists claim that social capital is central to social cohesion and a sense of community. As popularized by Putnam, a political scientist, the concept of social capital 'refers to the social connections, networks and interpersonal trust that occur in communities' (Keele, 2007, p. 243). It has been appropriated by political scientists and others concerned with trust in government to enrich their theorizing about trust and political outcomes. The concept has been used, for example, to analyse the relationship between trust and political behaviour at all levels of American government.

According to Keele (2007), in his study of the federal government, 'the empirical results [of my study] demonstrate that both government performance and social capital matter, but that social capital appears to be the force which accounts for the decline in trust over the last 40 years' (p. 241). He continues (p. 252):

> The basic statistical results are straightforward. First, trust is an evalua-
> tion of politicians and their management of the economy and responds
> immediately to any changes in government performance. But trust also
> reflects the lessons learned in civic activity and feelings of personal mis-
> anthropy. . . . While changes in social capital will not register an effect
> on trust immediately, the effect on trust is substantively important.

Of the sharp decline in Americans' trust in government, Keele says that social capital provides the best explanation yet: 'it declined over the same period [and] the evidence [in my study] demonstrates that social capital exerts a powerful effect on trust' (p. 252). Keele conjectures that 'when citizens disengage from civic life and its lessons of social reciprocity, they are unable to trust the institutions that govern political life' (p. 241). He tests this proposition and finds that 'while performance may be responsible for temporary increases in trust, without some change in social capital, trust will not return to the levels witnessed in the 1950s and 1960s' (2007, p. 251).

Based on his analysis at the state level, Knack (2002, p. 782) says that it 'provides strong evidence that social capital influences governmental perfor-mance. However, this result is highly qualified: some dimensions of social capital matter much more than others. Volunteering, census response and social trust are significant predictors of governmental performance.'[6] When citizens are willing to contribute to social welfare despite the cost of doing so, he continues, they

> are less likely to view government and public officials as dispensers of private benefits, and more likely to help keep government accountable to the broader public interest by staying informed and using voice mechanisms (signing petitions, contacting legislators, etc.) when they perceive incompetence or corruption in government. (pp. 782–783)

In another definition of social capital, Pierce, Lovrich and Moon (2002, p. 381) in their study of twenty American cities, say it may be

> broadly conceptualized as the shared resource produced by trust in others, which in turn enables individuals to participate in organized networks that maximize political influence on those in power. . . . According to the proponents of a social capital approach to explaining cross-jurisdictional differences in government performance, in those locations where social capital is in greater supply it can be expected that higher levels of government performance will be achieved.

A variety of social-psychological mechanisms link improved performance to trust-based social capital. Such social capital in turn enables citizens to collaborate in playing more active roles in governmental processes to secure public goods and services and to hold officials accountable for their performance. The authors' measure of trust had a robust correlation with government performance across the twenty cities in their study. 'Social capital remains a strong predictor of the quality of government performance' (Pierce, Lovrich and Moon 2002, p. 394), although other interpretations of causality are suggested.

So What Can We Say about Americans' Trust in Government?

It is arguable (cf. Hardin, 1998) that, with anti-statist and individualistic Americans, distrust in government is a consequence of Constitutional intention, institutional design and a pluralistic civic culture, a circumstantial reflection of America's separation of powers, federalism and checks and balances, rather than a phenomenon subject to the influences of public policy and political strategy. Anderson and Lo Tempio (2002, p. 350) conclude that 'in many ways, America's system of government frustrates voters because it is designed to muddle clarity of responsibility and accountability.' However, in reporting that 'Americans' trust in government is strongly affected by the presidential election, but not the congressional contest' (p. 335), Anderson and Lo Tempio (2002, p. 350) provide a more positive view of the relationship between trust in government and American democracy:

> The system provides a maximum sense that one is not shut out of the political process. While the diffusion and complexity of responsibility

makes it difficult to identify who is responsible, they also invite citizens to interpret the political process as one in which everyone is part of the game. Taken together, these results go a long way towards explaining the exceptional stability and vibrancy of American democracy.[7]

These views might seem to suggest that levels and trends in measures of Americans' trust in their government are far less consequential for governing than common sense and much research suggests, a point to which we will return in the concluding section. Hetherington (1998, p. 792) provides a balanced view:

> Some scholars suggest the trust measure correlates only with specific support [satisfaction with government outputs and the performance of political authorities], so trust's decline is of somewhat limited consequence. According to this view, an improvement in incumbent job performance should remedy low levels of political trust. In contrast, others provide evidence of a connection between political trust and some measures of diffuse support [support refers to the public's attitude toward regime-level political objects regardless of performance], implying that sustained low trust ultimately challenges regime legitimacy.

Hetherington continues, raising the issue of causality, 'To assess trust's relevance, it may be less important to know whether measures of specific or diffuse support explain political trust than whether political trust affects measures of specific and diffuse support. Viewed in this light, political trust can have system-level import regardless of which type of support it affects' (p. 792).

MEASURING TRUST

In academic and public discourse, trust is about numbers. Integral to empirical social science is devising measures that enable the testing of hypotheses derived from theories and models. Concurrently, public opinion polling by non-academic organizations such as Gallup, Roper and Harris, often in partnership with TV networks and newspapers, provides grist for media coverage of trust issues in politics. Scholars and pollsters depend on each other in various ways—scholars using polling data to test their models, pollsters using academic frameworks to organize and interpret their findings.

Measurement in Scholarly Research

Not surprisingly, definitions and measures of trust in academic research reflect the investigators' specific questions, the availability and quality of data, and methods for constructing particular measures.[8] Examples of diverse measures can be drawn from studies cited earlier. Keele (2007) 'constructed a trust in government time series with nearly 200 administrations of nine different survey questions from the data archive at the Roper Center for Public Opinion' (p. 245).[9] Pierce, Lovrich and Moon's measure of trust was created for their study by a marketing research firm.[10] In Knack's 2002 study, 'social trust' is measured as the percentage of survey respondents in a state who agree with the statement that 'most people are honest' (p. 776).

In addition to theory-based empirical measures, a substantial effort is devoted to the development of measures of trust in government that can serve as social indicators. Some of this effort is based in the academy and is concerned, among other things, with developing predictors of trust in government and understanding the meaning of trust and confidence in government in public-opinion surveys (Cook and Gronke, 2005). 'The best-known measures of political trust,' say Mutz and Reeves (2005), 'are those from the National Election Studies (NES) battery that are labeled under the rubric of support for the political system.'[11] The General Social Survey (GSS), a face-to-face sample survey of Americans' demographic characteristics and attitudes conducted regularly since 1972, proposes, 'I am going to name some institutions in this country.[12] As far as the people running these institutions are concerned, would you say that you have a great deal of confidence, quite a lot of confidence, only some confidence, or very little confidence in them?'

Issues of construct validity and consistency arise, however, especially when different constructs—trust, confidence, approval, satisfaction—are purported to be measured. Cook and Gronke (2005, p. 786) note the problem that 'the lowest category on each set of questions cannot distinguish between one person who is deeply cynical and expects a malicious response from another who is simply sceptical and withholds prejudgment.'[13] To analyse the meaning of such responses, the authors conducted a survey based on questions from both the National Election Studies (NES) and the General Social Survey (GSS). Their method enabled them to compare responses about trust in government with those about confidence in institutions. Based on their analysis, they argue that different measures of trust and confidence are empirically distinct. Declines in NES measures of trust in government, they say, are grossly exaggerated. But 'the NES trust-in-government question is unusually sensitive to contemporary political and economic circumstances' (p. 799). Substantively, they 'cannot equate cynicism (not to mention distrust, mistrust, alienation, disaffection and estrangement) . . . with a low score on the NES question of trust in government or a low score on the GSS battery of questions on confidence in institutions' (p. 799). The American public, in other words, is sceptical but not cynical about their government.[14]

Public Opinion Research

While scholars attempt to disentangle constructs, numerous public opinion polling firms and organizations conduct surveys of Americans' attitudes towards their governments and other institutions. In addition to survey research methodology, scientific and political interest in such surveys focuses on several issues: (1) their usefulness as social indicators, (2) how well they perform as predictors of mass political behaviour and (3) how and with what significance measures of public attitudes are correlated with evaluations of governments, public officials, public policies and programmes, and public institutions and agencies.

Important measurement issues arise, for example, when comparing the objects of measurement such as distrust, dissatisfaction and other negatives (Cook and Gronke, 2005). Although such constructs are not necessarily the inverse of their positive counterparts, they are often treated as such in popular discourse. The confusion does not end there. By August 2011, the Pew Center's measure of Americans' trust in government had declined to 19% (Pew, 2011b). At the same time, under the heading 'Anger and Distrust in Government', the Pew Center (2011a) reported, based on different survey questions, that only 11% of Americans polled were 'basically content' with the federal government; the rest were either angry (26%) or 'frustrated' (60%). At the same time, 59% of Americans polled regarded President Barack Obama as 'trustworthy'.

In public discourse, the number and frequency of public opinion reports can also be confusing. Results from distinct measures that use terms—trust, satisfaction, approval, confidence—that are indistinguishable in meaning to the general public may be misinterpreted. A 'historically low' result in one poll may not be a historic low in another, comparable poll. Some measures may, without real significance, be ticking upward when other measures thought to be caused by them are falling. In other words, public attitudes and their causes can be interpreted as changing when they are not.

The previously discussed long-term decline in American trust in government is clear in polling results, however. The 2010 report by the Pew Research Center, *The People and Their Government: Distrust, Discontent, Anger and Partisan Rancor*, quoted in this chapter's opening paragraph, included an analysis of trust in government in America from 1958 (when the NES first asked a question relating to respondents' trust in government) to 2010.[15] Of special interest is the report's analysis of the correlates of trust in government. The measure that most highly correlates with polls charting Americans' trust in government is the state of the country's economy, a result reported in many studies. The story is not so simple, however. Recoveries in general satisfaction with the state of the country and in consumer satisfaction and economic recoveries in the 1980s and 1990s have not arrested the steady decline in measures of trust in government.

A different use of poll results is made by Chanley, Rudolph and Rahn (2000). They base their own measure of trust in government on survey responses to six similar but somewhat different questions asked by polling organizations. Employing sophisticated modelling and estimation methods, their findings are of considerable interest (p. 253): 'our research finds that evaluations of Congress and congressional scandals are more closely linked to trust in government than are evaluations of the president and presidential scandals.' They also found a positive relationship between trust and 'public policy mood' using a measure which 'reflects the extent of public support for increased government spending and activity across a range of domestic policy areas, including education, health care, welfare, aid to cities and the environment' (p. 245). The findings imply that trust affects public willingness to commit resources to public policy achievement, a finding of particular importance, the authors say, to politicians advocating new and expanded programmes.

As already suggested, the interactions among these results and indicators are conceptually and statistically complex. Statistically, measures of trust may be correlated with ideology, policy preferences and personal interests. Thus a decline in trust in a central institution such as the presidency or in an individual leader such as the president might reflect a summation of the disappointed expectations of many different groups in an electorate, some who want more of something, some who want less of it. This, in turn, may be reflected in voting patterns, in voter turnout, in campaign contributions and in partisan activity on behalf of issues and candidates. These political behaviours will, in turn, affect governing outcomes.

TRUST, GOVERNING AND AMERICAN POLITICS

American politicians often claim that they listen carefully to their constituents but pay no attention to public opinion polls. Based on the discussion in this chapter, politicians should do just the opposite: ignore the 'squeaky wheels' of non-representative interests within their jurisdictions and try to find meaning in measurements that have some scientific justification. But would doing that really be a good idea? Would governing outcomes improve if public attitudes measured and interpreted in the ways discussed in this chapter were taken more seriously as a practical political matter?

Consider the following analysis of the 2010 American midterm election results (Galston, 2010):

> Although [Barack Obama] was warned just days after his victory that the public's mistrust of government would limit its tolerance for bold initiatives, he refused to trim his sails, in effect assuming that his personal credibility would outweigh the public's doubts about the competence and integrity of the government he led. As events proved, that was a significant misjudgment. . . . A major health care initiative was piled on top of the financial rescue plan and the stimulus package, exacerbating the public's sticker shock [alarm over the cost]. And initiatives such as climate change legislation and comprehensive immigration reform remained in play long after it should have been clear that they stood no serious chance of enactment while pervasive economic distress dominated the political landscape.

Based on research cited earlier, it is reasonable to conclude, as does Galston, that the low level of public trust in government—scepticism more than cynicism—was a significant influence on the 2010 midterm elections.

Such analysis can be elaborated. Prior to the US midterm elections in November 2010, the most accepted measures of trust in government were, as noted above, at or near their historic lows. At the same time, over 90% of those polled ranked the economy as important/extremely important to them, and the 'dismal economy' was the greatest source of public dissatisfaction with government, according to other poll results. Further, over 70% of those in another poll disapproved of President Obama's performance on the economy. If Obama is perceived as having failed to establish a clear, effective focus on the economy, deficits and debt by 2012, it almost surely will affect his and his party's prospects as it did in 2010.

A dramatic shift of voter preferences for conservatives and Republicans occurred in many states as well. Republicans took control of nineteen formerly Democrat-controlled legislatures, reaching a level of dominance not seen since 1928. Distrust of government awakens Americans' reflexive belief that governments that are closer to the people are more accountable and reliable, thus having a decentralizing effect. This result compounds the effects of the mistaken judgement Galston attributed to Obama: forty-four state legislatures will be responsible for redrawing Congressional district boundaries following the 2010 decennial census, and many more of these legislatures are now controlled by Republicans, whose redrawing of district boundaries will favour their party.

Consider, in addition, the evident increase in partisanship in the US Congress since the 1970s, the increased intensity of partisanship among Republican and conservatives, the seemingly corresponding disaffection of partisan Democrats and independents with President Obama and likely public scepticism towards their ability to influence government policies at the federal level. All reinforce the prospect that the political outcomes of the 2010 midterm election seem even more understandable and are harbingers of 2012.

The Pew Research Center's invoking the metaphor of 'perfect storm' to summarize the state of trust in government in 2010 may serve as a cautionary note, however. For nearly fifty years, several social indicators, including trust in government, voter participation and social capital, have been trending downward. Barack Obama and the Democratic Party arguably have misunderstood this fraught reality and are likely to continue to pay for their mistakes. If and when, for whatever reason, trust recovers to the point that trust exceeds scepticism, then a great many correlates of trust—approval, confidence, satisfaction, contentment—will come into play but in no predictable way. But then again, it may not matter because appropriate inferences about the return of trust will be drawn regardless of such correlations.

An appropriate apothegm for America's complex democracy might well be: trust in trust, but don't count on it.

NOTES

1. Among the most respected of American polling organizations, the Pew Research Center for the People and the Press is a non-partisan, non-profit organization that studies and reports on attitudes towards politics, the press and public policy issues. See: http://people-press.org/.
2. Pew's historical data on trust is compiled from six different surveys, with the measure from 1976 to the present based on a three-survey moving average. Thus, individual surveys might have reported lower or higher levels than the moving average. 'A CBS/New York Times poll conducted in October 2008 found just 17% trusting the federal government to do what is right—a low seen previously only in a June 1994 Gallup survey' (Pew, 2010, p. 13). Trust is defined as trusting the government to do the right thing all or most of the time.
3. Insufficient data are available to evaluate whether or not the high levels of trust in 1958–1966 were typical or, what seems more likely, an indication of cyclical movements in public confidence in government.
4. 'Regrettably,' says Di Maggio, 'they neglect generalized trust, which, unlike communal trust, does not risk corrosive particularism and they ignore ethnomethodologic trust, which may explain why people comply unreflectively with many government demands' (1999, p. 732).
5. Surveys reveal that those fiscal and social conservatives and evangelical Christians who have coalesced into the Tea Party movement are Republican partisans for the most part (Jones and Cox, 2010).
6. As assessed by the Government Performance Project of *Governing* magazine and the Maxwell School of Citizenship and Public Affairs at Syracuse University.
7. Anderson and Lo Tempio say America is not unique in this pattern of political behaviour, citing Anderson and Guillory (1997).
8. A 'World Database of Trust' (James, 2010) contains a lengthy list of definitions of trust compiled from academic literature as well as an extensive bibliography of trust publications.

    The wide variety of trust measures used in research raises questions both of construct validity (is it 'trust' or something else that is being measured?) and of the consistency of trust constructs across studies (are findings from different studies comparable—i.e. do they measure approximately the same thing?).
9. Creating the trust measure is a highly technical process. Keele uses a 'recursive dyadic dominance algorithm' to form a quarterly trust time series and assess how well the different survey questions tap the same underlying trust construct (2007, p. 245).
10. The trust measure is derived from data sets provided to the researchers by Leigh Stowell and Company of Seattle, a media marketing research company. Telephone surveys have been conducted in more than fifty US and Canadian cities over a decade. Among other things, data collected included more than fifty items relating to political and social trust, reflecting misanthropy, open-mindedness, efficacy and related social science concepts. Item scales were constructed from these data.
11. Available at: http://www.electionstudies.org/nesguide/toptable/tab5a_5.htm. Index to tables at: http://www.electionstudies.org/nesguide/gd-index.htm. This is one of the indexes used in the Pew study of trust.
12. Available at: http://www3.norc.org/GSS+Website/.
13. They cite Citrin: 'the cynical responses to the CPS [Census Population Survey] political trust items are hardly extreme. To believe that the government wastes "a lot" of money, can be trusted to "do what is right only some of

the time", and includes "quite a few" people who are "crooked" or "don't know what they're doing" need not bespeak a deep-seated hostility toward the political system' (Citrin, 1974, p. 975).

14. The 2010 Pew Research Center on trust in government uses the term 'scepticism' to depict the low level of trust in 2010.
15. To create such a time series, Pew analysts drew not only on Pew's own surveys but on the NES, the Gallup organization, polls regularly conducted by ABC/Washington Post, CBS/New York Times and CNN.

REFERENCES

Anderson, C. J. and Guillory, C. A. (1997) Political Institutions and Satisfaction with Democracy: A Cross-National Analysis of Consensus and Majoritarian Systems. *American Political Science Review*, 91(6), pp. 6–81.

Anderson, C. J. and Lo Tempio, A. J. (2002) Winning, Losing and Political Trust in America. *British Journal of Political Science*, 32(2), pp. 335–351.

Braithwaite, V. and Levi, M., eds. (1998) *Trust and Governance*. New York: Russell Sage Foundation. (One of a RSF series on Trust.) Available at: https://www.russellsage.org/publications/category/RSF%20Series%20on%20Trust.

Chanley, V. A., Rudolph T. J. and Rahn, W. M. (2000) The Origins and Consequences of Public Trust in Government: A Time Series Analysis. *Public Opinion Quarterly*, 64(3), pp. 239–256.

Citrin, J. (1974) Comment: The Political Relevance of Trust in Government. *American Political Science Review*, 68(3), pp. 973–988.

Cnaan, R. A. (1991) Neighbourhood-Representing Organizations: How Democratic Are They? *Social Service Review*, 65(4), pp. 614–634.

Cook, T. E. and Gronke, P. (2005) The Skeptical American: Revisiting the Meanings of Trust in Government and Confidence in Institutions. *Journal of Politics*, 67(3), pp. 784–803.

Di Maggio, P. (1999) Review: *Trust and Governance*, by Braithwaite, V. and Levi, M., eds. *Contemporary Sociology*, 28(6), pp. 731–732.

Galston, W. A. (2010) *President Barack Obama's First Two Years: Policy Accomplishments, Political Difficulties*. Washington, DC: The Brookings Institution. Available at: http://www.brookings.edu/papers/2010/1104_obama_galston.aspx.

Hardin, R. (1998) Trust in Government. In: Braithwaite, V. and Levi, M., eds. *Trust and Governance*. New York: Russell Sage Foundation, pp. 9–27.

Hetherington, M. J. (1998) The Political Relevance of Political Trust. *American Political Science Review*, 92(4), pp. 791–808.

——— (2006) *Why Trust Matters: Declining Political Trust and the Demise of American Liberalism*. Princeton, NJ: Princeton University Press.

James, Harvey S. (2010) *Database of Trust*. Available at: http://web.missouri.edu/~jamesha/trust/index.htm.

Jones, R. P. and Cox, D. (2010) *Religion and the Tea Party in the 2010 Election: An Analysis of the Third Biennial American Values Survey*. Washington, DC: Public Religion Research Institute.

Keele, L. (2005) The Authorities Really Do Matter: Party Control and Trust in Government. *Journal of Politics*, 67(3), pp. 873–886.

——— (2007) Social Capital and the Dynamics of Trust in Government. *American Journal of Political Science*, 51(2), pp. 241–254.

Keller, R. and Poferl, A. (2000) Habermas Fightin' Waste: Problems of Alternative Dispute Resolution in the Risk Society. *Journal of Environmental Policy and Planning*, 2(1), pp. 55–67.

Knack, S. (2002) Social Capital and the Quality of Government: Evidence from the States. *American Journal of Political Science*, 46(4), pp. 772–785.

Markham, W., Johnson, M. and Bonjean, C. (1999) Nonprofit Decision Making and Resource Allocation: The Importance of Membership Preferences, Community Needs, and Interorganizational Ties. *Nonprofit and Voluntary Sector Quarterly*, 28(2), pp. 152–184.

Mutz, D. C. and Reeves, B. (2005) The New Video Malaise: Effects of Televised Incivility on Political Trust. *American Political Science Review*, 99(1), pp. 1–15.

Nolan, L. and Zuvekas, A. (2001) Challenges to Early Development of Integrated Service Delivery Networks and Keys to Success: Lessons Learned from the Community Integrated Services Initiative. *Abstracts of Academy of Health Services Research Health Policy Meeting*, 18, 116.

Pew Research Center for the People and the Press (2010) *Public Trust in Government: 1958–2010*. Available at: http://people-press.org/trust/.

——— (2011a) *Beyond Red vs. Blue: Political Typology*. Available at: http://people-press.org/files/legacy-pdf/Beyond-Red-vs-Blue-The-Political-Typology.pdf.

——— (2011b) *Obama Leadership Image Takes a Hit, GOP Ratings Decline*. Available at: http://people-press.org/files/legacy-pdf/8-25-11%20Political%20Release.pdf.

Pierce, J. C., Lovrich N. P., Jr., and Moon, C. D. (2002) Social Capital and Government Performance: An Analysis of 20 American Cities. *Public Performance & Management Review*, 25(4), pp. 381–397.

Radin, B. A. (2006) *Challenging the Performance Movement: Accountability, Complexity and Democratic Values*. Washington, DC: Georgetown University Press.

Rice, T. W. (2001) Social Capital and Government Performance in Iowa Communities. *Journal of Urban Affairs*, 23(3/4), pp. 375–389.

Shapiro, A. (2010) *Distrusting Government: As American as Apple Pie*. NPR, April 19. Available at: http://www.npr.org/templates/story/story.php?storyId=126028106.

Tolbert, C. J. and Mossberg, K. (2006) The Effect of E-Government on Trust and Confidence in Government. *Public Administration Review*, 66(3), pp. 354–369.

Torney-Purta, J., Richardson, W. K. and Barber, C. H. (2004) *Trust in Government-Related Institutions and Civic Engagement among Adolescents: Analysis of Five Countries from the IEA Civic Education Study*. Working Paper 17, Center for Information and Research on Civic Learning and Engagement, Tufts University, Medford, MA.

Ulbig, S. G. (2008) Voice Is Not Enough: The Importance of Influence in Political Trust and Policy Assessments. *Public Opinion Quarterly*, 72(3), pp. 523–539.

Yang, K. and Holzer, M. (2006) The Performance-Trust Link: Implications for Performance Measurement. *Public Administration Review*, 66(1), pp. 114–126.

3 Evidence-Based Trust

A Contradiction in Terms?

Christopher Pollitt and Naomi Chambers

It is often claimed that the provision of positive performance information will increase the trust that users, in particular, and citizens, more generally, have in our public services (Van de Walle, 2010, pp. 310–312). This is one—though only one—of the reasons why so much time and effort has been invested in improving the provision of performance information throughout the public domain. In this chapter we argue that this simple equation (better performance information = higher public trust) is multiply mistaken. This chapter complements the contribution by Greasley, this volume, which also acknowledges the fallacy of a simplistic performance information–trust link, although he maintains that a composite summary score for government performance can solve cognitive problems faced by citizens in coming to a view and that the relationship between performance and trust is in some part accounted for by the effects of aggregating multiple views. We maintain that the circumstances under which performance information is likely to significantly increase public trust are fairly rare. We explain why we hold this pessimistic view but will eventually argue that the provision of evidence-based performance information is nonetheless a vital ingredient of public-service improvement, and, furthermore, it not only fits with the zeitgeist but is also the 'right' thing to do. We will confine our analysis to evidence from the developed liberal democratic states of north-west Europe and North America because research on this topic is particularly culturally contingent, although the underlining philosophical argument may be less so.

BACKGROUND

Our argument is not about trust in political leaders, or about general trust in government, it is about the citizen's trust in specific public services, such as the health service, schools or the police. It is important to keep these different 'targets' for trust distinct. There is evidence to show that the public is often quite capable of doing so—that, for example, falling trust in a prime minister may have little effect on trust in the police (or vice versa). Overall evaluations of public services are frequently quite different from evaluations of particular services, and satisfaction research concerning specific aspects of services draw out additionally nuanced judgements on the part of the public (Sitzia and Wood, 1997). Furthermore, citizens quite definitely distinguish between different public services—for example, Canadian citizens routinely think better of the fire brigade and the police than public transport or the postal service (Canadian Centre for Management Development, 2000; Erin Research, 2005). So we analysts need to be similarly discriminating.

It is also worth mentioning that our argument does *not* depend on the popular assumption that trust levels in public services have been falling dramatically throughout the western world, for example, as highlighted and then critiqued by Onora O'Neill (2002). Such evidence as is available does not seem to support such an assertion (O'Neill, 2002; Van de Walle et al., 2008), but, in any case, our argument simply concerns the likelihood of increasing trust by displaying good performance, irrespective of whether trust was previously static, falling or even increasing.

Why do we doubt whether better performance information about public services will increase public trust? The conditions that would have to be fulfilled before this could be the case include the following:

- The performance information would have to reach the citizen
- The citizen would have to pay attention to the performance information
- The performance information in question would need to show a good performance, not a weak one (or, to be more precise, it would have to show a performance equal to or higher than the public's expectations— a highly variable and subjective standard)
- The citizen would have to understand the performance information
- The performance information would have to be trusted by the citizen

Taken together, this is a very demanding set of conditions. The information we have about how the public use performance information is very patchy, but that which there is does not suggest that any of these stages is likely to be particularly easy.

THE PERFORMANCE INFORMATION WOULD HAVE TO REACH THE CITIZEN

One might think that reaching the citizen, in our Internet age, would be no problem. In practice, of course, things are far from easy. The public is assailed by a mass of often conflicting information (e.g. Are local health services safe or not? Is the incidence of crime going up or down?) from multiple sources. At the same time, some citizens, perhaps especially the elderly and children but also certain ethnic minorities, live within their own fairly closed networks of information and are hard to reach through formal government-controlled channels. Others still are highly mobile, or personally disorganized, or actually hiding from the authorities for one reason or another. In short, 'the public' is anything but a unity. Getting relevant performance information to such a diverse audience and getting it to them at times when it is pertinent to their decision-making is a considerable challenge.

THE PERFORMANCE INFORMATION WOULD HAVE TO BE PAID ATTENTION TO BY THE CITIZEN

When the British government put 100,000 copies of its annual performance report into supermarkets—priced at £2.99—only 12,000 copies were sold and the government was obliged to buy back most of the remainder (BBC News, 1999, 2000). The idea of such an annual report was quietly dropped. Many other pieces of research show that, even when public-service performance information is put in front of service users, only a minority pay it much attention (e.g. Mannion and Goddard, 2003; Marshall et al., 2000). From the United States (US) comes evidence that, even when citizens are deliberately and intimately involved in the design and operation of a local performance measurement system, 'citizens can easily lose patience and drop out of the process' (Ho and Coates, 2004, p. 47). There is also a challenge because certain public services tend to be regarded by citizens as having low interest, although they are nevertheless important prerequisites of civilized society. Refuse collection and public health inspection are among the examples of this category—in the general run of things, they would attract much less attention than, say, healthcare or education. We can hardly blame our good citizens for this lack of enthusiasm for performance data. Indeed, in this they are merely mirroring the behaviour of their elected representatives. Several studies have indicated low or only episodic use of public-services performance data by politicians (Ter Bogt, 2004; Bouckaert and Halligan, 2006; Moynihan, 2008; Pollitt, 2006).

THE PERFORMANCE INFORMATION IN QUESTION WOULD NEED TO SHOW A GOOD PERFORMANCE, NOT A WEAK ONE

There are at least two problems with this requirement. First, performance will be judged good or bad in relation to prior expectations (Zeithmal et al., 1990), and the prior expectations of citizens are both variable and, in many cases, unrealistic. As a rule of thumb, the less prior experience a citizen has with a service, the more unrealistic his or her expectations are likely to be. For some assessments—particularly those where tangible qualities are readily and directly observable, such as clean streets—citizen judgements may be rather accurate and, for others, not (Barnes and Gill, 2000; Bok, 1997; Van Ryzin, 2007). One cannot expect most lay members of the general public to be able to distinguish between the competence of an average neurosurgeon and that of an outstanding neurosurgeon (especially if the former has a wonderful 'bedside manner' and the latter is a little stiff and formal).

The second problem is that much if not most performance information reaches the citizen through the mass media, and the media, as we know, has a strong tendency to concentrate on negative extremes—'the worst school in England' and so on:

> Mass media that are characterized by a combination of political-economic antagonism towards public services and journalistic cynicism about politics form a difficult setting for the publication and celebration of 'success stories'. (Clarke, 2005, p. 226)

For a specific example about the negative treatment of international education league tables, see Grek (2008).

THE PERFORMANCE INFORMATION WOULD HAVE TO BE UNDERSTOOD BY THE CITIZEN

Psychologists and others have supplied us with a great deal of evidence about how most of us, most of the time, process information. And the news is not good. We readily misunderstand, take unwarranted shortcuts and arrive at inconsistent or downright contradictory conclusions (Hammond, 1996; Hibbard et al., 1997; Pollitt, 2010a; Tversky and Kahneman, 1974). Understanding the kind of composite measures which are regularly used to sum up the performance of hospitals or schools is especially problematic (Jacobs et al., 2006), and when aggregation is taken to the extreme represented by the World Bank's World Governance Indicators, then it is hard even for experts to understand what the scores are supposed to mean (Pollitt, 2010b).

THE PERFORMANCE INFORMATION WOULD HAVE TO BE TRUSTED BY THE CITIZEN

At this point it is necessary to refine our central concept. Some writers have distinguished between different types of trust, and we will here employ a three-fold categorization which originates with Lewicki and Bunker (1996) and which has subsequently been found useful in specific public sector applications (Van de Walle, 2010). Lewicki and Bunker distinguish between:

- *Calculus-based trust*, which is present when a conscious calculation takes place of the rewards and penalties of trusting or not trusting, and it is eventually decided to trust (we should note that some other writers on the subject would not regard this as trust at all)

- *Knowledge-based trust*, which is based on the provision of information ('our records show we have never had an accident', etc.) and confidence in the reliability of that information
- *Identification-based trust*, which lies beyond calculative or knowledge-based trust because it rests on an assumption of shared goals or values. Its foundations are thus emotional as well as, or instead of, cognitive

Performance information is presumably intended to reinforce knowledge-based trust, but we should immediately note that the trust which is said to be being lost is often of the identification-based type. We could argue that knowledge-based trust is thus closely related to confidence, with loss of confidence related to the provision of negative performance information, for example as the facts about failures of care have come to light with the inquiries into the failures of hospital care at Mid Staffordshire NHS Foundation Trust in the United Kingdom (UK) (Francis, 2010). We used to trust public service professionals because we believed that they shared our values and had our best interests at heart. Now, perhaps, we are less likely to extend that kind of trust to those public figures. Therefore, even if it was successful, spreading performance would not directly restore diminishing identification-based trust; rather it would replace it with another kind of trust.

Furthermore, the growth and shrinkage of the three types of trust is substantially different. The first type may be quickly formed (if it looks to be strongly in Agent A's interest to do what B wants, then B would calculatively trust A straight away). On the other hand, it also disappears quickly—as soon as the terms of the calculus appear to change, so does the trust. The second type may take longer to establish but may also be somewhat more durable. The relevant knowledge (performance information) has to be communicated and understood (for which difficulties, see previous sections), but once it is received and understood, trust should be maintained unless and until the performance information shows a substantial change for the worse. Identification-based trust takes the longest period to build up but is then so well rooted (an emotional component as well as cognitive acceptance) that it can survive short-term fluctuations and disappointments. This sturdiness makes it perhaps the most desirable kind of trust to have, at least from the point of view of the trustees.

This threefold categorization is indeed useful, but we should note that the categories are not entirely watertight and mutually exclusive. As mentioned in previous sections, psychological and other research has shown that acceptance of information/knowledge is by no means an exclusively cognitive process. Whether we trust a piece of performance information (whether we regard it as 'knowledge' at all) may well rest not so much on its statistical reliability as on our identification stance/emotional stance towards the presumed source.

Which brings us to a paradox. Trust is not just an *outcome* of government actions; it is simultaneously an *input* (Bouckaert and Halligan, 2008, pp. 20–21). If you trust in the third, identificatory sense, you are more likely to believe, comply, obey and accept. Indeed, one fundamental definition of that type of trust is that it is a form of confidence that goes *beyond* the immediate evidence. To the extent that this is useful, it could be argued that the terms 'trust' and 'confidence' are distinguishable by these two different sources of reliance. Performance measurement systems are, from this perspective, a low-trust alternative to low-transaction-cost, traditional, identification-based systems in which citizens assume that 'the authorities know best'.

A further twist to the story is that information about levels of trust is usually gathered by means of survey questionnaires. However, extensive research—mainly in general psychology, but some are also specifically focused on citizen satisfaction with public services—has clearly demonstrated a number of distortions in the way that many respondents answer such questions. In particular, they tend to 'anchor' or 'prime' on early questions and allow these to influence their responses to later questions. Thus, the responses obtained depend to some extent on the order in which the questions are posed (Tourangeau et al., 2000).

Evidence of the degree to which citizens trust government information and how this may be changing is very patchy indeed (Coulter et al., 2002). Such as it is, however, it is not particularly encouraging. In one focus group, for example, government information on the quality of health services was trusted less than information from for-profit consultancy, partly because it was from 'the government'—even though the consultancy's work was largely based on the same underlying official data (Magee et al., 2003). There is an obvious danger that, to the extent that performance measures become weapons that political parties fling at each other when vying for votes, those same measures are thereby tainted by association and, in the public mind, become part of untrustworthy party political hype. In a number of other cases, research indicated that citizens would place much more trust in what friends and families said about hospitals than what they were told either by government agencies or by patient surveys (e.g. Robinson and Brodie, 1997).

Another relevant consideration is timescale. Public confidence can be lost quite quickly when something goes wrong. However, the *creation* of trust—especially the most robust type of identificatory trust—is more commonly a gradual process, not the result of exposure to a single set of results. One substantial piece of research on this quotes the saying 'Confidence arrives on foot and departs on horseback' (Erin Research Inc., 2008, p. 9).

On the other hand, there is perhaps a sliver of hope in the fact that a number of surveys find that those American Internet users who regularly used government services websites tended to trust government services more, at least at the local level—and even preferred Internet contacts to face-to-face ones (Reddick, 2005; Tolbert and Mossberger, 2006). Recent UK research also shows that Internet users trust Internet services more than they do government (Dutton et al., 2009)—whatever that means! However, these results need to be interpreted with great caution, because they refer to Internet usage in general, not to any specific use of performance data.

Perhaps the most fundamental criticism of the effects of performance measurement on public accountability comes in Tsoukas's notion of the 'tyranny of light' (Tsoukas, 1997). Tsoukas argues that attempts to create measurement systems which will reassure the public that organizations and services are performing well eventually become self-defeating. This is because the process of measurement inevitably becomes a domain of experts, and a deep asymmetry of knowledge develops between these 'insiders' and the citizen and politician 'outsiders'. Ultimately, the strenuous efforts of the experts to cast light on the strengths and weaknesses of public policies has the paradoxical effect of *increasing* citizen distrust and the opposite of the effect that is intended (Tsoukas, 1997, p. 834).

This 'tyranny of light' may be partially mitigated by the advent of social media, and Web 2.0 technology has enabled the development of user-generated performance information, of which the Tripadvisor website, with its user-generated ratings of hotels, restaurants and so on, is probably the most famous example. The use of social media is now also percolating in the public sector sphere (Kawalek, 2010), although the performance information is more focused on views and opinions (e.g. www.patientopinion.org.uk) rather than on 'hard', quantitative data. Yet this more optimistic line of argument has some obvious limitations. For services of a complex, expertise-based type it would be positively foolhardy to trust popularly generated opinions and social media. If you want to find out as much as you can about aircraft safety, or climate change or the safety of a vaccine you would not be well advised to rely on Facebook, Twitter and the more sensational broadsheets and blogs. The unhappy saga of the combined mumps, measles and rubella (MMR) vaccine would be a case in point: information of very poor quality (because of the very small number of cases, which did not allow for statistical significance) about causality was repeatedly reported using popular media channels, augmented by accounts of individual stories of children who had become unwell after receiving the vaccine but without scientific basis for the causality that was inferred.

CONCLUSIONS: IS PERFORMANCE MEASUREMENT AND EVIDENCE-GATHERING A WASTE OF TIME?

Even if performance measures were definitively proven *not* to increase public trust under any circumstances, there would be many other powerful reasons for continuing to use them (see, e.g. Behn, 2003; OECD, 2005; Pollitt, 2010a). These include:

- To encourage the more efficient use of scarce resources (technical efficiency)
- To influence resource allocation between different services, units or activities (allocative efficiency)

- To inform local professionals and managers so that they can better identify, diagnose and solve local problems and weaknesses in service provision
- To serve as a basis for a performance pay system
- To guide inspectorates and external audit bodies to a problem's location for deeper investigation

In short, the main rationale for performance measurement is probably *not* to promote public trust. It is to help managers and professionals focus on critical dimensions and areas of change and, occasionally, to help inspectors and/or elected politicians hold organizations and individuals to account.

Although the arguments and evidence set out above may seem wholly pessimistic, it is important not to overstate the gloom. The argument is not that performance information can *never* influence trust, it is rather that the process of its doing so is delicate and complicated. Many conditions have to be met, and perhaps not all these conditions can be 'managed'—some are contextual factors where the context cannot really be altered, at least not in the short term. In other words, the argument here is a typical 'critical realist' analysis—that the policy (in this case publishing performance data with the aim of enhancing trust) only works in certain contexts under certain conditions (Pawson, 2002). The task of academics is to try to sort out what those conditions are. The evidence thus far is patchy, but it does contain some suggestive hints.

For example, in a situation of existing low trust, the deliberate marketing of performance measures by public authorities may be part of the problem rather than part of the solution. New messages from an untrusted source are themselves untrusted, and party political squabbling just amplifies this. On the other hand, citizens can themselves be involved in the design of the gathering, processing and dissemination of the performance information, particularly with the advent of social media and Web 2.0 technology. Presentation can be carefully crafted to minimize complex composite measures and widely unintelligible abstractions (such as 'good governance' or 'quality-adjusted life years'). Information can be timed so that it is delivered at the moment when citizens need it for pressing decisions (Which school for the child? Which surgeon for the operation?). It can be delivered by trained intermediaries who can assist in clarification and interpretation, and so on—these strategies will not make all the problems go away, but they are likely at least to help.

Performance measurement can never become the main driver of identification-based trust—and perhaps that is not a bad thing. But at least it should be possible to craft and disseminate performance information in a way that helps some citizens make important choices while not actually *undermining* existing trust (as some performance measurement efforts seem to have done in the recent past). Above all, the search for 'quick wins' should be abandoned. Trust is something that grows, over time, in a specific relationship. You cannot bottle it and sell it in the supermarkets or across the net. You have to earn it.

REFERENCES

Barnes, C. and Gill, D. (2000) *Declining Government Performance? Why Citizens Don't Trust Government.* State Services Commission, Working Paper 9, Auckland, New Zealand.

BBC News (1999) *UK Politics: Government Puts a Gloss on Its Goals*, 26 July. Available at: http://bbc.co.uk/1/hi/uk_politics/403993.stm.

——— (2000) Annual Report: A Hostage to Fortune? 13 July. Available at: http://bbc.co.uk/1/hi/uk_politics/831585.stm.

Behn, R. (2003) Why Measure Performance? Different Purposes Require Different Measures. *Public Administration Review*, 63(5), pp. 586–606.

Bok, D. (1997) Measuring the Performance of Government. In: Nye, S., Zelikow, P. and King, D., eds. *Why People Don't Trust Government.* Cambridge, MA: Harvard University Press, pp. 55–76.

Bouckaert, G. and Halligan, J. (2006) Performance and Performance Management. In: Peters, B. G. and Pierre, J., eds. *Handbook of Public Policy.* London: Sage, pp. 443–459.

——— (2008) *Managing Performance: International Comparisons.* London: Routledge/Taylor and Francis.

Canadian Centre for Management Development (2000) *Citizens First.* Research carried out by Erin Research Inc., Ottawa, Canada.

Clarke, J. (2005) Performing for the Public: Doubt, Desire and the Evaluation of Public Services. In: Du Gay, P., ed. *The Values of Bureaucracy.* Oxford: Oxford University Press, pp. 211–232.

Coulter, A., Fitzpatrick, R. and Davis, L-J. (2002) Patient and Public Perspectives on Health Care Performance. Unpublished report prepared for the Commission for Health Improvement, Oxford.

Dutton, W. H., Helsper, E. J. and Gerber, M. M. (2009) *Oxford Internet Survey 2009 Report: The Internet in Britain.* Oxford: Oxford Internet Institute, University of Oxford. Available at: http://microsites.oii.ox.ac.uk/oxis/publications.

Erin Research Inc. (2005) *Citizens First 4.* Toronto, Canada: Institute for Citizen-Centred Service.

——— (2008) *Citizens First 5.* Toronto, Canada: Institute for Citizen-Centred Service.

Francis, R. (2010) *Department of Health: Mid Staffordshire NHS Foundation Trust Inquiry.* London: The Stationery Office.

Grek, S. (2008) *PISA in the British Media: Leaning Tower or Robust Testing Tool?* Centre for Educational Sociology, Briefing 45, University of Edinburgh.

Hammond, K. (1996) *Human Judgement and Social Policy: Irreducible Uncertainty, Inevitable Error, Unavoidable Injustice.* New York: Oxford University Press.

Hibbard, J., Slovic, P. and Jewett, J. (1997) Informing Consumer Decisions in Health Care: Implications from Decision-Making Research. *The Milbank Quarterly*, 75(3), pp. 395–414.

Ho, A. and Coates, P. (2004) Citizen-Initiated Performance Assessment: The Initial Iowa Experience. *Public Performance and Management Review*, 27(3), pp. 29–50.

Jacobs, R., Goddard, M. and Smith, P. (2006) *Public Services: Are Composite Measures a Robust Reflection of Performance in the Public Sector?* Research Report. Centre for Health Economics Research Paper (16), Centre for Health Economics, York.

Kawalek, P. (2010) *Notes on Transparency: The Corporate and Society.* Available at: http://www.tm.mbs.ac.uk.

Lewicki, R. and Bunker, B. (1996) Developing and Maintaining Trust in Work Relationships. In: Kramer, R. and Tyler, T., eds. *Trust in Organizations: Frontiers of Theory and Research.* Thousand Oaks, CA: Sage, pp. 114–139.

Magee, H., Lucy-Davis, J. and Coulter, A. (2003) Public Views on Healthcare Performance Indicators and Patient Choice. *Journal of the Royal Society of Medicine*, 96, pp. 338–342.

Mannion, R. and Goddard, M. (2003) Public Disclosure of Comparative Clinical Performance Data: Lessons from the Scottish Experience. *Journal of Evaluation in Clinical Practice*, 9(2), pp. 277–286.

Marshall, M. et al. (2000) The Public Release of Performance Data: What Do We Expect to Gain? A Review of the Evidence. *Journal of the American Medical Association*, 283(14), pp. 1866–1874.

Moynihan, D. (2008) *The Dynamics of Performance Management: Constructing Information and Reform*. Washington, DC: Georgetown University Press.

OECD (2005) *Modernising Government—The Way Forward*. Paris: OECD.

O'Neill, O. (2002) *The Philosophy of Trust*. Reith Lectures, BBC—Radio 4, http://www.bbc.co.uk/radio4/reith2002/.

Pawson, R. (2002) Evidence and Policy and Naming and Shaming. *Policy Studies*, 23(3/4), pp. 211–230.

Pollitt, C. (2006) Performance Information for Democracy: The Missing Link? *Evaluation*, 12(1), pp. 39–56.

——— (2010a) Performance Blight and the Tyranny of Light? Accountability in Advanced Performance Measurement Regimes. In: Dubnick, M. J. and Frederickson, G. H., eds. *Accountable Governance: Problems and Promises*. Armonk, NY: M. E. Sharpe , pp. 81–110.

——— (2010b) Simply the Best? The International Benchmarking of Reform and Good Governance. In: Pierre, J. and Ingraham, P., eds. *Comparative Administrative Change and Reform: Lessons Learned* (Festschrift for Guy B. Peters). Montreal: McGill-Queens University Press, pp. 91–113.

Reddick, C. (2005) Citizen Interaction with E-Government: From the Streets to Servers? *Government Information Quarterly*, 22(1), pp. 38–57.

Robinson, S. and Brodie, M. (1997) Understanding the Quality Challenge for Health Consumers: The Kaiser/AHCPR Survey. *Journal of Quality Improvement*, 23(5), pp. 239–244.

Sitzia, J. and Wood, N. (1997) Patient Satisfaction: A Review of Issues and Concepts. *Social Science and Medicine*, 45(12), pp. 1829–1843.

Ter Bogt, H. (2004) Politicians in Search of Performance Information? Survey Research on Dutch Aldermen's Use of Performance Information. *Financial Accountability and Management*, 20(3), pp. 221–252.

Tolbert, C. and Mossberger, K. (2006) The Effects of E-Government on Trust and Confidence in Government. *Public Administration Review*, 66(3), pp. 354–369.

Tourangeau, R. et al. (2000) *The Psychology of Survey Response*. Cambridge: Cambridge University Press.

Tsoukas, H. (1997) The Tyranny of Light: The Temptations and Paradoxes of the Information Society. *Futures*, 29(9), pp. 827–843.

Tversky, A. and Kahneman, D. (1974) Judgement under Uncertainty: Heuristics and Biases. *Science*, 185, pp. 1124–1131.

Van de Walle, S. (2010) NPM: Restoring the Public Trust through Creating Distrust? In: Christensen, T. and Laegreid, P., eds. *The Ashgate Research Companion to the New Public Management*. Farnham: Ashgate, pp. 309–320.

Van de Walle, S., Van Roosbroek, S. and Bouckaert, G. (2008) Trust in the Public Sector: Is There Any Evidence for a Long Term Decline? *International Review of Administrative Sciences*, 74(1), pp. 47–64.

Van Ryzin, G. (2007) *Can Citizens Accurately Judge Public Performance? Evidence from New York City with Implications for Developing International Bureaumetrics*. Paper presented at the European Group of Public Administration Conference, Madrid, Spain, September.

Zeithmal, V., Parasuraman, A. and Berry, L. (1990) *Delivering Quality Service*. New York: Free Press.

4 Trust and Networks

Erik Hans Klijn and Jasper Eshuis

Trust is often mentioned as the core coordination mechanism of networks (Thomson et al., 1991). Trust is then contrasted with two other forms of governance: markets and hierarchies. Hierarchies are characterized by rules and central steering, while markets are dominated by the decentralized mechanism of prices as dictated by supply and demand.

The discussion of trust as a core coordination mechanism in networks is, however, somewhat misleading and confusing in that it places networks somewhere between markets and hierarchies when in fact this positioning reveals little about networks. In the first place, it is very questionable if networks are characterized by a high degree of trust because most authors on networks stress that networks consist of various actors with different perceptions and interests and that the complex interactions between these actors show a lot of conflict (see Gage and Mandell, 1990; Kickert et al., 1997; Rhodes, 1997). Secondly, the story about trust as a coordination mechanism of networks (Thomson et al., 1991) ignores that networks are coordinated by many coordination mechanisms (including rules and price mechanisms) and not necessarily only or even predominantly by trust.

This does not mean that there is no relation between networks or trust, but it is a different one than what is mostly proposed. Networks, or governance networks, as we will call them in this chapter, are characterized by both the self-organizing and intentional actions of multiple actors that are interdependent in tackling a policy problem or providing services or other public tasks. One could say that governance networks, as emerging structures of patterns of interactions, are a vehicle to build trust to achieve the minimum of coordination between otherwise autonomous actors with conflicting goals. Trust then, is the goal to achieve in interaction if one wants to facilitate the performance of networks.

In this chapter, we look conceptually at the meaning of trust, how it can facilitate interactions in networks and how it can grow, since trust has to be built. But first we must look at what we mean by networks and why trust could be an asset in these networks.

NETWORKS AS VEHICLE FOR POLICY-MAKING AND SERVICE DELIVERY

A mantra of modern public-administration theory is that many decision-making processes, including service delivery and implementation processes, take place within complex networks of actors (Hanf and Scharpf, 1978; Kaufmann et al., 1986; Marsh and Rhodes, 1992; Kickert et al., 1997; Rhodes, 1997). These networks emerge out of a necessity to interact and are, on the one hand, consciously planned in the sense that actors deliberately interact and attempt to structure these interactions with organizations and rules, but on the other hand, they are also unplanned as a result of coincidental interactions and strategies and previously created rules.

Governance networks can roughly be defined as 'more or less stable patterns of social relations between mutually dependent actors, which form around policy program and/or clusters of resources and which are formed, maintained and changed through series of (policy) games' (Koppenjan and Klijn, 2004, pp. 69–70).[1] Crucial to the emergence and existence of networks are dependency relations between actors (Hanf and Scharpf, 1978). The resource dependencies around policy problems or policy programs require actors to interact with one another and create more intensive and enduring interactions (Mandell, 2001; Agranoff and McGuire, 2003).

A governance network's perspective sees interaction in networks around policy and service delivery as a continuous set of strategic games between various actors who have their own perceptions of the problems to be addressed and the solutions to be accomplished (Rhodes, 1997). During these games, the actors attempt to influence the content and progress of the issue at stake on the basis of their perceptions. In doing so, their perceptions and actions are shaped and constrained by the institutional rules that they share with other actors within the network. But their perceptions and strategies are not determined by the network. To a certain extent, they re-interpret the available information and the applicability and content of the informal and formal network rules (Koppenjan and Klijn, 2004). Games are characterized by conflicts and stagnations but also by breakthroughs, negotiated package deals and innovative project definitions. Processes of decision-making in the context of project realization and implementation can be erratic and only partly controlled by management efforts. In short, decision-making in governance networks are characterized by a high degree of complexity and dynamics. This complexity stems from the variety and dynamics of perceptions and strategies in interaction processes but also from the fact that these interactions take place at different places (arenas). This fragmentation makes the game more than simply a negotiation game.

Thus, if we look at the characteristics of networks, we can see that actors in networks are dependent on each other, and the nature of the problems require cooperation but at the same time the interaction is characterized by conflict and different interests. This creates a high level of uncertainty for the actors. They have to find new solutions for complex problems, exchange information but at the same time be competitive. Thus is especially the situation where trust is difficult to establish but can have a very important function. After all, actors have to cooperate in a situation where other actors, who take advantage of cooperative efforts of others, might misuse cooperative strategies.

TRUST IN GOVERNANCE NETWORKS: WHAT AND HOW

Trust is defined in many ways in the literature. Before we start a discussion about trust, we have to narrow the range of what can be considered as trust. A key characteristic that emerges from the literature is the aspect of risk and vulnerability to opportunistic behaviour (see Edelenbos and Klijn, 2007; Eshuis and Van Woerkum, 2003): when an actor trusts another actor, he is in fact taking a risk and allowing himself to be vulnerable to opportunistic behaviour. If trust has developed, each actor expects the other actor to refrain from opportunistic behaviour, even if the opportunity for it arises (Deakin and Michie, 1997; Deakin and Wilkinson, 1998). He or she assumes that the partner will take their interests into account in the interaction, but he or she is not certain about it (Rousseau et al., 1998; Nooteboom, 2002). A conscious choice has to be made to take a risk, and this is usually done with the belief that the other party can be trusted. Interlinked with the previous argument is the idea that trust only arises in cases of interdependency. If an actor is not dependent on another actor but fully autonomous, there is no vulnerability involved. The other's behaviour does not pose a risk and therefore there is no real need for trust.

What Is Trust?

A (general) working definition for trust can thus be derived as follows: 'trust refers to the actors' more or less stable, positive perception of the intentions of other actors—that is, the perception that other actors will refrain from opportunistic behaviour' (Edelenbos and Klijn, 2007, p. 30). As the definition highlights, trust is a perception about intentions. It can thus be distinguished from institutional characteristics, such as rules and norms, which often serve to facilitate trustworthy behaviours. Trust can also be distinguished from action. However, trust and actions are mutually interrelated. Trust develops in action or, to put it more precisely, in interaction between actors (Eshuis, 2006). For example, trust develops when an actor communicates openly about his intentions, or when an actor hands over particular responsibilities, or when actors work together on a project without misusing each other's vulnerabilities. Trust is thus *active* trust in the sense that it needs to be developed and maintained actively through interaction (Giddens, 1984; Nooteboom, 2002). Without interaction, trust will easily diminish.

Trust Is Related to Risks

Most authors on trust agree that trust is inextricably related to risk. Without risk, the notion of trust is simply unnecessary (Rousseau et al., 1998; Lyons and Metha, 1997; Lane and Bachmann, 1998; Nooteboom, 2002). As demonstrated earlier, trust has much to do with the expectations an actor has of another actor. In contractual relations, partnerships and almost all cooperative relations involving private and public actors of various affiliations, actors are confronted with risks that can take various forms.

Some authors (see, for instance, Williamson, 1996) state that trust is a superfluous concept and that interactions in those uncertain situations can be explained by risk-taking (the actor perceives risks and decides whether to take the risk or not). Under this analysis, trust is seen as almost unnecessary, and the concept is viewed as being almost synonymous with risk-taking. But the risk-taking perspective assumes that a calculation can be made which then forms the basis for a rational decision. Without such a calculation, the assumption of risk becomes blind. However, this assumption cannot easily be squared with the idea of bounded rationality. If the possibility of gathering information is limited, then so are the opportunities to assess the behavioural alternatives that independent actors have. Interestingly, this argument holds even more strongly for larger governance networks with greater numbers of actors and where unexpected strategic moves take place more frequently and the possibilities are wider. The uncertainty over the strategic behaviour of actors is thus much greater than the term 'information insecurity' suggests, certainly as it is presented in the literature on governance networks. Thus, the idea of rational calculation of the risk in governance networks provides an unlikely perspective. Without a minimum level of trust, risk-taking behaviour of the actors will become very difficult and, thus, reaching satisfactory outcomes will not be easy to realize.

Trust as the Basis to Act in Networks

An important value of the concept of trust lies in the fact that through interaction in networks, strategic complexities (Koppenjan and Klijn, 2004) make it too difficult for the actors to foresee all the possible contingencies, reason them out or calculate them accurately (Deakin and Wilkinson, 1998). It is precisely the many possible contingencies which make the concept of trust such an interesting one to consider when appraising the performance of governance networks (Edelenbos and Klijn, 2007). In particular, in the case of trust, people no longer need to calculate all possible negative outcomes because they expect that the outcome will be positive (Luhmann, 1979; see also Edelenbos and Eshuis, 2012).

The fact that trust is *not* the same as calculation and cannot be entirely reduced to purely rational assessments does not mean that it is blind. Trust does in fact have a rational basis, and is it usually well considered. Most authors point to the fact that trust grows according to the actor's earlier experiences (Nooteboom et al., 1996; Lyons and Metha, 1997; Rousseau et al., 1998) and that trust will not be sustained when it is repeatedly violated (Rousseau et al., 1998; Nooteboom, 2002). Reciprocal behaviour is an essential condition for trust to emerge and to be sustained. This reciprocity is precisely what can be developed during the mutual interactions in governance networks.

So far we have argued that trust exists by virtue of dependency (Rousseau et al., 1998), and that it can develop in interactions, especially in relationships that are continued over time. This is exactly what can be done in governance networks. This is the reason why we stated in the introduction that one can see networks as a vehicle for achieving trust rather than assuming (as is done in some of the literature) that trust is an inherent characteristic of networks.

Understanding trust as something that is not inherently or automatically present in networks also clarifies why trust is something that needs to be worked upon and actively managed. But before we deal with managerial activities and trust, we will first discuss why trust would be worth the managerial efforts.

WHY TRUST IS BENEFICIAL IN GOVERNANCE NETWORKS

The literature, although mostly from fields other than governance, governance networks or public administration, provides various reasons why trust is important. The most important reasons are discussed below.

Transaction Costs and Durable Investments

The first argument concerns the reduction of transaction costs. Fukuyama (1995, p. 336) argues: 'Property rights, contracts and commercial law are all indispensable institutions for creating a modern market-oriented economic system, but it is possible to economize substantially on transaction costs if such institutions are supplemented by social capital and trust.' On the one hand, trust reduces the risk inherent in transactions and cooperative relations because it creates greater predictability (Kramer and Tyler, 1996). In a situation where one actor assumes good intentions on the part of the other, the likelihood of unexpected interactions as a consequence of opportunistic behaviour are smaller. Given the complexity of decision-making and inter-actions in governance networks, this could be a significant advantage. On the other hand, trust can also serve to reduce costs that are connected with contracts because contracts need fewer details and specifications when trust is present (Hindmoor, 1998; Sako, 1998; Ring and Van de Ven, 1992; Nooteboom, 2002). This could also be an advantage in governance networks, given the costs of complex cooperation processes (Agranoff and McGuire, 2003).

A second argument is that trust increases the probability that actors will invest their resources—such as money, knowledge and so on—in cooperation, thus creating stability in the relationship and providing them with a stronger basis for cooperation (Sako, 1998; Parker and Vaidya, 2001; Ring and Van de Ven, 1992; Nooteboom et al., 1996). Although this argument is made for private cooperative relationships between firms, it is likely that it applies to cooperation within governance networks. The complexity of decision-making and the multiplicity of actors require investments in forming and maintaining relations (Agranoff and McGuire, 2003). Trust can stimulate that investment and the effort actors put into those relations.

Trust as Facilitator for Learning and Innovation

A third argument in the literature is that trust stimulates learning and the exchange of information and knowledge. Knowledge is partly tacit and only available, for instance, in the form of human capital (Nooteboom, 2002). This type of knowledge can be acquired only by exchange and intensive cooperation.

Learning and discovering new things requires knowledge exchange and intensive interaction. Trust plays an important role in these types of interaction, for example, because trusting actors are more open towards each other (Zand, 1972), which facilitates the learning process. Nooteboom (2002) mentions the example of small companies that maintain a network of contacts with other organizations, which enables them to acquire the necessary specific knowledge they do not possess. These types of knowledge exchange require a minimum amount of trust, since drawing up a contract in such a network is far too costly, especially given the limited means of such companies (cf. Miles and Snow, 1986; Graeber, 1993; Parker and Vaidya, 2001). Most of the literature on governance and governance networks also emphasizes the importance of learning processes in which actors not only exchange information but also learn from each other the particular new solutions that satisfy their interests (Rein and Schön, 1992; Hajer and Wagenaar, 2003).

A fourth argument is that trust has the ability to stimulate innovation. The outcome of innovation processes is usually uncertain since innovations are novelties rather than proven developments. Therefore, actors are not certain that their efforts and investment in the innovation process will give any returns. Thus, trust is crucial. From a transaction cost perspective, vertical integration, bringing separate units under one heading to reduce the transaction costs, is quickly chosen in order to achieve innovation (Williamson, 1996); however, this has its disadvantages. An important disadvantage regarding innovations is that these emerge by confronting different ideas and expertise: vertical integration tends to minimize these differences, which has a negative impact on future innovation. Trust can facilitate innovation by reducing uncertainty about opportunistic behaviour and making vertical integration less necessary (Miles and Snow, 1986;

Alter and Hage, 1993; Lundval, 1993; Parker and Vaidya, 2001). This argument is interesting for governance networks because empirical research shows that vertical integration is hardly an option in these networks (Koppenjan and Klijn, 2004; Marcussen and Torfing, 2007). That means that trust as a horizontal coordinating mechanism is one of the few options left for innovation.

TRUST HAS TO BE BUILT AND MANAGED

Earlier on we argued that trust does not arise unaided. Most authors agree that trust has to grow gradually and needs to be sustained by the trustworthy behaviour of actors. This is where institutions or rules come in because rules structure behaviour (e.g. Giddens, 1984), which in turn enhances continuity and predictability of behaviour. Luhmann (1979) adds to this that the latent existence of rules means that actors need to be less afraid that their trust in others will be breached. As a consequence, trust between actors develops more easily.

Some authors speak of a 'trust cycle', in which more interactions lead to an inclination among actors to trust each other, which in its turn leads to more interactions (Huxham and Vangen, 2005). This generates a gradual process of trust-building (Huxham and Vangen, 2005; Rousseau et al., 1998). Thus, trust needs time to develop, and interaction between actors needs to grow and sustain. It develops in relationships between people. One could also say that trust can be the 'emergent outcome' of growing interdependency and interactions between actors in a network. But many authors also point out that trust is very vulnerable for 'untrustful' behaviour (Gambetta, 1988). Trust may lead to a certain forgiveness in interaction and giving other actors the benefit of the doubt, but repeatedly violating trust relations will certainly damage a trust relation.

But if trust develops during interactions, it follows that it can be fostered and managed. It is relevant to keep in mind that the management of trust is a form of indirect management; trust itself cannot be managed because it cannot be directly created or enforced. The manager can only facilitate certain behaviour and create conditions that facilitate the development of relationships.

In most network literature, much emphasis is laid on network management, that is, the deliberate governing and facilitating of interactions in governance networks. A significant amount of the literature emphasizes that network management is one of the most important factors to achieve good outcomes in governance networks (see Agranoff and McGuire, 2003; Meier and O'Toole, 2007; Provan et al., 2009; Klijn et al., 2010a).

The literature has dealt with an impressive number of the types of network-management strategies to guide interaction processes, so an exhaustive list cannot be provided here (see Gage and Mandell, 1990; O'Toole, 1988; Agranoff and McGuire, 2001, 2003). Table 4.1 provides a summary (albeit

Table 4.1 Overview of Network Management Strategies

Types of strategies	Process agreements	Exploring content	Arranging	Connecting
Main strategies mentioned in the literature	Rules for entrance into or exit from the process, conflict-regulating rules, rules that specify the interests of actors or veto possibilities, rules that inform actors about the availability of information about decision-making moments, etc.	Searching for goal congruency, creating variation in solutions, influencing (and explicating) perceptions, managing and collecting information and research, creating variation through creative competition	Creating new ad hoc organizational arrangements (boards, project organizations, etc.)	Selective (de)activation of actors, resource-mobilizing, initiating new series of interactions, coalition-building, mediation, appointment of process managers, removing obstacles to co-operation, creating incentives for co-operation

Source: Adapted from Klijn, 2005.

a non-exhaustive one) of the types of strategies that have been identified, providing examples of each of the categories. We shortly discuss the various types of network management strategies.

Connecting strategies such as the activation of actors or resources are required in order to start the game. The network-management literature stresses that the network manager has to identify the actors required for an initiative and actually create a situation in which they become interested in investing their resources (see Scharpf, 1978). The interactions within the game itself also have to be managed. This can be done by appointing a process manager, who invests time and energy in connecting the actions and strategies of actors to one another during the interactions. Once the game has begun, strategies for exploring content are necessary to clarify the goals and perceptions of actors (Fischer, 2003; Koppenjan and Klijn, 2004) and to try to invest time and money in developing solutions that create opportunities for actors' participation. However, the process is sometimes short of creative solutions to satisfy the various actors involved. In such cases, more variation is required, for instance, by using different teams of experts who compete against one another to create solutions. The managerial strategy of arranging means setting (temporary) structures for consultation, interaction and deliberation, like project organization, communication lines, etc. (Rogers and Whetten, 1982). The transaction costs of these arrangements must be kept as low as possible (Williamson, 1996), but at the same time the arrangements have to be acceptable to the actors involved. Another important strategy mentioned in the literature are strategies of process agreements that draft temporary sets of rules for interaction that structure the interactions and protect each actor's core values (Koppenjan and Klijn, 2004). The rules can be seen as ground rules for behaviour and interaction in the network that the actors in the network (explicitly) agreed on.

Thus network management is needed to bring actors together, increase their interactions, create organizational arrangements for interactions, organize joint fact-finding and search for innovative solutions that will satisfy preferences of actors, to list just a few of the network-management strategies mentioned in the literature. Since network management aims to bring actors together, increase their interactions and stimulate the development of a common perspective, network management is thought to have a positive effect on trust-building. More and active network management will then result in a higher level of trust in networks.

Although most of the literature on network management stresses the 'processual' character of the strategies (thus, the strategies mentioned in Table 4.1), there is also some literature that mentions creating institutional changes (see, for an overview, Klijn, 2008). Since trust can be fostered by influencing behaviour and relations of actors but also by creating rules and institutional arrangements that support trust relations, this could be an alternative route to stimulating trust. On the other hand, authors warn that strategies that are aimed at creating trust during changes in the institutional structure often will affect actors' power positions and core beliefs, and therefore they will not often be uncontested. Strong conflicts may in turn diminish trust relations in networks.

TRUST IN NETWORKS: SOME EMPIRICAL EVIDENCE

What do we know about the effects of trust and how it is generated if it comes to empirical findings? There are very few empirical studies of governance networks that examine the relationship between trust and network performance and network-management strategies. Although several studies suggest that increasing the intensity of the interactions and employing network-management strategies enhances the relations between actors in the governance network (see, for instance, Marcussen and Torfing, 2007; Huang and Provan, 2007), the level of trust has not been directly related to the intensity and character of the network-management strategies employed.

Does Trust Matter?

One of the exceptions is a study by Provan et al. (2009). They studied a centrally led, publicly funded mixed-sector health and human service network and examined over time the effect of network embeddedness (measured as

Box 4.1 Measuring Trust in Networks

To measure trust within the network, Klijn et all used five dimensions derived from business literature (see Sako, 1998; Nooteboom, 2002, Klijn et al., 2010b for more information on these dimensions). The five point Likert items are shown below.

Measurement of trust

Dimension	Item
1. Agreement trust	The parties in this project generally live up to the agreements made with each other
2. Benefit of the doubt	The parties in this project give one another the benefit of the doubt
3. Reliability	The parties in this project keep in mind the intentions of the other parties
4. Absence of opportunistic behaviour	Parties do not use the contributions of other actors for their own advantage
5. Goodwill trust	Parties in this project can assume that the intentions of the other parties are good in principle

centrality) on trustworthiness, reputation and influence of actors. They find that when embeddedness increases, this is positively related to the three social indicators of the network (trustworthiness, reputation and influence). They also found that when the network matured, the performance of the network became better.

Klijn, Steijn and Edelenbos (2010b) looked at the relationship between trust and outcomes in governance networks. Judging from their survey of actors involved in large environmental projects, there appears to be a high correlation between the level of trust (as measured by five items—see Box 4.1) and perceived outcomes. In this research a distinction was made between process (level of management, contact frequency achieved, conflict resolution etc.) and content outcomes (innovative character, effectiveness solutions, efficiency etc.). The researchers found in their regression analysis (which controlled for actor characteristics (e.g. public or private), phase of decision-making and the complexity of the issue) that trust has a very strong relationship with both content (Beta of .534) and process outcomes (Beta of .545). This shows that trust does matter in governance networks. This strong relation holds in later repeated surveys (Korthagen et al., 2011).

Impact of Network Management

In the same survey, Klijn, Edelenbos and Steijn (2010b) asked respondents about network-management strategies used in the project. They measured the amount of network management by using sixteen items that measured the four types of network-management activities mentioned in Table 1 (see Klijn et al., 2010a, 2010b). By dichotomizing the scores (only if the respondent answered positively about the presence of a certain activity was the strategy scored as 'present'), a score for the amount of network management was created (possible score from 0 [*no network management activities*] to 16 [*all identified activities present*]). The authors found a strong relation between the number of strategies employed in governance networks and the overall level of trust. Thus, networks which were characterized by a high level of network-management activities are also characterized by a high level of trust in general. Active network management, here seen as actively connecting actors, searching for solutions and new information and using process rules and organizational arrangements to facilitate interactions, seems to be good for achieving trust.

If we look at various types of strategies we mentioned in the previous section (exploring, connecting, arranging and process rules), we see that the strategies connecting and exploring have the most impact on the level of trust in networks, followed by the strategies of process rules. Arranging strategies have no significant effect.

How Does Trust Work in Practice: A Case Analysis

Thus, we see from survey material that trust matters and can be managed. How that works out in daily practice can be witnessed in a case study on Crooswijk, a large urban regeneration project in the Dutch city of Rotterdam.

The case study involved a radical restructuring project, including the demolition and rebuilding of 1,800 houses out of 2,100 houses in the community. It was implemented by a private partnership of three parties, namely a housing association, a developer and a building company. The municipality was at arm's length, mainly focusing on setting the preconditions of the project and on monitoring whether these preconditions were met during the development. The project was a big project, and its failure would almost certainly mean the direct bankruptcy of the developer and the builder while it would be a major blow to the housing association. In short, the project involved considerable risk.

From the beginning, the project was also politically sensitive because a significant part of the community protested against the large-scale demolition of houses. However, the municipality continued with the project because they thought that the high quality of the spatial plan and the planned houses would improve the community and benefit the city.

At the start of the project, a crucial step was that private parties were selected which were trusted by the municipality because the municipality had a long relationship with those parties. One respondent explains:

> WBRS (the housing association, authors) had involved ERA and Proper Stok (the developers) because they know that the municipality had trust

in these parties. We had earned our track record in Rotterdam if it comes to restructuring, they know how we operate.

During the implementation of the project, sustained, trustworthy behaviour was essential. This was realized by intensive cooperation of the directors of the three private parties, who mutually agreed on the strategy to show that they themselves, the top of the private organizations, were very committed to the project. They were present as much as possible, not only to show their commitment but also to enact intensive interactions with each other and the municipality during the implementation of the project.

> The CEOs are working very hard on the project. By doing so we try to reduce the risk of the project losing its credibility. We are present at many moments in the decision-making also in the political arena. That creates trust with politicians. This is more than a technocratic project.

Another aspect of the process gives some more insight in how particular trusting behaviour was applied to trigger reciprocal behaviour. The municipal project manager tells how this worked during the negotiations about the cooperation agreement.

> The general attitude was not that the other should give it first but that each of the parties now and then did the first step to come to an agreement and that creates a situation where the other party is also more willing.

Another respondent explains how the contract as an institutional arrangement did not function as a sign of distrust or as a substitute for trust, but that the development of this institutional arrangement was an important managerial activity because the contract actually facilitated further development of trust.

> You have to arrange some things in advance and later in the cooperation-agreement. Not the details but the general ideas. This to prevent that things will be interpreted differently during the process, especially when other people get involved . . . But in the period of drawing the cooperation-agreement the idea was how can we write down things to prevent problems, rather than we do not trust each other.

The quotes show how trust is built through intensified interactions and sustained in the negotiating process during implementation. It also exemplifies how trust is sustained by process rules, in this case, intentional agreements made among the actors that sustain the relation and provide a guideline and 'safety valve' in difficult times.

CONCLUSIONS AND REFLECTIONS: TRUST AS IMPORTANT CONDITION IN NETWORKS

In this chapter, we argued that trust is not something that is inherently present in governance networks, as a governance mechanism, as some authors argue. Trust is, rather, very scarce most of the time because governance networks are composed of various autonomous actors who are interdependent but nevertheless pursue their own strategies and interests. Thus, we are witnessing complex interaction and decision-making processes in these networks to achieve satisfying outcomes. Trust is thus something that needs to be built instead of something that can be assumed as a coordination mechanism.

We showed the importance of trust for the interactions and outcomes of governance networks. We elaborated why trust would be important for those networks—that is, because they can reduce transaction costs, enhance information-sharing and learning and solidify cooperation and that is very important because most governance networks are characterized by a high degree of uncertainty—uncertainty about the strategic moves of other actors, about the possible benefits that come from cooperation and about the institutional characteristics of networks.

Trust can provide a basis for cooperation and help to secure the possible benefits of it and prevent highly conflicting and costly interactions. Thus, not surprisingly, the available empirical material tends to show that networks that are characterized by higher levels of trust also show better performance. At least some of all the 'good things' that the literature attributes to trust actually hold in the empirical material.

We must, however, realize that trust is very vulnerable and can be easily damaged. Because there are no mechanisms to enforce trust, it can easily be broken. Thus, trust has to be built consciously and sustained during interaction. That is why network management, described as the deliberate attempt to guide and facilitate interactions in networks, is very important in order to achieve and sustain trust in networks.

NOTE

1. Games then are ongoing, coherent sets of (strategic) interactions between actors around specific issues or decisions that actors have interest in. Networks mostly consists of a wide variety of games that take place at the same time.

    We are aware that the term 'governance' is sometimes used in other ways (good governance, corporate governance, governance as new public management). However, governance is most often used for situations where governments operate in a multi-actor situation and use horizontal ways of steering/governance (Rhodes, 1997; Pierre and Peters, 2000), which fits our description of governance networks.

REFERENCES

Agranoff, R. and McGuire, M. (2001) Big Questions in Public Network Management Research. *Journal of Public Administration Research and Theory*, 11, pp. 295–326.
—— (2003) *Collaborative Public Management: New Strategies for Local Governments*. Washington, DC: Georgetown University Press.
Alter, C. and Hage, J. (1993) *Organizations Working Together*. Newbury Park, CA: Sage.
Deakin, S. and Michie, J., eds. (1997) *Contract, Co-Operation, and Competition; Studies in Economics, Management and Law*. Oxford: Oxford University Press.
Deakin, S. and Wilkinson, F. (1998) Contract Law and the Economics of Interorganizational Trust. In: Lane, C. and Bachman, R., eds. *Trust within and between Organizations: Conceptual Issues and Empirical Applications*. Oxford: Oxford University Press, pp. 146–172.
Edelenbos, J. and Eshuis, J. (2012). The Interplay between Trust and Control in Governance Processes: A Conceptual and Empirical Investigation. *Administration and Society*, 44(6), pp. 647–674.
Edelenbos, J. and Klijn, E. H. (2007) Trust in Complex Decision-Making Networks: A Theoretical and Empirical Exploration. *Administration and Society*, 39(1), pp. 25–50.
Eshuis, J. and Van Woerkum, C. (2003) Trust and Monitoring in Governance Processes: Lessons from Landscape Management by Farmers in a Dutch Municipality. *Journal of Environmental Policy and Planning*, 5(4), pp. 379–396.
Fischer, F. (2003) *Reframing Public Policy: Discursive Politics and Deliberative Practices*. Oxford: Oxford University Press.
Fukuyama, F. (1995) *Trust, the Social Virtues and the Creation of Prosperity*. New York: Free Press.
Gage, R. W. and Mandell, M. P. eds. (1990) *Strategies for Managing Intergovernmental Policies and Networks*. New York: Praeger.
Gambetta, D. (1988) *Trust: Making and Breaking of Cooperative Relations*. Oxford: Blackwell.
Giddens, A. (1984) *The Constitution of Society*. Berkeley: University of California Press.
Graeber, G. (1993) *The Embedded Firm: Understanding Networks: Actors, Resources and Processes in Interfirm Cooperation*. London: Routledge.
Hajer, M. and Wagenaar, H., eds. (2003) *Deliberative Policy Analysis: Understanding Governance in the Network Society*. Cambridge: Cambridge University Press.
Hanf, K. I. and Scharpf, F. W., eds. (1978) *Interorganizational Policy Making: Limits to Coordination and Central Control*. London: Sage.
Hindmoor, A. (1998) The Importance of Being Trusted: Transaction Costs and Policy Network Theory. *Public Administration*, 76(Spring), pp. 25–43.
Huang, K., and Provan, K. G. (2007) Structural Embeddedness and Organizational Social Outcomes in a Centrally Governed Mental Health Service Network. *Public Management Review*, 9(2), pp. 169–189.
Huxham, C. and Vangen, S. (2005) *Managing to Collaborate: The Theory and Practice of Collaborative Advantage*. London: Routledge.
Kaufmann, F. X., Majone, G. and Ostrom, V., eds. (1986) *Guidance, Control and Evaluation in the Public Sector: The Bielefeld Interdisciplinary Project*. Berlin: Walter de Gruyter.
Kickert, W.J.M., Klijn, E. H. and Koppenjan, J.F.M. (1997) *Managing Complex Networks: Strategies for the Public Sector*. London: Sage.
Klijn, E. H. (2005) Networks and Inter-Organisational Management: Challenging, Steering, Evaluation and the Role of Public Actors in Public Management. In: Ferlie, E., Lynn, L. and Pollitt, C., eds. *The Oxford Handbook of Public Management*. Oxford: Oxford University Press, pp. 257–281.

Klijn, E. H., Steijn, B. and Edelenbos, J. (2010a) The Impact of Network Management on Outcomes in Governance Networks. *Public Administration*, 88(4), pp. 1063–1082.

———— (2010b) Trust in Governance Networks: Its Implications on Outcomes. *Administration and Society*, 42(2), pp. 193–221.

Koppenjan, J.F.M. and Klijn, E. H. (2004) *Managing Uncertainties in Networks: A Network Perspective on Problem Solving and Decision Making*. London: Routledge.

Korthagen, I. A. et al. (2011) *Complex Decision Making in Mediatized Societies: The Effects of Media Attention on Network Performance*. Panel Session: Predicting the Performance of Public Networks, the International Society of Public Management Conference, Dublin, 11–13 April.

Kramer, R. M. and Tyler, T. R., eds. (1996) *Trust in Organizations: Frontiers of Theory and Research*. Thousand Oaks, CA: Sage.

Lane, C. and Bachman, R., eds. (1998) *Trust within and between Organizations: Conceptual Issues and Empirical Applications*. Oxford: Oxford University Press.

Luhmann, N. (1979) *Trust and Power*. Chichester: Wiley.

Lyons, B, and Metha, J. (1997) Private Sector Business Contracts: The Text between the Lines. In: Deakin, S. and Michie, J., eds. *Contract, Co-Operation, and Competition: Studies in Economics, Management and Law*. Oxford: Oxford University Press, pp. 43–66.

Mandell, M. P., ed. (2001) *Getting Results through Collaboration: Networks and Network Structures for Public Policy and Management*. Westport, CT: Quorum Books.

Marcussen, M. and Torfing, J., eds. (2007) *Democratic Network Governance in Europe*. Cheltenham: Edward Elgar.

Marsh, D. and Rhodes, R.A.W., eds. (1992) *Policy Networks in British Government*. Oxford: Clarendon Press.

Meier, K. J. and O'Toole, L. J. (2007) Modelling Public Management: Empirical Analysis of the Management-Performance Nexus. *Public Administration Review*, 9(4), pp. 503–527.

Miles, R. E. and Snow, C. C. (1986) Network Organizations: New Concepts for New Forms. *California Management Review*, 28(3), pp. 62–73.

Nooteboom, B. (2002) *Trust: Forms, Foundations, Functions, Failures and Figures*. Cheltenham: Edgar Elgar.

Nooteboom, B., Berger, H. and Noorderhaven, N. (1996) Effects of Trust and Governance on Relational Risk. *Academy of Management Journal*, 40(2), pp. 308–338.

O'Toole, L. J. (1988) Strategies for Intergovernmental Management: Implementing Programs in Interorganizational Networks. *Journal of Public Administration*, 11(4), pp. 417–441.

Parker, D. and Vaidya, K. (2001) An Economic Perspective on Innovation Networks. In: Jones, O., Conway, S. and Steward, F., eds. *Social Interaction and Organisational Change: Aston Perspectives on Innovation Networks*. London: Imperial College Press.

Pierre, J. and Peters, B. G. (2000) *Governance, Politics and the State*. Basingstoke: Macmillan.

Provan, K. G., Huang, K. and Milward, B. H. (2009) The Evolution of Structural Embeddedness and Organizational Social Outcomes in a Centrally Governed Health and Human Service Network. *Journal of Public Administration Research and Theory*, 19, pp. 873–893.

Rein, M. and Schön, D. A. (1992) Reframing Policy Discourse. In: Fischer, F. and Forester, J., eds. *The Argumentative Turn in Policy Analysis and Planning*. Durham, NC: Duke University Press, pp. 145–166.

Rhodes, R.A.W. 1997. *Understanding Governance: Policy Networks, Governance, Reflexivity and Accountability*. Buckingham and Philadelphia: Open University Press.

Ring, P. S. and Van de Ven, A. H. (1992) Structuring Cooperative Relations between Organizations. *Strategic Management Journal*, 13, pp. 483–498.

Rogers, D. L. and Whetten, D. A., eds. (1982) *Interorganizational Coordination: Theory, Research, and Implementation.* Ames: Iowa State University Press.

Rousseau, D. et al. (1998) Not So Different after All: A Cross Discipline View of Trust. *Academy of Management Review*, 23(3), pp. 393–404.

Sako, M. (1998) Does Trust Improve Business Performance? In: Lane, C. and Bachman, R., eds. *Trust within and between Organizations: Conceptual Issues and Empirical Applications.* Oxford: Oxford University Press, pp. 88–117.

Scharpf, F. W. (1978) Interorganizational Policy Studies: Issues, Concepts and Perspectives. In: Hanf, K. I. and Scharpf, F. W., eds. *Interorganizational Policy Making: Limits to Coordination and Central Control.* London: Sage, pp. 345–370.

Schön, D. A. and Rein, M. (1994) *Frame Reflection: Toward the Resolution of Intractable Policy Controversies.* New York: Basic Books.

Thomson, G., Frances, J., Levacic, R. and J. Mitchell, J., eds. (1991) *Markets, Hierarchies & Networks.* London: Sage.

Williamson, O. E. (1996) *The Mechanisms of Governance.* Oxford: Oxford University Press.

Zand, D. E. (1972) Trust and Managerial Problem Solving. *Administrative Science Quarterly*, 17(2), pp. 229–239.

Part II

Trust in Government and Major Public Institutions

5 Trust in Government, Performance Information and Democracy

Stephen Greasley

How does a public decide whether its government is trustworthy? How do government actions influence the public's perceptions of government trustworthiness? Answers to these questions are significant for public policy and democracy. If the public's perception is independent of the way a government acts, then it seems there is little that can be done to defend or restore perceived trustworthiness. It may be that trust in government is determined by psychological or sociological factors and government can only adapt to the fluctuations that occur. Similarly, if citizens' trust in their local governments is strongly influenced by events on the national political scene, then there is little that a local government can do to improve its perceived trustworthiness. If the link between government performance and political trust is to survive, some account is needed of how the public forms its political perceptions. This issue is a specific example of what has been called the 'street level epistemology of trust' (Hardin, 1993), the question of how actors use the information available to them to form their judgements about whether to trust or not to trust. In this chapter, I explore what role government performance and information about government performance plays in citizens' street-level epistemology of government trustworthiness. The question has been addressed before (Van de Walle and Bouckaert, 2003; Van Ryzin, 2007, 2011; Yang and Holzer, 2006). The previous literature has focused primarily on the formation of individual beliefs about government trustworthiness and has been pessimistic about the reliability of the process by which individuals form their beliefs. Here I argue that there are two ways of retaining the performance–trust link, even if citizens are inattentive. One is by structuring the information environment in which citizens operate, and the other is to argue that when attitudes about government trustworthiness are aggregated across populations, the summary scores for the population (mean, proportion, median) can carry meaningful information, even if they are based on partial ignorance at the individual level.

Here the focus is on the 'political-citizen', who judges the trustworthiness of general processes of collective decision-making and implementation, as opposed to the 'client-citizen', who uses specific public services as an individual. It is the citizen's general assessment of government that has been the main focus of debates about political trust and trust in governance (Levi and Stoker, 2000). The political-citizens will rarely make considerable effort to collect information on the quality of governments and will interact with their governments relatively infrequently.[1] We should expect them to have fairly limited information on which to base their judgements, but when asked in surveys about government performance or trustworthiness, these citizens do come to a view; the puzzle is how they do so.

Information about the reliability of government is at the heart of the issue of political trust. In a naïve understanding of trust, a truster would simply enter into a relationship on the basis of no information about the reliability of the trustee. Despite the word's positive connotation, this understanding of 'trust' is close to credulousness, and it is difficult to make a case for its normative appeal in a democratic system. Yet, at the other extreme, attempts to entirely eradicate uncertainty by detailed and comprehensive public scrutiny of government motives and competences may also entirely eradicate any need for political trust in the first place. These points leave a question mark over the role of information in the formation of trust judgements. Trust on the basis of no information seems gullible, but the collection of detailed information about government might be considered a substitute for trust rather than a basis for it. The next section looks at this puzzle in more depth.

After that, the chapter turns to the relationship between government performance and citizens' perceptions of government trustworthiness. As part of this discussion, I review a debate about the roles that performance and performance information might play in accounting for the perceived trustworthiness of governments. Considerable progress has been made on this question, particularly focusing on how individuals access and process performance information. The literature suggests that there are some reasons for pessimism about the reliability of this process—in particular, individuals are inattentive and biased when it comes to their understanding of public affairs in general. Even where an individual has a personal interest in a particular service, the chain that links government decision-making to an individual's judgement of that government's trustworthiness is long and fragile. However, thinking about the measure of trustworthiness as an aggregate of judgements sheds a different light on the relationship between government performance and trust; a robust connection may exist between government performance and aggregated trust judgements, even if the individual street-level epistemology is unreliable.

The relationship between political trust, the perceived trustworthiness of government and performance information will be explored in the context of English local governments. The experience of English local government is interesting because comparable performance information was collected and published across similar classes of local council for the major part of the last decade. The introduction of a high-profile summary assessment of performance should add to the information available for citizens to use in making political judgements (James and John, 2007) and judgements about how much to trust government. The data suggest a fairly robust relationship between a council's service performance and the proportion of citizens perceiving it to be trustworthy: a connection does exist between government performance and aggregated levels of trust, at least in this context. However, with this data, it is difficult to say much about how that trust in judgement is formed.

The final section summarizes the argument and concurs with the position of Yang and Holzer (2006) on the importance of performance for trust. However, it suggests that further research is required to explore the trade-offs associated with designing governance for an inattentive citizenry.

POLITICAL TRUST AND TRUSTWORTHINESS: SOME CONCEPTUAL ISSUES

There is a gap between conceptual discussions of political trust and the empirical data available to analysts. Over recent decades, the debate about political trust has been driven by opinion-poll and survey data (for a review, see Levi and Stoker, 2000), and such data can only inexactly reflect theoretical work. A common understanding of these data is that they reflect respondents' general feelings with regard to system legitimacy. This encompassing approach to the definition of trust is also apparent in public administration research; for example, when referring to one of the key objects of their study, Van de Walle and Bouckaert (2003, p. 892) advise their readers to 'call these: trust, support, perceptions, or whatever you like.' They claim that this 'catchall' meaning of trust reflects its usage in political debates. However, if this catchall definition of trust is to be adopted, we would need to reassess exactly why we care about trust in the first place. In this section I want to try to be precise about the meanings of trust and trustworthiness while recognizing that when it comes to survey data, interpretation may have to be a little more rough and ready.

When an actor 'trusts', she makes herself vulnerable to another in the hope of attaining some goal that would not otherwise be achieved. In forming a judgement about whether a government is trustworthy, citizens consider both motivation and competence (Levi and Stoker, 2000, p. 476). This does not mean that a trustworthy government will always succeed in satisfying the truster; it may simply experience bad luck, but the 'trustworthy will not betray the trust as a consequence of either bad faith or ineptitude' (Levi and Stoker, 2000, p. 476). I will work with this understanding of trustworthiness, although it is closely related to the concept of 'confidence' in government.

Both confidence and perceived trustworthiness are oriented to the future, but a distinction can start to be drawn between the two concepts by considering the role of knowledge and uncertainty (Newton, 1999, pp. 170–171). In one view, for example, the absence of information about the trustee's reliability is what makes 'trust' necessary (Barbalet, 2009). Additional information about the trustee does not increase trust; rather, it reduces the need for trust by allowing a transaction to occur in a context of greater confidence. In this view,

> trust includes only those asymmetrically dependent relations in which a person's expectations of another's contribution to the realization of an outcome otherwise not available is formed in the absence of confirming evidence concerning their reliability. (Barbalet, 2009, p. 371)

Although Barbalet (2009, pp. 369–370; see also Hardin, 1998) is doubtful that what is commonly meant by political trust is in fact 'trust', as he characterizes it, his emphasis on the definitional role of the 'absence of confirming evidence concerning the reliability of the trustee' does go to the core of what this chapter discusses. It raises a challenge to the way that trends and variation in political trust have been analysed: if patterns in political trust are to be understood as at least potentially influenced by a government's previous actions, then citizens must have some information on which to base their judgements. At first sight, and if Barbalet's view is accepted, this cannot be the case because additional information does not produce political trust but rather lessens the need for political trust; citizens and researchers must simply have misunderstood what the word 'trust' means. With this conceptualization, it seems to be incoherent to even ask whether performance 'causes' trust (Van de Walle and Bouckaert, 2003).

To try to get round this problem, I want to suggest that information on government performance can be used in two distinct ways. Extra information about past performance reduces uncertainty in relation to those functions satisfactorily delivered in the past and thus reduces the need for citizens to exercise trust in relation to those functions in the future. There is additional pertinent knowledge about government's competence and intentions, and there can be greater confidence in future performance in relation to the specific activity. But citizens may also use information from their past experience of government to draw inferences about the character of future government actions in different contexts, in different policy fields or relating to novel problems. A known record of good performance in specific fields can warrant greater government discretion in new fields of activity; that is, it can generate political trust, a tolerance on the part of citizens of vulnerability and uncertainty in pursuit of a goal, which would not otherwise be attainable. To make this idea concrete, imagine that a municipality faces some unpredicted natural disaster. Citizens will not have much pertinent prior knowledge about how the municipality will respond; however, they may infer from previous good performance in the routine work of government that it can be trusted in various ways (or at least more so than if previous performance had been poor). Alternatively, if some ambitious infrastructure project is proposed, such as a tram network or a road-charging scheme, citizens will rarely have previous specific experience of their government managing such projects, but they may use the accumulated knowledge of previous government actions across the range of other functions to generalize about whether or not to trust (or how much to trust) government with this new project.

In this view, political trust relates to how citizens generalize about future government behaviours on the basis of the specific information that they have available to them from past experience. This understanding of political trust as generalization retains both the possibility of a link between citizen knowledge of previous performance and trust and also retains the uncertainty that is part of a definition of trust. More information about government performance does not only erase the need for political trust by reducing uncertainty in specific areas of government activity, it may also increase the tolerance of citizens in accepting uncertainty or dependency in pursuit of some public goal in novel areas of government activity. It may also increase the range of goals that citizens are willing to see their governments pursue. In politics, the outcome being sought is often vaguely defined, and in such instances specific knowledge of government reliability will never be available. The generalized political trust of citizens may relate to goals as vague as 'good governance', 'social cohesion' or, recently in English local government, 'place-shaping'.[2] Here, 'trust' must be about more than keeping specific promises or delivering particular services because of 'the very indefiniteness of what we are counting on them [trustees] to do' (Baier, cited in Hardin, 1993, p. 506). This is not to say that political trust or any other type of trust is granted without boundaries being established (Hardin, 1993, p. 507); when survey respondents say they trust doctors, implicitly they mean they trust doctors with respect to their medical roles, not in relation to other functions. Presumably, when citizens say they trust government, they have some domain of functions in mind, even if the edges of the domain are moveable and a little blurry.

This section has discussed the meanings of political trust and trustworthiness. The main purpose has been to outline an understanding of political trust as citizens' willingness to allow different levels of discretion to governments in dealing with novel and unanticipated problems. Citizens' political trust and the perceived trustworthiness of government can be partially informed by previous experience, but by definition such experience cannot inform citizens directly or completely about novel or unanticipated challenges or about ambiguous goals. However, such experience can give some indication of the 'character' of a government or institution.

PERFORMANCE AND PERCEIVED TRUSTWORTHINESS

If it is sensible to think that previous performance might contribute to the formation of judgements about political trust, there remains the question of whether it actually does. At least since the work of Downs (1957), there have been questions about whether citizens have the incentives to inform themselves about political issues before they choose how to vote, and similar questions have also been raised about public opinion surveys (Page and Shapiro,

1992). Unsurprisingly, when the question is asked, 'How are perceptions of government trustworthiness influenced by government performance?' further questions are raised about the biases, knowledge and thought processes of citizens. In the case of government, the way that information about performance is presented may be crucial, allowing citizens to shortcut the information-gathering process and simplify the cognitive task involved in formulating a judgement (James and John, 2007; Yang and Holzer, 2006).

In their influential contribution, Van de Walle and Bouckaert (2003) provide a number of challenges to the link between performance and trust in government, and a number of scholars have responded to and developed these challenges further (Christensen and Laegreid, 2005; Yang and Holzer, 2006; Van Ryzin, 2007). The Van de Walle and Bouckaert paper sets out to examine an implicit hypothesis in discourses about the modernization of public services that 'better performing public services will lead to increased satisfaction among their users, and this, in turn, will lead to more trust in government' (2003, p. 892). They question whether citizens' (positive or negative) assessment of government performance influences their assessments of government trustworthiness, or whether the relationship is reversed, with assessments of government trustworthiness influencing perceived performance. Specifically, they criticize the 'micro-performance' approach because of its perceived dependence on a number of strict preconditions (2003, p. 895): citizens must have a clear perception of which organizations are governmental and which are not (the *object precondition*); there is a direct and linear relation between agency performance and perceptions of government, 'no other factors should be involved' (the *criteria precondition*); 'subjective performance perceptions should somehow correspond to (objective) reality'; here, the concern is about the direction of causality between performance, perceived performance and trust (the *causality precondition*).

Van de Walle and Bouckaert argue that these three preconditions will only be met under very rare circumstances. The complexity of government, multiple social factors and the prevalence of stereotypes regarding government all stand in the way. However, the case is overstated. What should interest us is whether better government performance is associated with higher perceived government trustworthiness than would be otherwise observed. The important issue is the marginal effect of performance on perceived government trustworthiness. It may be the case that there are other factors influencing perceived government trustworthiness, but the important question is, ceteris paribus, what effect does a change in the level of government performance have? The criteria precondition that 'no other factors should be involved' is much too strong. The possibility of a reliable and significant relationship between performance and perceived trustworthiness is not precluded by the involvement of other causal factors. Similarly, with the object precondition, it is important that citizens have an approximate understanding of which organizations are governmental and what their responsibilities are, but does there really have to be '*certainty and clarity*' (Van de Walle and Bouckaert, 2003, p. 895, emphasis added)?

The causality precondition is more of a problem; it 'takes a causality leading from performance to satisfaction to trust for granted, whereas it may well be that evaluations of the performance of public services are not based on actual performance, but on a stereotypical view on how government is said to function' (Van de Walle and Bouckaert, 2003, pp. 895–896). It is true that stereotypes can be important, but it does not follow from this that there is no connection between government performance and citizens' perceptions of government trustworthiness. Presumably, poor performance and information about poor performance will reinforce the stereotype, and good performance will make some progress on eroding the stereotype (or at least good performance will reinforce the stereotype to a lesser extent). The existence of stereotypes about government does not by itself fatally weaken the relationship between performance and perceived trustworthiness.

The target of Van de Walle and Bouckaert is a model where individuals accurately, and without prior bias or influence from other factors, judge the performance of individual agencies and then aggregate these (weighted) judgements into an overall score of trust in government. This implies a demanding level of engagement, even for the most committed citizen. The question of the performance–trust link has been picked up by other scholars; for example, Yang and Holzer (2006, p. 115) usefully summarize five typical arguments that question the performance–trust link: expectations about the appropriate size of government vary between citizens and will influence performance assessments; citizens' perceptions of performance are likely to be overly negative due to political discourse and framing; citizens may have difficulty attributing performance to the appropriate organization; criteria other than performance enter citizens' judgements; and, for some services, there is an asymmetry with bad performance generating distrust but good performance not leading to greater trust. When the focus is on individual cognition, the chain from government outcome via perceived outcome and satisfaction to trust is complex, prone to reverse causation and to external influence (Van Ryzin, 2007). In addition, Van Ryzin (2011) argues that the quality of democratic *process* can be more important than the outcomes of government activity.

All these arguments, in one way or another, threaten to weaken the link between administrative performance and political trust (Yang and Holzer, 2006, p. 115); the unresolved question is by how much do they weaken the link? In the messy world of government and public-administration research, we are generally quite impressed by relationships that fall a long way from perfection. The questions then are how much ignorance on the part of citizens can be allowed before the relationship between performance and perceived trustworthiness breaks down? How complex does government have to be before perceptions of its trustworthiness become either random or entirely determined by psychological or sociological factors? It may be possible to retain some confidence in a performance–trust link, even as the assumptions about citizens' knowledge are loosened.

There are two reasons why we may not need to make strong assumptions about individual-level cognition of citizens in order to retain a link between performance and trust, although there are problems with both. The first is that government can generate a high-profile and easily understood performance rating that bundles up a range of disparate data into a single summary score. This allows citizens to easily assess the quality of their government and, in the case of local government, compare it to other jurisdictions; it cuts down on the cognitive effort and the motivation required for citizens to reliably judge their governments. It would be unfair to criticize the early literature on the performance–trust link for not taking this into account. In the United Kingdom (UK) at least, the use of simplified performance reporting for local government only really took off in the early part of the century and, with respect to local government, the first wave of such ratings was calculated in 2002. There is now some good evidence that such performance measures have had an impact on the share of votes of incumbent political parties in English local government (James and John, 2007; Boyne et al., 2009). However, for this mechanism to be robust, two quite strong assumptions are required to be made about the performance-information framework. First, the performance information produced must reliably reflect the goals of citizens, otherwise the relationship may really be between 'government presentation of performance' and citizens' trust. Second, the citizens who are observing the performance scores must believe the process that generates the performance scores to be trustworthy. One way this may be achieved is by allocating the function to an independent body; in the case of English local government, this was the Audit Commission, but the independent body also has to somehow earn citizen trust. Still, as a result of recent trends in public administration (and also technological advances), citizens now find themselves in an information environment that is both richer and more easily understood than in the past. It is relatively easy to access and disseminate information about local governments or other public bodies. In their paper, Yang and Holzer (2006) discuss in detail the potential contribution of performance information in reinforcing the performance–trust link; they argue that performance measurement has to be more sophisticated and responsive to citizens' views than the technocratic norm. Whatever the virtues of their proposals, they contrast with the recent work in the UK which has focused on the simplicity and comparability of performance information (Boyne et al., 2009).

The second reason for being relatively sanguine about the existence of a robust relationship between government performance and perceived trustworthiness is analogous to an argument that is sometimes made in the public-opinion literature. As an influential book puts it, 'collective public opinion has properties quite different from those of the opinions of individual citizens, taken one at a time' (Page and Shapiro, 1992, p. 1). The idea is that even if individuals' beliefs about government activity are not based on detailed and reliable knowledge, when the survey answers of a large number of respondents are aggregated, the random fluctuations will balance each other out and something close to a 'true' value will be revealed.[3] Page and Shapiro's claims for the rational public have been subject to some criticism (e.g. Althaus, 2003), particularly in relation to the distributional assumptions that have to be made for the mechanism to work. I do not want to enter the detail of this argument here but only raise the possibility that some individual-level ignorance does not necessarily imply that aggregated judgements about government trustworthiness are meaningless.

PERFORMANCE, PERFORMANCE MEASUREMENT AND TRUSTWORTHINESS

To assess whether performance is related to trust, and to avoid the problem of a culture of distrust influencing perceived performance, we need to go beyond the responses to survey questions and look at the effect of independently measured performance on levels of political trust. Local government in England provides a useful setting to do this. Over the period 2001–2008, local authorities in England were required to periodically conduct surveys of their residents, asking for their views about council services. The design of these surveys was centralized, and consequently the questions and data are comparable in terms of wording and sampling strategy. In 2006, the General Household Survey asked residents if they felt that their local authority was trustworthy. Looking only at the 148 top-tier councils,[4] the proportion of citizens who perceived their council as trustworthy ranged from a low of 38% to a high of 79% of respondents. The mean was approximately 57% of respondents believing the council was trustworthy, and the standard deviation was 7.2. The distribution was not significantly different from normal (using a Shapiro-Wilks test, $p < 0.97$), but a boxplot did identify the maximum value of 79% as an extreme case. A regression, controlling for population density, a measure of area deprivation, the type of authority and whether there was a single-party majority in control, explained about 18% of the variation in the proportion of residents who perceived the council as trustworthy ($R^2 = 0.183$; Adj-$R^2 = 0.148$).[5] In this model, increased population density tended to increase council trustworthiness, deprivation tended to decrease council trustworthiness, County Councils scored nearly 7 percentage points higher and Metropolitan Boroughs 6.5 percentage points higher when compared to London Boroughs. Single-party control did not make a statistically significant difference, and unitary councils were not statistically different from the London Boroughs. Thus, after controlling for a number of potential explanatory factors, a large proportion of the variation in council trustworthiness went unexplained.[6]

Over the same period, this group of councils was also subject to a centralized performance-management framework based on a combination of inspections and performance indicators (the Comprehensive Performance

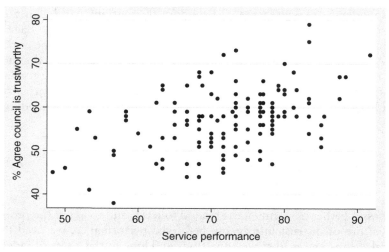

Graph 5.1 Councils' Trustworthiness and Service Performance

Assessment, or CPA). The CPA, as it was published, was a summary ranged from zero to four stars, but it was partly based on a series of service-specific assessments which can be aggregated to generate a 'service-performance' percentage score (see Andrews et al., 2005, p. 641, for details of how this is calculated). The two performance scores were highly correlated (Kendall's tau-b = 0.60, $p < 0.00005$), but the relationship was by no means perfect.[7] If data from the CPA helped to account for some of the unexplained variation in council trustworthiness, then this would be consistent with the claim that 'objective' government performance had exercised an influence on the public's subjective judgement of council trustworthiness.

Graph 5.1 shows the relationship between councils' service performance and councils' trustworthiness ($r = 0.436$, $p < 0.0005$). There was a moderately strong linear relationship between the performance measure and council trustworthiness; in general, higher performing councils were also the more trustworthy councils. There was also a positive and statistically significant relationship between the star rating a council received and its trustworthiness (Graph 5.2, Kendall's tau-b = 0.366, $p < 0.0005$).

Adding these performance variables to the earlier regression model produced the results in Table 5.1. The first point to note is that adding either 'service performance' or the 'star rating' variables to the model increased the R^2 value by over ten percentage points. Turning to the estimates of coefficients, in Model 1 each additional percentage point increase in service performance was associated with a 0.35-point increase in council trustworthiness. In Model 2, each CPA category is entered as a dummy variable (with '1 star' as the reference; no council received zero stars in 2006). Only those councils with a four-star CPA are statistically different from the reference category, scoring on average 8.65 points higher than the reference.

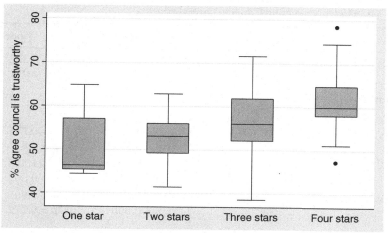

Graph 5.2 Boxplots of Trustworthiness over CPA Star Rating

Model 3 includes both the underlying performance score and the CPA, combined—it seems that the high-publicity star-rating measurements in this model do not explain any additional element of the variance of councils' trustworthiness when the service performance variable was controlled for. In Model 3, the level of trust in councils with four stars is now not significantly different from the level of trust in councils with one star whilst controlling for the other variables, and the CPA stars scores are not jointly significant either.

The analysis suggests there was a positive and fairly substantial relationship between both measures of a council's performance and its perceived trustworthiness. This relationship survived when a number of potentially confounding factors were controlled for. In fact, there was substantive increase in R^2 when either of the performance measures was included in the model. It appears that by some method residents learnt (at least collectively) about the councils' performance, and they used this knowledge to come to a judgement about the trustworthiness of the council. This may not be a surprise, but earlier some good a priori reasons for doubt about the link between performance and perceived trustworthiness were discussed, especially if the link relies only on individual citizens each becoming informed and then judging government performance (Yang and Holzer, 2006, p. 115; Van de Walle and Bouckaert, 2003). Finally, if a council having no single party with overall control is an indicator of disagreement among the public about the best policy and service options to choose, then it does not have a statistically significant effect on trustworthiness, although the coefficients are negative as expected.

Unless some unmeasured factor exists which are associated with both council performance and trustworthiness, there is a performance–trust link

Table 5.1 Models Predicting Council Trustworthiness

	Model 1	Model 2	Model 3
Service performance	0.3483*** $p = 0.000$		0.222** $p = 0.011$
Star rating			
1 star = reference			
2 stars		0.776 $p = 0.800$	−0.735 $p = 0.810$
3 stars		4.368 $p = 0.132$	1.580 $p = 0.603$
4 stars		8.650*** $p = 0.000$	3.809 $p = 0.272$
Controls:			
Area deprivation	−0.281***	0.288***	−0.2801***
Population density	0.001*	0.001*	0.001*
No majority control	−1.582	−1.591	−1.541
Authority type:			
Met	5.943**	6.372**	6.035**
County	6.129**	5.487*	5.635*
Unitary	4.126*	3.909	4.121*
Constant	33.219***	53.359***	40.444***
R^2 / Adj-R^2	.335 /.302	.328/.284	.359 /.312
	148	148	148

* $p < 0.05$; ** $p < 0.01$; *** $p < 0.001$

(For the service performance and star rating measures, the estimated p values are reported.)

in evidence at the aggregate level in English local government. The observed variation in local government performance is reflected in the variation in the proportion of the local populations perceiving their local government to be trustworthy. There is not much that can be said empirically about causal mechanisms from this analysis. It may be that the causality is reversed, with greater levels of trust generating better performance, but I would argue that, although the claim that council trustworthiness causes better objective performance (rather than only perceived performance) is plausible, it is less likely than the more intuitive story that better performance leads to higher perceived trustworthiness. It is perhaps still more likely, as suggested by Yang and Holzer (2006), that causality is more complex, with relations flowing in both directions and trust and performance reinforcing each other. The data from English local government is illuminating because it is quite rare to have comparable data across a reasonable number of similar units, but there is not the variation through time that would allow an analysis of the dynamics of the relationship between performance and trust.

A theory that requires large sections of local publics to individually pay close attention to the promises and performance of their councils would stretch credibility. Following the argument of James and John (2007), it might be claimed that the introduction of an independent, high-profile and simple summary indicator of performance (in the form of the CPA star rating) helps to smooth out wrinkles in the street-level epistemology of political trust, but these measures do not contribute statistically to the model when the underlying measure of performance is also controlled for. The low profile underlying performance score is statistically significant when the CPA scores are controlled for. As was mentioned earlier, these two measures are closely related, and it is difficult to disentangle their separate relationships with council trustworthiness. Are citizens really much better informed about government performance than we give them credit for? An alternative argument based on the aggregation of perceptions would account for the relationship between performance and perceived trustworthiness without the need for strong assumptions about individual political knowledge, as long as there are no systematic biases in the 'errors'.

CONCLUSION: GOVERNANCE FOR THE INATTENTIVE MASSES

The chapter started with a question about how a public learns to trust a government and how this is affected by government performance and performance measures. A fairly conventional definition of trust was used based on vulnerability, uncertainty and the necessity of trust for achieving a goal. A sketch of an argument about how knowledge of past government performance might be a basis for trust was presented.

There is an empirical association between performance and perceived council trustworthiness in the data on English local governments. In the data that were presented, the local publics approximately 'know' whether their governments can be trusted, or at least their judgements about government trustworthiness reflect objective measures of performance. This challenges some previous contributions, which suggested that such a link should be quite unlikely. Two arguments were proposed to explain the existence of the relationship: a simple summary score for government performance solved many of the cognitive problems faced by citizens in learning about the actions of government, and the relationship between performance and trust is, in some part, accounted for by the effects of aggregating the multiple views of survey respondents cancelling out the errors. Either way, the evidence provides some support to Yang and Holzer's imperative: 'to restore public trust, public administrators must improve their performance and communicate it to citizens' (2006, p. 116). However, the position developed in this paper suggests that performance should be communicated in as simple a way as possible to allow busy citizens to easily interpret it and form a judgement. This will no doubt generate error and unfairness in certain cases, but strategies for performance dissemination need to be designed for the inattentive public.

NOTES

1. Or at least they will not have the personal interactions that a client experiences. Political-citizens will, however, observe the cleanliness of the neighbourhood, the state of the roads or whether the rubbish has been collected (Van Ryzin, 2007).
2. 'The creative use of powers and influence to promote the general well-being of a community and its citizens' (Lyons, 2007, p. 3).
3. In *Vox Populi* (Galton, 1907), Francis Galton observed a similar effect as a crowd tried to estimate the weight of an ox.
4. Those with responsibility for the large-scale services of education and social services. A subsequent reorganization of council structures has increased this number.
5. From now on, I will use 'council trustworthiness' as shorthand for the proportion of residents considering the council to be trustworthy. The data used in this chapter are based on the database collected by Boyne et al. (2009); data on trustworthiness are taken from the Audit Commission website.
6. It should be noted that the average council trustworthiness is very highly correlated with citizens' assessment of its performance ($r = .872$).
7. In fact, the relationship between the star rating and the underlying performance assessments was changed in the 2006 round of the CPA and was no longer based on a weighted average score but on a system of threshold criteria (Audit Commission, 2007, p. 50).

REFERENCES

Althaus, S. (2003) *Collective Preferences in Democratic Politics: Opinions Surveys and the Will of the People.* Cambridge: Cambridge University Press.

Andrews, R. et al. (2005) External Constraints on Local Service Standards: The Case of Comprehensive Performance Assessment in English Local Government. *Public Administration*, 83(3), pp. 639–656.

Audit Commission (2007) *CPA—The Harder Test: Scores and Analysis of Performance in Single Tier and County Councils 2006.* London: Audit Commission.

Barbalet, J. (2009) A Characterization of Trust and Its Consequences. *Theory and Society*, 38, pp. 367–382.

Boyne, G. et al. (2009) Democracy and Government Performance: Holding Incumbents Accountable in English Local Government. *Journal of Politics*, 71, pp. 1273–1284.

Christensen, T. and Laegreid, P. (2005) Trust in Government: The Relative Importance of Service Satisfaction, Political Factors and Demography. *Public Performance and Management Review*, 28(4), pp. 487–511.

Downs, A. (1957) *An Economic Theory of Democracy.* New York: Harper & Row.

Galton, F. (1907) Vox Populi. In: *Nature*, March 7, 1997, pp. 450–451. Available at: http://galton.org/essays/1900–1911/galton-1907-vox-populi.pdf?page=7.

Hardin, R. (1993) The Street-Level Epistemology of Trust. *Politics and Society*, 21, pp. 505–529.

———— (1998) Trust in Government. In: Braithwaite, V. and Levi, M., eds. *Trust and Governance*. New York: Russell Sage Foundation, pp. 9–27.

James, O. and John, P. (2007) Public Management at the Ballot Box: Performance Information and Electoral Support for Incumbent English Local Governments. *Journal of Public Administration: Research and Theory*, 17, pp. 567–580.

Levi, M. and Stoker, L. (2000) Political Trust and Trustworthiness. *Annual Review of Political Science*, 3, pp. 475–507.

Lyons, M. (2007) *Place-Shaping: A Shared Ambition for the Future of Local Government. The Report of the Lyons Enquiry into Local Government*. Norwich: TSO.

Newton, K. (1999) Social and Political Trust in Established Democracies. In: Norris, P. *Critical Citizens: Global Support for Democratic Governance*. Oxford: Oxford University Press, pp. 169–187.

Page, B. and Shapiro, R. (1992) *The Rational Public: Fifty Years of Trends in Americans' Policy Preferences*. Chicago: Chicago University Press.

Van de Walle, S. and Bouckaert, G. (2003) Public Service Performance and Trust in Government: The Problem of Causality. *International Journal of Public Administration*, 26(8), pp. 891–913.

Van Ryzin, G. (2007) Pieces of a Puzzle: Linking Government Performance, Citizen Satisfaction and Trust. *Public Performance and Management Review*, 30(4), pp. 521–535.

———— (2011). Outcomes, Process and Trust in Civil Servants. *Journal of Public Administration Research and Theory*, 21(4), pp. 745–760.

Yang, K. and Holzer, M. (2006) The Performance-Trust Link: Implications for Performance Management. *Journal of Public Administration Research and Theory*, 66(1), pp. 114–126.

6 Why Do Politicians Reform? Do They Know Something about the Drivers of Trust in Government?

Nick Manning and Alejandro Guerrero

The concept of trust in government has gained attention in development institutions as a measure of the overall quality of governments and as a potential metric for good governance (Cheema and Popovsk, 2010; World Bank, 2011; Dalton et al., 2000). Trends in trust have been closely examined by several recent studies, often with a sense of alarm regarding a potential long-term decline of confidence in governments. However, little work has been done to understand and empirically measure the drivers of trust in public institutions.

Trust in government is a multidimensional concept in which citizens expect the government and public officials to be responsive, honest and competent, 'even in the absence of constant scrutiny' (Miller and Listhaug, 1990, p. 358). As Levi (1998, p. 78) puts it,

> trust is, in fact, a holding word for a variety of phenomena that enable individuals to take risks in dealing with others, solve collective action problems, or act in ways that seem contrary to standard definitions of self-interest . . . At issue is a cooperative venture, which implies that the truster possesses a reasonable belief that well-placed trust will yield positive returns and is willing to act upon that belief.

'Performance', 'trust', 'legitimacy' and 'trustworthiness' are terms that may be used interchangeably or may be mobilized through meanings that are very specific to the particular situation. Empirically, the various measures of trust in government that result from surveys are often unclear about the unit of analysis (What is being trusted?) and whether respondents understand trust and confidence in the same way as the interviewers.

To avoid the definitional problems, or at least to minimize ambiguity, this chapter will begin with some operational definitions of the terms (see Table 6.1). In essence, the assumption made here is that views of performance draw on assessments of the past, views of the trustworthiness of public institutions require an estimate about the future and views on trust and legitimacy draw on both of these and are about a current assessment of government.

This chapter reviews the broad literature on trust in government and concludes that while the national-level data seem portentous, it is hard to draw

Table 6.1 Definitions

Key concepts		Definition
Focus on the past	Government performance	An empirically observed pattern of past government behaviour: a view about how well government has delivered relative to its own or others' standards in, largely recent, history.
Focus on the present	Trust in government	An individual's or group's overall assessment of government's current entitlement to enforce its policy decisions, laws and regulations based on some aspects of past performance and its general trustworthiness—but with no specific criteria to be met.
	Legitimacy of government[1]	Citizens' current assessment of government's entitlement to a monopoly of the use of violence in the enforcement of its order—in the context of some (constitutional, electoral or other) test that it has passed.
Focus on the future	Trustworthiness of government[2]	A view of how government and its institutions are likely to act in the future: a view about whether government institutions and entities are likely to do the 'right' or 'best' thing in the months or years to come.

[1] Legitimacy and trust are closely related, but there are two distinctions. First, 'trust' is an individual judgement that requires no evidence or criteria to be met, while 'legitimacy' presupposes some test (legal, constitutional or otherwise) that has to be passed (see Rheinstein, 1968, pp. 212–216, and Levi and Sacks, 2005). Second, legitimacy is a more encompassing concept. Trust is often seen as a contributor to legitimacy (Lipset, 1963). Conversely, lack of legitimacy can be seen as evidence of lack of trust.

[2] '(A) trustworthy government (is) . . . competent and credible in its commitments to provide services and benefits that enhance citizens' welfare and motivated to implement laws and regulations effectively. . . . The trustworthy will not betray the trust as a consequence of either bad faith or ineptitude' (Levi and Stoker, 2000, p. 476). The unit of analysis for 'trustworthiness' is the institution or entity.

Source: This section draws on Manning et al., 2010b.

any specific policy conclusions. It then considers trust data at the local level, suggesting that these can tell a clearer story. It looks at the case of Medellin, Colombia—and some significant reforms that were undertaken in the early 2000s. It offers some hypotheses concerning the relationship between trust and government performance and then develops a working model which is tested using detailed survey data available from Medellin. It concludes that trust in government might be central to endogenously driven public sector reform and reviews the potential significance of this conclusion, reviewing how politicians might be interpreting the challenge that they face to maintain support and political capital while making institutional reforms.

WHY TRUST MATTERS AS A MEASURE
OF PUBLIC SECTOR PERFORMANCE

Trust in government matters because it reduces transaction costs between governments and cooperative citizens, facilitates tax collection and regulatory enforcement, and, to the extent that trust in government as an institution is linked with trust in the incumbent politicians, it offers the political capital necessary to support policy reform (Levi, 1988; Bergman, 2009). Bergman (2009) has shown empirically how tax enforcement costs decline in high-trusting societies, as trusting citizens' exhibit less resistance in the payment of taxes. This increase in quasi-voluntary compliance allows the tax administration to focus audits more efficiently on the predictable pockets of tax evasion instead of practicing mass audits across the table, confirming previous theoretical assumptions (Levi, 1988).

Citizen trust in government, in a functioning representative system, also arguably strengthens the social contract, improving compliance with regulations and legal obligations, making citizens less prone to use bribes and less tolerant of corrupt behaviours. It also leads to reciprocal actions beyond tax compliance, such as greater participation in public services and so on. There are also claims of a connection between trust in government and the exercise of political voice and other forms of civic engagement. Van De Walle et al. (2005, p. 16) and Kramer (1999) found that transaction costs within the public sector decline in high-trust environments, as trusting citizens are more willing to comply with regulations and procedures and provide useful feedback and participate in policy implementation, thus enhancing public sector effectiveness. Hall et al. (2001, p. 614) summarize an extensive literature supporting the argument that trust in medical institutions and physicians affects 'a host of important behaviours and attitudes, including patients' willingness to seek care, reveal sensitive information, submit to treatment, participate in research, adhere to treatment regimens, and remain with a physician.' Lieberman (2007) also notes the significance of trust concerning compliance with public health programs, as does Weatherford (1992), concerning redistributive programs.

However, Blind (2006) concludes, from a review of the literature, that *distrust* may contribute to some increased political involvement for some people, although he notes that prolonged periods of distrust diminish civic engagement.

ORGANISATION FOR ECONOMIC COOPERATION AND
DEVELOPMENT (OECD) AND GLOBAL STORIES ABOUT TRUST
ARE THE LEAST PROMISING

Trust Metrics Are Slippery

Trust in government and in other major institutions has been measured most often in the OECD, and the most common way to measure it has been through surveys. The popularization of survey questions asking people about their 'trust in government' as a measure of the performance and quality of government continues to generate active discussions in the literature concerning trends of trust in government and their significance.[1] Typically, the crucial variable is the trustworthiness of government in general and specific institutions under government control (such as the police, courts, hospitals, or the civil service).[2]

There is a significant caveat to make regarding the trustworthiness of trust surveys, as there can be significant problems in interpreting what survey results mean. How should we interpret survey results which indicate that 'Haitian citizens place greater trust in their political parties than U.S. citizens'[3]? Public surveys rarely define terms in advance, usually relying on respondents to infer a definition of trust and of the institutions of government in question (Pollitt and Bouckaert, 2004, p. 152). It is also unclear in most surveys whether trust is to be measured against some notional absolute of perfect trust or distrust or in relation to the level of trust that a sceptical citizen is intended to have in a democratic system. Overall, these broad and ambiguous measures of trust in 'government', and confidence in an abstract 'civil service', may be presenting other significant conceptual challenges to respondents who may be answering in very diverse ways.

These considerations make the interpretation of survey results particularly difficult, and this may be why 'many survey-based explanations of why trust in government changes across countries and population groups tend to give statistically poor results and can disagree with each other' (Manning et al., 2010a, p. 55).

The OECD 'Decline in Trust' Meta-Story Is Weak

To the extent that the data do have some meaning despite the conceptual uncertainties, it is not clear what is behind the decline in trustworthiness of OECD government officials and institutions, which is much discussed in the literature. If they are less trustworthy than several decades ago, as some scholars have argued (Nye et al., 1997; Norris, 1999; Dalton, 2005), then failing performance does not seem to be a likely reason; whereas trust in government has declined in OECD countries since the 1960s, citizens have experienced a long-term improvement in material well-being and freedoms during the same period (Hardin, 2006; Manning and Wetzel, 2010). It is possible that these long-term welfare gains may be discounted by a post-war 'entitlement generation' in the OECD, which takes improved living standards for granted (Inglehart, 1997, 2008) and that anything that governments do or achieve is swamped by broader anxieties that they seem incapable of responding to challenges such as terrorism, genetically modified crops or climate change, or that improvements are still seen as insufficient to justify current levels of taxation (and, through debt, taxation on subsequent generations).

It is also possible that the institutional and public-management reforms that have delivered the performance improvements carried the seeds of distrust within them, with some sense that to achieve them governments have become less moral and more preoccupied with ends rather than means (Warren, 2006), and that in order to explain why reforms are necessary, politicians have 'talked down' the competency of public institutions, making citizens doubt the honesty or the value of government overall (Goodsell, 1994). The confusing deluge of public sector reform over the last thirty years in the OECD (Light, 2006; Pollitt, 2007) may have exacerbated this. However, the declining trust claim itself should not be extrapolated beyond its evidence base in OECD countries and for the period 1960s–1980s in the United States (US), in particular.

Figure 6.1 illustrates the longest available time-series on 'trust in government' and 'public support for the bureaucracy'. Whilst the former shows the much-remarked-upon downward trend until around 1980, subsequently it shows significant variation and no specific trend during the 1980s and 1990s. 'Support for the bureaucracy' is only identified during this latter period, and it also shows no trend. These broad measures of trust in government or in the civil service seem to be volatile and affected by the role of political leaders, with public opinion about government's overall

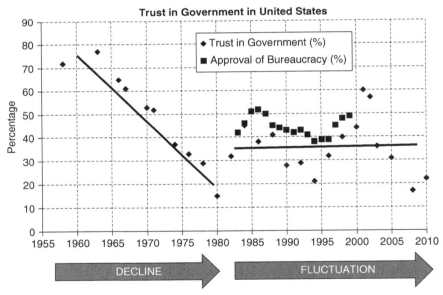

Figure 6.1 Trust in Government and Approval of the Bureaucracy, USA, 1958–2010

Sources: National Election Studies (http://www.umich.edu/~nes/) ; Yackee and Lowery, 2005.

Note: On 'trust in government', the National Election Studies survey asked citizens, 'How much of the time do you think you can trust the government in Washington to do what is right? Just about always, most of the time, or only some of the time?' The volunteered 'never' response is also recorded. On 'approval of the bureaucracy', Yackee and Lowery (2005) constructed an index using four questions from the archives of the Roper Center for Public Opinion Research that were asked more than one time over the time period from 1983 to 1999 and that reflected an overall level of public approval of the US bureaucracy.

Table 6.2 Percentage of Respondents Showing Confidence in the Civil Service

Country	1981	1990	1995–1997	1999–2000
Australia	47		38	
Austria		42		42
Belgium	46	42		45
Canada	51	50		50
Czech Republic		34		22
Denmark	47	51		55
Finland	53	33		41
France	52	49		46
Germany	32	38	48	29
Greece				14
Hungary	74	50		50
Iceland	34	46		56
Ireland	54	59		59
Italy	27	25		33
Japan	31	34	38	32
Republic of Korea	88	61	78	67
Luxembourg				59
Mexico	23	28	41	22
Netherlands	44	46		37
New Zealand			29	
Norway	58	44	51	
Poland		79	35	33
Portugal		36		54
Slovakia		30		39
Spain	39	35	42	41
Sweden	46	44	45	49
Switzerland			46	
Turkey		50	67	60
United Kingdom	47	46		46
United States	58	60	51	55
Northern Ireland	59	57		52

Note: Percentage showing a 'great deal' or 'quite a lot' of confidence in the civil service.
Source: Van De Walle, 2005.

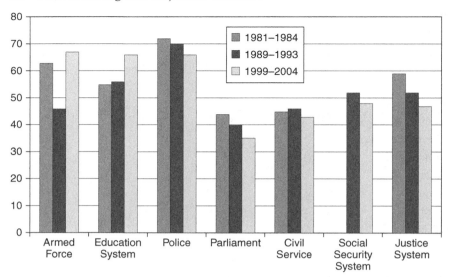

Figure 6.2 Recent Trends in Trust in Public Institutions in the OECD

Source: Arizti et al., 2010, using data from World Values Survey 1980–2005 and Eurobarometer 2002. Weighted averages for a sample of sixteen OECD countries.

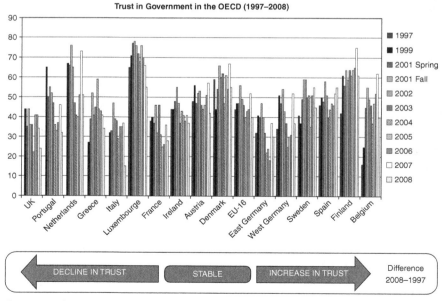

Figure 6.3 Trust in Government in the OECD (1997–2008)

Source: Norris (2011), using Eurobarometer 1997–2008 data.

trustworthiness sensitive to government's fiscal performance and specific agency scandals (Yackee and Lowery, 2005, p. 531).

More generally in the OECD, post-1970s trends of trust in government bureaucracy also fluctuate—with no consistent decline in levels of trust in the bureaucracy and significant variation across countries and across time (see Table 6.2).

Trust in different government institutions in OECD countries evolved in different directions, in some cases experiencing an upward trend in trust during the last decades (Figure 6.2). The picture for the trends of trust in government as a whole (see Figure 6.3) seems to be equally mixed and volatile, with some countries experiencing a progressive decline and other countries experiencing significant recovery in the levels of public confidence, suggesting that trust in government stories are quite country-specific. In a number of countries there simply are insufficient data to come to any conclusions at all about time trends in citizen trust in the public sector (Van de Walle, 2005; Van de Walle et al., 2008), and for most countries, no clear trend is evident post 1980.

National-Level Trust Measures Outside of the OECD Suggest Country-Specific Factors

Recent data for other groups of countries also confirm that the universal decline in trust in government institutions is not apparent. A review of similar trust measures from Africa and Latin America shows significant variance both within and between regions, again, not the universal downwards convergence suggested by the predominant OECD story. In Africa, trust in the incumbent seems to be extremely high in comparative terms, but very volatile (see Figure 6.4). In Latin America, presidents also enjoy fluctuating levels of

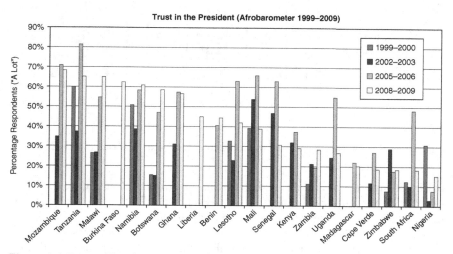

Figure 6.4 Recent Trends in Trust in the Incumbent in Africa (1999–2009)
Source: Afrobarometer 1999–2009.

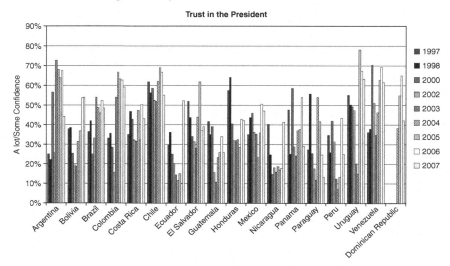

Figure 6.5 Recent Trends in Trust in the Incumbent in Latin America (1997–2007)
Source: Latinobarometer 1995–2009.

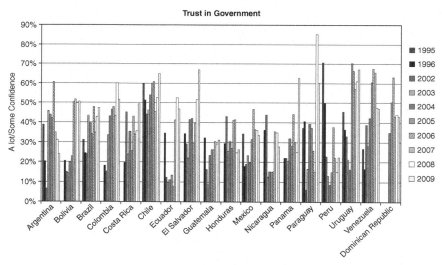

Figure 6.6 Recent Trends in Trust in Government in Latin America (1995–2009)

trust (see Figure 6.5) and trends in 'trust in government' (see Figure 6.6) and in 'trust in the public administration' (see Figure 6.7) also fluctuate across time and countries, according to country-specific factors.

There is a strong correlation between the different measures presented for Latin America—trust in the incumbent, in government in general and in the public administration, specifically, all tend to rise and fall together.

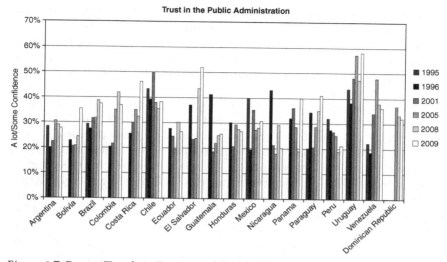

Figure 6.7 Recent Trends in Trust in Public Administration in Latin America (1995–2009)

Sources: Latinobarometer 1995–2009.

Arguably, this is consistent with a proposition that trust in government as an institution is very close to trust in the political incumbents, particularly in strongly presidential (or mayoral) systems where the president (mayor) is very closely identified with the government.[4]

IDENTIFYING SOME DRIVERS OF TRUST

Learning from the Literature

Public trust in the good faith of individuals belonging to complex organisations has been labelled as institutional-based trust—a diffuse, system-based type of trust (Blind, 2010). Public servants are usually in a position of significant power vis-à-vis citizens, and their relationships with citizens are transient because often they meet only occasionally. Given this power imbalance, and in the absence of a repeated interaction, an underlying level of institutional trust is needed in order to smooth government functioning (La Porta et al., 1997, p. 311; Cook et al., 2005). Many formal public sector institutional arrangements are concerned with enhancing trustworthiness, for example, the vote and recall mechanisms, checks and balances between different branches of government and the delegation of functions to specialized bodies, in particular, professional public administrations which limit the ability of politicians to interfere with their work (Shepherd, 2003, pp. 14–17; Silberman, 1993; Horn, 1995).[5] However, there are also less celebrated but robust institutional arrangements that enforce a credible commitment on the part of the otherwise unconstrained bureaucrat. These often take the form of clientelism, a lasting institution in which the expectations of (for example) bureaucratic favours being provided in exchange for votes has proven itself as a credible arrangement for enforcing commitments on both sides.[6]

Literature suggests that the level of institutional trust can be driven up by known factors. It assumes that because citizens have a difficult time interpreting the strength of these institutional arrangements for ensuring credible commitments, they are forced to look at the empirics of government behaviours. Various researchers have found evidence for this effect in comparative studies (Mishler and Rose, 1997, 2001; Miller and Listhaug, 1990; Seligson, 2002; Klingemann, 1999). Espinal et al. (2006) find specific empirical evidence for this effect over time in the Dominican Republic. Cheema and Popovsk (2010) provide a useful classification of five categories of government behaviours which plausibly drive trust: (1) *performance* of government policies; (2) committed and *inspiring political leaders*, able to build ample coalitions for change based on shared basic values; (3) *economic growth* providing new opportunities to citizens, which explains why some booming economies under authoritarian regimes express high levels of trust in government; (4) the *effective provision of basic public services* 'such as water, sanitation, health care and education are essential to inspire confidence and trust in government because these services affect citizens directly and in most cases immediately' (Cheema, 2010, p. 7); and (5) *administrative integrity*, or 'good governance', as expressed by honest bureaucrats doing their jobs effectively, in an impartial way and according to the rule of law.

The relative importance of these five sets of determinants of trust in government is shaped by the context in which they operate. Achieving economic growth or a successful implementation of some national government policy (such as one related to meeting national poverty-reduction targets, winning a war or expanding civil rights) could have a positive impact on the levels of trust in government in general, as these outcomes can be perceived as a government collective achievement. Conversely, the effective provision of public services by the specific government institutions which are responsible for delivering them, or the integrity and impartiality of street-level bureaucrats and public officers may increase trust in these specific institutions and government agencies and, only indirectly, in government in general.

However, it is important to note that there is also significant literature which is sceptical that changes in trust can be plausibly attributed to isolated performance changes.[7] Essentially, there are two arguments. Some note that the information about government behaviour or achievements is unlikely to register in the mind of the public as a significant variable. For example, Pollitt and Chambers (this volume) note that the cofactors necessary for information on improved performance to increase public trust are daunting: the information would have to reach the citizens and be noted by them, and it would have to be understood, perceived as a performance improvement higher than expectations and trusted. Many argue that the public have a very limited understanding of which services a particular government actually provides (Dinsdale and Marson, 2000; Swindell and Kelly, 2000; Van de Walle and Bouckaert, 2003). Another argument is that information about service-delivery performance is only part of the story. The performance information that matters to citizens is only partly to satisfy rational inquiry—it is also value-based (Taylor-Gooby and Wallace, 2009; Taylor-Gooby, 2006). Citizens can consider that the gains in service-delivery quality have been achieved at the expense of other public sector values, such as neutrality or kindness and, consequently, the overall level of trust can diminish. Similarly, Warren (2006) highlights that perceptions of ethical standards in government are likely more important factors. The performance that particularly matters for trust includes meeting prevailing standards of procedural fairness in delivering services, regulating behaviour and taxing citizens (Tyler, 1990; Levi, 1997; Rothstein, 1986, 2005). Trust in government could be the cause, rather than the consequence, of views about service delivery (Van de Walle and Bouckaert, 2003; Levi and Stoker, 2000). Inequality could also be implicated. Using surveys conducted in 2002–2003 in twenty European democracies, Anderson and Singer (2007) examine the effect of income inequality on people's attitudes about the functioning of the political system and trust in public institutions and find that citizens in countries with higher levels of income inequality express more negative attitudes towards public institutions.

Learning from Comparative Data

Guerrero-Ruiz and Manning (2010), examining the particular case of Latin America, found that both direct and indirect measures of trust in government seem to be strongly correlated with objective policy outcomes delivered by the government (see Figure 6.8). There are strong cross-country correlations between service-delivery measures and trust in government. Also, this preliminary evidence suggested that improving services which are strongly associated with the creation of opportunities for the next generation[8] has a particular impact on trust in government and correlates with the benefits associated with trust, such as less resistance to taxation.

However, using macro-survey data at the individual level from Africa, Latin America and several Arab countries, a comprehensive study (Sacks, 2011) confirms that other determinants matter as much, if not more, than service-delivery performance. She reviews how government's honesty and performance in the delivery of services affect different measures of trust in government and political support. To test the hypothesis, a multilevel model is estimated using different measures of trust, regressed against objective

Dimensions of government performance		Measures of Trust in Government			
		Perceived Level of Corrupt Bureaucrats	Trust in the Way Taxes are Spent	Tax Evasion is Totally Justified	State Effectiveness in Solving Problems
Inequality	Inequality of Outcome (Gini Index)	Not Significant Correlation	Moderate Negative Correlation	Not Significant Correlation	Not Significant Correlation
	Equality of Opportunities Index (World Bank)	Not Significant Correlation	Moderate Positive Correlation	Strong Negative Correlation	Strong Negative Correlation
Educational Outcomes	School Attendance (ages 10–14)	Moderate Negative Correlation	Moderate Positive Correlation	Moderate Negative Correlation	Strong Positive Correlation
	Sixth Grade on time	Not Significant Correlation	Not Significant Correlation	Moderate Negative Correlation	Moderate Positive Correlation
Basic Services Outcomes	Water Access (2005)	Strong Negative Correlation	Moderate Positive Correlation	Moderate Negative Correlation	Moderate Positive Correlation
	Sanitation Access (2005)	Strong Negative Correlation	Moderate Positive Correlation	Strong Negative Correlation	Strong Positive Correlation
	Electricity Access (2005)	Moderate Negative Correlation	Moderate Positive Correlation	Moderate Negative Correlation	Strong Positive Correlation

Figure 6.8 Correlation between Measures of Trust and Service Delivery in Latin America, for 2005

Source: Authors' calculations for nineteen major Latin American countries, using data from Latinobarometro Corporation, 2006; World Bank, 2010; Paes De Barros et al., 2009.

Note: *Lighter shades* for positive Pearson correlation coefficients; *darker shades* for negative coefficients.

and subjective measures of service delivery as well as against perceptions of administrative competence and honesty and procedural justice. Her comparative analysis reveals that, across the large sample of Latin American, African and Arab countries, citizens who perceive the bureaucracy to be honest and fair are far more likely to trust the government and approve the incumbent than are citizens holding a view of government officials as corrupt, inefficient and discriminatory. Sacks provides empirical evidence confirming the hypothesis that citizens are willing to trust in the state and express more consent to taxation and regulations if government civil servants are perceived as being effective and fair.

In sum, performance in the sense of service delivery and achievement of social outcomes matter for trust, but this effect is significantly moderated by the impact of procedural fairness. The data show that 'governments are more likely to elicit its citizens' approval, trust and legitimacy when bureaucrats treat those individuals with whom they interact on a day-to-day basis with dignity and provide services with a relatively low amount of red tape and corruption' (Sacks, 2011, p. 5). This combination of findings, while not mutually inconsistent, leaves us with a rather broad set of entry points for improving trust.

TRUST DATA FROM THE LOCAL LEVEL CAN TELL A CLEARER STORY

The difficulty in translating results from cross-country macro-surveys on trust in government into policy-relevant conclusions are mitigated by looking at the local level, where trust surveys are usually more comprehensive regarding the number of institutions and agencies involved in the local government and in service delivery, and where citizens can better identify these public institutions and officials and form a judgement of their trustworthiness based on direct and more frequent interaction with them.

The Case of Medellin: Background and Recent Reforms

The municipality of Medellin was historically both Colombia's traditional industrial centre and one of the most violent, crime-ridden cities in the world, especially with the drug cartel's takeover of the city's barrios during the 1980s and 1990s. The general retreat of the state in many fronts during these decades would characterize Medellin in the 1980s and most of the 1990s as a 'failed city'.

However, in step with the recent progress in reimposing the rule of law, with the near defeat of the drug cartels and the considerable reduction in murder rates, Medellin started to improve significantly the performance of all the services directly provided by the local government. By objective measures, Medellin improved the management of schools and hospitals, the police, and other service-delivery agencies, including the powerful, local, state-owned enterprise, Empresas Publicas de Medellin (EPM), which is responsible for the delivery of many key services at the subnational level.[9] The municipality also improved the services provided by Metro de Medellin, a transport system servicing the whole city, including the slums, and Empresas Varias de Medellín (EEVV), which provides Medellin with street-cleaning services. Metro system expansion to the slums, using innovative cable cars connecting marginalized uphill communities to the network, was a significant step in order to increase social cohesion in a city which had hitherto been divided geographically by income groups with few transport connections between the different areas. In addition, the municipality created a set of agencies and decentralized services in the neighbourhoods to improve citizen access, to offer social services and psychological support, and it developed oversight and accountability institutions to enhance civic transparency.

The mayor (Sergio Fajardo), elected in 2004, was seen as the instigator of these improvements (Devlin and Chaskel, 2010). The mayor led a comprehensive reform program during his period in office (2004–2007). His drive to break up clientelistic political networks, raise tax revenues and improve basic public services was accompanied by high-profile dissemination events and public formal commitments regarding service-delivery targets (such as transparency fairs and civil-society–municipality agreements),[10] all with the aim of 'restoring citizens' sense of hope',[11] and all to be captured in comprehensive, annual independent surveys.

To enable and sustain these reforms, the mayor oversaw improved financial and business management of the public sector agencies, in particular of the locally owned utility company (EPM), and it was the growing profits of this public firm which brought subsequent municipal fiscal buoyancy and financed the service-delivery improvements.[12] This budget expansion allowed for much of the urban upgrading taking place during the mid-2000s, including world-class schools in poor neighbourhoods, public libraries, parks and sport infrastructure, and a vibrant and year-round cultural agenda. Fajardo left office at the end of 2007, with an unprecedented approval rating of nearly 90% and a balanced budget.

Through its management of EPM, the municipality guaranteed almost universal access to relatively high-quality basic public services (energy, water and sewage, gas). For the less affluent customers, and in addition to Colombia's system of cross-subsidized tariffs according to income levels,[13] EPM designed a variety of innovative mechanisms, such as daily prepaid energy and water cards instead of bimonthly bills—a crucial mechanism for the many households that work in the informal sector for a small irregular wage earned on a daily basis and thus unable to face large bimonthly payments. On the other side, the municipality became very strict in cutting off access to those who would not pay their bills through establishing illegal connections to the grid, slowly imposing a civic culture of compliance and payment.[14] EPM's rate of collection is among the highest in the Latin American region, even in comparison with other privately owned competitors.

In sum, the improvements in the public services delivered by the municipal government and its dependent agencies were highly visible, and the local government's investments in schools and clinics, fighting crime, urban upgrading and in expanding the transport and basic infrastructure network to reach marginalized communities were easily recognized by citizens. These very basic services have a direct impact on citizens' welfare and prospects, and recent World Bank research has shown that these investment priorities are closely associated with wider equality in opportunities for the next generation (Molinas et al., 2010). Individual household access and quality to these services is a proxy for quality of life at the neighbourhood level because access to energy, water and other basic services is generally expanded cluster by cluster inside neighbourhoods rather than by household. As the arrival of basic infrastructure services in the neighbourhood has a simultaneous positive impact on the welfare of many local residents, neighbours tend to have a similar and accurate perception about the quantity and quality of service delivery in their area. The same applies for other public goods, such as crime levels, street lighting, paved roads or availability of parks and gardens.

How Trust Might Be Central to Endogenously Driven Public Sector Reform

The political dynamic of such rapid improvements in public sector management are hard to explain—generic phrases such as 'reform champion' and 'dynamic leader' obviously have some meaning in relation to the managerial style of the key actors, but they do nothing to help understand how a low-performing entity can 'pull itself up by its own bootstraps', taking the political risk of raising revenue collections before sustainability in service-delivery improvements can be assured, and destabilizing a culture of clientelistic practices within the public sector, which had previously proved itself to be a successful political strategy.

A recent study by Guerrero-Ruiz (2011) examined the relationship between service-delivery improvements in basic infrastructure, health, education and crime in Medellin municipality in Colombia and the levels of political and institutional support in the period 2003–2010. The qualitative analysis suggested that a rapid upgrading in the city's less favoured districts, combined with a stronger enforcement of the rule of law, may have successfully raised the traditionally low levels of support for politicians and for public institutions, breaking the equilibrium of distrust in government. This research also provides quantitative empirical evidence supporting these broad findings, and it distinguishes the relative contribution of procedural (or administrative) fairness, perceptions of improvements in service delivery, actual service delivery and satisfaction with services as possible alternative drivers of trust in institutions. The analysis also examines the spillover effects in trust between institutions. For this estimation, microdata from an extensive local opinion poll (Medellin Como Vamos) are used, covering citizens' assessments on service delivery and quality of government (Proantioquia, 2011). In sum, taking into account geographic and intertemporal disparities in the provision of services, the analysis unpacks how perceived improvements in different public services may have a distinct impact on citizens' perceptions of government trustworthiness.

This suggests is that such rapid turnarounds can be enabled by a virtuous circle in which political leaders respond to fast-changing signals that initial improvements in service delivery are associated with improvements in trust in the public sector and in them as incumbents—giving them reasons to assume that they have accumulated sufficient popularity to take political risks, such as those entailed in raising additional taxes and in limiting patronage and cronyism, and giving them the bonus of additional revenues, which can in turn further improve service delivery. Figure 6.9 shows that this is a set of linked hypotheses concerning trust-building and trust-utilization

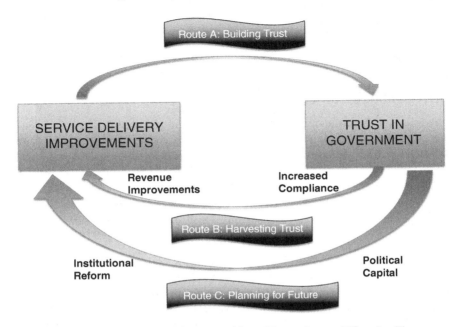

Figure 6.9 Three Linked Hypotheses: Building, Harvesting and Planning Trust
Source: Authors.

routes. Route A is the hypothesized relationship between service delivery and trust. Route B is the established linkage between trust and compliance with revenue administration. Route C is the reformers' additional route—using some of their political capital to pursue deeper institutional reforms with the risk of unpopularity that these bring—in order to improve service delivery more sustainably for the future.

Prima facie, this set of hypotheses seems to fit the observed facts in Medellin, where the visibility of the improved provision and greater coverage of high-quality, basic services was widely regarded as being associated with observed increased levels of trust in government and in several key public institutions, including EPM, the police and Metro de Medellin, the transport agency. The improvements in service delivery were also very publicly associated with improved public management and its connection, via the specific improvements in the management of EPM, with additional revenues, likely producing an increasingly strong disincentive for local politicians to continue patronage politics. The mayor was widely associated with the reforms in all the agencies, and he heads the Board of EPM,[15] and so any trust rewards for improved performance by these service-delivery agencies would likely also become a source of legitimacy and electoral support for him.

The question posed in the rest of this chapter is whether Route A is a practical possibility in the short term. Can service-delivery improvements drive trust and under what conditions? Route B is reasonably well established and needs little further support. Route C is supported anecdotally and in case studies—but we do not seek to validate this hypothesis here.

The data available from Medellin allow some testing of the Route-A hypothesis, deepening our understanding of the relationship between perceived improvements in service delivery and political support/trust in government institutions and the political incumbent in areas where previous literature on the performance–trust link was unclear. In particular, the data enable some testing of whether: (1) citizens reward all service-delivery improvement equally; (2) citizens are able to reward on the basis of their perception of ongoing improvements in service delivery, regardless of the current state of affairs in terms of access and quality; (3) citizens also factor other citizens' experiences into their assessment of government performance, beyond their personal experience with public services or the impact on their individual well-being.

A MODEL FOR THE DRIVERS OF TRUST AT THE LOCAL LEVEL

Some Assumptions

Pulling together the diverse strands of theory and laboratory and field research suggests a set of hypotheses about trust in particular governmental institutions and how it is developed from public-service improvements. These hypotheses rest on the premise that at the local level, in a strongly mayoral system, with a high-profile mayor who takes political responsibility for service-delivery improvements, the arguments against performance acting as a driver of trust, referred to earlier (performance information is unlikely to register in the mind of the public as a significant variable, and anyway is only one variable amongst many), weaken—especially when previous performance was distinctively low.[16]

Hypothesis 1: Citizens Are Able to Distinguish between Government Institutions and Reward Those Institutions for Improved Performance

We start by assuming that in a local/strongly mayoral context, the public can and do distinguish between institutions. Citizens may claim not to trust government in general but identify and trust specific institutions and individual agents of government with whom they personally interact (Klein, 1994; Van de Walle et al., 2008; Pollitt and Bouckaert, 2004). Medellin's recent history offers an interesting case of sudden service-delivery deterioration to test the validity of this particular assumption. After many years of a successful government fight against crime, Medellin has experienced a dramatic surge in gang-related homicides since 2008. In Figure 6.10, citizens' levels of trust in four visible service areas[17] are

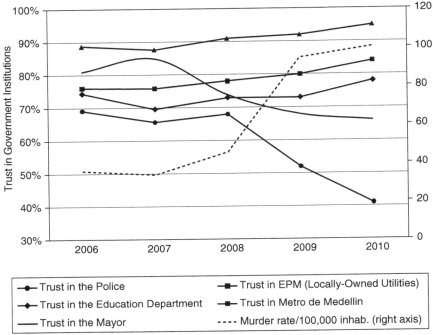

Figure 6.10 Perceptions of Trust in Specific Institutions Are Relatively Autonomous

Source: Data for 2006–2010 from Proantioquia, 2011, and Secretaria De Gobierno De Medellin, 2011.

displayed as well as trust in the mayor/local government. As one would expect, trust in the police experienced a significant drop due to the surge in violence.[18] This drop in a key service area also had a negative impact on the levels of trust in the incumbent government, although in a more moderate way. But, interestingly, trust levels in other well-performing institutions did not seem to be affected by the surge in crime or the drop in trust in the mayor/local government, thus providing some empirical support for the hypothesis that citizens' are able to discern between different institutions' performance.

We hypothesize that, when citizens are able to *perceive* the improvement in service delivery, ascribe it to a particular entity and consider that it is *significant* in size, performance improvements will be rewarded with proportional increases in trust.

Hypothesis 2: Trust Is a Sticky Measure

Previous experiences with government institutions determine the baseline level of trust, and although specific scandals or media commentary may create a deviation from this trend (Barnes and Gill, 2000), trust quickly reverts to its previous trajectory, which responds to new information slowly over time. Citizens base their assessment of government trustworthiness by looking in retrospect to previous experiences, and so the degree of trust in a certain institution or service area in previous periods marks the baseline from which trust improvements or deteriorations will start—providing a reservoir of trust which can be drawn on temporarily, despite setbacks, or providing a level of distrust which will survive initial attempts to improve (Graham and Pettinato, 2001).

Hypothesis 3: To Be Perceived as Significant, Service-Delivery Improvements Must Represent a Significant Gain from the Current Situation

If things are going well, services have to improve beyond trend in order to be noticed. What was achieved through much effort last year is simply this year's baseline. An implicit corollary here is that there are diminishing returns in the performance–trust link as services reach certain tipping points in quality and access (Graham and Pettinato, 2001). After that tipping point, increases in quality, although objectively significant, may be harder for the public to discern—a phenomenon that may be at work in to limit the ability of OECD governments to garner increased trust through service-delivery improvements.

Hypothesis 4: Citizens' Actual Perception of Performance Improvements Is Shaped by the Visibility and Salience of the Specific Service-Delivery Areas Experiencing Improvements

Concerning *visibility*; as citizens do not have perfect information regarding the actual performance in every service-delivery area where government is involved, and they may be unaware of the complete set of government agencies involved in the production chain of any given public service, they experience significant difficulties in correctly recognizing improvements in institutions which are little known or which function in the back office of government.[19] Conversely, citizens will not face the same problems in assessing well-known public institutions with a high degree of visibility and whose performance is as easy to verify as turning on the lights, running the tap, or walking through clean and safe streets (Van de Walle and Bouckaert, 2003). Figure 6.11 illustrates how citizens are better able to identify and have an opinion on public institutions and agencies they often interact with compared to back-office or core government departments.

Concerning *salience*; citizens may prioritize some service-delivery improvements versus others based on their needs, urgencies and preferences. For this reason, we hypothesize that citizens will weight the importance of different service-delivery improvements based on their priorities, and those improvements better matching their priorities will have the largest positive

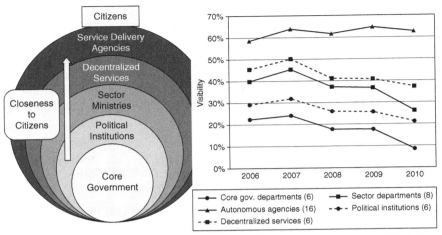

Figure 6.11 Visibility of Different Government Functions or Service Areas (Medellin)

N = 43 Institutions

Source: Authors' estimates using data for 2006–2010, from Proantioquia, 2011.

Note: Classification: '*Core Government*' include the Departments of Planning, Finance, Government, Administrative Services, Evaluation and Control, and the First Lady Office; '*Political or Public Institutions*' include councils and political authorities; '*Sector Ministries*' include the Departments of Health, Education, Transport, Public Works, Environment, Social Welfare, Culture and Social Development; '*Decentralized Services*' include specific government offices deployed at the neighbourhood level to provide closer services to the citizens; and '*Service Delivery Agencies*' include sixteen public agencies dependent on the mayor, providing infrastructure, transport, urban upgrading, as well as some distinctive autonomous institutions on health and education. *Visibility* is defined here as citizens being able to recognize the agency or institution *and* having either a positive or negative opinion on it. Notice that agencies delivering directly to citizens rank higher. Internal statistical homogeneity (average values) characterizes these five institutional sub-sets.

impact on trust. Conversely, improvements in areas that are not relevant for them may be deemed a waste of public resources.

Hypothesis 5: Heterogeneity in the Type of Service Provided Is Likely to Drive Down Views on Service-Delivery Performance

When citizens have had limited or no previous interactions with specific agencies of government, they rely on other people's subjective experiences (including 'gossip') from within their social network for information, drawing on relationships with strong ties, such as family members, and weaker ties, such as neighbours and friends.[20] Similarly, we assume that citizens estimate government performance not only in specific services by direct experience but also by means of their social network. Homogeneity in the service-delivery experience inside the individual's social environment determines the likely variation in feedback that the citizen will receive from peers, neighbours and family. As negative experiences count more than positive ones (Kampen et al., 2006), the more the individual experiences heterogeneity in the quality of services (e.g. doctors of different quality), and the more heterogeneous are opinions coming from his social network/geographic cluster, the greater the likelihood that negative opinions will prevail. Heterogeneity in service delivery tends to convince people that the service is worse than it really is, even though their own individual experience may have been positive. Heterogeneity in service quality and access could also be signalling inequalities in service delivery, which may shape the perception of fairness of the delivery institution.

Hypothesis 6: Procedural Fairness Matters as Much as Service Delivery

Because perceptions of fairness and honesty in the civil service raise citizens' trust in institutions (Sacks, 2011), when citizens perceive that they are operating in a context in which bureaucrats tend to abide by the rule of law, those institutions have a head start in terms of trust, which can provide some buffer against future deterioration.

Hypothesis 7: Overall 'Trust in Local Government' Is a Weighted Aggregation of Citizens' Trust in the Set of Public Institutions That Compose the Government, According to the Salience and Visibility of the Institution and the Service It Provides[21]

We suggest that the performance of very salient, visible government institutions is the main driver of trust in government, with the following caveats:

- The salience of specific service areas do not remain constant over time but fluctuates with citizens' evolving priorities
- The degree of visibility of specific government institutions can be altered over time to some extension by the incumbent government and the media

Thus, although citizens may factor in all government institutions when assessing the overall trustworthiness of government, we suggest that, in practice, the more visible institutions delivering services in policy areas that are current priorities for citizens play a major role in determining the degree of trust in government as a whole. The impact of less relevant, obscure public agencies, which usually operate in the back office of government, may be less clear or insignificant.

An interesting corollary from this last hypothesis is that citizens will tend to distrust public institutions that are little known or lack any visibility, as their real usefulness or performance would be hard to assess. Similarly, although citizens will generally appreciate good performance in any public agency, they will express more trust in public institutions when they are operating in policy areas that are relevant for them.

EMBEDDING THOSE ASSUMPTIONS WITHIN
A MODEL FOR EXPLAINING TRUST CHANGES

This section describes and empirically tests a model of the determinants of trust in local government, using data from Medellin. The model incorporates the hypotheses described in the previous section, in the same order. In essence, the model proposes that changes in the level of trust that an individual has towards government institutions can be explained as follows[22]:

$$Trust_{S_n,t} = Trust_{S_n,t-1} + \omega_{S_n}\left(\Delta_{S_n,t}\right)\cdot\left(H_{S_n}\right)\cdot\varepsilon$$

The terms mean that the current level of trust held by an individual towards any particular public institution or service-delivery agency ($Trust_{S_n,t}$) [hypothesis 1] is a function of *previous levels of trust* in that institution ($Trust_{S_n,t-1}$) [hypothesis 2], the *perceived performance* in service delivery in recent times (Δ_{S_n},t) [hypothesis 3], the *visibility* of the institution ω_{S_n} [hypothesis 4]. We are thus hypothesizing that public institutions are able to build up institutional trust by improving the perception of performance in delivering services, especially when these institutions are *very visible* and the services delivered rank amongst citizens' current *top priorities*. In addition, we also suggest that the perception of a *homogeneous* [hypothesis 5] delivery of services, H_{S_n} as well as a *fair, non-discriminatory* [hypothesis 6] service provision contributes to reinforce the performance–trust link[23].

The model then proposes that *Trust in Local Government Institutions*, as a whole, can be estimated as follows:

$$TiG = \begin{cases} \alpha_x Trust_{S_1,t} \\ \beta_x Trust_{S_2,t} \\ \gamma_x Trust_{S_3,t} \\ \delta_x Trust_{S_4,t} \\ \dots \\ \varphi_x Trust_{S_n,t} \end{cases} + \varepsilon$$

The terms mean that overall trust in government (*TiG*) is a function of the sum of current trust in the public institutions and agencies composing government ($Trust_{S_n,t}$), *weighted* by the salience and visibility of the services delivered by these institutions ($\alpha_x, \beta_x, \dots$)[hypothesis 7].

Testing the Model

To test this model, we first examine if trust in individual government institutions is indeed influenced by current and perceived performance in service delivery. We use a sample of 1,415 respondents for Medellin in 2007.

These respondents were asked questions regarding the trustworthiness of local government institutions and agencies, their knowledge about them as well as measures of perceptions, actual service delivery and satisfaction with seven main local service-delivery areas.[24]

To test the statistical strength of the hypotheses laid out above regarding the drivers of trust in individual government institutions, we use an ordinal probit model,[25] with clusters at the neighbourhood level and socio-demographic control variables.[26] The regressions for all seven government agencies, shown in the annex, consistently confirmed our earlier hypotheses:

- Trust in specific government institutions is mainly driven by the *perceived performance*. Perceived performance is, obviously, endogenously correlated to trust in the agency—people decide to trust the institution because they have the perception of being effectively served, and vice versa
- However, the degree of *visibility* and *salience* of the institution has a significant effect in generating trust in the government agency. This result suggests that perceived performance of any agency becomes a strong driver and generator of trust, especially when the delivery agency is very visible and salient. This evidence provides support to the proposition that, in order to have any significant impact on trust, performance needs to be both very visible and should happen in priority services. These conditions are determining the conversion rate from agency performance to institutional trust
- *Actual access* to these services was found not to be generally significant, from a purely statistical perspective, but satisfaction levels with current *degree of quality* in service provision were found moderately significant. In other words, as expected, satisfied citizens tend to show more trust for the delivery agency

These findings suggest that citizens seem to make their decision to trust mostly based on perceptions of performance by the delivery agency instead of on current levels of service provision. In other words, the expectations of future improvements derived from current perceived (visible) performance seem to drive trust in institutions, whereas current service levels play a more limited role.

The regression model presented in these tables allows us now to estimate the average marginal effect on institutional trust caused by perceived agency performance, agency visibility, and actual improvements in service access and quality. Table 6.3 summarizes the marginal effect of these four statistically significant drivers of trust in institutions, such as the metropolitan police, local clinics and hospitals, the transport agency or the locally owned utility providing basic services such as water, electricity or gas.

The bottom line is that perceived effort at the agency level, when the agency is very visible and salient, really matters. As mentioned, trust in the

Table 6.3 Calculated Average Marginal Effects of Independent Variables on Trust in Specific Sector Institutions

	Perceived impact		Perceived effort	
	Current service access	Satisfaction with current service quality	Visibility/salience of sector responsible institution	Performance of sector responsible institution
Education	5.53%	2.15%	2.15%	33.17%
Crime	0.77%	5.32%	4.93%	21.67%
Health	1.30%	0.65%	7.03%	25.67%
Parks and public spaces	2.55%	1.50%	18.29%	27.33%
Street cleaning	0.18%	0.93%	9.20%	14.79%
Basic infrastructure services	1.95%	0.84%	4.00%	16.00%
Transport	n.d.	n.d.	13.73%	29.59%

institutions in charge of the seven main policy areas at the local level is strongly driven by their perceived overall performance and, to varying degrees, by the actual visibility of these institutions. As predicted by the literature, trust in institutions seems to be more a question of expectations regarding an honest and responsive institutional behaviour than an assessment about the current objective level of service delivery. The fact that current access to services was not statistically significant in any case reinforces this interpretation of the results.

The importance of visibility/salience of the agency in generating agency-level trust can be more clearly seen in Figure 6.12. Apparently, citizens tend to distrust government agencies or departments when they do not know what exactly these institutions do and cannot come to conclusions about the actual performance, intentions, relevance or usefulness of the government agency.

The next stage is to review whether trust in government as a whole is an aggregative process of trust in government institutions, weighted by the importance that citizens attribute to the role of these institutions and by the actual visibility of these institutions (i.e. the knowledge that citizens can have about their existence and performance).

Table 6.4 tests if trust in local government (proxied here as 'trust in the mayor', given the high level of personalization of local politics) is partially driven by the weighted sum of the levels of trust in each local government institution. Citizens were asked to identify their three top priority sectors as well as their knowledge (visibility), opinion and trust regarding the delivery institutions that operate in these and other service-delivery areas. We then compared these three dimensions (i.e. trust, visibility and sector relevance). The regression results presented below examine the statistical relevance

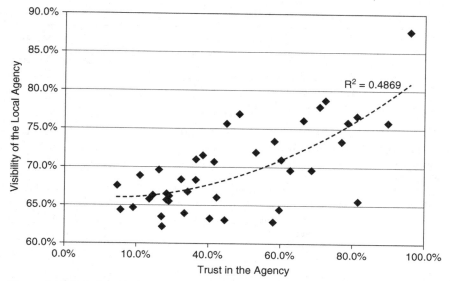

Figure 6.12 Relationship between Agency Visibility/Salience and Trust in 43 Agencies
Source: Authors' estimates using data for 2007, from Proantioquia, 2011.
N = 43 local government agencies.

and marginal effect for the seven sets of government institutions described in the annex.

The regression results suggest, as expected, that trust in individual institutions is positively correlated with trust in the mayor. But, interestingly, trust in institutions which are widely known and are operating in priority sectors have a more significant impact on trust in the mayor than less visible institutions delivering services in areas that citizens may consider to be already in good shape—in this case, local transportation.

In other words, the marginal effect of trust at the agency level on trust in general government is mediated (weighted) by the visibility of the agency, and the evolving priorities of citizens, to which politicians should respond if they want to maximize the 'trust return' on investments in public sector management reform.

In sum, in this one very time- and place-specific case (Medellin city, 2006–2007), we see that:

- Perceptions of performance at the institution/agency level are crucial in rebuilding trust in government, especially when better performance is perceived in policy areas that are amongst citizens' current priorities and are delivered by very visible agencies
- A significant impact on trust could be possible in a relatively short period of time, by focusing on service areas and institutions offering the largest trust pay-offs for performance improvements

Table 6.4 Determinants of Trust in the Mayor

		Coefficient	Significance	Maximum effect
Trust in sector institutions (weighted by relevance & visibility)	Trust in education institutions	0.022	***	6.11%
	Trust in crime-fighting institutions	0.033	***	9.20%
	Trust in basic services provider	0.022	***	6.07%
	Trust in healthcare institutions	0.024	***	6.67%
	Trust in street-cleaning agency	0.021	**	5.74%
	Trust in parks/public spaces agency	0.029	***	8.11%
	Trust in transport agencies	0.015		
	N	1410		
	Count *R*2	0.439		
	Log-likelihood full model	−1601.151		

*** 99%, ** 95%, * 90% significance level.

Note: A set of eight socio-economic and demographic controls was included in the model (gender, age, income level, educational level, newly arrived to the city, household with children, unemployment status, and poverty status). These control variables were not generally signifi-cant, or their explanatory power was weak. The coefficients presented above were estimated with the full model, including control variables and data clustered at the neighbourhood level.

- Current levels in access and quality of service delivery are somewhat important but are not crucial in building institutional trust; citizens care about the perceived effort more than they do the impact of the current levels of service delivery
- Perceived procedural or administrative fairness is an important contex-tual factor because it is highly correlated with trust in government—although the direction of causality is unclear

Did the Mayor Use This Model?

The model allows us to estimate how improvements in performance at the agency level would have been translated into higher levels of institutional-based trust and how they would have contributed to general levels of trust in government at specific points in time. Table 6.5 summarizes where the biggest trust pay-offs were to be found at that time (in 2007)—education,

Table 6.5 Predicted Set of Trust Pay-Offs for the Mayor for Investments in Sectors

Policy areas	Predicted impact of improvements in trust in sector institutions	Current level of institutional trust	Salience/visibility sector priority (% respondents)
Local education services	6.11%	62.20%	39.51%
Crime-fighting	9.20%	63.20%	23.60%
Basic infrastructure services	6.07%	75.30%	3.60%
Healthcare services	6.67%	66.90%	40.49%
Street-cleaning services	5.74%	73.10%	8.90%
Parks and public spaces	8.11%	69.80%	3.32%
Local public transportation	*Not significant*	78.90%	4.66%

Source: Authors' regression estimates using data for 2007, from Proantioquia, 2011.

health and crime-fighting—because citizens saw these services as particularly salient, and trust levels for the agencies in charge of these policies were relatively low.

Do politicians really have these considerations in mind when making the decision on where to focus reform efforts aimed at performance improvements? Table 6.5 suggested that education, healthcare and crime-fighting were three service-delivery areas with the biggest trust pay-offs in Medellin in 2007. Figure 6.13 tracks citizen views on the salience of two of those key priorities for citizens, the level of public expenditures devoted to them in the following year (the mayor's policy reaction) and how citizen trust the

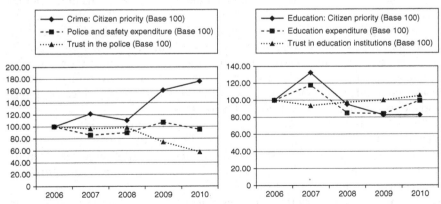

Figure 6.13 The Effect on Trust on Institutional Responsiveness: Crime and Education

Source: Authors' estimates using data for 2006–2010, from Proantioquia, 2011, and official budget publications from Medellin Municipality. Budgeted figures were lagged one year to account for government's responsiveness to changing citizens' priorities.

sector delivery agency. We interpret the trust changes as a consequence of the public's perception of changed government effort, as proxied by the changes in expenditure. Regarding education, public expenditures perfectly tracked citizens' demands for more attention on that sector and, consequently, trust in education institutions has slowly increased over time. In comparison, crime rates soared in 2008, and citizens' attention to crime almost doubled. However, the municipality did not react in the same way, and budgeted expenditures on crime prevention remained at the same level. The lack of reaction in an increasingly important sector, and the probably high visibility of the police in the media, contributed to the consequent halving in the levels of trust towards the police in less than two years.[27]

THE SIGNIFICANCE OF THE FINDINGS: VIRTUOUS CIRCLES AND INTRODUCING A CULTURE OF COMPLIANCE

The case of Medellin offers some particularly interesting insights on the relationship between government performance and political support/trust in institutions. As the headlines triggered by the intense levels of violence disappeared towards the mid-2000s, for internal and external reasons, Medellin became an interesting case of analysis as other limitations in the provision of public services became more obvious. Politicians faced the daunting challenge of rebuilding a dysfunctional city, restoring government's presence in marginalized areas previously controlled by drug cartels, and increasing fiscal compliance and social cohesion while at the same time reincorporating demobilized gangs and paramilitary in the city's economy. On balance, the successive governments of the city managed to develop a strategy of political survival based on providing very visible public goods in exchange for fiscal compliance, instead of the traditional clientelistic politics, which included offering positions in the public sector in exchange of votes, or selective transfers and pork-barrel investments to targeted groups of voters and neighbourhoods. Obviously, this process of improvements in specific, very visible government institutions (EPM, Metro de Medellin, schools) had already started during previous administrations, but the political payoffs associated with improvements in those government institutions were not feasible until crime levels had decreased to more tolerable levels and stopped being the main priority for most citizens.

We argue that one possible explanation for Medellin success (and recent partial decline) was that politicians knew how to build trust through service-delivery improvements (Route A) and how that trust could be used to further improve services through increased revenues (Route B), and through deeper institutional reform (Route C).

We cannot gauge whether this was indeed how politicians made their calculations—but we can assert that if they were relying on a predictable link between service-delivery improvements and trust, then such a link does in fact exist. As the evidence from Medellin suggested, the careful use of service-delivery improvement strategies for the services provided by autonomous, service-delivery, high-performing agencies, such as Metro de Medellin, the school system or the locally owned utility company were key to improving trust. Most services provided at the local level, and examined in the empirical section, are certainly service areas that rank among the highest in citizens' priorities and needs.

Trust in local government in Medellin (specifically, trust in the mayor) was built and remained high in a stable way because: (1) citizens were able to acknowledge the improvements in performance over time in specific services because they were both critical and very visible, in particular in comparison to much lower quality services in other Colombian cities; (2) performance information on these services was easy to gather at the individual level and easy to understand (as easy as turning the lights or the tap on); (3) these were service areas which are homogeneous in that most people receive a similar type of service in their geographic cluster, thus holding and reinforcing the same opinions on service quality inside their social networks;[28] (4) the performance change represented a significant improvement on the baseline, especially in the case of new coverage on areas and communities which were traditionally abandoned elsewhere in Colombia and may have been above the level of improvement to which citizens felt entitled.[29]

Consistent with the broader literature on consent and compliance, this context of improving trust meant that improvements in service delivery by Medellin could be met with higher compliance with regulations and taxes and through fees paid by the users to the public utilities and transport systems. As that context of performance improvement and innovation was accompanied by a strict policy of cutting services to non-compliant customers and sugar-coated with a flexible variety of payment mechanisms to ease the costs of compliance, many citizens perceived the government to operate in a moderately fair, responsive manner. This is likely to lie behind the high collection rates for the locally owned utility firm and other local public agencies, including the local tax administration as well as the baseline perception of generalized compliance in the public.

The case also suggests a couple of cautionary notes. First, expectations matter and innovations and performance improvements achieved through much effort last year may be the baseline this year in citizens' minds. If the public expectation is that services should consistently improve, then unless they improve particularly sharply, there is little credit for the achievement. Thus, as Medellin's well-performing agencies are reaching its limits in universal coverage and quality improvement in their core activities of service delivery, individuals may start facing increasing difficulties over time in experiencing identical satisfaction for similar rates of service improvement. On the one hand, Medellin's local government institutions are and will be facing diminishing returns as citizens will perceive less change than in earlier stages of policy development (Graham and Pettinato, 2001), except in the areas where these public agencies are actually building new 'markets' of public service delivery, such as in displaced communities or marginalized neighbourhoods and towns. On the other hand, at this point of Medellin's development, the efficiency gains and service innovations driven by new technology may be sufficient to keep up satisfaction with and trust in the government of Medellin for some time. If there is an 'entitlement frontier', beyond which citizens take for granted significant improvements in service delivery, Medellin has likely not yet reached it.

Second, because citizens seem to give a higher reward if they perceive increased performance effort in institutions that are responsible for services that they consider current priorities. As citizens priorities will evolve over time, the relative pay-off for improvements in each policy area will track these changes. Governments can focus public attention on some public agency (by announcing reforms related to the agency, or by increasing the visibility of that agency in the media) and this will increase the weight of that particular agency's performance in determining the total level of political capital. On the one hand, this higher visibility could maximize the trust pay-off associated to a successful reform of the agency. On the other, if the reform fails, the resulting high visibility of the involved agency may also amplify the resulting political damage.

CONCLUSIONS

In this chapter, we have speculated about the significance of trust in government. We note that broad measures of trust in OECD countries lend themselves to interesting debate but offer little that is immediately relevant to policy makers. By contrast, we note that trust in government at the local level seems to have a more precise meaning and may play a very significant part in some hypotheses with which reforming politicians may be working. These hypotheses might point the way towards some more systematic analysis of leadership in public sector reform, addressing the vexing question of why some politicians are prepared to abandon safe practices of clientelistic management of public sector agencies (like the discretionary selection practices of civil servants for political and electoral reasons) with its accompanying poor service-delivery outcomes but with the benefit of political stability, and to venture into new and politically unproven territory through institutional reforms which will be resisted and resented by many who gained from the previous system. The calculation for the politician or leader is whether trust improvements have provided sufficient political capital and public forbearance to counterbalance the loss of support that they will receive from the losers in reforms which seek to strengthen formal institutional arrangements (protests from patronage employees, corrupt bidders for contracts, etc., could be outweighed by the increased trust from the general public).

We have shown that, in one major city, a significant part of those hypotheses do indeed have some empirical basis because trust in government institutions can indeed be influenced by strategically improving key service areas. Showing that such a political calculation can be justified is not the same thing as showing that this was in fact the strategy adopted by reforming politicians. However, it does open up a new array of questions to understand why some politicians are prepared to take risks to achieve important gains—maybe they know something intuitively which we are slowly discovering econometrically, namely that reforms can form part of a virtuous circle of performance and trust which strengthens rather than weakens their position. The evidence provided in this chapter from one set of local experiences in Colombia suggests that this may be the case.

NOTES

1. Typical survey questions are variations of the following question: 'How much do you trust the government to do what is right?' For a comprehensive review on survey research on the levels of trust in government, see Hardin (2006, chapter 3).
2. Surveys tend to focus on the 'trustworthiness of those who are to be trusted or relied upon' (Hardin, 2006, p. 59).
3. Corral (2008, Figure 1) cited in Manning et al. (2010b).
4. It is not clear that the available data would allow this proposition to be currently tested.
5. As we will illustrate in the empirical section, the government's degree of success in enforcing fair, rule-abiding, non-discriminatory behaviour on the civil service is a precondition to any attempt to rebuild trust in institutions by increasing performance and service delivery.
6. A much discussed example of clientelism in Mexico was the system of *caciquismo* during the era of one-party rule, in which *caciques*, or local power brokers, provided plots of land and loans and generally provided services and security in exchange for the votes of the peasants. Senegal's *marabouts* are said to perform a similar function in delivering the votes of their followers to political leaders and repaying the voters with farm implements and other gifts. In the Philippines, the system of 'bossism' provides political leaders with discretion to use local funds and the appointment of officials to positions as rewards in exchange for political support. See Brinkerhoff and Goldsmith (2002).
7. Van De Walle et al. (2008) provide a review of the claimed drivers of trust in the OECD and find little empirical support for the significance of any particular variable.
8. Molinas et al. (2010) construct a Human Opportunity Index to measure how personal circumstances (birthplace, wealth, race or gender) impact a child's probability of accessing the services that are necessary to succeed in life. They conclude that the key factors are timely education, running water and connection to electricity. In the table presented here, these variables are generally correlated with more trust in government and less resistance to taxation.
9. This local state-owned enterprise is directly responsible for the delivery of key infrastructures, including electricity, water, sanitation, gas and, to some degree, telecommunications. EPM is also the main provider of specific social programs at the local level, such as scholarships and cultural activities. Importantly, a third of the municipal budget comes from EPM's annual profits.

10. The mayor took a series of initiatives aimed at increasing the transparency of local government performance by making available indicators on public sector performance in all key sectors, and establishing sector targets in local 'civic agreements'. Transparency fairs were a mechanism to publicly disclose these initiatives.
11. Devlin and Chaskel (2010, p. 1).
12. Around a third of the municipal budget has been regularly covered by EPM's transfers to the municipality, which are agreed at a minimum of 30% of the firm's annual profits, usually averaging 50% for the 2005–2010 period. Despite these significant transfers, EPM is one of the highest capitalized firms in Colombia.
13. According to the Colombian cross-subsidy scheme for service delivery, the population in each municipality is divided into six strata for utility rate purposes. The poorest users are in stratum 1, whereas the richest users fall in stratum 6. The utility tariffs are subsidized in strata 1 to 3. Stratum 4 is neutral in the sense that users of stratum 4 pay the marginal cost. Users belonging to strata 5 and 6 are charged at higher rates to compensate for the low rates charged from strata 1 to 3. It is not only the public sector companies which have followed this cross-subsidy approach to enhance access to utilities' services; private sector companies have in some cases also followed similar pricing strategies (Sotomayor, 2003).
14. This is also the case for the very high number of newcomers, displaced by violence in other parts of the country. Although they come from other regions where the culture of payment is less entrenched, there was no apparent variation in collection rates. This is consistent with other research suggesting that immigrants' adaptation to the values and culture of host societies is more effective when inclusive social policies are in place, and no significant cultural or ethnic cleavages exist between newcomers and locals, as it was the case in Medellin. See Berry (1997) for a review of main findings.
15. Candidates to become Medellin's mayor indicate their candidate to be chief executive of EPM during the municipal electoral campaign.
16. The hypotheses do not include any reference to public trust in the data concerning performance. It is at least plausible to imagine that performance information which comes from institutions that have been associated with overheated or over-claiming rhetoric on performance improvements may damage the credibility of any performance data that show an improvement.
17. The 'most visible institutions' means here that more than 90% of the people can *recognize* the existence of these institutions/agencies and they are *salient*, as people have and express a positive or negative opinion about them.
18. Specific questions on citizens' propensity to 'denounce' crimes after being victimized also confirm this point, showing a substantial drop in denounce rates, from 52% in 2006 to 35% in 2009 (Planning Department, 2011).
19. Assessing what citizens see as 'government' is relevant in order to select which institutions are regarded as part of government and therefore may influence on the general perceptions of government. As shown by Dinsdale and Marson (2000) and Swindell and Kelly (2000), citizens have increasing problems to correctly attribute services delivery to the public and private sectors. Evidence from Belgium revealed that some services (post, health services, education system) are seen as inherently government responsibilities more than other policy areas (such as telecommunication services, television and radio or, to a lesser degree, water and electricity distribution).
20. Granovetter (1983, p. 209) argues that 'weak ties provide people with access to information and resources beyond those available in their own social circle; but strong ties have greater motivation to be of assistance and are typically more easily available.'

21. This is a similar argument to that used by Van De Walle and Bouckaert (2003), who highlight the importance for this hypothesis of citizens understanding which agencies are in fact in the public sector.
22. A more comprehensive description of the formal model, including the way the hypotheses above have been incorporated, can be found in the Annex.
23. Next section will empirically test these hypotheses (with the exception of hypothesis 6, which is referred in recent literature but cannot not tested here given the lack of disaggregated data on perceived fairness at the agency level in our sample).
24. The survey covered seven main areas of service delivery at the local level, allowing for a comprehensive assessment of citizens' priorities and actual service delivery, the visibility of government institutions, and degree of geographical homogeneity in the quality of delivered services. This empirical test was complemented with fifty qualitative interviews with representatives from the local government, service delivery agencies, the media, business associations, and civil society organizations in order to identify inconsistencies with the interpretation of the results.
25. Given that trust is measured as an ordered categorical question ('How much do you trust . . . ?'), the model has been estimated using maximum likelihood and an ordered probit function. This approach allows us to estimate the probabilistic effect of each predictor variable for each possible response, as well as the marginal effects for selected specifications.
26. The detailed results for each institution can be found in the Annex, Tables 6.6 to 6.12.
27. Soaring crime levels and lack of police effectiveness not only hindered trust in the police, but this situation also indirectly impacted on trust in the mayor, as predicted by the model and illustrated by Figure 6.10.
28. This is important because if service delivery is heterogeneous, such as in the case of doctors' performance, the tipping point after which performance improvements are able to change people's bad image of some service area is much higher, as negative opinions count more than positive ones in people's mind and will usually outweigh new positive experiences associated with the improvements.
29. This last point was confirmed during the interviews with the media, civil society and public officials, as Sergio Fajardo ran for office as an outsider to the traditional clientelist parties and practices, with a new promise of rebuilding the city by focusing on the provision of public goods, instead of targeted patronage.

REFERENCES

Afrobarometer (1999–2009). "Afrobarometer Surveys" Afrobarometer. Retrieved 2012-05-30 from www.afrobarometer.org.

American National Election Studies (1955–2010). The ANES Guide to Public Opinion and Electoral Behavior. Ann Arbor, MI: University of Michigan, Center for Political Studies [Datasets].

Anderson, C. J. and Singer, M. M. (2008). The Sensitive Left and the Impervious Right: Multilevel Models and the Politics of Inequality, Ideology, and Legitimacy in Europe. *Comparative Political Studies, 41*(4–5), 564–599.

Arizti, P. et al., eds. (2010) *Results, Performance Budgeting and Trust in Government.* Washington, DC: World Bank.

Barnes, C. and Gill, D. (2000) *Declining Government Performance? Why Citizens Don't Trust Government.* Wellington: State Services Commission.

Bergman, M. (2009) *Tax Evasion and the Rule of Law in Latin America: The Political Culture of Cheating and Compliance in Argentina and Chile*. University Park: Pennsylvania University Press.

Berry, J. W. (1997) Immigration, Acculturation, and Adaptation. *Applied Psychology: An International Review*, 46(1), pp. 5–68.

Blind, P. K. (2006) *Building Trust in Government in the Twenty-First Century: Review of Literature and Emerging Issues*. Seventh Global Forum on Reinventing Government: Building Trust in Government, Vienna, Austria. 26–29 June. Available at: http://unpan1.un.org/intradoc/groups/public/documents/UN/UNPAN025062.pdf.

——— (2010) Building Trust in Government: Linking Theory with Practice. In: Cheema, G. S. and Popovsk, V., eds. *Building Trust in Government: Innovations in Governance Reform in Asia*. Tokyo: United Nations University Press, Chapter 2, pages 22–53.

Brinkerhoff, D. W. and Goldsmith, A. A. (2002) *Clientelism, Patrimonialism and Democratic Governance: An Overview and Framework for Assessment and Programming*. Bethesda, MD: Abt Associates.

Cheema, G. S. and Popovsk, V., eds. (2010) *Building Trust in Government: Innovations in Governance Reform in Asia*. Tokyo: United Nations University Press.

Cook, K. S., Levi, M. and Hardin, R. (2005) *Cooperation without Trust?* New York: Russell Sage Foundation.

Corral, M. (2008) (Mis)Trust in Political Parties in Latin America. *Americas Barometer Insights*, 2008, p. 2. Available at: http://sitemason.vanderbilt.edu/files/eWYTss/I0802Mis%20trust%20in%20political%20parties%20in%20Latin%20America%20English_V2.pdf.

Dalton, R. J. (2005) The Social Transformation of Trust in Government. *International Review of Sociology*, 15(1), pp. 133–154. Available at: http://www.socsci.uci.edu/~rdalton/archive/int_soc05a.pdf.

Dalton, R. J., Pharr, S. J. and Putnam, R. D. (2000) A Quarter Century of Declining Confidence. *Journal of Democracy*, 11(April), pp. 5–25.

Devlin, M. and Chaskel, S. (2010) *From Fear to Hope in Colombia: Sergio Fajardo and Medellin, 2004–2007*. Princeton, NJ: Princeton University Press.

Dinsdale, G. and Marson, B. D. (2000) *Citizen/Client Surveys: Dispelling Myths and Redrawing Maps*. Ottawa: Canadian Centre for Management Development.

Espinal, R., Hartlyn, J. and Kelly, J. M. (2006) Performance Still Matters: Explaining Trust in Government in the Dominican Republic. *Comparative Political Studies*, 39(2), pp. 200–223. Available at: http://www.unc.edu/depts/polisci/hartlyn/Perf%20Matters%20CPS%20March%2006.pdf.

Goodsell, C. T. (1994) *The Case for Bureaucracy*. London: Chatham House.

Graham, C. and Pettinato, S. (2001) *Happiness and Hardship: Opportunity and Insecurity in New Market Economies*. Washington, DC: Brookings University Press.

Granovetter, M. (1983) The Strength of Weak Ties: A Network Theory Revisited. *Sociological Theory*, 1, pp. 201–233.

Guerrero-Ruiz, A. (2011) Rebuilding Trust in Government via Service Delivery: The Case of Medellin, Colombia. *Public Sector Management Companion Notes*. Washington, DC: World Bank.

Guerrero-Ruiz, A. and Manning, N. (2010) Endogenous Model of Trust in Government. *Unpublished Working Paper*. Washington, DC: World Bank.

Hall, M. A. et al. (2001) Trust in Physicians and Medical Institutions: What Is It, Can It Be Measured, and Does It Matter? *The Milibank Quarterly*, 79(4), pp. 613–639.

Hardin, R. (2006) *Trust*. Cambridge: Polity Press.

Horn, M. J. (1995) *The Political Economy of Public Administration: Institutional Choice in the Public Sector*. Cambridge: Cambridge University Press.

Inglehart, R. F. (1997) Postmaterialist Values and the Erosion of Institutional Authority. In: Nye, S., Zelikow, P. D. and King, D. C., eds. *Why People Don't Trust Government.* Cambridge, MA: Harvard University Press, pp. 217–236.

——— (2008) Changing Values among Western Publics from 1970 to 2006. *West European Politics*, 31, pp. 1–2, 130–146.

Kampen, J. K., Van De Walle, S. and Bouckaert, G. (2006) Assessing the Relation between Satisfaction with Public Service Delivery and Trust in Government: The Impact of the Predisposition of Citizens toward Government on Evaluations of Its Performance. *Public Performance and Management Review*, 29(4), pp. 387–404.

Klein, D. B. (1994) If Government Is So Villainous, How Come Government Officials Don't Seem Like Villains? *Economics and Philosophy*, 10, pp. 91–106.

Klingemann, H. (1999) Mapping Political Support in the 1990s. In: Norris, P., ed. *Critical Citizens.* New York: Oxford University Press, pp. 31–56.

Kramer, R. (1999) Trust and Distrust in Organizations: Emerging Perspectives, Enduring Questions. *Annual Review of Psychology*, 50, pp. 569–598.

La Porta, R. et al. (1997) Trust in Large Organizations. *AEA Papers and Proceedings*, 87(2), pp. 310–321.

Latinobarometro Corporation (1997–2008), "Latinobarometro/Latinobarometer Data Files". Santiago, Chile: Latinobarometro Corporation. Retrieved 2012-05-30 from www.latinobarometro.org.

——— (2006) Latinobarometro/Latinobarometer 2005 Data Files. Santiago, Chile: Latinobarometro Corporation.

Levi, M. (1988) *Of Rule and Revenue.* Berkeley: University of California.

——— (1997) *Consent, Dissent and Patriotism.* New York: Cambridge University Press.

——— (1998) State of Trust. In: Braithwaite, V. and Levi, M., eds. *Trust and Governance.* New York: Russell Sage Foundation, pp. 77–101.

Levi, M. and Sacks, A. (2005). "Achieving Good Government—and, maybe, legitimacy". *Arusha Conference: 'New Frontiers of Social Policy'—December 12–15, 2005*, pp. 1–48.

Levi, M. and Stoker, L. (2000) Political Trust and Trustworthiness. *Annual Review of Political Science*, 3, pp. 475–507.

Lieberman, J. (2007) *Lieberman, Collins, Clinton Seek Answers in TB Case.* Press release. Washington, DC. Available at: http://lieberman.senate.gov.

Light, P. C. (2006) The Tides of Reform Revisited: Patterns in Making Government Work, 1945–2002. *Public Administration Review*, 66(1), pp. 6–19.

Lipset, S. (1963). *Political Man* (p. 440). Garden City, NY: Doubleday.

Manning, N., Shepherd, G. and Guerrero, A. (2010a) Performance and Trust in Government in the OECD and Latin America. In: Arizti, P. et al., eds. *Results, Performance Budgeting and Trust in Government.* Washington, DC: World Bank, pp. 201–222.

——— (2010b) Why Trust in Government Matters. In: Arizti, P. et al., eds. *Results, Performance Budgeting and Trust in Government.* Washington, DC: World Bank, pp. 49–74.

Manning, N. and Wetzel, D. (2010) Tales of the Unexpected: Re-Building Trust in Government. In: Canuto, O. and Giugale, M., eds. *The Day after Tomorrow: A Handbook on the Future of Economic Policy in the Developing World.* Washington, DC: World Bank, pp. 163–181.

Miller, A. H. and Listhaug, O. (1990) Political Parties and Confidence in Government: A Comparison of Norway, Sweden and the United States. *British Journal of Political Science*, 20, pp. 357–386.

Mishler, W. and Rose, R. (1997) Trust, Distrust and Scepticism: Popular Evaluations of Civil and Political Institutions in Post-Communist Societies. *Journal of Politics*, 59(2), pp. 418–451.

———— (2001) What Are the Origins of Political Trust: Testing Institutional and Cultural Theories in Post-Communist Societies. *Comparative Political Studies*, 34(1), pp. 30–62.

Molinas, J. R. et al. (2010) *Do Our Children Have a Chance? The 2010 Human Opportunity Report for Latin America and the Caribbean*. Washington, DC: World Bank.

Norris, P. ed. (1999) *Critical Citizens: Global Support for Democratic Government*. Oxford: Oxford University Press.

Norris, P. (2011) *Democratic Deficit: Critical Citizens Revisited*. Cambridge: Cambridge University Press.

Nye, S., Zelikow, P. D. and King, D. C. (1997) *Why People Don't Trust Government*. Cambridge, MA: Harvard University Press.

Paes De Barros, R. et al. (2009) *Measuring Inequality of Opportunities in Latin America and the Caribbean*. Washington, DC: World Bank.

Planning Department (2011) *Encuesta De Calidad De Vida 2010*. Medellin, Colombia: Municipality of Medellin.

Pollitt, C. (2007) New Labour's Re-Disorganization: Hyper Modernism and the Costs of Reform—A Cautionary Tale. *Public Management Review*, 9(4), pp. 529–544.

Pollitt, C. and Bouckaert, G. (2004) *Public Management Reform: A Comparative Analysis*. Oxford: Oxford University Press.

Proantioquia (2011) *Medellin Como Vamos Dataset*. Medellin, Colombia: Proantioquia Foundation.

Rheinstein, M., ed. (1968) *Max Weber on Law in Economy and Society*. New York: Simon and Schuster.

Rothstein, B. (1986) *Just Institutions Matter*. Cambridge: Cambridge University Press.

———— (2005) *Social Traps and the Problem of Trust*. Cambridge: Cambridge University Press.

Sacks, A. (2011) The Antecedents of Approval of the Incumbent Government and Trust in Government in Sub-Saharan Africa, Latin America and Six Arab Countries. *Public Sector Management Companion Notes*. Washington, DC: World Bank.

Secretaria De Gobierno De Medellin (2011) *Sistema De Información Para La Seguridad y Convivencia—Sisc*. Medellin, Colombia: Municipality of Medellin.

Seligson, M. (2002) The Impact of Corruption on Regime Legitimacy: A Comparative Study of Four Latin American Countries. *Journal of Politics*, 64(2), pp. 408–433.

Shepherd, G. (2003) *Civil Service Reform in Developing Countries: Why Is It Going Badly?* Eleventh International Anti-Corruption Conference, Seoul, Republic of Korea, 25–28 May.

Silberman, B. S. (1993) *Cages of Reason: The Rise of the Rational State in France, Japan, the United States, and Great Britain*. Chicago: University of Chicago Press.

Sotomayor, M. A. (2003) *Colombia: Expanding Services to Low Income Areas-Comparing Private and Public Water Utilities*. Washington, DC: World Bank.

Swindell, D. and Kelly, J. M. (2000) Linking Citizen Satisfaction to Performance Measures: A Preliminary Evaluation. *Public Performance and Management Review*, 24(1), pp. 30–52.

Taylor-Gooby, P. (2006) The Rational Actor Reform Paradigm: Delivering the Goods but Destroying Public Trust? *European Journal of Social Quality*, 6(2), pp. 121–141.

Taylor-Gooby, P. and Wallace, A. (2009) Public Values and Public Trust: Responses to Welfare State Reform in the UK. *Journal of Social Policy*, 38(3), pp. 1–19.

Tyler, T. R. (1990) *Why People Obey the Law*. New Haven, CT: Yale University Press.

Van De Walle, S. (2005) *Measuring Bureaucratic Quality in Governance Indicators*. Eighth Public Management Research Conference, Los Angeles, 29 September–1 October. Leuven, Netherlands: Public Management Institute.

Van De Walle, S. and Bouckaert, G. (2003) Public Service Performance and Trust in Government: The Problem of Causality. *International Journal of Public Administration*, 26(8/9), pp. 891–913.

Van De Walle, S., Van Roosbroek, S. and Bouckaert, G. (2005) *Annex: Data on Trust in the Public Sector.* OECD Ministerial Meeting, Strengthening Trust in Government, 28 November, 2005. Paris: OECD.

——— (2008) Trust in the Public Sector: Is There Any Evidence for a Long-Term Decline? *International Review of Administrative Sciences*, 74(1), pp. 45–62.

Warren, M. E. (2006) Democracy and Deceit: Regulating Appearances of Corruption. *American Journal of Political Science*, 50(1), pp. 160–74.

Weatherford, M. S. (1992) Measuring Political Legitimacy. *American Political Science Review*, 86(1), pp. 149–166.

World Bank (2010) *World Development Indicators Dataset.* Washington, DC: World Bank.

——— (2011) *World Development Report: Conflict, Security and Development.* Washington, DC: World Bank.

Yackee, S. W. and Lowery, D. (2005) Understanding Public Support for the US Bureaucracy. *Public Management Review*, 7(4), pp. 515–536.

ANNEX

Table 6.6 Determinants of Trust in Local Education Institutions

Dependent variable:
1. Trust in local education institutions
(Education)

		Coeficient significance
Socio-economic and demographic characteristics	Gender	0.138 *
	Age	−0.047 *
	Local (>3 years in city)	0.131 ***
	Income level	−0.001
	Education level	0.001
	Children	−0.049
	Unemployed	0.098
	Poor	0.097
Current service delivery	Access to education	0.379
	Quality of education	0.139 ***
Perceived effort	Visibility of education dept.	0.882 ***
	Performance of education dept.	1.682 ***
	Pseudo R2	0.5839
	N	1410

Table 6.7 Determinants of Trust in Local Healthcare Institutions

Dependent variable:
2. Trust in local healthcare institutions
(Health: Local clinics; General hospital) — *Coeficient significance*

Socio-economic and demographic characteristics	Gender	0.066
	Age	0.014
	Local (>3 years in city)	−0.015
	Income level	−0.001
	Education level	−0.023
	Children	0.041
	Unemployed	**0.206** **
	Poor	0.043
Current service delivery	Access to health	0.149
	Quality of health	**0.734** **
Perceived effort	Visibility of health institutions	**0.796** ***
	Performance of health institutions	**2.906** ***
	Pseudo R2	0.486
	N	1410

Table 6.8 Determinants of Trust in Local Transport Agencies

Dependent variable:
3. Trust in local transport agencies
(Transport: MetroMedellin; Bus system) — *Coeficient significance*

Socio-economic and demographic characteristics	Gender	0.072
	Age	0.006
	Local (>3 years in city)	0.138 **
	Income level	−0.048
	Education level	−0.003
	Children	0.038
	Unemployed	−0.003
	Poor	0.057
Current service delivery	Access to transport	n.d.
	Quality of transport	n.d.
Perceived effort	Visibility of transport institutions	**1.273** ***
	Performance of transport institutions	**2.744** ***
	Pseudo R2	0.4237
	N	1410

Table 6.9 Determinants of Trust in the Parks and Public Spaces Agency

Dependent variable:
4. Trust in parks and public spaces agency
(Parks: Metroparque)

		Coeficient significance
Socio-economic and demographic characteristics	Gender	0.312
	Age	0.023
	Local (>3 years in city)	0.027
	Income level	**−0.073** **
	Education level	0.001
	Children	0.059
	Unemployed	0.085
	Poor	0.062
Current service delivery	Access to parks and public spaces	−0.201
	Quality of parks and public spaces	**0.116** ***
Perceived effort	Visibility of related institution	**1.294** ***
	Performance of related institution	**2.08** ***
	Pseudo R2	0.602
	N	1410

Table 6.10 Determinants of Trust in Crime-Fighting Institutions

Dependent variable:
5. Trust in crime-fighting institutions
(Crime: Police stations; Metropolitan police)

		Coeficient significance
Socio-economic and demographic characteristics	Gender	0.046
	Age	0.022
	Local (>3 years in city)	0.007
	Income level	**−0.005**
	Education level	0.007
	Children	0.1
	Unemployed	0.228
	Poor	0.074
Current service delivery	Access: Victimization last year	−0.109
	Quality: Neighborhood safety	**0.044** **
	Quality: City safety	**0.102** **
Perceived effort	Visibility safety institutions	**0.676** ***
	Performance safety institutions	**2.971** ***
	Pseudo R2	0.468
	N	1410

Table 6.11 Determinants of Trust in the Street-Cleaning Agency (EEVV)

Dependent variable: 6. Trust in the street-cleaning agency (Education)		Coeficient significance
Socio-economic and demographic characteristics	Gender	0.065
	Age	−0.021
	Local (>3 years in city)	0.098
	Income level	0.064
	Education level	−0.068
	Children	0.074
	Unemployed	0.046
	Poor	−0.025
Current service delivery		n.d.
	Quality of street cleaning	0.122 **
Perceived effort	Visibility street-cleaning agency	0.859 ***
	Performance street-cleaning agency	1.948 ***
	Pseudo R2	0.519
	N	1407

Table 6.12 Determinants of Trust in Basic Infrastructure Services Provider (EPM)

Dependent variable: 7. Trust in basic services provider (Basic infrastructure services: EPM)		Coeficient significance
Socio-economic and demographic characteristics	Gender	0.034
	Age	0.008
	Local (>3 years in city)	0.358
	Income level	−0.052
	Education level	0.027
	Children	−0.015
	Unemployed	−0.108
	Poor	−0.052
Current service delivery	Access to water	−0.141
	Access to sewage	−0.016
	Access to electricity	−0.152
	Access to domestic gas	−0.507
	Quality of water provision	0.038
	Quality of sewage provision	0.057
	Quality of electricity provision	0.082 *
	Quality of gas provision	1.658 *
Perceived effort	Visibility basic services provider	0.468 ***
	Performance basic services provid.	1.681 ***
	Pseudo R2	0.431
	N	1410

*** 99%, ** 95%, * 90% significance level.

7 The British Broadcasting Corporation (BBC)

A Trusted Institution?

Greg Dyke and Nick Clifford

We rely on the media to assist us in making sense of the changing culture of the society in which we live (Barnett, 2011; Briggs, 1961, 1965, 1970, 1979, 1995; Coleman and Ross, 2010; Hajkowski, 2010). The media help generate the confidence we need to navigate our social relationships, and, therefore, we need to be able to trust its compass. However, a number of recent events have contributed to our losing this sense of trust. This chapter identifies some of the more significant of these events in the United Kingdom (UK) and discusses their implications for public trust and confidence more widely.

Public interest is increasing in this area. The Arts and Humanities Research Council recently funded a two-year project (Holland et al., 2010) that sought to achieve a clearer historical understanding of how the idea of 'no such thing as society' took hold in the decade from 1979 to 1990. The project scrutinized the broadcast media and its role in 'the transformation of politics into culture'. In addition there have been a number of inquiries scrutinizing key issues surrounding the role of the media. The inquiry into the circumstances surrounding the death of Dr. David Kelly, usually known in the UK as 'The Hutton Report' (Hutton, 2004), examined media reporting on whether the government report on weapons of mass destruction (WMD) in Iraq (The Stationery Office, 2002) had been over-influenced by the prime minister's office; the outcome of the inquiry was disastrous for those in executive positions in the BBC. The further report that followed soon after, usually known in the UK as 'The Butler Report' (Butler, 2004), was far more measured and investigated the intelligence surrounding the wider issues concerning the government's report on WMD. The impact on the BBC has been to see its role and management scrutinized over the course of the last decade, resulting in significant changes to the BBC's governance arrangements and the licence fee settlement. Its charter renewal was debated widely in the public domain before being renewed in 2006 (DCMS, Cm6925, 2006) and the 'agreement' (DCMS, Cm 6872, 2006) has been amended a number of times by the government. Now, in 2012, a new inquiry into the relationship between governments, other public bodies and the media in the UK has been triggered by the discovery of widespread phone-hacking by journalists (Leveson, 2011–2012).[1] Public trust and confidence, in its written media, has appeared to falter, whereas public trust in broadcasting, and particularly the BBC, has not declined—in fact, quite the opposite. The possible reasons for this will be the subject of this chapter. By taking the BBC as a case example, we examine the impact of all these events on trust and confidence in the current British media. We review the prospects for the BBC for the coming decade and in a postscript discuss the resignation of the director general (DG), George Entwistle in the wake of the a Newsnight programme broadcast in October 2012'.

THE BBC AND THE MEDIA

Uniquely, the formation of the BBC nearly eighty years ago (1927), resulted in a British institution coming into existence that even today retains much of its original form (see Briggs, 1961–1995). It is independent of the government of the day, yet its funding is set by that same government (DCMS Cm6925, 2006 and DCMS Cm6872, 2006). It is not a profit-making enterprise, yet it acts, and has to act at times, in a commercial way. Any poll conducted into the relationship between the public and the BBC suggests that the corporation is held in very high esteem—achieving approval figures such as 95% for its radio and nearly 85% for its television programmes (Ipsos MORI, 2008). Somehow, the nation has evolved an institution that enjoys the trust and confidence of its citizenry. This chapter seeks to explain why that relationship, and the high regard in which the BBC is held by the public, came about. It then explores a little further why the changing logic and the widening spread of funding of television along with the erosion of advertising revenues have contributed to the growing criticism of the BBC. The chapter goes on to explore the likely future for the BBC from both the perspective of those that criticize it and those who continue to support the old regime.

We re-examine the events of 2003–2004, when the BBC found itself at the centre of a storm. In the aftermath of this, during the course of nearly a decade, the BBC lost its director general and its chair of governors; a new charter was agreed; a new constitution was put in place, which brought a new trust board to the BBC; and, finally, a new financial settlement was agreed, which anticipated a rapid reduction in funding and placed new responsibilities on the BBC to provide services previously funded by the government. In all, a radical set of initiatives was put in place which will have a significant impact on the BBC as it goes forward.

HISTORY OF THE BBC

The history of the BBC needs to be contextualized—up until the 1920s the 'media' relied on the technology of the printed word. Those words could be produced into multiple copies quickly via printing presses. Ownership of the media was through private-sector owners (press 'barons') who controlled them. Editorial freedom was an understood objective but, even so, individual owners could direct the kind of output each paper adopted. A 'free' press was a clear democratic principle that was generally understood and supported in the UK. However, during the early part of the twentieth century, electronic media was emerging. Telecommunications grew rapidly, firstly through radio and later through television. With this change of technology, two key issues emerged—firstly, a network of transmission could only be achieved through the installation of an infrastructure to support it; secondly, a system of receiving those transmissions required individual household possession of radios (and later televisions) to enable the output of the broadcaster to be received. This level of investment could have been left to the market with some form of roll-out over a number of years. A private sector experiment between six electronic companies was tried first (1922), but after five years the UK adopted a more elegant solution that also avoided a 'state-controlled' monopoly service (1927). It did this by meeting the investment costs on the transmission side through those receiving the service paying a licence 'fee' to permit them to receive the output. On the reception side, each individual household would purchase its own receiver (the radio, or 'wireless'), which would be provided by the market. Set in the heart of this neat solution was the invention of a broadcasting corporation which would not only take on the costs of the transmission infrastructure but also be responsible for the making of the programmes.

The outcome of this was the rapid development of private sector interest in the 'hardware'—because there was now a clear 'market opportunity' that could be exploited for the radio producers. Names such as Baird figure large here. On the other hand, the 'software'—the broadcast material—could now be justified because there was an expectant audience 'out there' who wanted to use the new, superior technology of radio broadcasting. What grew up was a production corporation that became extremely competent at making programmes and broadcasting them to a growing audience. The early development of television was therefore ready to exploit this unique relationship of receivers of the output (the listeners and the viewers) buying their own kit and at the same time funding the costs of the infrastructure development through paying their licence fees. The glue that held this all together was the BBC charter. This broadly amounted to a guarantee that the corporation would provide an output that would be worthwhile in both quantity and quality and would be reliable. If the BBC output had been poor or the broadcasting infrastructure had been subject to too many failures, the whole enterprise would never have succeeded. Into this mix emerged a man of vision and leadership, Lord Reith, whose obsession lay with quality, probity, high standards and a passion for achieving the very best for this country. He would go on to establish a reputation for the BBC and for himself which has lasted the whole of its lifetime. The old adage about standing on the shoulders of giants is genuinely apposite here. What Lord Reith's influence achieved in no small measure was a 'reputation' for the BBC. The words 'this is the BBC' would take on huge significance during the middle part of the century when linked to 'this is the news'. What lay behind them was a platform of trust through which the public could have complete confidence in 'their' broadcaster to 'tell them how it was, without fear or favour', and in particular by resisting the interference of government—'it must be realized that such pressures are inevitable, for the aims of political parties and those of broadcasting organizations are not the same' (Wyndham Goldie, 1977, p. 22).

The development of early television, therefore, was moulded on a model where the producer/provider 'enjoyed' this position of privilege through the state's enforcement of a licence fee on each household that received the output but which was then collected by the producer/provider itself. The fee was an interesting form of accountability that appeared to be highly tuned to customer satisfaction—if the licence payer felt they were not getting value for money, they would not buy the licence. The fact that they did, with a very low level of non-compliance, was testament to the quality of the service. Based on this successful model, the transition from radio technology to television production was made. The later addition of a private sector network of independent television (ITV), based on commercial exploitation of the advertising potential of television followed—the key economic element of this, however, was that the 'cost of the box' was now spread over the extended choice of programme providers who benefited from the initial set-up costs being met through the licence fee.

The BBC's position became established as the independent provider, free of commercial owners, supported effectively by the recipient of the service and therefore uniquely positioned to take advantage of stability, continuity and a lack of interference. What grew out of this was a corporation that acted as a honey-pot for talented programme makers, producers and directors, who could mine the huge cultural heritage of the nation to make programmes, to provide the news, to inform, educate and entertain all at the same time. Alongside this, there was a ready-made industry that could exploit the technological talent of those who would develop better picture quality, introduce colour and begin to investigate the next leap forward into digital technology and broadcasting—a fusion of artistic creativity and technological innovation.

The rich atmosphere of creativity and innovation that was a hallmark of the BBC during the mid and later twentieth century, not just technologically but in terms of the programme-making as well, turned into criticism towards the end of the century. The private sector looked enviously at the BBC charter that provided a level of protection to the corporation (the licence fee was seen as guaranteed income which did not need to be 'earned'). Advertising revenues were no longer the 'easy money' of the early days of ITV. The private sector part of the industry was restructuring with takeovers and mergers. The argument was, surely the start-up costs of broadcasting had been paid off long ago? Into this mix entered the world of digital technology, where both film and tape would be consigned to history. Most of all, the owners of newspaper groups in Britain increased their criticism of the BBC, partly because they themselves took a more ideological view of the media and partly because they blamed the BBC as their own revenues began to decline[2].

At the turn of the century, the BBC was struggling. The book *Inside Story* (Dyke, 2005) outlined the difficulty of seeking to run the 'Best Managed Public Sector Organisation in the World'. This was the legacy of the outgoing director general, John (now Lord) Birt. He introduced internal markets, role separation, hierarchical management and many of the ideas imported from private sector techniques and styles on how best to run the public sector—a form of 'new public management' (Hood, 1991, 2005). Appointed to the position of director general in 2000, I was confronted by a demoralized organization where the staff hadn't 'bought in' to the strategy the management was implementing. In the book (Dyke, 2005) I explain the fundamental thinking about radical organizational reform that I adopted during my time at the BBC, based largely on the ideas of transformational leadership. In a chapter I called 'Why Did They Cry?' I explained the journey from engendering a sense of urgency for change, forming a guiding coalition of senior executives and setting a new vision (the highly popular 'One BBC' idea), to communicating the vision, trying things out, embedding change and finally beginning to institutionalize it into the structures of the BBC. Across all this reform, outside events were eventually to play an instrumental role in disturbing the path of change.

On 11 September 2001, in New York and Washington, the attacks of 9/11 took place. The BBC website, still in its infancy as a news platform, was besieged. The reputation for integrity, investigative journalism, tenacity and the quality of its broadcasts set it apart on the world stage. Here was a news story of unprecedented proportion in peacetime. The BBC went onto full-time news delivery on its broadcasting terrestrial network as well as online. Its reputation was reinforced. The privately owned, huge corporate media organizations (especially in America) were unable to provide the level of balance and breadth of understanding and analysis that were needed in such circumstances.

In discussing the reputation of the BBC, John Simpson in his autobiography (Simpson, 2002) points out the way that a dedicated team of BBC people seek to report the news accurately and quickly. Rightly, they earn respect for their work.

> As a result of the events of 11 September 2001, the BBC became the most praised, and the most relied-on, source of information around the world. . . . Newspapers almost everywhere, and especially in the United States, carried articles praising the BBC. This scarcely got a mention in Britain; praise for the BBC isn't something most British newspapers feel is worth reporting. (Simpson, 2002, p. 14)

However, in a particularly British way, our reticence to acknowledge when we really do things well ends up playing very badly when an institution such as the BBC comes under pressure.

In organizing their response to the devastating attacks in New York and Washington, world leaders began the process of forming alliances and understandings around a series of propositions on what they needed to do next. The BBC reported on the growing focus on Iraq and its alleged weapons of mass destruction—the work of United Nations (UN) weapons inspectors appeared to be ambivalent. They could not be sure that such weapons existed. As the UK government prepared its case, a document was reported to Parliament by the prime minister that appeared to suggest that these weapons, which could be extremely harmful to Britain and British interests, could be deployed very quickly (The Stationery Office, 2002). On 29 May 2003, after the war in Iraq had started, the now well-documented 'Today' programme on Radio 4 carried an item on the possibility that the report had been 'sexed up'. It led to a determination by the government 'machine' to undermine the BBC.

The fact that subsequently the veracity of the statement was found to be largely true is now irrelevant. In fact, Tony Blair says as much:

> The Gilligan broadcast led the news because it alleged misconduct, a lie, in effect . . . In any event, a mere mistake was never going to lead the news. Now, in actual fact, it should do. The intelligence was wrong and we should have, and I have, apologized for it. So the real story is a story and a true one. But in today's environment, it doesn't have that sensational, outrage-provoking 'wow' factor of scandal. Hence an error is made into a deception. And it is this relationship between politics and media which then defines the political debate. (Blair, 2010, p. 463)

This claim by members of the political classes that the media misrepresents them has been particularly challenging to the BBC. Although the evidence is clear that whereas public trust in the BBC in the light of the 'Today' programme item and its aftermath has not moved, public trust in the Blair government was damaged. In short, the public believed the BBC more than they believed the politicians, a fact which is very scary for the political classes.

In the case of the recent inquiries, either within the House of Commons, to Parliamentary Select Committees or outside the House to public inquiries, the BBC has been attacked. For example, the head of communications for the government under Tony Blair sat in a parliamentary foreign affairs select committee and castigated BBC journalism for being inaccurate and prejudiced (House of Commons, 25 June 2003, Question no. 1131). 'I think if we carry on with this constant denigration of politics, the political process, we are going down a very bad route . . . I tell you, until the BBC acknowledge that is a lie, I will keep banging on, that correspondence file will get thicker and they had better issue an apology pretty quickly.' The aim of this was not simply to place the role of the government, and in particular some of its ministers, in a better light but more importantly to challenge the accepted view of the BBC as a trusted and reliable organization in which the public could have confidence. In fact much of the vehemence of the attack appeared to be aimed at deliberately undermining the trust and confidence of the public in 'their' BBC in order to attempt to erode the strength of that support.

The government's policy response was to seek a systematic 'rebalancing' of the relationship between the BBC, the licence fee and the financial underpinning of the BBC's revenue streams. What followed was a fundamental restructuring of the BBC's finances. Where, in the past, the licence fee had been linked to the scale of the investment needed to maintain the BBC's leading technological edge in both broadcasting and the Internet, it became frozen at an arbitrary level. Where the licence fee had been channelled into funding BBC activities, it was now used to fund subsidies to elderly households needing to switch over to digital reception and the provision of the World Service, both previously the responsibility of government (Department of Work and Pension and the Foreign and Commonwealth Office). Where corporate management had been left to the Board of Governors and its senior executives, financial reductions of specific percentages were now imposed by government ministers. Where the Board of Governors were mainly appointments of known 'worthies' from the establishment, a form of benign oversight, a new BBC trust was formed and expected to manage the corporation with more hands-on pressure and regulation.

BALANCING PUBLIC SERVICE BROADCASTING AND THE PUBLIC INTEREST

What we now want to discuss, therefore, is the fundamental balance between the need to provide a full daily output of programmes which inform, educate and entertain (as was the original charter ideals) and the need to broadcast and publish material of the highest possible journalistic integrity.

Public service broadcasting (PSB) has an important role to play. As the United Nations Educational, Scientific and Cultural Organisation (UNESCO) asserts: 'Neither commercial nor State-controlled, public broadcasting's only *raison d'être* is public service. It is the public's broadcasting organization; it speaks to everyone as a citizen. Public broadcasters encourage access to and participation in public life. They develop knowledge, broaden horizons and enable people to better understand themselves by better understanding the world and others' (World Radio and Television Council, 2001, p. 7). To be seen as a public service broadcaster, a provider should ideally demonstrate a number of specific characteristics. These include: universal (geographic) accessibility; universal appeal (covering general tastes and interests), paying particular attention to minorities; contributing to a sense of national identity and community; distancing from vested interests; funding directly with universality of price, competing on the basis of good programming and quality based on objective values and not simply viewer and listener figures; and adopting guidelines that liberate rather than restrict programme makers (Broadcasting Research Unit, 1985). Ofcom's chief executive, Ed Richards, defined PSB as broadcasting that aimed to do four things: to increase our understanding of the world, to stimulate knowledge and learning, to reflect the cultural identity of the UK and to ensure diversity and alternative viewpoints (Ofcom, 2008). David Attenborough (2008) has reflected on the apparently popular view that PSB programmes should only expect to attract small-niche small audiences; he argued strongly there should be no contradiction between popularity and public-service interests. It is a measure of the overall quality of the BBC that it has been able to continue as a PSB while at the same time to retain its popularity.

To take the fundamental criticisms 'head on', the key charges are:

- The BBC is too large
- The BBC is too ubiquitous; it is spread across too many channels, from radio to television, to the Internet, to the BBC's wide range of websites, to the iPlayer and so on
- The BBC is too difficult to manage
- The BBC is out of touch with its customers

The dominant logic of all these criticisms appears to be that the occupation by one player/provider in the market, with 'too high' a share, leads inevitably to a situation that is fundamentally anti-competitive, and this results in a public loss. The benefits of an early, relatively protected market, while the huge initial start-up costs were dealt with, have now been discharged. There is no more need to protect the market and therefore the fundamental economics of the BBC position have now changed—and it's time to 'move on'.

The BBC Is Too Large

'The Corporation is incapable of distinguishing between what is good for it, and what is good for the country. . . Funded by a hypothecated tax, the BBC feels empowered to offer something for everyone, even in areas well served by the market. The scope of its activities and ambitions is chilling' (Murdoch, 2009, p. 14). The corporation is a significant player in the whole media and communications market—it has multi-channel offerings through BBC1, BBC2, BBC3 and BBC4 before any of the niche channels are taken into account, such as CBBC. It has multiple platforms, such as digital audio broadcasting (DAB), Internet, Freesat, Freeserve, and so on. It can post its back catalogue on YouTube as well as provide play-again facilities through the iPlayer. It has extensive web capability with the capacity to provide live broadcasting via the Internet and mobile phones. It has a large staff of news and current-affairs correspondents who cover world news reporting on a twenty-four-hour basis. It is a £4 billion business—it is the largest public broadcasting service in the world of its type. In terms of its competitors, it is much larger and better resourced that its rivals in the private sector.

However, how is the size of such an institution to be measured, and by which criteria would 'too large' be judged? Would a programme, such as Live Aid, pulled together in what might have appeared to be an unrealistic but in the end. achievable, timescale have been possible without a BBC to throw all its resources into it? Would it have been possible to provide coverage as comprehensive and detailed on the events of the first Iraq war, 9/11, or 7/7 with a small-niche PSB? The London Olympics of 2012 brought a great deal of this capability to the fore with use of multi-platforms to broadcast live as well as through repeated programmes for selection later by viewers.[3]

The BBC Is Too Ubiquitous

One other way of asking this question would be to ask why the different parts of the BBC grew up in the first place. The broad objectives of the BBC have been to inform, educate and entertain. The BBC has developed a range of radio and television programmes spread across the different networks that entertain (from comedy, to drama and entertainment generally); that educate (from specific wildlife programmes to language, documentary and cultural/ minority programmes) and that inform (through news, current affairs and politics programmes). It has grown in response to need and demand. Whereas the BBC has to run as a business with an agreed rationale and cost for each programme, its overall remit does not come down to simple profit. The news and current-affairs correspondents are expected to provide more than just 'adequate' coverage of an issue—depth and scale are needed. Correspondents link their normal reporting 'pieces to camera', with their analysis in the studio, discussion pieces on the web page, individual blog pages, information and research within the BBC website, plus interactive correspondence through the web service. All these different channels provide an integrated service. When issues arise that are complex and fast moving—such as the recent banking collapse of 2007–2008—the BBC is able to provide a comprehensive means by which the consumer (listener, viewer, Internet user) can form their own view about a world or domestic issue. Only through its width and depth of reporting and analysis can the BBC build its trust with the British public; to limit this would be to diminish its important role.

The BBC Is Too Difficult to Manage

Managing the BBC is a huge task and therefore would simplification, streamlining and cost reduction assist in re-forming it? Are top executives' salaries too high? Can new managerial talent only be attracted to the BBC by offering salaries comparable to private sector companies? Are key star presenters/broadcasters being over-remunerated, or is there simply a market rate for such talent? I took the view, when director general, that actually managing the BBC was not that difficult—the business model then was that we got £3.5 billion in, and then we spent it. We were essentially a spending organization, not a business. I found myself asking in my early days, when still very much in my old 'business thinking mode', does anyone know the value of a million pounds? Of course a million on an overall profit of £20 million on a turnover of £400 million is a lot of money. But a million in a budget of £3.5 billion is not. Management of the BBC is actually difficult, but not in the traditional sense. Its difficulty is in thinking about how staff, in a considerable number of different settings—from the regional offices, to the specialist units, to the newsrooms, to outside broadcast—can all give of their best to the whole organization and to the whole of the listening, viewing and online-using public. Having a unified understanding of pulling together—such as working within the 'One BBC' mantra we developed while I was DG—can be a difficult managerial challenge. However, it is not solved using traditional business-management techniques; it requires much more creativity and leadership and full recognition of the public service ethos that lies at the heart of the organization.

The BBC Is Out of Touch with Its Customers

James Murdoch (Murdoch, 2009, p. 19) argued that 'there is an inescapable conclusion that we must reach if we are to have a better society. . . . The only reliable, durable, and perpetual guarantor of independence is profit. . . . Independence is sustained by true accountability—the accountability owed to customers.' We take 'customers' to mean those who are prepared to pay for a service. This argument appears to be increasingly flawed and comes down to expectations (Lankton and McKnight, 2012). Mainstream teaching on customer satisfaction suggests that people are satisfied when their expectations are met; that is, if your expectations are to have a BBC much as it is at the moment, then the likelihood is that you will be satisfied with what you currently receive. However, it is when there is 'disconfirmation' between your expectations and what you receive that complications can arise. Thus, if your expectations are wildly exceeded, you may be disproportionately happy, and similarly if your expectations are strongly under-realized, then you will be extremely unhappy. There tends to be a disproportionate move away from the mean, depending on the extent of the disconfirmation. However, this traditional way of seeking to meet people's expectations—as you would in a business where you segment your 'customers' and focus your production on meeting those customers' needs—seems irrelevant in PSB. As I said to the House of Lords Select Committee, 'I have never met a licence-fee payer' (House of Lords, 2011, Question 514, p. 221). What I meant was that no one defines themselves as a 'licence-fee payer' in the way they might describe themselves as a 'Manchester United fan'. There are, however, thousands of people who define themselves as Radio Four listeners. In other words, they identify with the service, not the means of paying for it. Licence-fee payers do not exist in the sense that they are customers of the BBC. In some respects, the BBC, when it's on the top of its game, is 'out of touch' because it is focusing on something that does not yet exist; the public's understanding of itself. And yet, on the whole, the BBC clearly meets and often exceeds public expectations.

TRUST AND CONFIDENCE IN PUBLIC SERVICE BROADCASTING

We feel, therefore, that trust and confidence in relation to public service broadcasting need to be discussed in the context of the impact that new media might be having on the relationship the public has with its institutions.

For journalists, their stories need to be based on facts and the basis for their opinions needs to be transparent—strengthening trust will come from bringing together the accuracy of the reporting alongside the sense of shared values of the organization—in a way a reflection of the organization's character.

For the public to trust broadcasters' character they need to feel that the production is accurate, it is considered, properly researched, referenced and so on. In the same way that an academic provides their sources for making assertions on issues of understood knowledge, so with a public broadcaster—its information sources need to be clear. There has to be capability within the resources provided to fully cover current 'stories'. This means ensuring that both the quality and quantity of people employed by an organization can provide the range and depth of information and comment that will build trust in its overall reporting.

For the public to begin to form their own view on emerging events within society, they rely heavily on the media to provide two forms of coverage. The first is the 'news', and this requires investigative journalism to provide a form of reporting that identifies 'what is going on'—in colloquial parlance, 'the facts'. The second is commentary on those emerging events in the form of opinions.

When a BBC 'correspondent' is reporting on a story, 'trust' in their report needs to meet three criteria—it is based on first-hand knowledge (they have to be there), it is told in a balanced way, and it is properly 'thought through' as an issue. 'Correspondents' are required to try and achieve a mix between 'facts' that are genuine and reliable and 'opinion' that is formed through experience and skills, which together inform 'their view' of a situation. In this way broadcasters' news and current affairs output provides listeners, viewers and Internet users with a basis on which they can form their own understanding and begin to come to 'their own view'. Confidence in this 'view' is underpinned by trust in both the correspondent (their training, selection, accuracy rates, judgement and experience) and the character and corporate standards of the organization. In the case of an organization like the BBC, the values and objectives of the organization, being a publicly accountable body, tend to be more explicit and clear. This provides a backdrop to the work of all those employed within the organization. Much of the praise for the BBC during the reporting of the second Iraq war came in part because, for many in the United States, their national coverage was overtly pro-government and, in particular, pro–White House.

John Simpson, still the BBC's brilliant world affairs editor, alluded to these battles when, in the weeks leading up to the Iraq War, he wrote: 'At the times of Suez, Biafra, Vietnam, the Falklands, the American bombing of Libya and the NATO attacks on Kosovo and Serbia, the BBC reported the opposition to these wars fully. On every occasion the government—Labour or Conservative—tried to bully the BBC into supporting the official line. On every occasion the BBC resisted; sometimes energetically, sometimes not as energetically as it ought to have done . . . Governments have as much right as anyone to put pressure on the BBC; it's only a problem if the BBC caves in' (Simpson, 2003, para. 13). He is right; it is only a problem if the BBC loses some of its character and gives in to this pressure.

Ownership of a media organ—whether it is print, electronic media, or broadcasting—needs to be independent of the editorial judgement. Lord Justice Leveson (2011–2012) has been charged to enquire into the relationships between the establishment (be they politicians or key people in the private or public sector) and the large media owners. We do not yet know the result. Part of his inquiry concerned the public expectation that establishment relationships were conducted properly. Editorial separation between the providers of news and current affairs and the owners of the different media channels is obviously essential. The decision to provide a unique public channel, through the BBC, by the British establishment over eighty years ago has been one that has stood this test through a considerable period of turbulent times.

However, new technology and its resulting new media have fundamentally broadened our access to information and opinion. No longer do you have to wait for a news bulletin to obtain 'news'—it is available throughout each day via a number of media channels and can be accessed 'out of time' by using the Internet. Increasingly, broadcasts are available to 'listen again' and linked to the Internet, journalists can use print media, links to other web pages and valuable background (e.g. archived material, analysis, etc.) to provide additional information in support of their views. Thus 'publication' has been taken away from a periodic 'event', when perhaps much of what was being discussed had become 'history', to a position where much of the discussion is capable of taking place close to 'real time'.

In the months following the revelations concerning investigative tactics used in the UK (that may still prove to have been both illegal and unethical) British journalism has been under intense scrutiny (Leveson, 2011–2012). The newspaper industry faces a dramatic loss in public confidence as the relationships between owners, editors and journalists are forensically picked apart for evidence of possible wrongdoing. In this new world order, the BBC is re-emerging; its independence from government is being reasserted. Institutionally its position is strengthening whereas those of press 'barons' and politicians are eroding. The unique settlement between broadcasting as a public service separated from political interference or commercial pressures through its charter appears to be assured. In this environment the BBC has an opportunity—it can take advantage of a landscape in which its size, complexity, capability and international reputation can lead it forward, with confidence, for the next decade; or it can 'freeze in the headlights' and risk considerable damage. The history of leadership at the BBC suggests that it will take advantage of this opportunity. Directors General (such as Reith), key production executives (such as Wyndham Goldie), key presenter/journalists (such as Dimbleby) and the host of household names whose careers have been embedded within the BBC (such as Attenborough, Simpson and Redhead) all stand testament to the culture of the BBC summed up in the idea that 'nation shall speak to nation', free of political and commercial pressures to bend and shape those nations' voices.

How might advantage be taken of such new opportunities? One recent example was the BBC's lead in forming a consortium to be awarded the Digital Terrestrial Television (DTT) licence which established 'Freeview'. This became a new digital broadcasting platform and rescued it from the debacle of the collapse of 'ITV Digital'. The vision behind this free-to-air service has been described as 'a remarkable illustration of how a range of diverse players can identify and launch an idea within a very short period of time . . . It is an excellent example of public-private partnership in practice' (Boyfield and Mather, 2006, p. 21). The take-off of digital receivership has borne out the confidence shown by the BBC executives at the time that the BBC was capable of leading itself and others into new broadcasting territory while fully including the private sector involvement in the project. In 2006, Boyfield and Mather identified three 'key challenges' for Freeview—overcoming the limited spectrum capacity, especially in the context of HD (high definition); the future of pay-TV; and the exploitation of Freeview as a brand. With the hindsight of just six years, these were clearly not the key challenges; HD is now a regular alternative channel for both the BBC and ITV; pay-TV has settled down to specific customer needs, for example sport and shopping; and Freeview occupies a whole two-page spread in the *Radio Times* for each day's programming.

So what might be the real challenges? The first is the nature of data; data are the building blocks of information, and in a digital world it can be both captured and copied extremely quickly. It can appear in formats such as text, pictures, video, code and programs. It can also be accessed very quickly and efficiently. But data on its own is of little use. It only becomes knowledge when it helps people to make sense of the world. 'OurDemocracy', a website devoted to encouraging global debate on matters on public concern, launched 'OurBeeb' in 2012 to stimulate debate on the future of the BBC in the advent of the new director general taking up office[4]. Google has grasped an important insight about the use of data. As Emily Bell, Professor of Professional Practice and Director, Tow Center for Digital Journalism at Columbia University's Journalism School, explained recently, 'Google organizes and helps you discover things that are going on the world right now—(yet) this is the function of journalism.' She argues that those who feel that Google is 'not the same' as the media businesses of newspapers and broadcasting are making a 'fundamental type of error' (Bell, 2010). She gives the example of Matt Waite, the co-creator of PolitiFact.com,[5] who dramatically turned round the fortunes of the St. Petersburg Times in Florida by offering an immediate check on the likely veracity of claims made by politicians through building a website containing 'truth-o-meters'. Interestingly, Waite's career has moved into academia (Professor of Practice at the College of Journalism and Mass Communication at University of Nebraska–Lincoln)[6] mirroring Emily Bell, who moved recently from being director of digital content at the *Guardian*.[7] It is therefore all the more interesting to note the beginnings of a recognition that academia and journalism might not be too far apart. Ken Doctor at Harvard asks such questions as: What's the difference between being informed and being educated? What's the line between learning something new and being *taught* (his italics) something new? Are news media and universities just two ways to do the same thing: gain knowledge? His argument is: 'Become the go-to source, globally, nationally or locally for something people value and the digital world rewards you'. And he goes on 'So where is the money here? Is there a business model to be found? The facile Silicon Valley answer may seem unpalatable to *current* (his italics) newspaper company owners: Become more essential to people and the money will follow . . . what can be more essential, and more relationship-building, than lifelong education?' (Doctor, 2012).

Part of the 'data' challenge is to recognize the new models for using information. Alistair Croll argues that 'big data' presents a problem for the citizen. Surprisingly it's not the volume that presents the problem; it's the speed at which it can be analysed. In the past, securing all the '3 V's of data' (volume, variety and velocity) at the same time, was a problem. With the advent of clouds, platforms and speedy technological innovation the analyses of data 'become so cheap they are practically free . . . Abundance replaces scarcity, and we invent new business models'. Croll's argument (Croll, 2012) is that 'big data' now means that we supply data in all sorts of ways without controlling what is done with it. 'Data doesn't invade people's lives. *Lack of control over how it's used does*' (his italics). Croll suggests that the decision on what data is stored, how and why, is 'called designing the schema', and this defines what the data is about: 'It's the instant of context'. He argues that protecting the schema from possible abuse by organizations is becoming a 'civil rights issue'. In the same way that Google 'anticipates' our searches and sets up the algorithms to aid our searching, organizations can link data that might indicate certain preferences or even ethnicity or gender.

In this way they can devise marketing plans designed to target (or discriminate against) these individuals—all made possible with huge amounts of data—or 'big data'.

Tesco used this plan with success in introducing their 'Clubcard'. As the adoption by the individual of a 'harmless' loyalty card took off, so Tesco developed a 'big data' set of 'who, where, when and what' for a large majority of its sales. It was enough to provide a good indication of where and when middle-class people bought high-end purchases, and it did this by simply matching addresses of card-holders and purchases made at its stores. This enabled it to invade retail areas long held by traditional pharmacies (e.g. Boots), electrical retailers (e.g. Currys) and clothes, linens and internal decorations (e.g. Marks and Spencer) and to take market share from high-end food purveyors through introducing Tesco 'Finest' as a brand.

As the legacy of the last two decades becomes more and more apparent, the impact of digital technology has been recognized as profound. It has changed the definition of businesses from 'sectors' or 'industries' to 'business models'. Much of the argument about the failure of the banking sector to realize its own folly, in time to avoid a disaster, was their disconnection from customers, local communities and the basic principles of banking. They built systems which eroded trust, confidence and a clear understanding of their accountability to public standards. The newsprint media has similarly failed to recognize this. Emily Bell narrates a Google executive admonishing her when she was still at the *Guardian* for not listening to their key stakeholders. She believes, like Google, that those who are the first to recognize the nature of high connectivity—what will become possible through using different platforms, channels, means of access and locations to reach vast markets—will be the ones who can capture the benefits of innovation most effectively. This will clearly not only be a technological issue but an ethical one as well.

The notion of 'algorithmic authority' discussed by Clay Shirky (2009) suggests that the public need to feel some confidence that their knowledge base is reliable, or at worse they will not feel isolated if it turns out to be wrong. Compared to personal or institutional authority, algorithmic authority is 'the decision to regard as authoritative an unmanaged process of extracting value from diverse, untrustworthy sources without any human standing beside the result saying "Trust this because you trust me".' Jonathan Stray (2012) discusses the difficulty of this in the news media world:

> What we see, and what we don't see, is heavily mediated by information filtering algorithms . . . [which] . . . shape our knowledge and our society. They are a permanent part of what it means to perceive the world . . . we don't yet really know how to combine the pragmatic demands of technology with the social aspirations of the humanities. But it's also an exciting time to be working in the digital journalism, where these two cultures meet every day.

It is possible that 'the web' is searching for a means to reconcile the tension between these two cultures and that rather than invent such a means on its own, painfully, the experience of the BBC may well be able to provide a smoother learning curve in the way it approaches the whole issue.

The second challenge is the dramatic fall in reputation experienced by major institutions/industries, such as politics, media and financial services. For example, since 2007–2008, it has become apparent that banking institutions were being hopelessly mismanaged. The old principles of caution and rectitude, based on much of the older heritage of 'our word is our bond' were lost. The old principles of integrity espoused by many early banks' founders (such as Barclays and Lloyds, both Quakers) were overtaken by greed. The 'casino atmosphere' generated in the years leading up to the crash fatally undermined confidence in the sector. This extended to the banks themselves, who could no longer trust each other to know the value of their debts, which meant they were no longer prepared to trade with each other. This led to the 'credit crunch' of 2008–2009. Alongside this, the Leveson Inquiry (Leveson, 2011–2012) has revealed a world of intertwined relationships between politicians and the newspaper and broadcasting media that has genuinely shocked the British public. A brand strength which contains genuine reputation, full of authenticity and trust, will be required to achieve levels of reassurance with the public for the future. The BBC is poised to take advantage of this, should it have the confidence in its own worth, its heritage and its creativity.

C. P. Scott (1921), in his now famous essay reflecting on 100 years of the *Guardian* and the social and institutional position of a newspaper, saw a newspaper as 'much more than a business; it is an institution; it reflects and it influences the life of a whole community; it may affect even wider destinies. It is, in its way, an instrument of government. It plays on the minds and consciences of men' (Scott, 1921, para. 2). He felt a newspaper should have a moral as well as a material existence, and its character and influence were determined by the balance of these two forces. He was perhaps prescient in arguing: '(a newspaper) may make profit or power its first object, or it may conceive itself as fulfilling a higher and more exacting function.' In seeking to achieve the latter he saw character as crucial. Character was a slow deposit of past actions and ideals and 'for each man his most precious possession' (Scott, 1921, para. 4), and so it was for a newspaper's 'character'. For him a good character implied

> honesty, cleanness, courage, fairness, a sense of duty to the reader and the community . . . nothing should satisfy short of the best, and the best must always seem a little ahead of the actual. It is here that ability counts and that character counts, and it is on these that a newspaper, like every great undertaking, if it is to be worthy of its power and duty, must rely. (Scott, 1921, para. 7)

Could this be a future guiding principle for the BBC? Maybe the essence of an institution's character is in its constant search for a mechanism through which the public can build and maintain their trust and confidence—something that the BBC has striven for since its early beginnings?

CONCLUSION

In 2008, the BBC attempted to develop a public debate over the future of public service broadcasting. It commissioned a series of lectures on the subject and published them in a booklet entitled *The Creative Perspective* (BBC, 2008). In each case, the lecturers sought to discern the essence of 'public' in broadcasting. For one, it was a 'miraculous advance, still not a century old that allows a whole society, a whole nation, to see itself and to talk to itself. It enables people, no matter who they are, to share insights and illuminations, to become aware of problems and collectively consider solutions. It is one of the wonders of our age' (Attenborough, 2008, p. 36). For another, public service broadcasting, via the BBC, 'got here by an unusual route that stretches back to Reith. We have evolved extraordinarily, like our parliament and other institutions, such is the British way; . . . to reduce its economies of scale, its artistic, social and national reach for misbegotten reasons of ideology or thrift would be a tragedy' (Fry, 2008, p. 54). Finally, the third felt that the spirit of the Enlightenment in 'daring to know' could only be attained where a public space existed in which such daring to know could take place—'an independent public space which allows us to compensate by freely challenging and testing these partial truths—and sometimes actual lies (of the powerful)—so that we can arrive at the truth. Parliament, courts and universities are part of this public space, but so crucially is an independent media' (Hutton, 2008, p. 58).

We conclude that as the first decade of the century has closed and the second one has begun, there appears to be two distinct narratives being written in British culture. The first is a longer one, which stretches back to the post-war period in the middle of the last century and contains the essence of British attitudes to public service that grew out of the lessons drawn from that century—a sense of 'institutional character'. Both Reith and C. P. Scott were steeped in this narrative and defended independence in both private business (the *Guardian*) and public corporation (the BBC) as a core principle of a democracy. The second is a shorter one that absorbs short-term values which suggest there is less to be gained from public services and their support—the BSkyB, News Corp and Murdoch narrative. The question is now whether this short-term narrative will survive into the longer term or whether the older long-term narrative will re-emerge as the dominant one of a mature democracy. Public service broadcasting is likely to lie at the heart of such a debate.

The BBC, has variety around locality, channels, means of access and a multiplicity of platforms including broadcasting; the 'Red Button'; iPlayer; and its print, picture and video capability through its website, as well as hard copy through its publications. It has size and credibility, it has experience and creativity. However, it will need to be willing to innovate, willing to move at speed and take positive action to get their staff onside. It will also need to have a means with which to accommodate change—to change more, and faster, than many have been prepared or able to do in the past. I have said elsewhere (Dyke, 2012b), what they cannot do is just sit and wait and lament the passing of an earlier age. That way lies decline and fall. Time is of the essence. What it will need above all else is ambition and confidence based on its organizational 'character'. The BBC's 'longer narrative' should enable it to take full advantage of the opportunity that now presents itself at this exciting moment in broadcasting history.

POSTSCRIPT: 25 NOVEMBER 2012

In the autumn of 2012, shortly after the newly appointed director general George Entwistle took up his post, the BBC was overtaken by another controversy. Most crises seem to appear from nowhere and arrive with a speed that leaves most people unprepared—so it was with this crisis at the BBC. Within a few weeks it led to the resignation of the new director general and a loss of confidence in the BBC. Polls taken during this time showed a marked downswing. 'For the first time since YouGov started tracking public trust in British institutions, more people distrust BBC journalists (47%) than trust them (44%)' (Kellner, 2012). The essence of the crisis was an accusation that the BBC had dropped a proposed Newsnight programme on the alleged paedophilic activities of an entertainer who had died recently (Sir Jimmy Savile), in favour of films celebrating his career and charitable fundraising, to be shown during the Christmas schedules of 2011. A subsequent ITV programme, made about a year later, suggested the Savile allegations were correct. Criticism of the BBC grew. The BBC's Panorama programme then made a film that was critical of the decision to drop the original Newsnight film. In the wake of this, the most senior BBC news editors 'stepped aside' while two internal BBC inquiries took place. However, perhaps in the hope of redeeming its reputation, Newsnight then made another film, based on the evidence of someone sexually abused when young, that implied a senior politician had been the perpetrator. This later turned out to be a case of mistaken identity. In seeking to be thorough in its investigation of the story, the BBC aired a challenging live interview between one of its highly regarded radio journalists, John Humphrys, and the director general. In the aftermath of the flawed Newsnight programme and unable to cope with the intensity of this personal examination in public, the director general felt obliged to resign—the same day. He may have been unsuited for the post, but there was a deeper problem. I said in 2004 that there needed to be 'a separation of powers with a BBC Board, made up of executives and knowledgeable non-executives, responsible for running the BBC and an outside regulator with the job of checking on it' (Dyke, 2005, p. 320). Instead, the government created a BBC Trust. It was a disaster waiting to happen. The chair of the trust does not know whether to stand back and regulate or step forward and get involved as an executive. Caught between these two, he effectively hung the beleaguered director general out to dry. At the next charter renewal this governance structure should be abandoned, and Ofcom should take on a light-touch regulatory role, and a board should be established—with a chairman, a chief executive (director general) and a mix of executive and non-executive directors—like almost every organization in the world.

Ironically, the BBC became impaled on a dilemma—in this crisis, the more it subjected itself to its own high-quality investigative journalism (usually a public benefit), the more it risked damaging its reputation (a potential public harm). Humphrys's view, expressed at this time, was interesting. In a YouGov comment column, Humphrys noted that society's response to some recent breaches of public trust, for example the setting of inter-bank lending rates, the setting of wholesale gas prices, and newspapers hacking into people's phones, had been calls for more regulation and supervision. However, he argued, there were dangers in such a response. If, for example, schools set up systems to watch over teachers more closely to protect pupils from abuse, even though it is only a tiny handful who ever pose a risk, then children will grow up being suspicious of all teachers as potential abusers. Similarly, adults, fearful of being thought of as potential child abusers, might disengage into unsmiling and unfriendly people unwilling to volunteer for any children's activities. 'We need to trust our trustfulness, no matter how much the world seems to be undermining it . . . or our world will become . . . colder, harder and devoid of trust . . . we should not allow ourselves to believe there is a crisis of trust. To think otherwise is to succumb to a moral panic got up by the media. Our only way to fight back is to go on trusting. And if our trust is sometimes betrayed, then so be it, that's life' (Humphrys, 2012).

During my time at the Corporation, we tried to define its basic values and came up with the overriding one that 'trust is the foundation of the BBC' (Dyke, 2012a). I felt in 2005, in the wake of the Hutton report, that 'the great loser in the whole story (had been) public trust in the political process overall and in politicians in particular' (Tucker, 2005, p. 14). But these recent opinion figures show that trust in the BBC has now been fractured and short term it is clearly damaged. Long term, however, I suspect it will recover, and the biggest job for the new director general will be to rebuild the trust the British public rightly expect in organizations such as the BBC.

NOTES

1. The prime minister announced an inquiry investigating the role of the press and police in the phone-hacking scandal, on 13 July 2011. Lord Justice Leveson was appointed as chairman of the inquiry. He is assisted by a panel of six independent assessors. The inquiry was established under the Inquiries Act 2005. Further information available at: http://www.levesoninquiry.org.uk/.

2. See both Rupert Murdoch in 1989, and son James in 2009, delivering their McTaggert Lectures.
3. 'Red Button Olympics—the BBC's Olympic coverage has been hailed as the new century's "Coronation moment" as it switched millions of us onto digital viewing.' Gideon Spanier, *London Evening Standard*, 13 August 2012.
4. 'Running May-October 2012 as an independent section of openDemocracy, OurBeeb is a digital challenge to the old order, seeking to make the BBC's next director general truly accountable to the public, and debate the future of *our* BBC. This is a critical time for public service broadcasting, and the challenges of massive cuts and rapid technological change must be addressed head on'. More information available at: http://www.opendemocracy.net/about.
5. http://www.politifact.com/. Tampa Bay Times PolitifactCom, accessed October 2012.
6. http://journalism.unl.edu/cojmc/about/bios/waite.shtml.
7. Emily Bell was director of digital content for Britain's Guardian News and Media from 2006 to 2010. Previous to that post, Bell was editor-in-chief of Guardian Unlimited from 2001 to 2006. Under Bell, the *Guardian* received numerous awards, including the Webby Award for a newspaper website in 2005, 2006, 2007 and 2009, and British Press Awards for Website of the Year in 2006, 2008 and 2009.

REFERENCES

Attenborough, D. (2008) In: BBC, *The Creative Perspective—The Future Role of Public Sector Broadcasting*. London: Premium, pp. 24–36.
Barnett, S. (2011) *The Rise and Fall of Television Journalism: Just Wires and Lights in a Box?* London: Bloomsbury.
BBC (2008) *The Creative Perspective—The Future Role of Public Sector Broadcasting*. London: Premium.
Bell, E. (2010) *Emily Bell on the Future of Digital Media, Social Media and Journalism Training* [Video]. Available at: http://www.youtube.com/watch?v=-tiMu04XJ0M.
——— (2011) *Emily Bell on an Embarrassing Moment with Google* [Video]. Available at: http://www.youtube.com/watch?v=GOCNjeYuhNI.
Blair, T. (2010) *A Journey*. London: Hutchinson.
Boyfield, K. and Mather, G. (2006) *Freeview, the Free Broadcasting Formula That Clicked*. London: European Media Forum.
Briggs, A. (1961–1995) *The History of Broadcasting in the United Kingdom*, Volume 1: *The Birth of Broadcasting* (1961); Volume 2: *The Golden Age of Wireless* (1965); Volume 3: *The War of Words* (1970); Volume 4: *Sound and Vision* (1979); Volume 5: *Competition 1955–1974* (1995). Oxford: Oxford University Press.
Broadcasting Research Unit (1985) *The Public Service Idea in British Broadcasting*. London: Broadcasting Research Unit.
Butler, R. (2004) *Review of Intelligence on Weapons of Mass Destruction*. HC 989. Report of a Committee of Privy Counsellors chaired by The Rt. Hon. The Lord Butler of Brockwell KG, GCB, CVO on behalf of the House of Commons. London: The Stationery Office.
Coleman, S. and Ross, K. (2010) *The Media and the Public: 'Them' and 'Us' in Media Discourse*. Oxford: Wiley Blackwell.
Croll, A. (2012) Big Data Is Our Generation's Civil Rights Issue, and We Don't Know It—What the Data Is Must Be Linked to How It Can Be Used. *O'Reilly Radar*, 2 August. Available at: http://radar.oreilly.com/2012/08/big-data-is-our-generations-civil-rights-issue-and-we-dont-know-it.html#more-50087.

Department for Culture, Media and Sport (2006) *Broadcasting: Copy of Royal Charter for the Continuance of the British Broadcasting Corporation.* Cm 6925. London: The Stationery Office. Available at: http://www.official-documents.gov. uk/document/cm69/6925/6925.asp.

Department for Culture, Media and Sport (2006, with amendments 2010 and 2011) *Broadcasting: An Agreement between Her Majesty's Secretary of State for Culture, Media and Sport and the British Broadcasting Corporation.* Cm 6872. London: The Stationery Office.

Doctor, K. (2012) The Newsonomics of News U—Journalism and Education Are Both about Knowledge: Could Their Post-Disruption Business Models Start to Blur? *Nieman Journalism Lab,* 17 May. Available at: http://www.niemanlab. org/2012/05/the-newsonomics-of-news-u/.

Dyke, G. (2005) *Inside Story.* London: Harper Perennial.

—— (2012a) The BBC Can Get Out of This Hole. *Daily Telegraph,* 24 November.

—— (2012b) Change or Die: The Future of the BBC. Keynote speech given to the European Broadcasting Union, Copenhagen, Denmark, on 27 April 2012. Edited version, 15 May.

Fry, S. (2008) In: BBC, *The Creative Perspective—The Future Role of Public Sector Broadcasting.* London: Premium, pp. 38–54.

Hajkowski, T. (2010) *The BBC and National Identity in Britain 1922–53.* Manchester, UK: Manchester University Press.

Holland, P. et al. (2010) *"No Such" Research.* Available at: http://www.nosuch-research.co.uk/.

Hood, C. (1991) A Public Management for All Seasons. *Public Administration,* 69(1), pp. 3–19.

—— (2005) Public Management: The Word, the Movement, the Science. In: Ferlie, E., Lynn, L. and Pollitt, C., eds. *The Oxford Handbook of Public Management.* Oxford: Oxford University Press, pp. 7–26.

House of Commons (2003) Foreign Affairs Select Committee Minutes of Evidence (Session 2002/3) ordered by the House of Commons to be printed 3 July 2003. Examination of Witness (Questions 1120–1139) Mr Alistair Campbell 25 June 2003. London: The Stationery Office.

House of Lords (2011) Select Committee on Communications—Inquiry into the Governance and Regulation of the BBC, March–May 2011. Available at: http://www. parliament.uk/documents/lords-committees/communications/BBCgovernance/ BBCGRallev.pdf.

Humphrys, J. (2012) Trust, Is This a Crisis? Comment piece, 16 November, on YouGov website. Available at: http://yougov.co.uk/news/2012/11/16/trust-crisis/.

Hutton, B. (2004) *Report of the Inquiry into the Circumstances Surrounding the Death of Dr David Kelly CMG.* HC 247. Report of a Committee of Privy Counsellors chaired by The Rt Hon Lord Hutton on behalf of the House of Commons. London: The Stationery Office.

Hutton, W. (2008) In: BBC, *The Creative Perspective—The Future Role of Public Sector Broadcasting.* London: Premium, pp. 56–68.

Ipsos MORI (2008) *BBC Survey on Trust Issues,* 22 January. Available at: http:// www.ipsos-mori.com/Assets/Docs/Archive/Polls/bbc.pdf.

Kellner, P. (2012) The Problem with Trust. Comment piece, 13 November, on YouGov website. Available at: http://yougov.co.uk/news/2012/11/13/problem-trust/.

Lankton, N. K. and McKnight, H. D. (2012) Examining Two Expectation Disconfirmation Theory Models: Assimilation and Asymmetry Effects. *Journal of the Association for Information Systems,* 13(2). Available at: http://aisel.aisnet.org/ jais/vol13/iss2/1.

Leveson, B. (2011–2012) *Leveson Inquiry: Culture, Practice and Ethics of the Press.* Available at: http://www.levesoninquiry.org.uk/.

Murdoch, J. (2009) *The Absence of Trust*. MacTaggart Lecture at 2009 Edinburgh International Television Festival, Edinburgh, 28 August. Available at: http://image.guardian.co.uk/sys-files/Media/documents/2009/08/28/JamesMurdoch-MacTaggartLecture.pdf.

Ofcom (2008) *Ofcom's Second Public Service Broadcasting Review, Phase Two: Preparing for the Digital Future*. London: Ofcom. Available at: http://comment.ofcom.org.uk/phase2summary/glossary.html.

Scott, C. P. (1921) *A Hundred Years*. Reprinted in: *The Guardian*, 29 November.

Shirky, C. (2009) A Speculative Post on the Idea of Algorithmic Authority. *Clay Shirky* (Weblog), 15 November. Available at: http://www.shirky.com/weblog/2009/11/a-speculative-post-on-the-idea-of-algorithmic-authority/.

Simpson, J. (2002) *News from No Man's Land—Reporting the World*. London: Macmillan.

——— (2003) Simpson on Sunday: My Part in the Fall and Rise of Freddy Forsyth. *Sunday Telegraph*, 2 March.

The Stationery Office (2002) *Iraq's Weapons of Mass Destruction: The Assessment of the British Government*. London: The Stationery Office. Available at: http://www.archive2.official-documents.co.uk/document/reps/iraq/iraqdossier.pdf.

Stray, J. (2012) There's No Such Thing as an Objective Filter: Why Designing Algorithms That Tell Us the News Is Hard. *Nieman Journalism Lab*, 18 June. Available at: http://www.niemanlab.org/2012/06/theres-no-such-thing-as-an-objective-filter/.

Tucker, L. (2005) Leading by Example—Louise Tucker Talks to Greg Dyke. In Dyke, G. *Inside Story*. London: Harper Perennial, pp. 2–9.

World Radio and Television Council (2001) *Public* Broadcasting—*Why? How?* Paris: UNESCO. Available at: http://unesdoc.unesco.org/images/0012/001240/124058eo.pdf .

Wyndham Goldie, G. (1977) *Facing the Nation: Television and Politics 1936–76*. London: Bodley Head.

8 Trust between the UK Government, the Nation and Its Armed Forces
The Military Covenant

Mike Dunn

Herbert Spencer, the Victorian philosopher and sociologist, when informed that British troops were in danger during the Second Afghan War (1878–1880), responded, 'When men hire themselves out to shoot other men to order, asking nothing about the justice of their cause, I don't care if they are shot themselves' (Spencer, 1902, p. 126).

Spencer's view, heavily criticized at the time as unpatriotic, contrasts strongly with the current debate about whether a privileged military covenant or civil-military contract (McCartney, 2010) exists between the members and veterans of the United Kingdom's (UK) armed forces, the government and the nation. The Strategic Defence and Security Review in October 2010 stated that:

> ultimately it is our people that really make the difference. As a country, we have failed to give them the support they deserve. We are putting that right, even in the very difficult economic circumstances we face. We will renew the *military covenant* (author's emphasis), that vital contract between the armed forces, their families, our veterans and the country they sacrifice so much to keep safe. (HM Government, 2010, foreword, Cm 7948)

A more detailed explanation of the military, or armed forces, covenant and its provenance will be given later, but the schematic below at Figure 8.1 explains the broad concept. It shows the three parties of government, armed forces and the nation involved in a mutual support relationship, the output from which is trust and goodwill.

The chapter firstly examines the complex context within which the UK's armed forces serve and the role of Clausewitz's trinitarian theory. Briefly, this theory holds that, to achieve military success, the nation, government and the military commander and his forces must operate in harmony. The chapter goes on to discuss the fields of psychological contract and trust and conduct a limited review of the academic literature. The concept of a covenant is defined and the military covenant discourse and its history charted. This is primarily through the grey literature and media output generated by

Figure 8.1 The Military Covenant (MOD, 2011c, p. 10)

this debate. Finally, the military covenant is analysed using the concepts of the psychological contract and trust. Within this context, and as developed in this chapter, the following definition of trust is most apposite: 'a psychological state comprising the intention to accept vulnerability based on positive expectations of the intentions or behaviour of another'[1] (Rousseau et al., 1998, p. 395).

The chapter concludes that the covenant is a separate concept to the psychological contract, although it may have relevance to what Rousseau (1989) terms an implied contract. However, because the terms of the covenant are drawn so broadly, it is unenforceable. Furthermore, given that trust has been conceptualized as dyadic in nature, the triadic nature of the covenant is also problematic. The chapter concludes that the covenant may be better understood as a restatement of Clausewitzian thinking and the outcome of a series of exchanges within a transient network of powerful political actors, where trust between these actors has waxed and waned over time.

The chapter also argues that there have been possible unintended consequences to the covenant phenomenon. Firstly, the triadic nature of covenant may obscure rather than clarify employer responsibilities. Secondly, it may have weakened the ability of government to use its armed forces as an instrument of policy. Overall, therefore, the covenant phenomenon may have reduced, rather than built, trust within and between the armed forces, the government and the nation.

CONTEXT

The UK's regular armed forces numbered a total of 186,360 at 1 April 2011, of which 31,830 were officers and 154,520 were other ranks (DASA, 2011). The British Army has the highest number of personnel at 106,230, with the Royal Air Force (RAF) employing 42,460 and the Royal Navy 37,660. These numbers and the number of military bases will reduce as a result of the Strategic Defence and Security Review (HM Government, 2010) conducted by the government and published in October 2010. There is a complex, dynamic and sometimes uneasy relationship between the UK's armed forces, the British people and government, mediated through the press and other stakeholders.

An example of this complexity is the role of the UK's head of state, HM Queen Elizabeth II. Constitutionally, she is the commander-in-chief of the UK's armed forces. Members of the forces, on attestation, swear a loyal oath of allegiance to her, rather than to the state. This contrasts with the political reality that the armed forces are an instrument of government. As Clarke (2011, p. 6) comments: 'The (service) chiefs also understand they are officers of the crown, not the government, and have some responsibility to an independent sense of national interest.' This contrasts with the de facto role of the armed forces as an instrument of government.

Although the armed forces are subordinate to the Crown, the Bill of Rights (1689) forbids the Crown from funding standing forces in peacetime. These can be maintained only by Parliament's continuing consent. To resolve this constitutional impasse, Parliament approves their continuance through a quinquennial Armed Forces Bill. The last bill received royal assent in November 2006, and therefore a new bill was required in the 2010–2011 session, to renew the 2006 Armed Forces Act for a further five years.[2]

Since the ending of the Cold War, the lack of any existential threat to Britain, combined with a series of controversial and unpopular military interventions, plus an increasing lack of first-hand experience of military life by the public, have raised concerns that public support for the military and its work is diminishing (Forsyth, 2008, p. 11). Murrison (2011), in discussing the gap between the public and the armed forces, quotes a YouGov poll in 2007 that showed only 18% of the population could recall a friend or relation in the armed forces. There has been particular concern about a range of incidents (McCartney, 2010, p. 425) where members of the armed forces have been subject to abuse by the British public, for example, by Muslim groups during military parades in Luton.

In the context of this expressed opposition to recent armed conflicts, the question of whether the demographic of the armed forces should and does reflect the UK's changing demographic is significant. The Ministry of Defence (MOD) believes it should. According to Taylor and Croucher (2009), MOD aims to employ forces staff 'from all of the UK's diverse communities, so we reflect the society we serve.' The Taylor and Croucher article was an account of a series of racist comments on Facebook, allegedly written by soldiers, and followed the publication of a video of Prince Harry describing another soldier as a 'Paki'.

The demographic make-up of the UK's armed forces and its attitudinal posture is therefore an important issue, because we now live in a multicultural, diverse and, in public affairs, largely secular culture. As Alistair Campbell advised Tony Blair, 'we don't do God' (Brown, 2003). One consequence is that marked differences between the demographic make-up of the armed forces and mainstream society could become a divisive issue. Population growth is increasing; between 2001 and 2010 the UK population increased by 3.1 million people. The Office for National Statistics (ONS) says that two factors are significant—rising fertility among UK-born women and more inward migration of women of childbearing age.[3] There are now large and established Muslim communities in the UK (ONS, 2011) having ties both through kinship and religion with those same regions of the world in which the UK is conducting military operations.

Gender inequalities in the British Army have been written about elsewhere (Dunn, 2007) but, in addition to this, the demographic make-up of the armed forces is some way adrift from the developing UK demographic. At 1 April 2011, only 2.4% of the officer cadre was classed as black and minority ethnic (BME), with an overall total of 6.7% of armed forces personnel classed in this category (DASA, 2011, Table 1A). This figure includes Gurkhas, who have transferred into the UK regular army and Foreign and Commonwealth soldiers, for example, some 2,000 Fijians (McDougall, 2009).

Sands (2006) interviewed General Lord Dannatt for the *Daily Mail*, shortly after his appointment as chief of the general staff in succession to General Sir Michael Jackson.[4] She reported that 'the General is a practising Christian and this informs his views on the army's role and place in society.' General Lord Dannatt, perhaps unaware of the UK's demographic situation, was further quoted in the interview as saying, 'The Judaic-Christian tradition has underpinned British society. It underpins the British Army.'

Carl von Clausewitz (1780–1831), the Prussian military thinker, in his magnum opus *On War* (1993), states, according to the popular interpretation of the text, that a trinitarian model exists between the nation, the commander and his forces, and the government which, to achieve success, must work in harmony. Although this interpretation is contested (Van Creveld, 1991; Gillie, 2009), it remains widely held. It is argued that if any of these parties are in disagreement, it will eventually prove fatal to military endeavours. Public protests against the armed forces are therefore a serious issue to both the service chiefs and government. As McCartney puts it (2010, p. 412), 'A damaged relationship between civilian society and the armed forces represents a challenge to the effective defence and security of the UK.'

In December 2007, Gordon Brown asked Quentin Davies MP, Bill Clark OBE of the MOD and Air Commodore Martin Sharp of the RAF, to investigate and report on how to encourage greater understanding and appreciation of the armed forces by the British public. The report (Davies et al., 2008), delivered in May 2008 after a consultation that involved a review of arrangements in the United States (US), Canada and Australia, recommended a range of measures including increasing visibility of armed forces personnel, wider use of uniforms in public, a more systematic approach to homecoming parades, the institution of a British Armed Forces and Veterans Day and public outreach programmes by the armed forces. The government's response in October 2008 (MOD, 2008a) was to accept, with some modifications, the report's recommendations.

Following this, homecoming parades for military units returning from deployment have become a regular feature. The repatriation ceremonies for military personnel killed in action, routed from RAF Lyneham through Wootton Bassett, now Royal Wootton Bassett, to Oxford's John Radcliffe Hospital, became public spectacles. However, public spectacles also provide a platform for other voices. In January 2010, Anjem Choudary, the leader of the Islam4UK group, announced plans, later cancelled, to hold a parade through Royal Wootton Bassett, carrying up to 500 coffins symbolizing the Muslim dead from the invasion and occupation of Afghanistan. This in turn provoked a protest rally in the town by the right-wing English Defence League (EDL) movement. An estimated 200 gathered around the town's war memorial waving St George flags and chanting 'Muslim bombers off our streets'.[5]

General Sir Robert Fry, a former commander of British forces in Iraq, dissents from the view that public displays of support for the armed forces are to be wholeheartedly welcomed. He is quoted in a *Times* article (Coghlan, 2010) stating, 'I think the British people hold the armed forces in a state of excessive reverence at the present time. It is a greater infatuation than at any other stage of recent military history that I can recall . . . There is some of this that is good and laudable and there is some that is pretty mawkish . . . it is a question of trying to celebrate what is good and trying to avoid the Diana, Graceland stuff.' In the same piece, Michael Clarke, director of the Royal United Services Institute (RUSI), agreed: 'We have moved into an age of recreational grief in our society and the armed forces are the recipients of it in the most direct form.'

In summary, the context of the armed forces is complex and dynamic. They occupy a vexed constitutional position, their demographic make-up is not reflective of society and few members of the public have any connection with them. There are also nascent indications of a rift between sections of the public and the armed forces caused by the expeditionary nature of current engagements, particularly in Muslim countries such as Iraq and Afghanistan. I return later in the piece to the significance of the trinitarian model for the concept of the military covenant and will now examine the concepts of the psychological contract and trust. I have adopted these two lenses because it seems to me that the military covenant debate centres on the informal trust relationship between the three parties; at an initial sweep, they would appear the most obvious to explore and establish whether, as analysis frameworks, they have any explanatory utility.

THE PSYCHOLOGICAL CONTRACT AND TRUST

Rousseau (1989) holds that the typical parties to a psychological contract are the employee and the organization and goes on to define the psychological contract as referring to an individual's beliefs regarding the terms and conditions of a reciprocal exchange agreement between the focal person and another party. As she points out (Rousseau, 1989, p. 122), 'parties to a contract written or otherwise can have very different perceptions regarding its terms.'

She draws a distinction with equity theory (Adams, 1965), which juxtaposes exchange and fairness and argues a fine point that an individual can experience unfairness, for example, someone of a lesser calibre being promoted in their place yet without causing any specific contract violation. As she says (Rousseau, 1989, p. 127), 'Inequity can be remedied e.g. through a pay rise, however contract violation, which causes mistrust, cannot be so easily repaired. An individual paid less than the market rates might feel inequitably treated; one who was promised a raise for hard work and fails to get it is likely to feel wronged.'

Other leading writers, such as Argyris (1960) and Schein (1980), conceptualized the psychological contract as the unwritten expectations on exchange that accrete over time between employers and employees, but Rousseau argues that a psychological contract focuses on the employee's experience. 'Individuals have psychological contracts, organizations do not' (Rousseau, 1989, p. 126).

Rousseau (1990) develops the concept of the psychological contract into two forms: transactional and relational. The transactional form focuses on the exchange between employer and employee of money and other specified benefits for completion of specified tasks over a finite period. A relational psychological contract, although involving the basic exchange elements, also extends to issues such as training career development and long-term employment expectations. The period of the contract is indefinite and the rights and obligations both unclear and subject to change.

Rousseau (1989, p. 124) draws a distinction between what she terms *implied* contracts and *psychological* contracts.

> Psychological contracts exist between employer and employee. Implied contract is a mutual obligation existing at the level of the relationship (e.g. dyadic, interorganizational). Unlike psychological contracts which are subjective patterns held by individual parties to a relationship, implied contracts are patterns of obligations arising from interactions between parties (e.g. individuals and organizations) that become part of the social structure of which the relationship is part (e.g. legal, cultural) . . . Implied contracts reside in the social structure in which the relationship occurs and can be assessed by observers to a relationship (e.g. third parties, courts, the public). (Rousseau, 1989, p. 124)

Although she places this concept in a working environment and on a quasi-legal basis in relation to the law of contract, it resonates to an extent with the concept of the military covenant, save that she implies that such contracts are dyadic in nature. As she concludes (p. 132), 'Moreover, researchers examining implied contracts in employment and other organizational relationships must address the emergent nature of implied contracts. Such contracts often require historical analysis to capture the pattern of interactions which contracts reflect.' This will be discussed further.

There has not been extensive research conducted on the impact of the psychological contract in a military environment, but there is some relevant work. Bartone (1998), Britt (1998, 1999), Britt and Adler (1999) and Litz (1996) have all examined the linkage between psychological stress endured on military operations as it relates to the norms of their organizations. Chambel and Olivera-Cruz (2010) focused on soldiers involved in peacekeeping missions to analyse the extent to which a breach of the psychological contract could be used to explain the effect of soldier burnout and their level of engagement. This positivistic longitudinal study concluded that there was a clear linkage between breach of psychological contract and the development of burnout during the mission. They state that (Chambel and Olivera-Cruz, 2010, p. 122) when soldiers believed that the army was not complying with its obligations, 'it gave rise to a situation of unpredictability and a lack of control for the soldiers because they no longer knew what to expect.' These obligations would include financial compensation and the upkeep of their well-being.

Moving now to trust, the linkage between trust and the psychological contract has been extensively researched (Robinson, 1996; Rousseau et al., 1998). Guest and Conway (1997) identified the content of the psychological contract as: trust, fairness and delivery on the deal. Nicolson and Johns (1985) identified trust as a defining characteristic of psychological contracts and developed the notion of high- and low-trust psychological contracts. This is further developed by Street (2009), who also focuses on the outcomes of the psychological contract, crucially, the degree of commitment the employee develops, which similarly can range between high and low. Sullivan et al. (2009, p. 18) position trust as 'part of the fuel that keeps a healthy psychological contract alive.'

The salience of trust both within and between organizations as a cultural enabler for organizational performance has also been an area for intensive academic study (Gibbs, 1964; Knack and Keefer 1997; Kramer and Cook, 2007; Chiles and McMackin, 1996). Sullivan et al. (2009) argue that the focus on trust has increased as organizations shift away from people management, based on hierarchy, bureaucracy and control, towards more cooperative working environments. A number of popular works have also been published on the topic of trust. Examples are Stephen Covey's text *The Speed of Trust* (2006) and *Trust* by Anthony Seldon (2010). Covey (2006, p. 14) posits that a lack of trust in organizations incurs a tax whereas trust provides dividends. He quotes Emile Durkheim (Covey, 2006, p. 254) defining the essential conundrum of trust as: 'When mores (cultural values) are sufficient, laws are unnecessary, when mores are insufficient, laws are unenforceable.' Much that has been written on trust focuses on long-term relationship management (Das and Teng, 2001; Knights et al., 2001; Bachmann et al., 2001; Lewicki et al., 1998), although interest is now turning to the issue of trust in hastily formed networks (HFNs), typically required in postconflict or crisis contexts between organizations (Burt and Knez, 1995).

Trust is of paramount importance in the armed forces, but my initial focus of discussion is on trust between the individual and the chain of command. The values and standards of the British Army (MOD, 2000b, p. 5) states that the ethos of the army comprises 'commitment, self-sacrifice and mutual trust.' Kearney (2010), writing from a New Zealand Army perspective, holds that, despite the well-defined authority structure, military leaders need to nurture and develop trust for operational success. He reports on Canadian Defence Force research that suggests there are four 'pillars' that will determine team members' trust in their leaders. The first pillar is competence: are the leaders and teams good at their job? The second is integrity, or issues around the use or misuse of trust. The third is benevolence, or 'are my needs valued?' It brings in, for example, 'am I being exposed to more risk than is necessary?' The fourth is predictability, or, does my leader act in a consistent manner?

This brief examination of academic thinking on the linked concepts of the psychological contract and trust has identified that the two concepts are linked but operate dyadically. The chapter now examines the development of the military covenant discourse.

THE MILITARY COVENANT DISCOURSE

This section will focus on analysing the extensive grey literature produced by the phenomenon, coupled with selected media sources that reflect, amongst other points, its emotive nature. To begin, the term 'covenant' is value-laden (Mileham, 2010). It has a Judaeo-Christian association being defined as 'an agreement, a contract . . . the agreement between God and the Israelites' (OEED, 1991, p. 334). It also has strong politico-religious connotations in the UK, with particular resonance in Scotland through the Scottish Covenants of 1638 and 1949, and the Ulster Covenant of 1912 that was used by loyalists in Northern Ireland as part of their resistance to home rule proposals for Ireland at the turn of the last century (Dunn, 2010). It also has legal and contractual meaning, particularly in registering property covenants that limit an owner's rights and the conveyancing of covenanted property.

Its provenance in a military context is recent. The term first appears in 2000 in *Soldiering: The Military Covenant* (Army Doctrine Publication No. 5), shortened to ADP 5 (MOD, 2000a). Mileham (2010) argues that the term was carefully chosen by the publication's three authors[6] to demonstrate the 'institutional uniqueness' of the British Army. It was followed by the British Army doctrinal publication (MOD, 2000b) entitled *The Values and Standards of the British Army*. It stated:

> For those in positions of authority it also requires them to discharge in full their responsibilities and their duty of care to subordinates whether in peace time or on operations. This two-way obligation *forms a covenant* (author's emphasis) between the army and its soldiers. Both share a common bond of identity of loyalty and responsibility for each other which is unwritten but unbreakable and which has sustained the army throughout its history. Soldiers volunteering for the British Army accept that by putting the needs of the service before their own, they will forego some of the rights enjoyed by those outside the armed forces. But in return they can at all times expect fair treatment, to be respected and valued as an individual and to be rewarded by reasonable terms and conditions of service. *By extension, this covenant also exists between the army and the nation it serves.* (MOD, 2000b, p. 7; author's emphasis)

The significant point is that a third party, the nation, has now been added to the conventional employer–employee relationship. The authors of this emotive, and heroically unevidenced, claim, presumably took the view that 'by extension' required no further explanation, but it begs the question.

The term developed traction some six years later, at a time when the government's handling of the armed forces was coming under criticism. McCartney (2007, p. 15), reporting on the retiring chief of the general staff Sir Michael Jackson's Dimbleby lecture in November 2006, quotes him speaking of the nation 'letting the Covenant down' by refusing to pay the true cost of military operations. 'Military operations cost in blood and treasure . . . It is our soldiers who pay the cost in blood; the nation must therefore pay the cost in treasure.' General Lord Dannatt talked shortly after his appointment as chief of the general staff (Sands, 2006) about the 'military covenant between a nation and its armed forces'. This extended the reach of the concept beyond the army to all the armed forces. On 13 September 2007, the Royal British Legion launched a campaign, *It's Time to Honour the Covenant*, to 'restore the Covenant and improve conditions for the Service community in the areas of care, compensation and coroners' inquests.'[7]

Members of the UK's armed forces are not allowed to communicate with the public on military matters, are bound by the Official Secrets Act and are not permitted to join a trade union. Consequently, their voice in any debate is absent, or claimed by proxies such as the Royal British Legion and the British Armed Forces Federation. However, the MOD operates an annual Armed Forces Continuous Attitude Survey (AFCAS). In the latest survey (AFCAS, 2010), although there were no specific questions on the covenant, some relevant responses are given in Table 8.1.

Table 8.1 Selected Responses from the Armed Forces Continuous Attitude Survey (AFCAS, 2010)

Issue	AFCAS Table Ref
85% of those surveyed claimed they were proud to be in their service	B2.8
69% agreed that they were treated fairly in the service	B4.1
68% stated that the frequency of their operational deployments were about right	B3.8
79% were satisfied with medical facilities	B9.2
52% overall and 71% of officers are satisfied with their pay	B1.1
55% are satisfied with their allowances*	B1.5
29% agree that senior officers understand and represent their interests	B4.51
68% agree that their immediate superior understands and represents their interests	B4.53

* The military has a complex set of allowances, the intent of which is to compensate for deployment to operations and the subsequent disruption to family life.

These results do not appear indicative of any crisis in the attitude of those surveyed to their employment, although trust in senior officers is low. In fact, Ursula Brennan, MOD permanent undersecretary, told the Commons Defence Select Committee on 9 February 2011 that 'as a whole, we have a programme which still provides for the armed forces challenging and exciting careers with a regime of pay and reward, which still offers a good level of pay, a good level of allowances and a good level of pensions.'[8] However it should be noted that, as McCartney (2007, p. 9) advises, 'the soldier does not sign a formal contract on joining the army. There are terms and conditions of service written down for the soldiers and a plethora of rules which they are required to follow.'

Other commentators picked up the term 'military covenant'. The DEMOS think tank report (Edmunds and Foster, 2007) published in November 2007 claimed that:

> the military covenant—the contract between the nation and service personnel and their families who make personal sacrifices in return for fair treatment and commensurate terms and conditions of service has been *damaged almost beyond repair* (author's emphasis). A new civil-military compact is necessary—first, to restore the military covenant between the army and the nation, and second, the military covenant must be a tri-service rather than army pledge between the government on behalf of its citizens, the military as an employer and individual serving personnel. (Edmunds and Foster, 2007, p. 13)

Tipping (2008) further argued that the military covenant is not an agreement between government and the armed forces. She states (p. 12), possibly reflecting Rousseau's thinking on implied contracts, that 'this fails to capture the true nature of the covenant—it is an implicit contract that exists between the nation and the armed forces.' She goes on to claim that, if it is in danger of being breached, not only the government and the service chains of command must bear most of the responsibility but also Parliament. She claims, rather boldly, that 'a hitherto apathetic public' is also culpable. This may be overstating the case; the legal definition of a contract, under English law, is an agreement between two or more parties that is legally binding (Poole, 2001; Chen-Wishart, 2005).

The Conservative Party and the Liberal Democratic Party then became involved, so transforming the debate into an overtly political one. At the Conservative Party Conference on 3 October 2007, David Cameron referred to the covenant and said:[9]

> And our prime minister likes to say that nothing in Britain is broken but I would refer him to a piece of paper which is all about the sacrifices our troops are prepared to make on our behalf, including the ultimate sacrifice and our duties and obligations to them. It's called the military covenant and Mr Brown, I believe your government has broken it.

In March 2008, he launched a Military Covenant Commission, chaired by Frederick Forsyth and with Andrew Murrison MP as Parliamentary advisor. Its function was to 'offer advice to the Leader of the Opposition on the health of the military covenant' (Forsyth, 2008, p. 2).

The government, in the meantime, was endeavouring to limit the damage from this political attack. In early 2008, Gordon Brown requested a pan-departmental review of 'what more could be and should be done to demonstrate our commitment to the armed forces and our gratitude for their service and sacrifice' (MOD, 2008b, p. 6). Whereas the resulting Service Personnel Command Paper (MOD, 2008b) made no explicit reference to a military covenant, Gordon Brown stated that the armed forces 'by reason of the demands we impose on them in the course of their duty are unique. These obligations set them apart from others who serve and protect society' (MOD, 2008b, p. 5). Other uniformed security organizations, e.g. the police, fire and rescue services and, increasingly, private contractors deployed on military operations, might contest this assertion.

It also explicitly widened the debate beyond an employer–employee relationship to encompass a whole of government approach, including the devolved administrations and, not simply serving personnel and cadets, but also their families, reservists and their families, and veterans. Veterans are defined as having served at least one day in uniform. Including widows and the extended families of these groups, the paper estimated this would involve over ten million people in total. It also stated as a principle that

Table 8.2 Key Personnel Themes Identified in the Service Personnel Command Paper (Ministry of Defence, 2008, p. 6)

Access to NHS dentistry
Standard of service housing and housing entitlement rules
Desire for stability, wish for choice in buying a home, home location and supporting allowances
Children's schooling and the problems of disruption caused by mobility
Perceived lack of welfare support when partner is deployed, compounded by a lack of information on how to access support mechanisms
Single personnel's sense of disadvantage compared to married colleagues
Career opportunities and continuity for spouses of serving personnel

those who serve must not be disadvantaged by what they do in terms of lifestyle choice, continuity of public services and a proper return for sacrifice concerning physical and mental injury. This paper was evidence-based and a forensic analysis of the current provision of conditions of service. It established an external reference group and consulted serving personnel and other stakeholders. The outcomes included an action plan to remedy the shortfalls and gaps in service employment conditions. The main themes of concern that emerged are shown below in Table 8.2.

One could argue that these are basic employment-condition concerns that should be resolved between the employee and the employer, or issues such as schooling and access to NHS dentistry, which are common to the nation.

The general election in May 2010 saw a Conservative–Liberal Democratic coalition government. The prime minister commissioned an Armed Forces Covenant Task Force to discharge an election commitment to 'rebuild the military covenant'. However, the term 'military covenant' was dropped and replaced by 'Armed Forces Covenant' for the task force's work. This was to deal with the semantic point that the term 'military' is held to be descriptive of the British Army, to the exclusion of the Royal Navy and Royal Air Force (Murrison, 2011). Professor Hew Strachan chaired this task force with a brief to develop a series of innovative, low-cost, policy ideas to rebuild the covenant. The Armed Forces Covenant Task Force reported in September 2010 (Strachan, 2010); the government responded to the report by issuing three documents:

- The government's response to the report of the task force on the military covenant (MOD, 2011a). This was a detailed response to each recommendation
- The Armed Forces Covenant: today and tomorrow (MOD, 2011b) and the Armed Forces Covenant (MOD, 2011c). These two documents are intended to be read together. The former is a detailed coverage of policy intent, and the latter is a series of definitions of the Armed Forces

Covenant and Armed Forces Community and Scope of the Covenant obligations and principles

MOD (2011c) contains a model of the covenant showing the parties to it and their respective rights and obligations. This was shown in Figure 8.1 earlier in the chapter. The Armed Forces Bill 2011, after some heated debate, now includes the term 'armed forces covenant', and the Minister for Defence is required to report annually on it.

Summarizing the covenant discourse, the concept originated as an unevidenced doctrinal statement in an army publication, then, over a period of five to six years, was adopted as doctrine for the entire armed forces. In the same period, it became a major political issue involving the whole of government, the political opposition, ten million citizens, the media and stakeholders, such as the Royal British Legion and a range of other charitable organizations. The net result has been a set of management actions for MOD, some broad directives to local government and devolved administrations, plus a requirement for the Secretary of State for Defence each year to report to Parliament on the armed forces covenant.

ANALYSIS

Can the covenant, in particular its development and significance, be more clearly understood through the lens of the psychological contract and trust? If we analyse the concept of the psychological contract, it would appear that the military covenant does not read across. Psychological contracts are held to exist between the focal person and the employer, so the triadic nature of the covenant does not conform. In examining Table 8.2, it would appear that the issues are mainly within the employer's scope to resolve. It might be argued that it is more compliant with Rousseau's concept of an implied contract, which operates at the level of a relationship and can involve interorganizational issues. However, the term 'implied contract' is a quasi-legal one and would need to stand the legal tests of whether a contract exists. Furthermore, her inference is that such contracts are also dyadic in nature, so again it would not comply with the triadic nature of the military covenant.

On trust, the issue, as with the psychological contract, is that research and writings on trust focus more on the dyadic relationship between those leading and those being led. The definition of trust at the beginning of the chapter talks about a psychological state comprising the intention to accept vulnerability based on positive expectations of the intentions or behaviour of another. The triadic nature of the covenant again does not easily read across to this conceptualization of trust. What is at issue here is the trust between the armed forces government and the public. This triangular relationship is difficult to establish and maintain. As Bassford (2011, p. 4) comments, 'Juggling the meaning of and implications of three interacting realities makes even splitting the difference obnoxiously difficult and is utterly beyond the pale of acceptable political analysis.' So, if the concepts of trust and the psychological contract do not appear relevant to the military covenant, are there additional lenses that might aid analysis, such as Clausewitz's trinitarian model?

Clausewitz and the Trinitarian Model

When we analyse the covenant model in Figure 8.1 through the lens of the trinitarian concept, as defined earlier in the chapter, there is a good fit. The three parties—the government, the nation and the armed forces—are present and positioned so that their mutual obligations enable them to work in harmony. However, and setting aside the complexity of any triangular relationship, there is a fallacy in the model. It assumes that the armed forces, by virtue of their conduct and service, will merit respect, gratitude and solidarity from the nation. This is wishful thinking.

There is evidence that sections of the UK population are deeply unhappy with both the nature and conduct of military operations and an emergent unwillingness to distinguish between armed forces personnel and the operations they conduct. This may be compounded by the unrepresentative demographic profile of the armed forces. The discourse that the UK's armed forces are a force for good is contested and likely to become more so, as demographic change progressively alters national identity. Finally, the exact nature of armed conflict operations is often not transparent for security reasons, so, if for this reason alone, any notion of contract cannot apply.

In summary, a conclusion is that the concept of the military covenant is not explicable by existing thinking on either trust or the psychological contract. A tentative argument is that the phenomenon became prominent during a febrile period in British politics where certain players, e.g. the opposition, saw potential advantage in promoting it. Certainly it is based on highly contestable premises: it is unevidenced, so begs the question, and is wishful thinking. The military covenant may therefore be better understood as a political device and the outcome of a series of exchanges within a transient network of powerful political actors, where trust between these actors has waxed and waned over time. However, and apart from its continuing impact, it is an important phenomenon for these possible consequences:

Lack of Clarity on Accountability for Terms and Conditions of Employment

The military covenant phenomenon and its triadic nature may result in a more confused rather than clearer responsibility for the employment conditions of service personnel. These concerns partly drove the military covenant debate in the first place. The triadic relationship may confuse responsibility and accountability to service personnel for their conditions of service: is it their service, the MOD, government in its widest sense or the nation? In the continued absence of formal employment contracts, their armed service employer could argue that responsibility lies with the whole of government and the nation. If so, this might intensify the existing lack of trust in senior officers.

Emergent Politicization of Service Chiefs

Michael Clark (Coghlan, 2010) has remarked, 'Service personnel who die on operations are seen as yet more victims of government policy, as opposed to instruments of that policy.' This may be partly due to service chiefs, such as General Lord Dannatt, communicating through the popular media on emotive issues like the covenant and military 'overstretch'. A further example is Admiral Mark Stanhope's public assertion that the Royal Navy would struggle to fulfil its duties if the Libyan conflict went beyond September 2011. This latter instance met with the robust response of Prime Minister David Cameron: 'You do the fighting and I'll do the talking' (Clarke, 2011, p. 6). The media appetite for the views of service chiefs may complicate their already vexed constitutional position referred to in the introduction and reduce trust between them and government. Ultimately, it may prove a constraint on government's ability to use the armed forces as an instrument of government policy. In conclusion then, far from building trust, the military covenant phenomenon may, as an unintended consequence, be acting to reduce what already existed between the three parties.

NOTES

1. 'Another', as understood here, can be either an individual or a collective.
2. Armed Forces Act 2010–2012, UK Parliament website, available at: http://services.parliament.uk/bills/2010–11/armedforces.html.
3. UK Population Sees Biggest Increase in Half a Century, BBC News, 30 June 2011, available at: http://www.bbc.co.uk/news/uk-13975481.
4. The Chief of the General Staff is the head of the British Army.
5. Right Wing Extremists Descend on Wootton Bassett, *The Telegraph*, 11 January 2010, available at: http://www.telegraph.co.uk/news/uknews/terrorism-in-the-uk/6962386/Right-wing-extremists-descend-on-Wootton-Bassett.html.
6. Reserve Forces chaplain Reverend Iain Torrence, later moderator (principal) of the General Assembly of the Church of Scotland, Major General Sir Sebastian Roberts and Major General Andrew Ritchie (Mileham, p. 38).
7. Legion Launches Campaign: 'Its Time to Honour the Covenant,' Royal British Legion website, 13 September 2007, available at: http://www.britishlegion.org.uk/about-us/media-centre/news/honour-the-covenant/legion-launches-campaign-its-time-to-honour-the-covenant.
8. MOD Defend Defence Cuts, British Forces News, 9 February 2011, available at: http://www.bfbs.com/news/mod-defend-defence-cuts-43926.html.
9. Cameron Speech in Full, BBC News, 3 October 2007, available at: http://news.bbc.co.uk/1/hi/uk_politics/7026435.stm.

REFERENCES

Adams, J. S. (1965) Inequity in Social Exchange. In: Berkowitz, L., ed. *Advances in Experimental Social Psychology.* New York: Academic Press, vol. 2, pp. 267–299.

AFCAS (2010) *Armed Forces Continuous Attitude Survey—Deputy Chief of Defence Staff Personnel and Training.* London: Ministry of Defence.

Argyris, C. (1960) *Understanding Organizational Behaviour.* Homewood, IL: Dorsey Press.

Bachmann, R., Knights R. and Sydow, J. (2001) Trust and Control in Organizational Relations (Editorial). *Organization Studies*, 22(2), pp. v to viii.

Bartone, P. (1998) Dimensions of Psychological Stress in Peacekeeping Missions. *Military Medicine*, 163, pp. 587–593.

Bassford, C. (2011) *Tip-Toe through the Trinity or The Strange Persistence of Trinitarian Warfare.* Working Paper. Available at: http://www.clausewitz.com/readings/Bassford/Trinity/Trinity8.html.

Britt, T. W. (1998) Psychological Ambiguities in Peacekeeping. In: Langholtz, H. J., ed. *The Psychology of Peacekeeping.* Westport, CT: Praeger, pp. 111–128.

——— (1999) Engaging the Self in the Field: Testing the Triangle Model of Responsibility. *Personality and Social Psychology Bulletin*, 25, pp. 696–706.

Britt, T. W. and Adler, A. B. (1999) Stress and Health during Medical Humanitarian Assistance Missions. *Military Medicine*, 164, pp. 275–279.

Brown, C. (2003) Campbell Interrupted Blair as He Spoke of His Faith: 'We Don't Do God'. *The Daily Telegraph*, 4 May. Available at: http://www.telegraph.co.uk/news/uknews/1429109/Campbell-interrupted-Blair-as-he-spoke-of-his-faith-We-dont-do-God.html.

Burt, R. and Knez, M. (1995) Kinds of Third Party Effects on Trust. *Rationality and Society*, 7(3), pp. 225–292.

Chambel, M. J. and Olivera-Cruz, F. (2010) Breach of Psychological Contract and Development of Burnout and Engagement: A Longitudinal Study among Soldiers on a Peacekeeping Mission. *Military Psychology*, 22(2), pp. 110–127.

Chen-Wishart, M. (2005) *Contract Law.* Oxford: Oxford University Press.

Chiles, T. H. and McMackin, J. F. (1996) Integrating Variable Risk Preferences, Trust and Transaction Cost Economics. *The Academy of Management Review*, 21(10), pp. 73–99.

Clarke, M. (2011) At War with the Taliban and No 10. *Sunday Times*, 3 July, p. 6.

Clausewitz, Carl von (1993) *On War.* Howard, M. and Paret, P., eds. New York: Everyman's Library–Alfred A. Knopf.

Coghlan, T. (2010) General Fears 'Mawkish' View of Military; Veterans Unhappy with Celebrity Subversion of Armistice Day. *The Times*, 13 November.

Covey, S. (2006) *The Speed of Trust: The One Thing that Changes Everything.* London: Simon and Schuster.

Das, T. K. and Teng, B. S. (2001) Trust Risk and Control in Strategic Alliances: An Integrated Framework. *Organization Studies*, 22(2), pp. 251–283.

DASA (2011) *UK Armed Forces Annual Manning Report Analysis by Rank and Age.* London: Ministry of Defence, Defence Analysis and Statistics Agency, 26 May.

Davies, Q., Clark, W. and Sharp, M. (2008) *Report of Inquiry into National Recognition of Our Armed Forces.* London: Report to the Prime Minister, May 2008.

Dunn, M. D. (2007) British Army Leadership—Is It Gendered? *Women in Management Review*, 22(6), pp. 468–481.

Dunn, P. J. (2010) Forsaking Their 'Own Flesh and Blood'? Ulster Unionism, Scotland and Home Rule, 1886–1914. *Irish Historical Studies*, XXXVII (146/November), pp. 203–220.

Edmunds, T. and Foster, A. (2007) *Out of Step: The Case for Change in the British Armed Forces.* DEMOS Report. London: Demos

Forsyth, F. (2008) *Restoring the Covenant: The Military Covenant Commission's Report to the Leader of the Conservative Party*. London: Military Covenant Commission.

Gibbs, J. R. (1964) Climate for Trust Formation. In: Bradford, L. P., Gibb, J. R. and Benne, K. D., eds. *T-Group Theory and Laboratory Method*. New York: Wiley, pp. 279–309.

Gillie, D. R (2009) *Interpreting Clausewitz's Miraculous Trinity. Thesis, Antithesis, Synthesis. A Study of the Essential Intellectual Content and Didactic Purpose of the Trinitarian Model*. Available at: http://www.clausewitz.com/readings/Gillie-ThesisAntithesisSynthesis.html.

Guest, D. and Conway, N. (1997) Employee Motivation and the Psychological Contract. *Issues in People Management*, 21, p. 6.

HM Government (2010) *Securing Britain in an Age of Uncertainty: The Strategic Defence and Security Review*. Cm 7948. Norwich: The Stationery Office. Available at: http://www.direct.gov.uk/prod_consum_dg/groups/dg_digitalassets/@dg/@en/documents/digitalasset/dg_191634.pdf?CID=PDF&PLA=furl&CRE=sdsr.

Kearney, S. (2010) Trust, Threat, and Leadership: What Military Experience Can Tell Leaders about Trust in Times of Change. *Human Resources*, June/July, pp. 8–9.

Knack, S. and Keefer, P. (1997) Does Social Capital Have an Economic Payoff? A Cross-Country Investigation. *Quarterly Journal of Economics*, 112(4) pp. 1251–1288.

Knights, D., Noble, F., Vurdubakis, T. and Willmott, H. (2001) Chasing Shadows: Control Virtuality and the Production of Trust. *Organization Studies*, 22(2), pp. 311–336.

Kramer, R. M. and Cook, K. S. (2007) *Trust and Distrust in Organizations: Dilemmas and Approaches*. Thousand Oaks, CA: Sage.

Lewicki, R. L., McAllister, D. J. and Bies, R. J. (1998) Trust and Distrust: New Relationships and Realities. *Academy of Management Review*, 23(3), pp. 438–458.

Litz, B. (1996) The Psychological Demands of Peacekeeping for Military Personnel. *NCP Clinical Quarterly*, 6, pp. 1–8.

McCartney, H. (2007) *Audit of the Military Covenant: Report for the Directorate of Army Personnel Strategy*. London: Kings College and Defence Academy of the UK, September 2007.

McCartney, H. (2010) The Military Covenant and the Civil-Military Contract in Britain. *International Affairs*, 86(2), pp. 411–428.

McDougall, D. (2009) To Helmand and Back. *Guardian*, 26 April. Available at: http://www.guardian.co.uk/uk/2009/apr/26/fijians-british-army-iraq.

Mileham, P. (2010) Unlimited Liability and the Military Covenant. *Journal of Military Ethics*, 9(1), pp. 23–40.

Ministry of Defence (MOD) (2000a) *Soldiering: The Military Covenant*. British Army Doctrine Publication No 5. London: British Army.

——— (2000b) *The Values and Standards of the British Army*. Commanders' Edition. ACNo63813. London: British Army.

——— (2008a) *The Government's Response to the Report of Inquiry into National Recognition of Our Armed Forces*. October. London: HMSO.

——— (2008b) *The Nation's Commitment: Cross-Government Support to our Armed Forces, Their Families and Veterans*. Cm 7424. Norwich: The Stationery Office. Available at: http://www.official-documents.gov.uk/document/cm74/7424/7424.pdf.

——— (2011a) *The Government's Response to the Report of the Task Force on the Military Covenant*. London: HMSO.

——— (2011b) *The Armed Forces Covenant: Today and Tomorrow*. London: HMSO.

——— (2011c) *The Armed Forces Covenant*. London: HMSO.

Murrison, A. (2011) *Tommy This an' Tommy That. The Military Covenant*. London: Biteback.

Nicolson, N. and Johns, G. (1985) The Absence Culture and the Psychological Contract—Who's in Control of Absence. *Academy of Management Review*, 10, pp. 397–407.

OEED (1991) *The Oxford Encyclopaedic English Dictionary*. Oxford: Oxford University Press.

ONS (2011) *Population Estimates by Ethnic Group 2002–2009*. Statistical Bulletin, 18 May. Available at: http://www.ons.gov.uk/ons/search/index.html?newq uery=population+estimates+by+ethnic+group+2002-2009.

Poole, J. (2001) *Contract Law*. London: Blackstone Press.

Robinson, S. L. (1996) Trust and Breach of Psychological Contract. *Administrative Science Quarterly*, 41, pp. 574–599.

Rousseau, D. M. (1989) Psychological and Implied Contracts in Organizations. *Employee Responsibilities and Rights Journal*, 2(2), pp. 121–139.

Rousseau, D. M. (1990) New Hire Perceptions of Their Own and Their Employers' Obligations: A Study of Psychological Contracts. *Journal of Organizational Behaviour*, 11, pp. 389–400.

Rousseau, D. M., Sitkin, B., Burt, R. and Camerer, C. (1998) Not So Different after All: A Cross- Discipline View of Trust. *Academy of Management Review*, 23, pp. 393–404.

Sands, S. (2006) Sir Richard Dannatt: A Very Honest General. *Daily Mail*, 12 October. Available at: http://www.dailymail.co.uk/news/article-410175/Sir-Richard-Dannatt--A-honest-General.html.

Schein, E. H. (1980) *Organizational Psychology*. Englewood Cliffs, NJ: Prentice-Hall.

Seldon, A. (2010) *Trust: How We Lost It and How to Get It Back*. London: Biteback.

Spencer, H. (1902) *Facts and Comments*. New York: D. Appleton and Company.

Strachan, H. (2010) *Report of the Task Force on the Military Covenant*. Available at: http://www.mod.uk/NR/rdonlyres/3C6A501D-5A85-47C9-9D89-B99C5E428061/0/militarycovenanttaskforcerpt.pdf.

Street, J. N. (2009) The Implications of the Cultural Values of individualism and Collectivism in the Formation of the Psychological Contract and Employee Commitment. *Journal of Behavioral & Applied Management*, 10(3), pp. 433–448.

Sullivan, J., Wong, W., Adusumilli, D., Albert, A., Blazey, L., Huggett, M. and Parkin, J. (2009) Deal or No Deal? An Exploration of the Modern Employment Relationship. In: *The Future of HR*. Working Paper. London: The Work Foundation, pp. 1–43.

Taylor, M. and Croucher, S. (2009) MoD Investigates Race Hate on Web. *Guardian*, 19 January. Available at: http://www.guardian.co.uk/politics/2009/jan/19/ministry-defence-race?INTCMP=SRCH.

Tipping, C. (2008) Understanding the Military Covenant. *RUSI Journal*, 153(3), pp. 12–15.

Van Creveld, M. (1991) *The Transformation of War: The Most Radical Reinterpretation of Armed Conflict since Clausewitz*. New York: Free Press.

9 Trust at the Interface between the Third and Public Sectors

Alex Murdock

Recent developments in the United Kingdom (UK) and other countries have seen a change in the relationship between the public and the third sector (Anheier, 2005). The third sector has increasingly come to be a provider of public services, and the funding basis of that provision has moved from a traditional grants-funded mode to a contract-based mode (NCVO, 2006).

These developments have been regarded by each sector from somewhat different perspectives. The public sector view on third sector provision is based upon such factors as public value, equity and choice in provision. Some public officials regard the third sector as representing a lower cost option than that of either state provision or private providers.

The third sector perceives the growth in service provision and contractual relations with the public sector with mixed feelings. For some—especially the larger and more commercially orientated organizations—it is seen as an opportunity. For others it is seen as jeopardizing deeply held organizational values and organizational independence. This is exemplified in the UK by a debate over whether the third sector should take contracts involving loss of liberty or benefits to clients (such as running custodial facilities or assessing disability).[1]

For third sector organizations which have a campaigning or advocacy role, accepting government contracts is seen as restricting (either implicitly or explicitly) their freedom of action to engage in this aspect of their role. A key characteristic accepted as defining the nature of the third sector is that of independence. This independence is often construed in terms of a mission, which has an underpinning set of values. Charities which work with, for example, pregnancy, may have a value set which acknowledges the woman's 'right to choose' a termination. Yet if such an organization is to seek government funding or contracts, then a clash of values may appear—as was identified by Etzioni (1973), writing about the United States (US). In the UK and much of the English-speaking commonwealth there has been the growth of devices such as 'compacts' to try and acknowledge the independence issue (Murdock, 2006).

The value differences may appear not just at a 'mission level' but also in terms of operational practices. Many public servants are expected to adopt a position of 'neutrality' and professional detachment in the conduct of their activities. Indeed, this may even extend to their activities outside the work-place, and joining the boards of outside organizations may lead to questions of their impartiality. In contrast, the third sector use of networks and 'cross memberships' are part of the organizational landscape. At the strategic level non-profit organizations tend to run on a high level of informal contact and trust as opposed to the rules and accountability which are part of the public sector landscape. Indeed, members of charity boards are called 'trustees'—a term not used to describe their political equivalents in the public sector.

So how might these potentially conflicting worlds interact without erosion of their core value systems? This chapter will seek to explore the normative and ethical boundaries of this debate, making use of the discourses which are already taking place.

THE CONCEPT OF TRUST AND VALUE: THE EVOLVING NATURE OF THE RELATIONSHIP BETWEEN GOVERNMENT AND THE THIRD SECTOR

On 12 December 2006, Nicholas Deakin gave a lecture hosted by the Baring Foundation (Deakin, 2006). This lecture was significant in terms of both the lecturer and the hosting organization. The date was chosen as it represented the tenth anniversary of a major report on the third sector. Professor Deakin's name is well known to the voluntary sector as the prime participant in a major review of the voluntary sector (Commission on the Future of the Voluntary Sector, 1996). Indeed, his name became synonymous with the report produced by the commission.

The commission highlighted changes in the nature of the relationship between government and the third sector. It recognized that moving towards contractual relationships between government and the third sector was having a major impact upon the way in which third sector organizations had to work. The commission also highlighted the diverse nature of the third sector, offering enormous potential and challenge to the both government and the third sector. Perhaps unusually for a number of such commissions, the recommendations had a significant impact. The incumbent government (which had rejected the recommendations) was soon to be replaced by the Labour government in 1997. The thinking of the incoming government had much in common with the recommendations and sentiments of the commission.

The Voluntary Sector Compact—a formal memorandum setting out the nature of the relationships between government and the sector—was perhaps the most tangible result (Osborne and McLaughlin, 2002, 2004). This compact has had implications not just for the UK but has had significant policy impacts in other countries (Murdock, 2006). The compact could be described as an attempt to enable the government and third sector to agree a set of rules for behaviour which enables trust to be constructed in a fashion which is not dependent upon contractual agreements. Indeed, it could be regarded as an endeavour to ensure that as contracts become more embedded the third sector is recognized as having 'rights' and also a degree of independence of movement. Although the government may be the partner 'who leads' in the relationship, the third sector is not a passive partner but one seen as worthy of respect (NCVO, 2005, 2006; Osborne, 2005).

The compact principles recognized that the third sector had a right to be consulted and indeed to criticize in terms of both the current and proposed movements on the dance floor. Indeed, the sector was recognized as possessing areas of expertise (Osborne and McLaughlin, 2002, 2004; Murdock, 2006). The compact has been continued under the coalition government, although it has been revised and simplified. There have been clearer terms introduced with a focus upon transparency (Cabinet Office, 2010; National Audit Office, 2012). However, this is in the context of austerity and cuts in funding to the third sector. As the 'Big Society' policy of the coalition government comes under increasing adverse comments following these cuts in public expenditure, the compact represents a tangible, although often unacknowledged, aspect of policy continuity in terms of acknowledging the contribution, value set and independence of the third sector (Civil Exchange, 2012; The Commission on Big Society, 2011; Ipsos MORI, 2010).

A critical question is whether the development of contractual relationships between the government and the third sector is affected by a fundamental difference occasioned by the different value and ethical sets of the respective parties. The third sector is described as 'diverse' by Deakin and as a 'loose and baggy monster'[2] by academics and researchers (Kendall and Knapp, 1995). It is important to note that the term is not necessarily used in a negative fashion to describe the sector. However, it does create the image of sector diversity and problems in establishing clear categories and defining rules of behaviour. It implies a lack of predictability and conformity. This imagery is not commensurate with the formalism of regulated government.

ARE THE SECTORS IN FACT SEPARATE ENTITIES?

The conventional image is of three sectors—public, private and 'third'. The implication is that there is some kind of boundary. This may convey some sector imagery from the days of a divided Berlin with Soviet, American, British and French sectors. By implication when something is divided into sectors then a boundary can be established.

However, this can be challenged and the divisions seen more as overlaps between the sectors. It is suggested that there are in fact four sectors which need to be considered. The informal sector represents the concept of civil society, which is to be found in the everyday activities which do not come within the measured bounds of the other sectors but which nevertheless represent a vital element in the generation of social capital (Putnam, 2000). Figure 9.1 illustrates this.

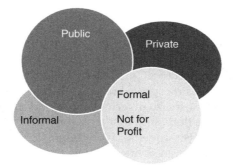

Figure 9.1 The Different Sectors

Pestoff (2005) has depicted the relationship diagrammatically as a series of triangles (Figure 9.2). This diagram places the third sector at the centre of a typology embracing the state, market (private sector) and the community sector. Pestoff suggests that in the areas of overlap, 'mixed' organizational forms can be found.

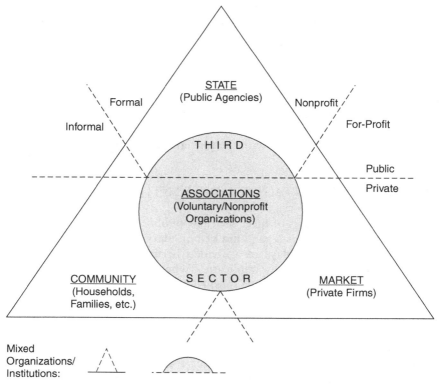

Figure 9.2 The Third Sector in the Welfare Triangle (Pestoff, 2005)

This conception has significant implications for the concept of values that are specific to a particular sector. If the boundaries are unclear and there are overlaps, then the implication is that the value sets similarly might overlap or lack sector distinctiveness at the boundaries (Evers, 2005; Brandsen, van de Donk and Putters, 2005).

HOW MIGHT THE VALUES OF THE PUBLIC AND THIRD SECTORS BE SIMILAR?

Both the public sector and the third sector have been described as possessing strong value sets. Writers such as Anheier (2005) and Etzioni (1973) have examined the nature of the values and mission of the third sector. The public sector value literature is extensive; Beck Jørgensen and Bozeman (2007) provided a useful bibliography for the public value panel at the 2006 European Group of Public Administration (EGPA) conference.[3] The question of public values has been linked to the reform agenda (Van de Walle, 2005). Public values (as described by others within this volume) are also seen as associated with 'taking tough choices' (O'Kelly and Dubnick, 2005).

Tijsterman (2006) suggested that there were five aspects of public values. He proposed that:

- They should make sense
- They should enable policy choice
- They should be collective
- They raise issues in application
- They should be upheld by public institutions

These five aspects would probably be largely accepted by third sector organizations (maybe with a textual amendment to the last one). Perhaps the implication here is of 'motherhood and apple pie'? Who can be against values that express simple and obvious truths? If so then the difference between the public and third sector in values may be less than the shared territory. Perhaps the public and third sector problems at the dance are along the lines of the oft cited comment about the UK and the US—two countries separated by a common language.[4]

Organizational values sometimes get wrapped up with the idea of culture and indeed this is true for all three formal sectors (private, public and third) (Aiken, 2001). The conception that values are transmittable—in effect, tangible objects—implies that managers can control them. This, however, understates the importance of the tacit and intangible quality attached to value. Nevertheless, governments and the public sector bodies associated with government have sought to expressly set out what the 'public sector values' are in tangible form (HM Treasury, 2004). Concern in the early 1990s in the UK about standards of public officials led to what has become known as the Nolan Report (Francis, 1995). For the UK it represents perhaps a common denominator of what should guide the behaviour of those in public office. The Nolan principles are as follows:

Box 9.1 The Seven Principles of Public Life

The Seven Principles of Public Life

Selflessness

Holders of public office should take decisions solely in terms of the public interest. They should not do so in order to gain financial or other material benefits for themselves, their family, or their friends.

Integrity

Holders of public office should not place themselves under any financial or other obligation to outside individuals or organizations that might influence them in the performance of their official duties.

Objectivity

In carrying out public business, including making public appointments, awarding contracts, or recommending individuals for rewards and benefits, holders of public office should make choices on merit.

Accountability

Holders of public office are accountable for their decisions and actions to the public and must submit themselves to whatever scrutiny is appropriate to their office.

Openness

Holders of public office should be as open as possible about all the decisions and actions that they take. They should give reasons for their decisions and restrict information only when the wider public interest clearly demands.

Honesty

Holders of public office have a duty to declare any private interests relating to their public duties and to take steps to resolve any conflicts arising in a way that protects the public interest.

Leadership

Holders of public office should promote and support these principles by leadership and example.

It is worthy of note that these principles have also been accepted by some of the major third sector umbrella organizations in the UK third sector as relevant for their members in the exercise of their third sector responsibilities. Therefore, there is a case for arguing that the Nolan principles may represent a base set of guidelines, which can be referred in this context as the 'rules of the dance'.

A number of these principles are in fact explicit in the governance of charitable bodies and in particular with respect to the board members (trustees) of such organizations. Selflessness, integrity, accountability, honesty and objectivity are enshrined in the legal expectation of how trustees of charities will conduct themselves. Openness and leadership are implicit (Hudson, 2004), and both of these are critical for trust.

THIRD SECTOR VALUES AND THE IMPLICATIONS FOR TRUST

Aiken (2001, 2002) has set out what he regards as distinctive about the values of voluntary and cooperative organizations. He indicates that for such organizations their values are often the core of their being. There is no private sector 'business bottom line' to fall back on. The values cannot be maintained by reference to an 'official government line'—they need to be sustained and renewed or the organizations concerned will deteriorate. Aiken notes that such organizations do not operate in a social and political vacuum and refers to commentators who question the continued distinctiveness and independence of the sector (Six and Vidal, 1994). Elson (2006), in a working paper from the London School of Economics, undertook a review of the nature of the values in the voluntary sector. This is reproduced as Table 9.1.

Many of the values adduced from the literature by Elson find close echoes in the Nolan principles set out above. Indeed, in governance terms, some authors have successfully written to encompass both sectors in the same text (Cornforth, 2003).

However, there are a number of values that are not associated with the Nolan principles and, indeed, are arguably potentially in conflict with them. Batsleer, Cornforth and Paton (1992) refer to values of 'devotion, compassion, enthusiasm, solidarity and defiance'. These are values that may not sit well with such Nolan principles as 'objectivity and accountability'. Other values referred to in Elson's impressive collation of authorities include 'sociability', 'reciprocity', 'collaboration', 'loyalty' and 'trust'. Such values are highly pertinent to many charitable and voluntary organizations.

The actual concept of 'charity' itself is worthy of exploration as a value. A Wikipedia-based definition describes it as 'an unlimited loving-kindness towards all others'.[5] For some charities this is inherent in the way in which they conduct themselves. As a small example, two apparent alcoholics entered a social enterprise run as a café in a church. They were carrying a bag full of tins of strong lager and were drinking at 9 a.m. They politely advised the cook that they had no money but they would like some food. The cook offered them a free meal (which one accepted and the other declined). The response of the cook was entirely in keeping with the charitable and community values of the café. However, if the café had been a public sector establishment, then this action would have been almost certainly counter to

Table 9.1 Synopsis of Values Profiled in Voluntary Sector Literature

Source (reference)	Values	Context
Cheung-Judge, M-Y. Henley, A. (1994) Equalty in Action – Introducing Equal Opportunities in Voluntary Organisations	Fairness, (social) Justice, Accessibility Accountability	Foundation for equal opportunities UK legislation
* **Gerard, D.** (1983) Charities in Britain: conservatism or change?	Authority, Hierarchy, Equity, Compassion, Freedom, Beneficence	Context: organisations – social order (adherence to moral and spiritual values) [stability, unity, cohesion] and *service to* those in need
	Democracy, Participation, Equality, Tolerance, Individual rights, Solidarity	Social change – (secular and material values) and *identify with* those in need
Jeavons. T.H. (1994) Ethics in nonprofit management: Creating a culture of integrity	Integrity, Openness, Accountability, Service, Charity, Reciprocity	Organisational ethical values
Jeavons. T.H. (1992) When the Management is the Message: relating values to management practice in non-profit organisations	Organisational honesty, Accountability, Service (to public good), Dignity and respect (for workers and volunteers)	Critical importance of consistency between values in organisational purpose and management
Leat, D. (1595) Challenging Management: An exploratory study of perceptions of managers moving from for-profit to voluntary organisations	Sociability, Equality, Participation, "business-like", Trust, altruism	Perceptions of managers moving from for-profit to voluntary organisations
Mason, D.E. (1995) Leading and Managing the Expressive Dimension	Accountability, Caring, Citizenship, Excellence, Fairness, Honesty, Integrity, Loyalty, Promise keeping, Respect	Managing nonprofit organizations
O'Connell, B. (1988) Values underlying non-profit endeavour	Commitment beyond self (altruism), Worth and dignity of individual, Responsibility, Tolerance, Freedom, Justice, Responsibilities of citizenship	Values espoused by Independent Sector (US)

(*Continued*)

Table 9.1 (Continued)

Source (reference)	Values	Context
O'Neill, M. (1992) Ethical Dimensions of Nonprofit Administration	Societal responsibility, Service to vulnerable, Honesty, Environmental protection	Ethical aspects of nonprofit management (US)
* Otto, S. (1997) Comparative Study of role issues and structures in voluntary and statutory organisations	Power combined with commitment to public good, personal and professional development, Empowerment, Collaboration	Trustee Chairs and senior managers in agencies for the homeless and statutory schools (UK)
Paton, R. (1996) How are values handled in the voluntary sector?	Equal opportunity, User empowerment, Social Justice	Social ideals Organisational values Personal conduct
Paton, R. (1992) The Social Economy: Value-based Organisations in the Wider Society	Devotion, Compassion, Enthusiasm, Solidarity, Defiance	Commitment to a common or public benefit
* Tonkiss, F. Passey, A. (1999) Trust, Confidence and Voluntary Organisations: Between Values and Institutions	Honesty, Fairness, Trust	Trust-base relations in civil society

* Empirical evidence provided

Source: Elson (2006)

the explicit values of the organization and could have been regarded as a manifest abuse of public assets.

Milbourne and Cushman (2010a, 2010b) have explored the implications of more recent coalition government policy (in particular, the Big Society and changing funding relationships in the context of recession). They note that public bodies often 'behave as if trust in their actions is a given, whereas all too often, trust is a masquerade' (Milbourne and Cushman, 2010b, p. 21). The implications of their research is that trust in the public sector by the third sector has been eroded by the recent actions of government, and attempts through government policy to engage voluntary effort may fail as a result. The use of contractual relationships may not be sufficient to enable delivery in a context where trust is missing (Murdock, 2006).

In a recent study, Murdock, Benz and O'Neill (2011) examined the activities of the Inuit tribal council in the delivery of services to Native Alaskans. The tribal council was in a position of high trust in that it possessed credibility with the Native Alaskan community. Thus, government relied upon the tribal council to deliver services which, in the case of non-tribal recipients, were largely delivered by the state. The direction of trust in this situation was significantly different in that the state 'trusted' the tribal council as an organization which was seen as close to the recipients and which had an understanding of their needs and an empathy with their values.

The Relationship as Separation

If the third sector and the public sector operate separately and their paths do not cross, then the potential for value conflict is quite limited. Some charities do not take any money from the public purse whether in the form of grants or contracts. They observe the legal formalities and are relatively detached from the processes of the public sector. It is as if they are on a separate floor of a building but are only affected if a major event happens (such as the building catching fire). Where a charity engages in an activity where the public sector would not become involved (such as the meeting of specific religious needs) then the relationship can be distant unless the values of the organization impinge on public law or cause public disquiet. In the UK post-9/11 there has been a greater public concern about the nature of the activities of imams in mosques, for example. However, the activities of other religious sects may pass without public comment.

The activities of 'below the radar' organizations raise an interesting question in the context of the 'Big Society' agenda of the government. Such organizations are not formally recorded in that they are typically not registered as charities and do not receive public funding. Nevertheless, with the focus on community engagement implicit in the Big Society agenda, there has been a considerable interest in such organizations, many of which would not have regarded themselves as 'part of public policy'. This is succinctly expressed in a briefing paper from the Third Sector Research Centre.

> Clubs, societies, village fetes etc. all make significant contributions to social cohesion as well as to combating isolation and promoting health and mental wellbeing. These are all Government agendas (both now and in the recent past) but this is not why those groups exist. They are there to meet basic human needs, not deliver on policy agendas. (McCabe, 2010, p. 13)

A Linked Relationship: The Third Sector Takes the Lead

For some third sector organizations, the inherent aim is to leverage some kind of change from a potentially labile or unwilling public sector. This may take a number of forms. The third sector organization may possess an asset or attribute which can be used to effect change. Some medical charities in the UK have a large donor base and use the financial leverage to pressure the government to change policy and enhance service provision. They are in effect the lead partner, and the public sector may have to change its step to accommodate them. In short, the third sector is able to 'pay for the piper and call the tune', and the public sector has to take account of this.

In other situations the third sector possesses resources—perhaps access to celebrities or to a large membership base—which enables it to influence or even threaten the public sector in order to get what it wants on the dance floor. The impact of individuals such as Bob Geldof and the power of media and music are well understood by charities. The public sector is not immune to being seduced by fame and glamour.

If seduction does not work, then in some cases the third sector is able to exploit the threat of exposure and political vulnerability. A local issue raised by a charity may threaten the security of re-election of a politician who then accepts the need to 'dance to a different tune'. This has been exemplified by the spectre of government ministers joining protests against policies in which they had, in cabinet, acquiesced. Campaigning charities are often adept at applying pressure through carefully targeted media coverage and letter-writing. Amnesty international is able to bring considerable pressure on apparently intransigent foreign governments over the treatment of prisoners by such means.

This is evidenced in the development in the UK of the movement and social enterprise represented by Emmaus. It was started by Abbé Pierre in Paris after the Second World War and now has spread to over thirty countries (Murdock, 2010; Murdock, Glemain and Meyer, 2011). The concept in value terms has been variously described but can be summed up as a living community encompassing the following principles:

- Work—all should work to the best of their ability
- A home and supportive setting—the strapline in UK has become 'a bed and a reason to get out of it'
- A family setting with meals taken communally
- Solidarity with a commitment to 'help those more in need'

The relationship between Abbé Pierre and the French government was certainly not one of deference or dependence. Emmaus raised its own funds through sale of donated goods and asserted an independence from the state. When the model extended to the UK, it took the form of a social business. In the UK, Emmaus was initially founded in 1992 as a community in Cambridge by a businessman, Selwyn Image. He had experienced Emmaus in France and commented on the influence of Abbé Pierre as follows:

I was an ordinary businessman excited by the power of the social enterprise he had almost inadvertently created and was convinced it could address some of the same problems in the UK as in France. I wrote a business plan and appealed to the good sense of enablers in the UK.[6]

Selwyn Image spoke of the process of creating Emmaus in the UK as involving effort and activity on both sides of the Channel. Selwyn Image had been advanced some initial funding through Abbé Pierre.[7]

Emmaus in the UK has now grown to some twenty-one communities, with further communities in the pipeline. Arguably, Emmaus has features of a broader based model that that of homelessness. The concept of solidarity is strongly embedded and the organization also espouses recycling. The fact that 'companions' come off all state benefits other than housing support has proven a strong argument with politicians. The concept of work is embedded in the model, and that work is linked to the activities of the Emmaus community. A companion who secures work outside of the community is still seen as part of the Emmaus movement but will (after a period of time to adjust) have to find accommodation elsewhere. Emmaus is more than an organization for the homeless but more restricted than a conventional hostel or housing provider because of the explicit expectation of both work and also of living as part of a community.

The concept of work is essential to an Emmaus community. All individuals or companions who join agree to give up all state support in terms of income related benefits and to work in the community to the best of their ability (Clarke et al., 2008, p. 4).

The characteristic of Emmaus in the UK as involving not just accommodation but also work and being part of a family and 'social movement' means that the organization reaches across a range of social and economic agendas. The recycling (and repair) of donated goods makes Emmaus a 'green and environmentally focused' organization. This potential of multiple impacts of Emmaus communities across a range of government policy agendas is presented below. These are shown in Figure 9.3.

Government Policy Agenda	Emmaus impact
Homelessness	All companions have a place to live
Welfare to work	All companions work
Health	Common meals with focus on diet and lifestyle
Social Inclusion	Companions encouraged to move on to reintegrate into broader community
Recycling	Community earns through recycled goods
Regeneration	Disused Buildings and brown field sites brought into use
Justice	Many companions come via justice system
Drugs and Alcohol	Many companions have drug /alcohol problems

Figure 9.3 The Policy Impacts of Emmaus

A Linked Relationship: The Public Sector Takes the Lead

The area of provision of public services is where a major focus has been in recent years in the UK (National Audit Office, 2005). The government has seen the third sector as a potential 'partner' in provision of services on behalf of the state. Many charities have the history in the identification of a need for service provision followed by the actual provision to meet that need (Kendall, 2003). Indeed, there is one major organization in the UK which provides a rescue service for those at peril on the sea and does it without recourse to public funds, namely, The Royal National Lifeboat Institution.[8] However, in general the pattern has been of a charitable provision being set up to meet a particular need (hospitals and orphanages, for example), and over time, the state steps in to take over the provision.

In a context of austerity and reduced public finance, the state is keen for the third sector to take a more active role in delivery of many of these services through contracts, grants or other arrangements. There are commentators on the third sector which have also explored this (Blake, Robinson and Smerdon, 2006; Cairns, Harris and Young, 2005).

One lure for the third sector in the UK has been something described as 'full cost recovery'[9]—this means not just the disbursement of the immediate costs of provision of the service but also what has been described by sector organizations as 'core costs', such as:

- Management and leadership
- Infrastructure and accommodation
- Finance, governance and controls
- Strategic development

There are also those who feel that the loss of independence associated with joining in contracts determined by the public sector is a price too great to pay. The constraints of government contracts are seen as restricting the ability of charities to offer a range of services and also may limit the choice of beneficiary. Furthermore, many charities see themselves as agents of societal change. The ability to criticize and pressure the government may be affected by having a substantial dependency on that same government for income.

The Charity Commission, the regulatory body for charities in England and Wales, recently published a key report examining the effects of charities accepting a greater role in public-service delivery. A large number of charities took part (circa 3,800). The report, perhaps quixotically entitled *Stand and Deliver*, was published in February 2007, and the findings make disturbing reading. Over 60% of the charities that responded with an income of over £0.5 million were involved in public-service delivery. Of the charities involved in public-service delivery, a third were dependent on this for 80% or more of their total income. However, only 12% reported that they were getting full cost recovery (Charity Commission, 2007b). Figure 9.4 shows

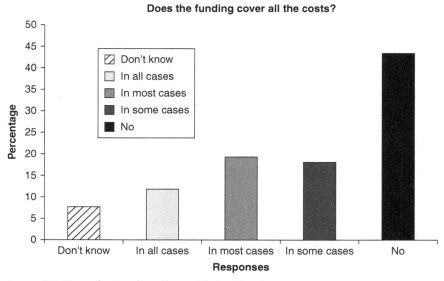

Figure 9.4 Does the Funding Cover All the Costs?

this and also shows that by far the largest proportion (43%) report that they did not recover full costs in any case.

It could be assumed that the stronger (i.e. largest) third sector organizations might be more likely to achieve full cost recovery. Table 9.2 suggests that this is not the case for the very largest (although they are less likely to report not getting any full cost recovery). What is also surprising is that the very largest organizations appear more likely to report not even knowing if their funding had covered their costs.

Possibly the nature of the service-delivery arrangement was a factor. Maybe there might be a difference between contract, grants, service level agreements[10] and a 'mixture' of these? The results reported in Table 9.3 prove interesting. Grants are most likely to be associated with a failure to meet full cost recovery, with service-level agreements coming second. The commentary on the report suggests that it may be possible that some respondents were unclear as to what was the nature of the agreements they had with the public sector. In any event, it suggests that participation had not been to the economic benefit of the third sector.

One argument advanced by third sector leaders is a plea for longer duration funding. This seems eminently sensible. It is seen as offering an assurance that the public sector will give a degree of continuity. However the Charity Commission findings suggest that longer duration contracts may be associated with poorer financial returns. Figure 9.5 shows that contracts longer than three years appear to be a worse deal than those which are shorter. It looks like 'longer commitments' may not always necessarily be to the third sectors' benefit. Due possibly to the value set of third sector organizations, they may be reluc-

Table 9.2

| | Does funding cover the full cost of services provided? | | | | | | | | | |
| | Don't know | | In all cases | | In most cases | | In some cases | | No | |
	Number	%	Number	%	Number	%	Number	%	Number	%
Under £10,000	19	19	16	16	9	9	9	9	47	47
£10,000 - £100,000	37	11.97	44	14.24	43	13.92	44	14.24	141	45.63
£100,000 - £250,000	14	5.71	19	7.76	43	17.55	34	13.88	135	55.1
£250,000 - £500,000	7	3.7	17	8.99	44	23.28	48	25.4	73	38.62
£500,000- £1 million	4	2.17	22	11.96	52	28.26	43	23.37	63	34.24
£1 million - £10 million	4	4.26	14	14.89	24	25.53	21	22.34	31	32.98
Over £10 million	2	9.52	1	4.76	6	28.57	8	38.1	4	19.05
Total	87	8	133	12	221	19	207	18	494	43

Note: The percentage total is the average of the column.

Table 9.3

		Type of funding agreement									
		Don't know		Grant(s)		Service level Contract(s)		A mixture/ agreement(s)		more than one		Other	
		No	%	No	%	No	%	No	%	No	%	No	%
	Don't know	17	51.52	13	7.78	5	2.99	10	5.24	12	2.82	30	18.87
	In all cases	3	9.09	19	11.38	32	19.16	33	17.28	28	6.59	18	11.32
Full cost	In most cases	3	9.09	23	13.77	37	22.16	37	19.37	110	25.88	11	6.92
recovery?	In some cases	2	6.06	21	12.57	28	16.77	23	12.04	114	26.82	19	11.95
	No	8	24.24	91	54.49	65	38.92	88	46.07	161	37.88	81	50.94
	Total	33	100	167	100	167	100	191	100	425	100	159	100

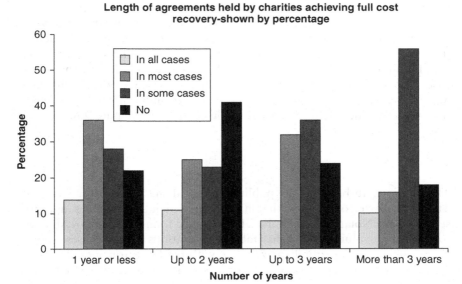

Figure 9.5 Length of Agreements Held by Charities Achieving Full Cost Recovery—Shown by Percentage

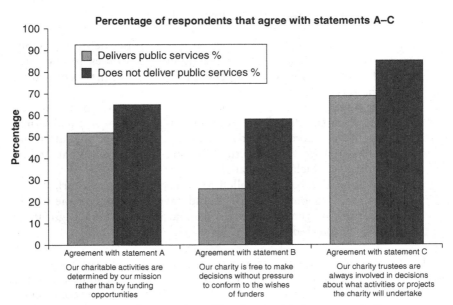

Figure 9.6 Percentage of Respondents That Agree with Statements A–C

tant to 'walk away' from contracts which turn out to be loss-making. Rather, the contract is cross-subsidized by donations or use of the charities' reserves.

Finally, there is the question as to whether the third sector's independence has been compromised through entering into public-service delivery. The findings from the survey suggest that respondents do feel this is the case. Organizations which did not deliver public services were more likely to agree to statements showing mission conformity, independence and trustee involvement in decisions on activities. This is shown in Figure 9.6.

CONCLUSION

The relationship between the public sector and the third sector is varied. There is a sharing of values in that many of the public sector values (as represented by the Nolan Report in the UK) would be found in the charitable sector. However, voluntary and charitable organizations in many cases espouse values which are potentially at variance with public sector ones. This may not be a problem. In some cases, the parties do not interfere with each other beyond the usual civilities. In other cases, the third sector may be more influential and possess desired resources. Here the balance of power may even rest significantly with the third sector partner. However, the increasing involvement of the third sector in the delivery of public services seems to be associated with both inadequate resourcing and a perceived loss of independence. This is clearly a source of concern to the chair of the Charity Commission, Dame Suzy Leather, who made the following observation as part of her speech introducing the findings of the survey:

> Under-funding threatens the very survival of charities delivering public services. Charities themselves, commissioning authorities and Government all have to address this urgently. If they don't, they will end up killing the very thing they believe in.
> Does our report entitled Stand and deliver signify a sector taken hostage, or a sector standing firm to deliver public services on equal terms? Everyone in this room instinctively knows it should be the latter, but many will fear that we are actually facing the former. What factors might influence which way it falls?
> Much as John Donne's bell tolled for everyone, so one charity's loss of reputation, mission or integrity could have an impact on the way in which charities are generally viewed. Reputation at best is a fragile thing and must be protected.[11]

The third sector organizations may be engaging in 'high-risk' behaviour in terms of taking on contracts which are loss-making. In some cases, the organization may know this at the outset but still enters into the contract on the basis that the values of the organization mandate it to do this. It is likely that some may leave saddened through financial losses which may—at the extreme—threaten their viability.

Perhaps, however, the more insidious threat is the loss of independence or compromise of core values that, as some might argue, have no price because, once lost, they cannot be repurchased. Furthermore, such loss may serve not just to damage the repute of the immediate owner but to erode that of other third sector organizations seen as partaking in a similar activity. The role of trust is critical. In a context of austerity and retrenchment the actions of government in both cutting funding for third sector organizations whilst also expecting (trusting?) civil society organizations to step up and take the strain for meeting needs where funding has been reduced may be jeopardized by a loss of trust in government by such organizations.

The findings of polls suggest in terms of the publicly expressed trust that people report they trust third sector organizations far more than they trust government (Ipsos MORI, 2010). Government and politicians would ignore this at their peril.

NOTES

1. Presentation by Stuart Etherington, CEO of National Council for Voluntary Organisations (NCVO), at London South Bank University, October 2005.
2. The original term was probably from the novelist Henry James, who referred to Tolstoy's *War and Peace* as a 'loose and baggy monster'.
3. See URL for European Group of Public Administration (EGPA) 2006: http://soc.kuleuven.be/io/egpa2006/.
4. Attributed variously to George Bernard Shaw and to Winston Churchill.
5. *Source:* wikipedia.com.
6. Selwyn Image (personal communication to Alex Murdock, 20 May 2009).
7. Abbé Pierre gave Selwyn Image £30,000 to establish the Cambridge Community with the injunction to 'pass on the money' to establish further communities once Cambridge was self-sustaining (personal communication with Selwyn Image, 20 May 2009).
8. See http://www.rnli.org.uk.
9. For more information on the nature of full cost recovery, see http://www.acevo.org.uk.
10. Service-level agreements are typically agreements where professional services (such as expert social work input or legal advice) are being provided. They are usually costed on a different basis to conventional contracts.
11. Dame Suzy Leather (charity commissioner), speech to NCVO Annual Conference, 21 February 2007.

REFERENCES

Aiken, M. (2001) *Keeping Close to Your Values: Lessons from a Study Examining How Voluntary and Co-Operative Organizations Reproduce Their Organizational Values.* Milton Keynes, UK: Open University. Available at: http://technology.open.ac.uk/cru/NCVO%20Paper.pdf.

—— (2002) *What Strategies Do Value Based Organizations Adopt to Resist Incursions on Their Organizational Values from Public or Private Sector Markets?* Dilemmas Facing the Public Sector: Sixth International Research Conference, London, September.

Anheier, H. (2005) *Non Profit Organizations: Theory, Management, Policy.* London: Routledge.

Batsleer, J., Cornforth, C. and Paton, R., eds. *Issues in Voluntary and Non Profit Management.* Wokingham, UK: Addison Wesley.

Beck Jørgensen, T. and Bozeman, B. (2007) The Public Value Universe: An Inventory. *Administration & Society*, 39(3), pp. 354–381.

Blake, G., Robinson, D. and Smerdon, D. (2006) *Living Values: A Report Encouraging Boldness in Third Sector Organizations.* (London: Community Links.

Brandsen, T., van de Donk, W. and Putters, K. (2005) Griffins or Chameleons? Hybridity as a Permanent and Inevitable Characteristic of the Third Sector. *International Journal of Public Administration*, 28(9/10), pp. 749–765.

Cabinet Office (2010) *The Compact.* London: Cabinet Office.

Cairns, B., Harris, M. and Young, P. (2005) Building the Capacity of the Voluntary Non-Profit Sector: Challenges of Theory and Practice. *International Journal of Public Administration*, 28(9/10), pp. 869–885.

Charity Commission (2007a) *Charities and Public Service Delivery.* Report Number CC37. London: Charity Commission of England and Wales. Available at: http://www.charitycommission.gov.uk/publications/cc37.aspx.

—— (2007b) *Stand and Deliver.* Report Number RS 15. London: Charity Commission of England and Wales. Available at: http://www.charitycommission.gov.uk/publications/rs15.aspx.

Civil Exchange (2012) *The Big Society Audit 2012.* London: Civil Exchange. Available at: http://www.civilexhange.org.uk.

Clarke, A., Markkanen, S. and Whitehead, C. (2008) *Evaluating Success: An Economic Evaluation of Emmaus Village Carlton.* Cambridge: Emmaus UK.

Commission on Big Society (2011) *Powerful People, Responsible Society: The Report of the Commission on Big Society.* London: ACEVO. Available at: http://www.acevo.org.uk/document.doc?id=1515.

Commission on the Future of the Voluntary Sector (1996) *Meeting the Challenge of Change: Voluntary Action in the 21st Century.* London: NCVO.

Cornforth, C. (2003) *The Governance of Public and Non-Profit Organizations.* London: Routledge.

Deakin, N. (2006) *Gains and Strains: The Voluntary Sector in the UK 1996–2006.* Baring Foundation Lecture, London, December. Available at: http://www.baring-foundation.org.uk/.

Elson, P. (2006) *Ties That Bind: An Empirical Exploration of Values in the Voluntary Sector: Value Importance, Hierarchy and Consensus in Independent Hospices in the UK.* London: Centre for Civil Society, Working Paper, London School of Economics.

Etzioni, A. (1973) The Third Sector and Domestic Missions. *Public Administration Review*, 33(4), pp. 314–323.

Evers, A. (2005) Mixed Welfare Systems and Hybrid Organizations: Changes in the Governance and Provision of Social Services. *International Journal of Public Administration*, 28(9/10), pp. 737–748.

HM Treasury (2004) *Regularity, Propriety and Value for Money.* London: HM Treasury. Available at: http://www.hm-treasury.gov.uk/d/Reg_Prop_and_VfM-November04.pdf.

Hudson, M. (2004) Managing without Profit. *Directory of Social Change.* London.

Ipsos MORI (2010) *Public Trust and Confidence in Charities: Research Study Conducted by Ipsos MORI on Behalf of the Charity Commission.* London: Ipsos MORI.

Kendall, J. (2003) *The Voluntary Sector.* London: Routledge

Kendall, J. and Knapp, M. (1995) A Loose and Baggy Monster: Boundaries, Definitions and Typologies. In: Davis Smith, J., Rochester, C. and Hedley, R., eds. *An Introduction to the Voluntary Sector.* London: Routledge, pp. 65–95.

McCabe, A. (2010) *Below the Radar in a Big Society? Reflections on Community Engagement, Empowerment and Social Action in a Changing Policy Context.* Third Sector Research Centre, Briefing Paper 51, Third Sector Research Centre, Birmingham, UK. Available at: http://www.tsrc.ac.uk.

Milbourne, L. and Cushman, M. (2010a) *Challenges to Trust in a Changing Third Sector.* Fifth Workshop on Trust within and between Organizations, Madrid, Spain, 28–29 January.

——— (2010b) *From the Third Sector to the Big Society: How Changing UK Government Policies Have Eroded Third Sector Trust.* Critical Management Studies Conference, Naples, Italy, 11–13 July.

Murdock, A. (2006) *Lessons from the Delivery of Public Services by the Third Sector and the Increasing Links to Citizenship: The Emergence and Development of Contractual Partnerships between the Third Sector and Government.* Third Sino-US International Conference for Public Administration, Beijing, People's Republic of China, 8–9 June.

——— (2010) *The Evolution of Emmaus in the UK.* Ninth International Conference of the International Society for Third Sector Research (ISTR), Istanbul, Turkey, 7–10 July.

Murdock, A., Benz, P. and O'Neill, G. (2011) *Social Enterprise Models and the Cook Inlet Tribal Council: An Assessment of the Applicability of Alter Model of Social Enterprise.* Social Innovation through Social Entrepreneurship in Civil Society, Third EMES International Research Conference on Social Enterprise, Roskilde, Denmark, 4–7 July.

Murdock, A., Glemain, P. and Meyer, M. (2011) De l'enterprise en economie sociale. *Economie et Societes,* 21(4), pp. 641–656.

Murdock, A., Parra, C. and Glemain, P. (2011) *Evaluating Solidarity for Emmaus International Groups around the World.* Association for Research on Nonprofit Organizations and Voluntary Action (Arnova) Conference, Toronto, Canada, November.

National Audit Office (2005) *Working with the Third Sector.* London: The Stationery Office. Available at: http://www.nao.org.uk/publications/0506/working_with_the_third_sector.aspx.

——— (2012) *Central Government's Implementation of the National Compact.* London: NAO. Available at: http://www.nao.org.uk/publications/1012/national_compact.aspx.

NCVO (2005) *Voluntary Action: Meeting the Challenges of the 21st Century.* London: NCVO.

——— (2006) *The UK Voluntary Sector Almanac 2006: The State of the Sector.* London: NCVO.

O'Kelly, C. and Dubnick, M. (2005) *Taking Tough Choices Seriously: Public Administration and Individual Moral Agency.* Institute of Governance, Public Policy and Social Research, Working Paper, Queens University, Belfast.

Osborne, S. (2005) Voluntary Action in a Changing Europe: Critical Perspectives. *International Journal of Public Administration,* 28(9/10), pp. 733–735.

Osborne, S. and McLaughlin, K. (2002) Trends and Issues in the Implementation of Local Voluntary Sector Compacts in England. *Public Money and Management,* Jan/Mar. 22.1: 55–64.

——— (2004) The Cross Cutting Review of the Voluntary Sector: Where Next for Local Government-Voluntary Sector Relationships? *Regional Studies,* 38(5), pp. 573–582.

Pestoff, V. (2005) *Beyond the Market and the State: Social Enterprises and Civil Democracy in a Welfare State*. Aldershot: Ashgate.

Pirson, M. and Malhotra, D. (2007) *What Matters to Whom? Managing Trust across Multiple Stakeholder Groups*. Cambridge, MA: The Hauser Center for Nonprofit Organizations, Harvard University, May.

Putnam, R. (2000) *Bowling Alone: The Collapse and Revival of American Community*. New York: Simon and Schuster.

Roberts, J. (2011) Trust and Early Years Childcare: Parents' Relationships with Private, State and Third Sector Providers in England. *Journal of Social Policy*, 40, pp. 695–715.

Six, P. and Vidal, I., eds. (1994) *Delivering Welfare: Repositioning Non-Profit and Co-Operative Action in Western European Welfare States*. Barcelona: Centre d'Iniciatives de l'Economica Social (CIES).

Tijsterman, S. (2006) *Public Values and the Idea of the State*. Netherlands Institute of Government Conference, Amsterdam, November.

Van de Walle, S. (2005) *The Impact of Public Service Values on Services of General Interest Reform Debates*. International Research Society for Public Management Conference IX, Bocconi University, Milan, Italy, April.

Part III

Trust and Citizens' Confidence in Public Services

10 Relationships in Healthcare
Trust in Transition?

Ann Mahon

Rudolf Klein offers an eloquent and persuasive account of the political context that resulted in the creation of the National Health Service (NHS) in the United Kingdom (UK) in 1948 (Klein, 2010). Although the events leading up to the creation of the NHS are inevitably open to interpretation, the outcome is subject to less debate—namely that the system placed the medical profession at the centre of the NHS power base, with various concessions to autonomy and self-regulation and, as a consequence, created a system demanding high levels of trust by patients, government and other stakeholders in the medical profession. Indeed:

> The post war consensus was underpinned by trust in professionalism with the state and patients tending to trust the norms of professional self-regulation and state licensing procedures to ensure that health professionals and health care institutions operated in the best interests of patients and citizens. (Rowe and Calnan, 2006, p. 376)

During the 1970s, however, matters began to change, as at least four key concerns were debated. First there were questions about how effective healthcare interventions actually were. Archibald Cochrane found that many decisions made by doctors were based as much on custom and practice as on scientific evidence, and his book criticized the lack of reliable scientific evidence for the effectiveness of many healthcare interventions at that time (Cochrane, 1972; Hill, 2000; Shah and Chung, 2009). Second, despite expectations that the introduction of the NHS would improve the health of the population and reduce inequalities, evidence began to emerge about persisting inequalities in health status and in unequal access to good medical care (Tudor-Hart, 1971). Third was the suggestion that the contribution of medical care to the health of the population had been overestimated, and that other factors, such as nutrition and housing, had a greater impact on increased life expectancy and reduced mortality rates than did medical interventions (McKeown, 1976). Finally, the adverse effects of healthcare, or iatrogenesis, on individual patients, on communities and on society as a whole was raised in Illich's polemic and arguably prophetic book, in, for example, the context of the personal, financial and socio-economic costs of hospital-acquired and -related infections (Illich, 1976; Plowman et al., 2001). These publications can, in retrospect, be seen as representing a watershed in the hitherto largely unchallenged trust and confidence held by patients and the public in doctors and other practitioners and healthcare institutions. The NHS as an institution and its workforce was not quite living up to expectations.

For the purposes of this chapter, an adaptation of the social ecology model provides a useful framework to begin an exploration of the literature relating to definitions of trust in healthcare relationships and how these may be changing in response to changes within and outside of the institutions setting and implementing health policy. At the micro level, the focus is on the individual in the system, on personal characteristics or attributes and on interpersonal relationships. At the meso level, the focus is on the organizational and institutional context where micro-level interactions take place. These are the systems and processes in place in healthcare organizations, the rules and processes that govern activity and the culture that shapes the norms and values of these institutions. In turn, such meso-level factors can impact on micro-level experiences. At the macro level are the broader social, political and cultural contexts that might be regarded as having an impact on trust by stimulating an institutional response, which in turn impacts on individuals in the system or by stimulating individual responses, which demand changes in institutional structures. Here, factors such as the media, government policy and broader social trends can be seen as relevant in discussions about trust in healthcare relationships. Applying the social ecology framework to healthcare relationships, the macro level relates to the external factors driving transitions in trust in institutions at the meso level and in individuals and their relationships at the micro level.

However, conceptual models of trust relationships in healthcare are much more sophisticated and plausible than the availability of empirical evidence to support them. The focus of empirical work has tended to be on the micro level of trust and from a patient perspective and, specifically, the doctor–patient relationship. Given the traditional and long-recognized centrality of the doctor–patient relationship in healthcare, this is not surprising (Mechanic and Schlesinger, 1996; Parsons, 1951; Freidson, 1975). More recently, attention has turned to meso levels of trust in healthcare relationships. Here there are more questions than answers, reflecting both the changing focus of health services research and the enduring methodological problems of attributing cause and effect when researching trust in complex systems.

The chapter begins by identifying a range of factors that can be regarded as influencing how we define and experience trust in healthcare relationships. How trust is defined at individual and institutional levels is then considered, focusing primarily on how trust has been defined and conceptualized. Focus then turns from theoretical concerns to the enactment of trust and what we know about trust from empirical studies looking at trust relationships in healthcare. Although it has been common to talk about a generalized decline or erosion in trust in healthcare relationships, it is argued in this chapter that it is more useful and perhaps more accurate to talk about trust in transition (Chin, 2001; Shore, 2006; Imber, 2008; Mechanic and Schlesinger, 1996). Notwithstanding the lack of longitudinal evidence supporting the 'erosion of trust thesis', the scale and nature of change at societal and system level demand a more nuanced approach than merely focusing on absolute levels of trust as a discrete indicator of what are a web of complex, interrelated sets of relationships in a range of different contexts. The importance of trust in healthcare relationships is then explored, followed by a consideration of the implications of the transitional nature of trust in healthcare for healthcare practitioners and managers.

TRUST RELATIONSHIPS IN HEALTHCARE: MACRO-LEVEL DRIVERS AND MESO-LEVEL ISSUES

For public services in general and health policy and management in particular, the drivers for reform, in the context of less reliance on trust, are well rehearsed (Baggott, 2007; OECD, 2005; Dubois et al., 2006; Walshe and Smith, 2010; Mahon et al., 2009). Studies or commentaries on trust in healthcare relationships often explore some of the wider factors impacting upon trust and are often discussed in the context of its apparent erosion. The macro-level drivers of particular relevance here include extensive media scrutiny, economic factors, workforce developments, consumerism and marketization. As noted earlier, the NHS was created within a bureaucratic, technocratic and professionally dominated paradigm, which came under increasing scrutiny from the 1970s onwards. Successive decades have witnessed a series of clinical 'scandals', where trust between patients and doctors, nurses, managers and institutions has been breached. These have received extensive scrutiny by the media and have often been subject to lengthy reviews. The media therefore is a significant factor in creating and reflecting concerns about trust in healthcare. Examples of inquiries subject to extensive media coverage and review and often producing recommendations resulting in institutional reform to secure greater governance and accountability, include the Bristol Royal Infirmary Inquiry (2001), the Shipman Inquiry (2005), the Royal Liverpool Children's Inquiry (2001) and the Mid Staffordshire NHS Foundation Trust Inquiry (2010).

Few, if any, healthcare systems in the developed world could have escaped the impact of the increased costs of healthcare. These relate to the rising costs of pharmaceuticals, new technologies and increases in public sector pay as well as an increased demand for healthcare associated with an aging population and the rising prevalence of long-term conditions. Concerns about efficiency, effectiveness and productivity in the context of scarce resources may be putting pressure on the relationship between patients, practitioners and institutions. In the United States, for example, there is some evidence that managed care has placed strains on the doctor–patient relationship and patients' trust in their doctors to act in their interests (Mechanic and Schlesinger 1996; Hall et al., 2001). In the UK, the changing role of general practitioners (GPs) as part of current healthcare reforms are also raising questions about how their new commissioning role might impact upon the doctor–patient relationship.

Medicine, along with law, was traditionally viewed as the archetypal profession. The study of the professions by sociologists, particularly from 'The Chicago School', produced some classic texts on the nature of professions and socialization into professional roles (Becker et al., 1961; Freidson, 1975). With some notable exceptions, such as Sinclair's anthropological study of medical socialization, research in this field has been neglected, and whilst there is widespread recognition that professions are being transformed, the empirical basis of this claim is weak (Sinclair, 1997). However, it can be argued that increased standardization of working hours and tasks has reduced autonomy. Changes in governance, including clinical governance and the implementation of policies such as the European Working Time Directive, have altered both the nature of clinical work and the status of the medical profession. Published work on trust, however, appears to be growing independently of any attempts to modernize the classical but inevitably outdated accounts of professions (Goudge and Gilson, 2005). Transformations in how the healthcare workforce is organized means that the boundaries between professional groups are becoming blurred and activities associated with particular roles are less steeped in status, hierarchy and tradition and are more open and explicit. Finally there is a generalized public decline in deference to authority, which may be linked to an overall decline in social trust due to the breakdown of communities, social cohesion and social networks (Rowe and Calnan, 2006) but also to a rise in consumerism.

As deference to authority declines and patients and the public have increasing access to healthcare information, including from web-based sources, there may be less reliance on professionals to gain information or reassurance. Thus, the power balance between patients, the public and health practitioners and institutions is shifting. As health policy increasingly emphasizes self-care; in the management of diabetes for example, the onus may begin to shift towards the trust that doctors and other healthcare practitioners must have in their patients to assess their own needs and care for themselves. Relationships are then transformed according to the clinicians' trust in patients to care for themselves. Increasing consumerism, including self-reliance, engenders more symmetrical relationships. Consumerism 'may have produced a shift in the balance of power within which trust relationships are formed, changing public and professional vulnerabilities and the requirement for trust in their relationships' (Rowe and Calnan, 2006, p. 378). Finally, the marketization of healthcare through the introduction of market-type mechanisms, such as competition, contestability, choice and the separation of the purchaser/provider function in services, along with outsourcing and public–private partnerships, has introduced new mechanisms and relationships that represent radical changes to traditional ways of working.

Although little direct evidence has been cited to demonstrate a direct causal relationship between the macro-level factors discussed and their impact on healthcare institutions and individual relationships within healthcare, the relationships have strong face validity and are generally well established in the literature (Baggott, 2007; OECD, 2005; Dubois et al., 2006; Walshe and Smith, 2010; Mahon et al., 2009). Taken together these various factors have engendered reduced tolerance for the professional paternalism traditionally associated with healthcare, and systems of self-regulation are now seen as inadequate (the Bristol Royal Infirmary Inquiry, 2001; the Shipman Inquiry, 2005; the Royal Liverpool Children's Inquiry, 2001; the Mid Staffordshire NHS Foundation Trust Inquiry, 2010; Rowe and Calnan, 2006). Alternative forms of regulation and governance that instil greater public confidence are now evolving in response to these drivers. The emphasis has shifted from internally focussed and closed systems of regulation, with an emphasis on individual competence and voluntary participation, towards more external scrutiny, with a greater emphasis on patient perspectives, teams and systems, performance and regulatory frameworks. Rowe and Calnan (2006, pp. 379–380) state:

> Political concerns about a loss of public trust in professionalism as a guarantor of high standards of conduct and competence, has prompted a debate about the accountability of clinicians, challenged the legitimacy of their power as enshrined in their right to clinical autonomy and high levels of discretion in their work and has prompted a search for new mechanisms of governance to hold institutions and professionals to account.

TRUST RELATIONSHIPS IN HEALTHCARE: DEFINITIONS OF TRUST

Trust is a multidimensional concept. Variation in how trust is defined is partly due to the theoretical heterogeneity of the academic disciplines that research in this area (Pearson and Raeke, 2000). There seems to be some consensus that trust is not just, or at least not primarily, a personal psychological attribute or disposition associated with personality type. A full consideration of an individual's propensity to trust or indeed to be trustworthy is outside the scope of this chapter. Rather at the micro level or personal level of trust, concern is about the nature and the quality of relationships between various stakeholders within the healthcare system. However, in a review, it was noted that most studies focused on patient–clinician relations from the perspective of patients rather than from other relationships and settings (Calnan and Rowe, 2006). In relation to inter-personal trust, the definition and dimensions of trust are routinely adapted to the behaviours that play out in particular settings (Goudge and Gilson, 2005). It may be that trust in healthcare has a stronger affective element than in other areas because of the emotional context of health and illness and the relationship with healthcare professionals and, in particular, with doctors. In this context, in addition to technical competence, trust is built through the creation of rapport between doctors and patients. A number of features are of note here. First, the emotional context relating to the vulnerability of a patient in a healthcare setting and, second, the distinction between trust in different dimensions of the trustees skills and behaviours.

Many writers refer to heightened emotional aspects of care, with the vulnerability of patients in a healthcare setting where illness, frailty and the uncertainty of treatment and outcomes create the propensity to trust in the treating doctor or practitioner. In this context for Hall et al. (2001) trust is: 'the optimistic acceptance of a vulnerable situation in which the truster believes the trustee will care for the truster's interests' (p. 615).

Indeed, it may be that the vulnerability associated with illness engenders the stronger emotional and instinctive component to trust in medical settings.

> Trust relationships are therefore characterized by one party, the trustor, having positive expectations regarding both the competence of the other party, the trustee, and that they will work in their best interests. As Porter et al. (1975) suggest 'where there is trust there is the feeling that others will not take advantage of me'. (Rowe and Calnan, 2006, p. 377)

Looking at the concept of trust at the micro level, it is clear that trust is an overarching concept with many dimensions. Some consider patients' trust to be a set of beliefs or expectations about how a healthcare practitioner will behave; others emphasize a feeling of confidence in practitioners' intentions (Pearson and Raeke, 2000). Goudge and Gilson (2005) distinguish between intuitive and calculated judgements about trust whilst Rowe and Calnan (2006) refer to cognitive and affective judgements. Cognitive or calculated judgements may be more concerned with the technical skills, knowledge and the competence of a practitioner. Interpersonal trust seems to be more driven by affective or intuitive judgement with commonly described dimensions, including satisfaction, communication, privacy, confidentiality, honesty, benevolence, integrity, listening skills, empathy, caring and showing respect (Pearson and Raeke, 2000; Goudge and Gilson, 2005; Rowe and Calnan, 2006; Calnan and Rowe, 2006; Gilson, 2006).

So, in the context of healthcare the evidence suggests the concept seems to embrace confidence in competence (skills and knowledge) as well as whether the trustee is working in the best interests of the truster. Confidence in competence is more concerned with the technical skills and knowledge of the practitioner. Pearson and Raeke (2000) note one key distinction in the conceptualization of trust—the distinction between interpersonal and social trust. Whilst interpersonal trust refers to the trust built up through social interactions, with expectations about a person's trustworthiness being tested over time, social trust in healthcare is trust in the collective institutions concerned with delivering healthcare and is influenced by the media and wider confidence in particular institutions at a community or societal level. This raises another key distinction that is the difference between trust and confidence in healthcare relationships. Trust judgements are made in the context of uncertainty, whereas confidence 'implies a situation of relative stability and security, where judgements about others are based on what is predictable' rather than what is unknown (Gilson, 2006, p. 361).

Meso levels of trust relate to organizational or corporate contexts where structures, financing and organizational features are associated with the corporate professionals leading and managing public sector and healthcare organizations. The role of trust in organizational performance (Goudge and Gilson, 2005) is also pertinent here: trust may be expressed in different ways in the same setting according to what people are relating to. In consequence, trust in relation to individual providers may operate differently from trust in a whole organization. Although trust is discussed primarily in terms of interpersonal one to one relationships in healthcare the various dimensions identified are equally applicable to relationships beyond practitioners and can be applied to relationships with managers and management, teams and others interactions within healthcare. In these settings an understanding of the rules, laws, norms and customs provide the basis for trusting others and generate a collective interest (Gilson, 2006). This kind of collective trust at an organizational level originates in the interpersonal relationships and illustrates the interconnectedness between micro and meso levels of trusts. One of the findings reported in the Mid Staffordshire NHS Trust Foundation Trust Inquiry was the disengagement of the doctors from management in the hospital—the consultants as a group dissociated itself from management and were described as 'fatalistic' in their approach to management issues and plans: 'There was also a lack of trust in management leading to a reluctance to raise concerns' (2010, vol. 1, p. 16).

In this context, doctors failed to engaged effectively at an interpersonal level with individual managers and at a system level with management processes because they were distrustful of managers and management. Chambers and Smith point to board dynamics as an emerging area of interest in the exploration of factors that influence performance in healthcare organizations and refer specifically to cultures characterized by high trust, high challenge and high engagement. In addition, the NHS Confederation identifies 'trust and corporate working' as one of the key characteristics of effective boards (Chambers and Smith, 2011).

THE NATURE AND EXTENT OF TRUST IN HEALTHCARE RELATIONSHIPS

Although the theoretical frameworks about trust in healthcare relations at micro and meso levels are fairly sophisticated and diverse, the empirical evidence is weak. What research there is tends to focus on assessing levels of trust in general populations. Perhaps the best example of this is the work undertaken by Ipsos MORI. The key findings are perhaps best summed up in the words of the founder of MORI, Sir Robert Worcester:

> Ever since 1983, when we first started asking the public's view of who they trust, more people have said they trust doctors than any other profession or occupation, and they remain so today. It just goes to show how much faith the public place in doctors. It will be interesting to see if the public's trust in doctors is maintained following the proposed changes to their role in the reforms of the NHS.[1]

Worcester's reference to the changing role of doctors and the NHS reforms makes the clear connection between how changes in functions and roles at the meso level can impact on levels of trust at the micro level.

As noted by Worcester, Ipsos MORI has carried out regular surveys drawing on samples of the general population. Respondents are asked the following: 'Now I will read out a list of different people. For each, would you tell me whether you generally trust them to tell the truth or not'. Table 10.1 summarizes the responses to this question, for selected groups of professions and for selected years between 1983 and 2011.

The evidence presented in Table 10.1 shows remarkably high and stable levels of trust in the medical profession over the past ten years. Doctors remain the most trusted profession to tell the truth and they have consistently being rated more trusted than all of the other professions across all of the years, with the exception of 1993, where teachers were rated at the same level as doctors. There are several peaks and troughs over time, and a recent decline between 2009 and 2011. However, looking at the overall trends from 1983 to the present day, the overall picture is one of high and enduring levels of trust in individual practitioners and certainly no solid evidence of a decline in trust. Turning to the data in the second part of the table—relating to 'not trust to tell the truth'—a similar pattern emerges. Again, with one exception in the year 1993, respondents were less likely to say they do not trust doctors to tell the truth than any other professional group. Again, there is a slight increase in the proportion responding they do not trust their doctors to tell the truth between 2009 and 2011, but it is unclear and unlikely, given previous trends, whether this is evidence of a decline in trust.

If we accept general levels of satisfaction as a proxy for trust or a related variable, then public opinion about satisfaction with how well people do their jobs may shed some light on trust in healthcare professionals. In another series of regular surveys conducted by Ipsos MORI, 2,000 British adults aged 15+ were surveyed between 1999 and 2004. Respondents were asked: 'How satisfied are you with the way the following types of people do their jobs?' Responses for selected groups of people are reported in Table 10.2.

Respondents were more satisfied with how well healthcare practitioners did their job than any other professional group. Interestingly, nurses are

Table 10.1 Trust to Tell the Truth/Not Trust to Tell the Truth

| | Trust to tell the truth | | | | | | |
	Doctors (%)	Teachers (%)	Professors (%)	Judges (%)	Police (%)	Government ministers (%)	Politicians in general (%)
1983	82	79	N/A	77	61	16	18
1993	84	84	70	68	63	11	14
1997	86	83	70	72	61	12	15
1999	91	89	79	77	61	23	23
2000	87	85	76	77	60	21	20
2001	89	86	78	78	63	20	17
2002	91	85	77	77	59	20	19
2003	91	87	74	72	64	20	18
2004	92	89	80	75	63	23	22
2005	91	88	77	76	58	20	20
2006	92	88	80	75	61	22	20
2007	90	86	78	78	59	22	18
2008	92	87	79	78	65	24	21
2009	92	88	80	80	60	16	13
2011	88	81	74	72	63	17	14

| | Do not trust to tell the truth | | | | | | |
	Doctors (%)	Teachers (%)	Professors (%)	Judges (%)	Police (%)	Government ministers (%)	Politicians in general (%)
1983	14	14	N/A	18	32	74	75
1993	11	9	12	21	26	81	79
1997	10	11	12	19	30	80	78
1999	7	7	10	16	31	70	72
2000	9	10	11	15	33	72	74
2001	7	10	10	15	27	73	77
2002	6	10	11	15	31	72	73
2003	6	8	11	19	26	73	75
2004	5	7	9	16	28	70	71
2005	6	8	10	16	32	71	73
2006	5	7	8	16	29	70	72
2007	6	9	10	14	31	71	76
2008	6	8	9	14	27	74	73
2009	5	8	9	13	31	79	82
2011	8	12	13	17	27	74	80

Source: Table contents extracted from Ipsos MORI: http://www.Ipsos-mori.com/.

Table 10.2 Opinions of Professions: How Well Do They Do Their Job?

	Doctors (%)	Nurses (%)	Teachers (%)	Judges (%)	Police (%)	Government ministers (%)	Politicians in general (%)
Satisfied							
1999	91	96	85	59	71	33	33
2000	90	95	83	59	65	28	27
2001	89	94	82	61	66	27	25
2002	91	94	84	60	68	30	31
2003	91	95	85	52	70	26	28
2004	92	96	86	58	67	27	27
Dissatisfied							
1999	5	2	5	15	39	39	39
2000	6	1	6	14	44	42	44
2001	5	2	6	14	48	47	48
2002	4	2	6	15	44	45	44
2003	5	2	4	21	51	51	51
2004	4	1	5	18	48	47	48

Source: Table contents extracted from Ipsos MORI: http://www.Ipsos-mori.com/.

rated more highly than doctors, but both doctors and nurses have high and stable levels of satisfaction. Although satisfaction is a distinct concept from trust, it is often reported as one dimension of it and in this context can be viewed as a proxy for trust, providing valuable comparative data about perceptions of trust in nurses. Although data is only available up to 2004, one might predict similar levels of satisfaction given the stability in responses to trust in professions to tell the truth/trust not to tell the truth, reported in Table 10.1.

However, when looking at the interface between micro and meso levels of trust, it seems that there are lower levels of trust in systems than in individual practitioners. Calnan and Rowe's study, with a sample of 1,187 adults in England and Wales and conducted in 2002–2003, found high levels of trust in individual practitioners such as doctors and nurses, but lower for managers and lower for specific aspects of a service such as waiting times. The following proposition was put to respondents; that they would trust NHS practitioners to: 'always or most of the time trust [practitioner] to put their interests above the convenience of the hospital'.

The positive responses were highest for practice nurses (87%) and hospital nurses (85%) followed by GPs (83%) and hospital doctors (76%). When asked about trust in hospital managers, levels of trust were lower so that 59% of respondents said they would always or most of the time trust private hospital managers to put their interests above the convenience of the hospital compared to 38% for NHS managers (Calnan and Rowe, 2006), suggesting lower trust (than healthcare professionals) in managers in a public setting. The findings relating to doctors and nurses are broadly comparable to the findings from Ipsos MORI, with slightly more positive responses relating to nurses but overall high levels of trust in doctors and, interestingly, slightly higher reported levels of trust in GPs compared with hospital doctors.

Turning to modes of governance and accountability, (Rowe and Calnan 2006, p. 379) 'set out a theoretical framework that seeks to explain how changes in public trust in the health system may have been generated by different modes of governance of healthcare'. The model, summarized in Table 10.3, is based on the idea 'that changes in trust relations reflect changes to the distribution of power, modes of governance and accountability within the health service' (p. 379). The framework suggests 'changes in trust are driven by the relationship between trust, power, governance and accountability' (p. 370) in an iterative process. Those who have power can demonstrate different levels of trust—and indeed distrust—through the extent to which they impose rules and regulations and limit discretion (p. 379). So that:

> Trust has an inverse relationship with demands for explicit account-ability, high trust relations result in limited demands for evidence of accountability, and low trust relations produce increased demands for explicit evidence of the same. (Rowe and Calnan, 2006, p. 379)

The introduction of 'clinical governance in 1997 was a policy that produced unprecedented changes in the nature of relationships between doctors and managers in the UK (Rowe and Calnan, 2006; Klein, 2010). Under the traditional model of accountability professionals operated 'within a network of governance with authority' which was based on 'professional status, coordinative competence' and control of resources (Rowe and Calnan, 2006, p. 382). Accountability sustained through associated relations relied on shared values and norms:

> Trust was central to this system. To be effective it required patients and politicians to have high levels of trust in the expertise of doctors and the effectiveness of professional self-regulation as a mechanism for ensuring high standards of care. For in effect, self –regulation protected physicians from accounting to anyone other than their professional colleagues for their clinical activity and performance or use of resources, essentially rendering them invisible to public scrutiny. (Rowe and Calnan, 2006, p. 382)

The introduction of clinical governance has represented a fundamental challenge to the authority of doctors because it means they are accountable

Table 10.3 Governance Models and Their Impact on Public Trust in the UK NHS

Model	Organizational structure	Form of governance	Trust	Power	Accountability mechanisms	Lay power
Bureaucratic	Integrated hierarchy	Command and control	High: trust in public service ethos and professionalism	Centralized: under political control	Political: ministerial accountability, line management, trust in public services ethos	Indirect: holding to account through periodic voting
Professional	Self-regulating (autonomous) groups of professionals	Network relations based on trust and reciprocity	High: trust in professional expertise and norms	Dispersed: professional control	Professional: integrity guaranteed by licensing and disciplinary procedures	Passive: recipients of care hold to account by complaints system
Market	Self-governing units in competition with each other	Exchange relations	Low: trust of professional and public service norms	Dispersed: consumer control	Economic: reliant on market forces to ensure responsiveness	Direct: choice and exit
New Public Management	Devolved operational units under centralized strategic control	"Tight-loose" relations with central "steering"	Low: trust performance to be explicitly accounted for	Centralized: managerial control	Managerial: reliant on performance management/targets	Indirect: public views mediated by professionals
Stakeholder	Local agencies led by frontline providers with devolved autonomy but under central strategic control	Partnership work involving network relations based on trust and mutual reciprocity	High: trust in partner's respect of reciprocal rights and duties	Dispersed: stakeholder control	Multiple accountabilities: reliant on consultation, effective reporting and active involvement of stakeholders	Direct: active citizen involvement in service planning

Source: Adapted from Rowe and Calnan, 2006.

for the organization and delivery of care and the criteria of standards not determined exclusively by the profession.

> Increasing managerial monitoring of clinical activity linked to the clinical governance initiative has obvious consequences for trust relationships between providers and managers and potentially between local healthcare delivery organizations and the centre. (Rowe and Calnan, 2006, p. 383)

Rowe and Calnan (2006) go on to develop a framework based on the proposition that changes in the organizational structure of medical care and the culture of healthcare delivery have changed the experiences of healthcare for individual patients. They argue 'current policy discourses suggest that new forms of trust relations are emerging in this new context of healthcare delivery, reflecting a change in motivations for trust' from affect/intuition-based judgments to cognitive/instrumental-based ones 'as patients, clinicians and managers become more active partners in trust relations' (p. 376). Embodied trust is therefore less relevant now than in the past. This thesis suggests that trust relations in all interpersonal types of relationship in healthcare might rely more on the provision of information and evidence to support decisions in a more reciprocal relationship, characterized by a negotiated alliance between patients and practitioners (Rowe and Calnan, 2006).

WHY IS TRUST AND CONFIDENCE IMPORTANT IN HEALTHCARE?

Trust is important in healthcare relationships for instrumental reasons in terms of the impact that it might have on health outcomes and the quality of interpersonal and organizational relationships. It can also be seen as intrinsically important in its own right. For Hall et al. (2001), trust is the core and defining characteristic that gives the doctor–patient relationship its 'meaning, importance and substance' (p. 613). They go on to say:

> Preserving, enhancing and justifying trust are the fundamental goals of much of medical ethics . . . and are prominent objectives in health care law and public policy.

In instrumental terms, trust has been identified as important in healthcare relationships in several aspects. Trust influences health and illness behaviours so that patients are more likely to seek help if they trust a practitioner and generally engage more fully with all aspects of care, including participating in research trials, complying with treatment regimes and remaining loyal to a particular doctor. Trust may have a positive impact on health outcomes both directly and indirectly (Calnan and Rowe, 2006; Hill et al., 2003). Again, as in the relationship between trust, health and illness behaviour, the impact of trust on health outcomes may be accounted for as trust may mediate therapeutic processes as it has an impact on patient satisfaction, compliance and continuity of care (Hill et al., 2003; Calnan and Rowe, 2006; Gilson, 2006). In the US, Hill and colleagues found that by establishing enduring and trusting relationships with at-risk young black men, a healthcare team successfully encouraged them to make changes to their lifestyle and to cooperate with treatment regimens that improved the management of their high blood pressure (Hill et al., 2003).

The impact of trust from a practitioner, managerial or organizational perspective or a system perspective has been neglected in comparison to trust from a patient perspective (Calnan and Rowe, 2006). However, in studies that have looked at the impact of trust on workplace relations, trust has facilitated commitment to the organizations and enhanced collaboration between clinicians. Inquiries into failures in healthcare report similar findings, such as those reported in the Mid Staffordshire NHS Foundation Trust Inquiry (2010), discussed earlier. Certain macro-level factors, including the marketization of healthcare and the increasing role of patients in self-management, may engender the situation where doctors need to learn to trust the decisions made by patients and to demonstrate confidence in their ability to manage their care. In this context, the current emphasis on self-management and expert patients in long-term conditions is a good example of how the trust relationship in healthcare care relationships is in transition. The emphasis now is more on partnership and collaborative working than was the case in the traditional doctor–patient relationship, and the notion of vulnerability and dependence in this context is different.

> Trust appears to depend not just on provider's demonstration of care and concern for the patient as an individual. It also requires providers to show confidence in a patient's ability to manage their diseases.
>
> Being viewed as competent by a health care professional encouraged patients to feel more confident in their ability to control and manage their illness and at the same time, increased patient trust in the provider. (Rowe and Calnan, 2006, p. 386)

Gilson (2006) identifies two answers to the question of why trust matters. First, it enables the cooperation required across the multiple relationships needed to produce healthcare and health and thus underpins the behaviours important for effective treatment, on the part not just of patients but also of practitioners and other stakeholders involved in healthcare provision. Second, a health system founded in trusted relationships can contribute to generating wider social value by providing the basis for generalized trust at a societal level and above and beyond the provision of healthcare (Gilson, 2006; Perry et al., 2006).

Despite the emphasis on the publication of various indicators of individual and organizational performance, it remains unclear what impact this type of data has on trust and confidence in healthcare practitioners and organization or the extent to which it is used by patients in forming judgements. This theme is explored more fully by Pollitt and Chambers in chapter three of this volume.

Finally, it is important to remember that trust is not intrinsically good. Trust can have a negative impact because it provides legitimacy for the exercise of power: 'trusting too much without caution may enable the abuse of power in the form of exploitation, domination or conspiracy against others' (Gilson, 2006, p. 364) and in extreme cases, the abuse of power can lead to serious mistreatment, death or, in the extreme case of Harold Shipman, mass murder (Shipman, 2005). Some level of distrust may therefore be both necessary and functional within a healthcare system.

IMPLICATIONS OF THEORETICAL AND EMPIRICAL CONSIDERATIONS OF TRUST FOR HEALTHCARE PRACTITIONERS

An understanding of the theoretical and empirical aspects of trust and confidence in health discussed in this chapter has direct and practical implications for managing and delivering healthcare in contemporary healthcare systems. Focusing attention on trust in healthcare systems allows a deeper understanding of healthcare systems and focuses thinking on issues of equity and justice at a societal level (Perry et al., 2006; Gilson, 2006). In terms of enabling a deeper understanding of health systems, Gilson argues that because work in this area focuses on relationships and values, this in itself is important in countering the tendency to see health systems as machines through which biomedical interventions are delivered. Thus, a focus on trust and confidence in healthcare offers an alternative perspective through which managers and practitioners can be helped to see the complexity of health systems.

> Thinking about the role of trust in health systems points instead to the need to consider the institutions and behaviours that shape performance, the sets of relationships that must be managed to deliver outcomes and the importance of developing shared meanings to sustain delivery. Such actions require different policy and managerial interventions commonly identified and great humility about the difficulties of managing change. (Gilson, 2006, p. 365)

It also reframes thinking about equity and justice, where concern about trust reflects concern for the interests of the trusters, which reflects a broader understanding of social value derived from being a member of the community:

> These insights about the ethical bases of health systems and how they contribute to social justice are particularly important given the types of pressures currently placed on health systems worldwide (Gilson, 2006, p. 365).

In terms of the more practical implications for healthcare managers and practitioners, five key themes emerge from the analysis in this chapter. First, interpersonal relationships and attitudes in healthcare are of vital importance, not just intrinsically but also instrumentally. Good, therapeutic relationships may well improve health outcomes, both as a direct and as a mediating variable. This applies to the patient–practitioner relationship as well as to relationships between different practitioners and, indeed, between managers. Practitioners, as we have seen already, evoke high levels of trusts in patients and the public. The challenge is to sustain this and to explore how trust in managers and management systems may also be enhanced.

Second, notwithstanding the importance of interpersonal relationships and the existence of rapport between key stakeholders in healthcare as a basis for trust, it may be that cognitive and calculated judgements of trust assume greater significance in decision-making. In addition to interpersonal factors, patients may increasingly expect evidence of competence and access to information to inform decisions. In turn, the power balance between doctors and patients will continue to move towards a more symmetrical relationship. This appears to be an inevitable part of the changing nature of relationships.

Third, as we begin to accept the limitations of medicine alongside the increasing prevalence of long-term conditions in society, then doctors and other practitioners will need to learn how to trust patients to make decisions about their own care and to accept the consequences of these decisions. Healthcare professionals and managers must learn to adapt to the changing nature of relationships with patients in order to work more collaboratively.

Fourth, organizational systems and processes are not only shaped by external factors but may well, in turn, help to shape trust in institutions as well as in individuals. Rowe and Calnan's (2006) conceptual model of the relationships between trust and modes of governance offers an intriguing and important thesis about how organizational structures may determine the nature of trust. This has implications for how governance, performance and quality procedures are designed and implemented in organizations. This could be extended to consider what styles of leadership and management might generate and sustain trust and confidence in the healthcare workforce. The relationship between culture and performance is worthy of further inquiry, with some promising hypotheses emerging in relation to board dynamics (Chambers and Smith, 2011).

Finally, it is clear that considerations of trust and confidence in healthcare relationships have considerable practical implications for how managers and clinicians enact their roles, how they develop systems and mechanisms and for training and development. Few studies, however, have paid attention to these concerns. Future research, in addition to developing more robust theoretical and empirical bases of our understanding of trust and confidence in healthcare, should also consider the implications for developing and sustaining trust and confidence at a time of continuous and considerable change in society and in healthcare institutions.

CONCLUSIONS

There are gaps in our understanding of trust and confidence in healthcare relationships. At the micro level, whilst we know of the importance of trust in clinical encounters, there is little empirical evidence to support various theoretical propositions, and attention has tended to focus on trust between doctors and patients. Similarly, at the meso level, trust is both intrinsically and instrumentally important, but its potential to influence health outcome, organizational culture or organizational performance is poorly understood. Research can support the policy and management action required to generate trust within and through health systems, including approaches to training and the institutional context needed to sustain change (Chambers and Smith, 2011; Gilson 2006).

The evidence available suggests that levels of trust in healthcare practitioners is high, and the majority of patients and the public continue to trust doctors and nurses to act in their best interests. Compared to healthcare managers, practitioners are highly trusted. However, change is happening at a fast pace, and, in response to various macro-level drivers, healthcare organizations and the roles of healthcare practitioners are subject to extensive change initiatives and new roles. Traditional ways of working and traditional roles are being transformed. In turn, this places pressure on the traditional trust relationships in healthcare. Rather than talking about a decline or erosion in trust, it is argued that it is more appropriate to talk about the transition of trust in healthcare relationships. There is little empirical evidence to support the 'erosion of trust thesis'. 'Transition' captures the more nuanced and dynamic nature of changes in trust relationships in healthcare.

NOTE

1. Sir Robert Worcester, founder of MORI, http://www.Ipsos-mori.com/.

REFERENCES

Baggott, R. (2007) *Understanding Health Policy.* Bristol: Policy Press and the Social Policy Association.

Becker, H. et al. (1961) *Boys in White.* Chicago: University of Chicago Press.

Bristol Royal Infirmary Inquiry (2001) Available at: http://www.bristol-inquiry.org.uk/final.

Calnan, M. and Rowe, R. (2006) Researching Trust Relations in Healthcare: Conceptual and Methodological Challenges—An Introduction. *Journal of Health Organization and Management,* 20(5), pp. 349–358.

Chambers, N. and Smith, J. (2011) *Issues in the Training and Development for Effective Boards in the NHS*. Briefing Paper for the Mid Staffordshire NHS Foundation Trust Public Inquiry: Seminar on Development and Training of Trust Leaders, Leeds, October. Available at: https://www.escholar.manchester.ac.uk/api/datastream?publicationPid=uk-ac-man-scw:166477&datastreamId=FULL-TEXT.PDF.

Chin, J. J. (2001) Doctor-Patient Relationships: A Covenant of Trust. *Singapore Medical Journal*, 42(12), pp. 579–581.

Cochrane, A. (1972) *Effectiveness and Efficiency*. Abingdon: Burgess and Son.

Dubois, C. A., McKee, M. and Nolte, E. (2006) *Human Resources for Health in Europe*. Maidenhead: Open University Press.

Freidson, E. (1975) *Profession of Medicine A Study of the Sociology of Applied Knowledge*. New York: Dodd, Mead.

Gilson, L. (2006) Trust in Health Care: Theoretical Perspectives and Research Needs. *Journal of Health Organisation and Management*, 20(5), pp. 359–375.

Goudge, J. and Gilson, L. (2005) How Can Trust Be Investigated? Drawing Lessons from Past Experience. *Social Science and Medicine*, 61, pp. 1439–1451.

Hall, M. A. et al. (2001) Trust in Physicians and Medical Institutions: What Is It, Can It Be Measured and Does It Matter? *Milbank Quarterly*, 79(4), pp. 613–639.

Hill, G. (2000) Archie Cochrane and His Legacy: An Internal Challenge to Physicians' Autonomy. *Journal of Clinical Epidemiology*, 53(12), pp. 1189–1192.

Hill, M. N. et al. (2003). Hypertension Care and Control in Underserved Urban African American Men: Behavioral and Physiologic Outcomes at 36 Months. *American Journal of Hypertension*, 16, pp. 906–913.

Illich, I. (1976) *Limits to Medicine: Medical Nemesis, the Expropriation of Health*. London: Marion Davies.

Imber, J. B. (2008) *Trusting Doctors: The Decline of Moral Authority in American Medicine*. Princeton, NJ: Princeton University Press.

Ipsos MORI. http://www.Ipsos-mori.com.

Klein, R. (2010) *The New Politics of the NHS*. 6th ed. Oxford: Radcliffe.

Mahon, A., Walshe, K. and Chambers, N. (2009) *A Reader in Health Policy and Management*. Maidenhead: Open University Press.

McKeown, T. (1976) *The Role of Medicine: Dream, Mirage or Nemesis?* New York: Academic Press.

Mechanic, D. and Schlesinger, M. (1996) The Impact of Managed Care on Patients' Trust in the Provision of Medical Care. *Journal of the American Medical Association*, 275(21), pp. 1693–1697.

Mid Staffordshire NHS Foundation Trust Inquiry (2010) Available at: http://www.midstaffsinquiry.com.

OECD (2005) *Modernising Government—The Way Forward*. Paris: OECD.

Parsons, T. (1951) *The Social System*. Glencoe, IL: Free Press.

Pearson, S. D. and Raeke, L. H. (2000) Patients' Trust in Physicians: Many Theories, Few Measures and Little Data. *Journal of General Internal Medicine*, 15, pp. 509–513.

Perry, M., Williams, R. L., Wallerstein, N. and Waitzkin, H. (2006) Social Capital and Health Care Experiences among Low-Income Individuals. *American Journal of Public Health*, 98, pp. 330–336.

Plowman, R. et al. (2001) The Rate and Cost of Hospital Acquired Infections Occurring in Patients Admitted to Selected Specialties of a District General Hospital in England and the National Burden Imposed. *Journal of Hospital Infection*, 47(3), pp. 198–209.

Rowe, R. and Calnan, M. (2006) Trust Relations in Health Care: Developing a Theoretical Framework for the 'New' NHS. *Journal of Health Organization and Management*, 20(5), pp. 376–396.

Royal Liverpool Children's Inquiry (2001) Available at: http://www.rclinquiry.org.uk/.

Shah, H. M. and Chung, K. C. (2009) Archie Cochrane and His Vision for Evidence-Based Medicine. *Plastic Reconstructive Surgery*, 124(3), pp. 982–988.

Shipman: Shipman Inquiry (2005) The Final Report. Available at: http://www.shipman-inquiry.org.uk/reports.asp.

Shore, D. (2006) *The Trust Crisis in Healthcare: Causes, Consequences and Cures*. Oxford: Oxford University Press.

Sinclair, S. (1997) *Making Doctors: An Institutional Apprenticeship*. Oxford: Berg.

Tudor-Hart, J. (1971) The Inverse Care Law. *The Lancet*, 27 February, pp. 406–412.

Walshe, K. and Smith, J. (2010) *Healthcare Management*. Maidenhead: Open University Press.

11 Public Trust and Education

Teachers and Their Work

Helen Gunter and David Hall

Research in England (e.g. Ball, 2003) and internationally (e.g. Codd, 2005) over the past thirty years shows that teachers have been positioned as a 'not to be trusted' profession, with daily newspaper headlines presenting stories of poor standards and inappropriate conduct (e.g. Lightfoot, 1991, reports on how the government plans to improve standards). The argument has been made that teachers, like other public sector workers, have lost public confidence by operating in their own interests with a 'professional image of infallibility' (Bottery, 1998, p. 173) and so need to be more transparent about and accountable for the conduct and outcomes of professional practice. Drawing on data from the Economic and Social Research Council (ESRC) funded *Distributed Leadership and the Social Practices of School Organisation* (RES-000–22–3610) project (Hall et al., 2011),[1] we examine the consequences of this positioning of teachers during the New Labour governments (1997–2010)—specifically, we engage with O'Neill's (2002) arguments that technical forms of accountability and transparency in public services can generate perverse outcomes. Specifically, O'Neill (2002) argues that such managerial processes not only generate deceptions but also miss the point because 'if we want to increase trust we need to avoid *deception* rather than *secrecy*' (p. 72, emphasis in original). In other words, league tables, inspectors in classrooms and contextual value-added calculations are designed to open up the teaching and learning process to scrutiny, but, in reality, a data-rich school may not produce truthful truths about standards and processes and, in attempting to do so, may operate in ways that are not educational. So we begin by examining the situation in education by developing a framework for analysing the way in which teachers' and the public's trust and confidence have developed. We then examine the issues generated through three case studies of schools and how they demonstrate the way deception works, even at a time of high accountability and transparency and in schools that are officially meeting national standards.

TRUSTING TEACHERS, TRUSTING TIMES?

The borderline between what is the responsibility of the 'private' (e.g. parents) and the 'public' (e.g. citizens) in regard to education is unclear and shifting, and so we share the Newman and Clarke (2009, p. 2) position about what they call 'publicness':

> As a way of talking about the combination of things, ideas, issues, people, relationships, practices and sites that have been made public. Such things, people, and issues get made public by a variety of means, but all of them involve processes of making visible matters of connective concern. Public issues or problems (objects) imply publics to take an interest in them (subjects) and these are connected by institutions, relationships and practices (mediums).

The education of children has been made public through, first, political, social, cultural and economic needs, in order to produce culturally interconnected and economically productive citizens as objects for improvement; second, investment by the public as interested and stakeholder subjects; and, third, mediation between objects and subjects within homes, schools, local authorities, central government offices and through networks of professional and interest groups with knowledge and codes of practices. So, as Newman and Clarke (2009) go on to argue, the 'publicness' of education is not just that it is funded by the public and regulated through public institutions but because it is imagined and constructed 'in which publicness is constantly being remade through the practices of public service work and the technologies of public governance' (p. 4). Our study of education as a public service from post-1945 in England illustrates three main positions in regard to this ongoing reconstruction of 'publicness'; first, the *neoliberal*, where education is a private matter for families to provide (e.g. home schooling, fee paying), with rationales about how the state should withdraw in order to enable the market to deliver more efficient and effective services, including narratives about choice, consumer satisfaction and economic productivity; second, the *neoconservative*, where families inculcate codes of practice enabled by public funding, with rationales about faith, single-sex and sponsored schools, generating narratives that transmit approved social and cultural norms through the curriculum, pedagogy and organizational structure and ethos; and third, the *civic*, where education is a public good that is integral to social, political, economic and cultural cohesion, with rationales about enabling equality of opportunity through shared learning and access to credentials, and communicated through narratives about aspirations, citizenship and fairness (Gunter, 2011, 2012; Raffo et al., 2010).

Each of these positions approaches trust as a relational process in different ways. In order to develop this, we are adopting Bottery's (2003, p. 249) four forms of trust hierarchy:

- **Calculative:** whether someone can be trusted is about undertaking a risk calculation
- **Practice:** 'repeated encounters' (p. 251) improves the calculation as people become better known to each other

- **Role:** the formation of groups, e.g. professional occupations, can speed up and enable the calculation because of the expectation and knowledge about ethics and practices
- **Identificatory:** when people work together over time, then they become known to each other and so 'feel that they can intuitively trust one another' (p. 253)

Tilly's (2005) conceptualization of 'trust networks' develops these ideas because he shows how people make connections or 'ties' with each other and where trust operates through how 'members' relations to each other put major long-term collective enterprises at risk to the malfeasance, mistakes, or failures of other network members' (p. 4). Bottery (2003) argues that humans lose confidence and feel hurt by any breaches of trust, and because different values are ascribed to these forms of trust (identificatory is more valued than calculative), then people will be personally hurt: 'people may never get over the breakage, may seek revenge, may attempt to physically harm the trust breaker' (p. 254). He goes on to show how trust operates:

- **Meso:** at the level of the organization, people can experience the four forms of trust in their working relationships as 'the belief or disbelief in the culture and ethos of the organization' (p. 255) and how professional practice is a site for the interplay between the organization and society
- **Macro:** at the level of the state, people can experience the four forms of trust in their social, political, economic and cultural relationships, particularly through the visible conduct of elite groups, such as politicians, the media and business
- **Existential:** the relationship between the self and others is more than a risk-calculation process, 'it is instead a long-term and deeply existential process, more felt than reasoned, but one which underpins much of the individual's confidence in the rightness of the world' (p. 256)

So trust involves the exercise of judgement prior to, within and after exchange processes, and within the public domain 'we need social and political institutions that allow us to judge where to place our trust' (O'Neill, 2002, p. vii).

Table 11.1 presents a summary of the conceptual framework we have now constructed through juxtaposing positions with forms of trust, and we intend to now go on to examining this in relation to publicly funded education.

From the end of the Second World War, the civic position dominated politics in England. In relation to education, this can be illuminated by legislation in 1944 that introduced 'secondary education for all', with a range of projects over the following forty years to deliver this: first, the tradition of comprehensive primary schools was extended to include secondary education, so that all children from a neighbourhood could attend the same school

Table 11.1 Political Positions and Trust

	Neoliberal	Neoconservative	Civic
Calculative	Risk management through decision to invest/disinvest	Risk management through identifying what is morally right and wrong, with clear boundaries	Risk management through social insurance of citizenship and welfare
Practice	A trade contract regulates relationships, and repeat business builds brand loyalty	A belief-based contract regulates relationships, with loyalty based on shared morality	A social contract regulates relationships, with loyalty based on social interdependence.
Role	Occupational ethics based on individual or company codes of practice	Occupational ethics based on compliance with belief-based codes of practice	Occupational ethics based on professional codes of practice known to and supported by the public
Identificatory	Identification with business partners to develop and trade products	Identification with espoused beliefs, and so partnerships formed to support and defend beliefs	Identification between individual and society, where pluralism is tolerated and regulated through rule of law

and experience inclusive learning; second, the use of mixed ability teaching, whereby within the classroom there was social mixing and respect for all learners; third, the establishment of teaching as a graduate and trained profession; and fourth, the ascendancy of local government in administering the national system locally. The profession in schools and local authorities were trusted through practice, roles and through identificatory association to run education as a public service and were accountable daily to parents and children, and educational decisions by local councillors could be challenged or supported through the ballot box. Consequently, as Carr and Hartnett (1996) have argued, the relationship between schools and democratic development is not 'to *defend* democracy by *reproducing* society, but to *create* democracy by *transforming* society' (p. 199, emphasis in original).

The neoliberal and neoconservative positions broke away from the post-war consensus generated by the civic approach and did so by challenging public confidence in the profession. Prime Minister Callaghan's Ruskin speech in 1976 argued that teachers 'must satisfy the parents and industry that what you are doing meets their requirements and the needs of the children' (James Callaghan, speech at Ruskin College, Oxford, October 1976, quoted in Chitty, 1989, pp. 93–94). For the neoconservatives, teachers and local authorities could not be trusted because they generated a curriculum that was considered to be too progressive and transformative. Roles and professional identification had generated producer capture, where teachers operated in their own rather than parental and business interests, and indeed had created a privileged position over the control of the curriculum. So whereas Christian religious education was the only part of the curriculum required by law and the public funded religious schools, other parts of the curriculum gave recognition to belief systems that were not supported, e.g. the shift away from discrete subjects towards integrated projects and learning schemes and from teacher-led pedagogy towards individual, group and place-based learning. Cox and Dyson (1968) launched a *Fight for Education*, in which they exposed that 'at primary school some teachers are taking to an extreme belief that children must not be told anything, but must find it for themselves. At the post-eleven stage there is a strong impetus to abolish streaming, and the grammar school concepts of discipline and hard work are treated with contempt' (p. 1). The National Curriculum from 1988 was a victory for this position as it laid out and encoded the knowledge, skills and understanding that all children had to be taught and tested against, and together with performance management of teachers, it presented strong moral and social control over professional practice.

For the neoliberals, the state being involved in the delivery of what is essentially a private matter is at the core of the problem of public education. High-profile and influential texts illustrated this internationally (e.g. Chubb and Moe, 1990; Osborne and Gaebler, 1993; Bobbitt, 2002) and in England (Tooley, 1996). Democratic politicians and the experts they employed (e.g. teachers) were regarded as *the* problem, with arguments 'castigating teachers for their professional self-interest, their monopolisation of provision, their constant expansion of the curriculum and demands for greater resources' (Ozga, 1995, p. 27). The solution was through markets, where the quality of provision improves when parents 'voice' their needs and 'exit' a service if it is not meeting them. Without this, all that a person can do is put up with the situation or perhaps complain (Tooley, 1995). This position generated projects designed to ensure that schools and staff accepted and embraced this modernized professionalism, and so a number of reforms took place: first, from 1988, schools were turned into small businesses located in a quasi-market, with the right to hire and fire staff, with income based on pupil enrolment; second, teachers were re-cultured as entrepreneurs, running a business based on calculative and repeat-business forms of trust, and so performance targets and pay was introduced together with regulatory inspections by Ofsted from 1992; third, the composition of the school workforce was remodelled with teachers' work (e.g. their caring and pastoral responsibilities) taken away, and training was used to inculcate the preferred model of delivering externally codified and accredited curriculum programmes; and, fourth, the school became data rich, enabling schools and teachers to compare both internally and externally (see DfES, 2004) and to enable children and parents to calculate and demand improvements in performance. More radical projects were also generated, where the aim was not to just improve publicly funded schools but to remove them from local public control. This has two features: schools were 'taken over' by private interests through leaving the local authority, e.g. Grant Maintained Status based on a public ballot from 1988; and from 2000, private individuals and companies could replace local authority schools as academies and, in return for a modest investment, were able to access public funding (Gunter, 2011). The second feature is a 'start-up' approach, where the Conservative-led coalition from 2010 have allowed new schools to be set up based on groups making a case for public investment along the lines of the 'free' schools in Sweden (Gunter, 2011). Importantly, nationally agreed terms and conditions of service for teachers do not automatically apply in these schools, and non-qualified people may be teaching children.

The challenge to teachers that they could not be trusted through practice, role and identificatory processes saw a return to a basic calculative form of trust, which in turn demanded risk management. In order to trust a teacher, the opportunity to exercise judgement and discretion had to be controlled. So there has been 'direct integration' (Tilly, 2005, p. 7) of the teaching profession (composition, identity and practice) into government policy and the 'indirect integration' (Tilly, 2005, p. 7) of the teaching profession into contracted providers of educational services, where they can 'bargain with each other and with governments over the allocation of politically mediated costs and benefits.' Therefore, from 1988 there was strong centralization through the national curriculum, data collection and performance tables combined with decentralization with the school located in a marketplace seeking advantage and distinction. New Labour, from 1997, sought to revitalize and modernize the status of the profession through making a case for more centralization, and Morris's (2001) *Professionalism and Trust* speech lays out the requirement for the local leadership of reforms (Gunter, 2012), and 'her pamphlet suggests little more than that the enormous raft of legislative and accountability checks put in place over the last 20 years will now make professional action so predictable and controllable that they can be "trusted" to be autonomous, because they will hardly dare to venture (or even to think) out of line' (Bottery, 2003, p. 248). Consequently, teachers now work within an environment where trust is likely to be in short supply, and Bottery (2003) is helpful in understanding this because he identifies a difference between 'trusting to' and 'being trusted' because 'trusting someone can be little more than a pragmatic calculation, whereas *being trusted* evokes very different emotions, being seen by many of those upon whom the judgement is made as being a moral judgement about them and their character' (Bottery, 2003, p. 246, emphasis in original). Highly centralized regulation of the curriculum, teaching and learning outcomes show that the profession is trusted to deliver through a combination of training and performance management and fear because schools and individuals were blamed, shamed or closed/sacked if they got it wrong.

TRUST AND DECEPTION

The reality of how teachers have positioned themselves at a time of regulated trust is varied. There is evidence of enthusiasm, rejection and mediation. Often, the teacher tries to protect what they believe in, and using remodelling the school workforce as an example, they make a poorly thought through and/or hurried reform work, without too much damage to children and learning (see Gunter, 2005; Gunter and Forrester, 2009). There is a range of writing and research that shows the problematics of the current situation, with broad meta-analysis of the impact of data-driven forms of accountability on the social fabric (Judt, 2010) and on organizational processes (Inglis, 1985). For education there are accounts about the detrimental impact on the system (e.g. Beckett, 2007; Ravitch, 2010), professional practice (e.g. Arrowsmith, 2001) and children as learners (e.g. Fielding, 1999). As O'Neill (2002) has argued, the drive towards more technical accountability and transparency has generated a situation where '*perverse incentives are real incentives*' (p. 55, emphasis in original):

> In the end, the new culture of accountability provides incentives for arbitrary and unprofessional choices. Lecturers may publish prematurely because their department's research rating and its funding require it. Schools may promote certain subjects in which it is easier to get 'As' in public examinations. Hospital trusts have to focus on waiting lists even where these are not the most significant measures of medical quality. To add to their grief, the Sisyphean task of pushing institutional performance up the league tables is made harder by constantly redefining and adding targets and introductive initiatives, and of course with no account taken of the costs of competing for initiative funding (p. 56).

Consequently, claims to reduce state power have actually seen it increase, largely because neoliberal markets need the state to protect and enhance private activity (Marquand, 2004), and claims that markets deliver more opportunity have faced evidence of the widening of the equity gap, with implications for health, education and the social fabric (Wilkinson and Pickett, 2009). Such perverse effects are clearly evident at school level: first, the New Labour investment in the profession to improve status has also seen fewer graduates wanting to be trained or to stay in the profession (Butt and Gunter, 2007), with continued equity issues regarding race and gender (McNamara et al., 2009, 2010); second, the increase in testing with data about performance, where children and teachers learn to do just what is needed to pass and no more (Galton, 2007) and where performance-related pay generates suspicion rather than teamwork (Cutler and Waine, 2000); third, a school can pass an Ofsted inspection, and yet staff and students can find themselves told to improve by reaching politically established benchmarks (such as 30% A*–C grades at Key Stage 4) or close down (Maddern, 2010); fourth, parents who are positioned as the determinants of educational quality through choice and voice but are no longer allowed to vote for changes to the ownership of schools (Gunter, 2011). What seems to be at the core of the problem is the emphasis on transparency, and O'Neill (2002) argues that:

> unless the individuals and institutions who sort, process and assess information are themselves already trusted, there is little reason to think that transparency and openness are going to increase trust. Transparency can encourage people to be less honest, so increasing deception and reducing reasons for trust: those who know that everything they say or write is to be made public may massage the truth. Public reports may underplay sensitive information; head teachers and employers may write blandly uninformative reports and references; evasive and uninformative statements may substitute for truth-telling. Demands for universal transparency are likely to encourage the evasions, hypocrisies and half-truths that we usually refer to as 'political correctness', but which might more forthrightly be called either 'self-censorship' or 'deception'. (p. 73)

We intend taking this forward by examining the evidence and impact of deception on and by the teaching profession through the use of technical forms of accountability and transparency in New Labour educational reforms. We will do this by drawing on data collected through the Social Practices of School Organisation (SPSO) project (Hall et al., 2011), where we completed three stages of data collection, including interviews with a stratified sample staff; a case study of a decision-making process, including documentary analysis, observations and interviews; and an analysis of individual views through a Q-sort, including follow-up interviews. Based on this data, we have developed five portraits of secondary schools in regard to the discursive practices of leadership, and whereas all these schools are accountable and transparent in regard to data and professional practice, with careful checking for compliance, we intend to use edited extracts from three of these to illuminate how deception operates.

Lime Tree

Our study of the approach to leadership and management has focused on consultation in the decision-making process. In terms of role and structure, the head teacher is senior to other members of staff, and externally driven reforms require the head teacher to implement and be accountable.

The deception being promoted in this school is that all staff are consulted through a form of what is called 'dispersed leadership', because the form of trust is generally calculative and practice based, and only senior leaders show forms of role and identificatory trust.

One of the key forms of staff consultation is after-school group sessions that include the entire teaching and support staff. The head described it as a 'tried and tested' method that they have used for a number of different developments, and for what he has described as some 'quite substantial changes'. He argues that it leads to more lasting outcomes because people can't say they have been railroaded into something that they disagree with:

> no one can say they haven't been consulted and, at the end of the day, while you will always get criticism and a cynical view, no one, hand on heart, can say 'this had been done to me' . . . its quite powerful to be able to say 'as we discussed', 'as we've agreed', so in terms of making the policy work then there is a feeling that you've got the critical mass of opinion that is very much for it.

Implicit within this approach is a form of control by contract, whereby those who have engaged in the compulsory consultative process are not legitimately able to subsequently complain about the nature of the decision-making process or, by implication, the decision itself. However, staff reported that senior leaders made major decisions, often without consultation, with a sense of resignation that change will happen regardless. Others are more dissatisfied:

> I think there's a danger sometimes that the people at the top think it's being cascaded down and it isn't necessarily. So they are under the impression we all know the rationale but we don't . . . that's why you don't feel valued because you're just being told what to do and no one's asking you 'do you see any value in it?' And I think that's what's perhaps the biggest—that's what's changing.

The overall interpretation of our research at Lime Tree is that the foregrounding of concepts such as dispersed leadership, consultation and empowerment do not reflect the actuality of the decision-making process which continues to be dominated by both the head teacher and key externally determined factors. The process is largely linked to matters of operational rather than strategic matters and is best viewed primarily as a tool for making staff 'feel' that they are being consulted. It is a technique that is viewed both by designated leaders and some others as preferable to enforcing new policies and changes in practice. This contradiction between the directive nature of school policies and the use of consultations is understood by many teachers, especially those lower in the organizational hierarchy. This has not resulted in widespread dissent within the school, although this is evident in some responses—indeed, the confidence in the leadership of the school is high—nor has it resulted in widespread enthusiasm to participate in more meaningful consultations; a number of those surveyed were content for school-level decision-making to remain centralized and closed off.

Cherry Tree

Our study of leadership and management has focused on how change has taken place since the appointment of a new head following a decline in standards and poor Ofsted grading. The deception operating in this school is that teaching and learning had to improve, but the real emphasis was on securing head teacher control, and the approach to trust is mainly based on calculation and practice.

Cherry Tree was widely described by interviewees as being on the verge of going into Special Measures when the previous head left in 2006. Following his appointment, the new head's judgement of the situation was that peer assessments of teaching were unrealistically high, given that levels of student performance were so low. He made initial changes to the school; a key moment then arose, in the form of a financial crisis: 'six weeks into the job I uncovered a projected deficit that nobody in the authority (LA) or the governors or anybody knew about' (head teacher). This had two main consequences: first, the staffing of the school was significantly reduced; and, second, the leadership of the school was significantly restructured: 'I made the entire row of assistant head teachers redundant which solved some leadership issues and some financial issues and then was able to create a new layer of directors' (head teacher). He was able to do this without negative responses: 'nobody blamed me . . . I was right at the eye of the storm.'

The head's strong, engaging and relentlessly enthusiastic character has been central to the changes that have occurred at Cherry Tree. His leadership has been very much in the transformative mould, where the sheer force and energy of his personality have been used to galvanize the school. The central importance of the head's vision was strongly underlined by a senior leader: 'I mean Mike's absolutely stunning with the vision, he's absolutely brilliant at knowing where he wants to be and inspiring' (senior leader). Indeed, the head confirms this: 'to begin with I wore my underpants on the outside of my trousers and flew around like superman but that's an unsustainable model' (head teacher). Staff now have the autonomy to complete tasks and undertake responsibilities, and staff are positive about this: 'I think you are given room, areas where you can you know you are given freedom to lead and you're given that space' (middle leader). The head is passionate about distributed leadership and preaches this philosophy to his staff, although the term is used in the school much more by the head than by other members of staff. Whilst staff are happy to recognize the presence of distributed leadership in the school, there are comments, usually delivered in a humorous manner, suggesting that this approach to leadership enables the head to pass responsibilities to others and free himself up. It seems that the head has two approaches: one that is about getting things done and underway, what he calls 'splattered leadership', and one that is tightly controlled, where practice is about delivering the vision. The head's aim is to become an executive head at Cherry Tree, gradually moving back from a more hands-on approach and leaving two deputy heads, 'two people working at headship level', in charge of the school.

Birch Tree

Our study of leadership and management focused on how the head teacher has led and established a new school as an academy in an area of socio-economic disadvantage. An inspection in 2009 highlighted strengths in the school leadership and reported good progress in raising levels of student attainment. The deception operating in this school is that effectiveness and improvement are based on a head teacher who is benign and inclusive, whereas in reality it has been through the exclusion of staff who did not fit with what the head teacher wanted to do. The approach is to manufacture the role and identificatory forms of trust through the exclusion of people who do not fit, hence avoiding the need for calculation and to practice forms of trust.

Since Birch Tree was created, there has been a significant turnover of staff. By 2008 just 25% of the teaching staff and 50% of the support staff remained from the predecessor schools. Comments from the head teacher strongly suggest that this high level of turnover was viewed positively:

> I absolutely 100% knew that I was not taking all them shit people out of the predecessor schools . . . I wasn't prepared to have them because I know that if you give me two rusty sheds at the bottom of the garden and excellent people, I'll give you a school. You can't give me a building like this and crap teachers, the kids will wreck the building.

Self-presentation by the head is as someone who is highly knowledge-able: 'so, I've been a head teacher before and I turned around one of the worst schools in the country and made it one of the most improved,' with official recognition of the approach taken: '[Ofsted] came in on the target setting visit, I mean I had a letter from the Prime Minister and everything saying "brilliant, well done".' External validation of standards is central to the school and permeates teacher discourse, and one senior leader states: 'The remit I've been given from [the head] is that at the next Ofsted we have outstanding at teaching and learning, so basically my job description is to get us there.' Key to this is a reaffirmation of success is by repeatedly making negative statements about local authorities and the predecessor schools, emphasizing how bad things were before, which serves to exaggerate how good things are now. The following statements were made within the first eight minutes of the first interview: 'the two schools the academy replaced were dreadful; . . . the predecessor school, where they all came from, the one that was truly shit where most of them came from; I knew that local authorities were about levelling down, and I really relish the independence of the academy.'

This is underlined by comments from other staff approving of the removal of staff regarded as being unable or unwilling to 'sign up' to the vision or remaining 'on message'. There are frequent references to turnover of 'off-message staff':

> we've only been together a few years, lots of the really negative people either didn't come and also to be fair your traditional skivers, you know the ones who always seem to have quite a few Mondays off or don't do their reports ever or skive meetings, the head won't tolerate . . . I can think of 20 people who have started here but are no longer here for that very reason . . . you know staff . . . just didn't fit into the ethos (senior leader).

The morale of those interviewed appeared high, and they spoke with real enthusiasm about the school and what they believe is being achieved there. This sense of being part of a successful school was intimately tied to the almost exclusively highly affirmative statements about the head's leadership and an understanding of leadership as hierarchical: 'I think the leadership here is really good; it's the way; you feel very supported and very managed in a good way, in a safe way that you are given the opportunities to further your career which in many schools you wouldn't' (emergent leader). Notions of distribution are, in fact, delegation, where the hierarchically endowed leader passes down authority to those lower in the organizational structure: 'what distributed leadership isn't is a democracy, and sometimes I'll say the problem you've all got is you think this is a democracy and it ain't because frankly I get paid a lot of money and the reason I get paid a lot of money is because the buck stops here' (head teacher).

The staff are incredibly, almost unnaturally, cohesive—at all stages of the research, the degree of dissent from authorized and approved views of the school was very limited: 'if you are not seen as being supportive on school policies and you are not supporting the school ethos, it doesn't really look very good' (middle leader). One senior leader described how it was acceptable to disagree with the head but that it was not done in an open arena; staff moaning is not done in the staff room but quietly behind closed doors. Any 'underground' activity is regarded as rather subversive, and one middle leader felt it to be damaging to the school: 'I think some people will just happily go along with the flow and then some people get very frustrated and I think when people get very frustrated obviously they just leave and move on.'

These three stories illuminate that there are elements of the civic position, particularly the humanist and collegial discourse of caring for and about people's views (Jeffrey, 2002), but, overall, across the three schools an alliance of neoliberal and neoconservative positions is evident. It seems that public confidence must be established in Birch Tree, secured in Cherry Tree and maintained at Lime Tree through strong leadership.

Schools are businesses required to deliver standards, and private interests must be protected; communities who do not have the resources to secure this themselves are presented with and compelled to accept the identified higher standards brought about by radical reforms of teachers and their work. Calculative forms of trust are used, and the profession is largely found wanting, and so investment by private philanthropy and by parents who expect their values to underpin education is conditional on a form of regulatory trust. It is what Scott and Dinham (2002) have characterized as teachers finding 'themselves subjected to "carrots" and "sticks" designed to entice or force them into activities believed to facilitate "quality improvement"' (p. 30). Our cases show that risk management of non- or partial compliance is handled either through the exclusion of people or by the compulsory participation of people in decision-making events, and this creates a fear-dependency by other staff. There is clear evidence of conformity with a leader-centric disposition. Control of schools is through heads who are highly knowledgeable about what needs to be done, who respond to the heroic model of headship presented as good practice from the 1980s onwards (Grace, 1995), and who can respond locally to what is needed. At Lime Tree, the head teacher knows that autocracy will not work in a school where standards have been generally good, and so staff have to be brought along in any major change; whereas at Cherry Tree and Birch Tree, the situation is such that the heads have a licence to clear out and appoint new staff that will be compliant with the new regime.

Whereas research for New Labour governments repeatedly showed that the most important people in a school are the teachers (e.g. Leithwood et al., 2006), the emphasis was put on the head teacher as the local deliverer of reform, and heads were given the status, pay and training to do this. Practice and identificatory forms of trust are narrowly defined around the type of professionals who are allowed or possibly tolerated, and the communication of the vision is used to speak into existence what the situation is and how it needs to be better. Avis (2003) identifies this as a form of 'conditional trust', with the teacher seen as a 'trusted servant' (p. 329), or, to reuse Bottery's (2003) distinction, it seems that staff are *trusted to* deliver, but there is little or no evidence of staff *being trusted*. Indeed, New Labour's rebranding of delegation as distributed leadership is used in the schools to move work down the line and ensure that all are accountable and transparent for examination results. The deception created by this is evident in the schools: at Lime Tree, strategy for key decisions such as the budget and staffing remains centralized, and consultation on operational matters acts as a disciplinary process. At Cherry Tree, the external demand to improve teaching and learning is an opportunity for the head teacher to demonstrate an approved of leadership style that will not only meet Ofsted requirements but also generate a professional portfolio that will improve his career opportunities. At Birch Tree, the external demand to make the New Labour Academies Programme work and the career aspirations of the head teacher to run a number of schools has enabled the control of the workforce through a 'shape up or ship out' culture. Heads are repositories of leadership, and they give it out, take it back, praise and criticize, as a means of delivering their goals. It seems that reforms over the past thirty years are based on a regulatory trust of heads to deliver, and the data-led system of tests and league tables have made this transparent. The perverse incentives are that heads have replicated the external regulation of themselves internally, and whereas the data may show improvement, the net effect has been to remove opportunities for discretion, or 'teacher proof' schools, where approved-of practice generates and constitutes dependency on those who are organizationally privileged and powerful.

The respondents in our project have worked hard to be officially and technically accountable and transparent, but in yielding to external and developing internal regulation they have in reality brought into existence some serious deceptions; only a few (e.g. in Lime Tree) have the confidence to see and speak things differently. Whereas data abound within and about schools regarding test outcomes and are used to calculate the worth of teachers to continue in the job, it is highly problematic. As O'Neill (2002) states:

> *Well-placed trust grows out of active inquiry rather than blind acceptance.* In traditional relations of trust, active inquiry was usually extended over time by talking and asking questions, by listening and seeing how well claims to know and undertakings to act held up. That was the world in which Socrates placed his trust . . . where we can check the information we receive, and when we can go back to those who put it into circulation, we may gain confidence about placing or refusing trust. (p. 76)

It seems to us that this is not in play currently in English schools; at best, there are some cynics who may voice issues but who may be prepared to just get on with the job on the basis that life is easier and after all, 'you win some, you lose some'. But in reality, schools are being cleansed of thinkers who link their practice to wider civic concerns, and, consequently, teachers who cannot display a soul (Ball, 2003) may speak about and in favour of data, but they are unable to speak about pedagogy and learning.

SUMMARY

The attack on civic approaches to trust in teachers is different to Scotland, where there is a 'greater confidence in teachers' in enabling education to be key to nation-building (Menter et al., 2004, p. 211). It seems that teachers in England are politically located at an intersection between civic, neoliberal and neoconservative positions, and this is creating a confusing and complex situation where conformity brings simplicity, and at a time of accountability and transparency, the way power is being exercised reveals some challenging deceptions. Hard-working and well-meaning people are located in situations where they both manipulate and are manipulated on the basis that they are not to be trusted. O'Neill (2002) argues that what we need to work towards is a form of 'intelligent accountability' (p. 58), based on 'good governance and fewer fantasies about total control' (p. 58), and that is only possible if people are trusted to serve the public. The implication of this for accountability is that there is a need to enable people 'who are called to account . . . to give an account of what they have done, and of their successes or failures, to others who have sufficient time and experience to assess the evidence and report on it' (p. 58). The everyday process of accountability and transparency of activity in classrooms, corridors and playgrounds is a space where investment can be made in pedagogy as a relational and often unmeasurable process.

NOTE

1. We would like to acknowledge the ESRC funding of the project (RES-000-22-3610) and Joanna Bragg, who as research assistant and co-applicant worked intensively on data collection and analysis.

REFERENCES

Arrowsmith, R. (2001) A Right Performance. In: Gleeson, D. and Husbands, C., eds. *The Performing School*. London: Routledge Falmer, pp. 33–43.
Avis, J. (2003) Re-Thinking Trust in a Performative Culture: The Case of EDUCA-Tion. *Journal of Education Policy*, 18(3), pp. 315–332.
Ball, S. J. (2003) The Teacher's Soul and the Terrors of Performativity. *Journal of Education Policy*, 18(2), pp. 215–228.
Beckett, F. (2007) *The Great City Academy Fraud*. London: Continuum.
Bobbitt, P. (2002) *The Shield of Achilles*. London: Penguin.
Bottery, M. (1998) *Professionals and Policy*. London: Cassell.
——— (2003) The Management and Mismanagement of Trust. *Educational Management and Administration*, 31(3), pp. 245–261.
Butt, G. and Gunter, H. M., eds. (2007) *Modernizing Schools: People, Learning and Organizations*. London: Continuum.
Carr, W. and Hartnett, A. (1996) *Education and the Struggle for Democracy*. Buckingham: Oxford University Press.
Chitty, C. (1989) *Towards a New Education System: The Victory of the New Right?* London: Falmer Press.
Chubb, J. E. and Moe, T. M. (1990) *Politics, Markets and America's Schools*. Washington, DC: The Brookings Institution.
Codd, J. (2005) Teachers as 'Managed Professionals' in the Global Education Industry: The New Zealand Experience. *Educational Review*, 57(2), pp. 193–206.

Cox, C. B. and Dyson, A. E., eds. (1968) *Fight for Education: A Black Paper*. London: The Critical Quarterly Society.

Cutler, T. and Waine, B. (2000) Mutual Benefits or Managerial Control? The Role of Appraisal in Performance Related Pay for Teachers. *British Journal of Educational Studies*, 48(2), pp. 170–182.

DfES (2004) *Smoking Out Underachievement, Guidance and Advice to Help Secondary Schools Use Value Added Approaches with Data*. London: DfES.

Fielding, M. (1999) Target Setting, Policy Pathology and Student Perspectives: Learning to Labour in New Times. *Cambridge Journal of Education*, 29(2), pp. 277–287.

Galton, M. (2007) New Labour and Education: An Evidence-Based Analysis. *Forum*, 49(1/2), pp. 157–177.

Grace, G. (1995) *School Leadership: Beyond Educational Management*. London: Falmer Press.

Gunter, H. M. (2005) *Leading Teachers*. London: Continuum.

Gunter, H. M., ed. (2011) *The State and Education Policy: The Academies Programme*. London: Continuum.

Gunter, H. M. (2012) *Leadership and the Reform of Education*. Bristol: Policy Press.

Gunter, H. M. and Forrester, G. (2009) Education Reform and School Leadership. In: Brookes, S. and Grint, K., eds. *The Public Sector Leadership Challenge*. London: Palgrave, pp. 54–69.

Hall, D., Gunter, H. M. and Bragg, J. (2011) *Distributed Leadership and the Social Practices of School Organisation*. Report to the ESRC. Swindon: ESRC.

Inglis, F. (1985) *The Management of Ignorance*. Oxford: Blackwell.

Jeffrey, B. (2002) Performativity and Primary Teacher Relations. *Journal of Education Policy*, 17(5), pp. 531–546.

Judt, T. (2010) *Ill Fares the Land*. New York: Penguin Press.

Leithwood, K., Day, C., Sammons, P., Harris, A. and Hopkins, D. (2006) *Seven Strong Claims about Successful School Leadership*. Nottingham: NCSL.

Lightfoot, L. (1991) Back to the Blackboard. *The Mail on Sunday*, 10 November, p. 1.

Maddern, K. (2010) Outstanding School Is a National Challenge Failure. *The Times Educational Supplement*, 3 June. Available at: http://www.tes.co.uk/article.aspx?storycode=6045164.

Marquand, D. (2004) *Decline of the Public*. Cambridge: Polity Press.

McNamara, O., Howson, J., Gunter, H. M. and Fryers, A. (2009) *The Leadership Aspirations and Careers of Black and Ethnic Minority Teachers*. Birmingham: NASUWT.

McNamara, O., Howson, J., Gunter, H. M. and Fryers, A. (2010) *No Job for a Woman: The Impact of Gender in School Leadership*. Birmingham: NASUWT.

Menter, I., Mahony, P. and Hextall, I. (2004) Ne'er the Twain Shall Meet? Modernizing the Teaching Profession in Scotland and England. *Journal of Education Policy*, 19(2), pp. 195–214.

Morris, E. (2001) *Professionalism and Trust: Social Market Foundation Speech*. London: DfES.

Newman, J. and Clarke, J. (2009) *Publics, Politics and Power*. London: Sage.

O'Neill, O. (2002) *A Question of Trust*. Cambridge: Cambridge University Press.

Osborne, D. and Gaebler, T. (1993) *Reinventing Government*. New York: Plume.

Ozga, J. (1995) Deskilling a Profession: Professionalism, Deprofessionalism and the New Managerialism. In: Busher, H. and Saran, R., eds. *Managing Teachers as Professionals in Schools*. London: Kogan Page, pp. 21–37.

Raffo, C., Dyson, A., Gunter, H. M, Hall, D., Jones, L. and Kalambouka, A., eds. (2010) *Education and Poverty in Affluent Countries*. London: Routledge.

Ravitch, D. (2010) *The Death and Life of the Great American School System*. New York: Basic Books.

Scott, C. and Dinham, S. (2002) The Beatings Will Continue until Quality Improves: Using Carrots and Sticks in the Quest for Educational Improvement. *Teacher Development*, 6(1), pp. 15–31.

Tilly, C. (2005) *Trust and Rule*. Cambridge: Cambridge University Press.

Tooley, J. (1995) Markets or Democracy for Education? A Reply to Stewart Ranson. *British Journal of Educational Studies*, 43(1), pp. 21–34.

Tooley, J. (1996) *Education without the State*. London: IJEA.

Wilkinson, R. and Pickett, K. (2009) *The Spirit Level*. London: Allen Lane.

12 Trust and Control in Children's Services

Adina Dudau and Georgios Kominis

This chapter explores the relationship between trust and control. We adopt a contingency perspective on this relationship as we argue that the United Kingdom (UK) government's choice, to either formally control or trust professionals working in children's services, is reliant on the level of uncertainty experienced in the policy realm. Extensive documentary research and a three-year-long observation of the work undertaken in a children's services partnership (between agencies providing outcomes for children in the local borough) in England revealed that, in an area where uncertainty about what keeps children safe from harm is considerable (and has arguably always been so), the government is embracing a philosophy of trust that departs quite fundamentally from the traditional 'mechanistic' system of control. Whereas the latter is still in place, there is an increasing body of evidence suggesting a shift towards trusting children's services professionals.

To speak of trust and control in children's services is rather timely in the midst of important policy developments in the area of children and families in England. All policy reviews since 2009 (e.g. Laming, 2009; HM Government, 2010; Munro, 2011) address the issue of public confidence in the front-line professionals and in the government as well as the trust and control links between the government and the professionals in children's services. The topic is most relevant in the aftermath of a thirty-year-long chain of adverse events with child victims (e.g. Department of Health [DoH], 1991; Laming, 2003), when the reputation of both the government and the front-line professionals is under close scrutiny. Whether these recent policy developments are a means to recover from a crisis of legitimation (Smith, 1990) or are part of a more fundamental and more sustainable change is yet to be seen. For what it is worth, however, some interesting conceptual changes seem to be emerging, and we contextualize these in a way that illuminates the trust and control nexus (e.g. Bijlsma-Frankema and Costa, 2005) in this policy context.

The evidence we have used to make our case consists mainly of policy documents (Children's Act 1989, Children's Act 2004, HM Government 2006), government-commissioned reports (Laming, 2009; Munro, 2011) and national inquiry reports into the death of two children: Maria Colwell

(Department of Health and Social Security [DHSS], 1974) and Victoria Climbié (Laming, 2003). This body of documentary evidence was corroborated with the conclusions of a three-year period of observation of the work undertaken in a Local Safeguarding Children's Board (LSCB) in north-west England by professionals, including social workers, police constables, health professionals and teachers.

UNPACKING THE CONCEPTS

To justify the conceptual suitability of using a theory of control systems to inform our study of trust and control in children's services, we need to reveal a number of key assumptions we are making in this chapter. First, we assume governments to be not only regulators of organizations, but also large and complex organizations in their own right (Murray, 1975); hence, organizational theories apply to them. Indeed, governments function on the same principles as any organization. There are leadership strategies which have followers as well as opposition, implementers, operations, beneficiaries and management-control systems to keep organizational elements aligned. More important, governments, like all organizations, are placed within an ever-changing external environment to which they must react to 'survive'. The recent economic crisis in Europe revealed clearly how poor appraisal of the external environment can lead to bankruptcy of the state and resort to unpopular financial policies that can further lead to loss of political mandate.

If governments are large organizations where citizens are stakeholders who can hire or fire their managers, it is important for the latter to ensure that their strategies have the desired impact at the implementation point. One way to ensure that is through control: 'a regulatory process through which work outcomes are made more predictable through the establishment of standards set up towards desired objective' (Bijlsma-Frankema and Costa, 2005, p. 259). In line with our first assumption, that the government is an organization itself, regulation is taken to be the type of control (bureaucratic control—see Edwards, 1979) that is exercised to determine policy outcomes (Simpson, 1985; Hood et al., 2000). Does this mean that trust, which, semantically speaking, is the opposite of control, occurs when regulation is absent?

In this chapter, we speak of trust in professionals when government regulations either are minimal or leave considerable 'grey areas' where professionals can exercise autonomy by interpreting general regulations to fit the specific contexts in which they work. Conversely, when the government issues vast amount of regulations to ensure that professionals deal with these appropriately, we face a situation of distrust in professionals where control is tight (e.g. Harlow and Shardlow, 2006). Conceptually, trust and control are therefore taken to be substitutes, in line with most of the literature on the trust and control (e.g. Costa and Bijlsma-Frankema, 2007; Edelenbos and

Eshuis, 2009), yet their usage in organizations can overlap to some extent, as formal control systems are likely to exist in organizations where a level of trust to organizational members is recognized (Weibel, 2007). This happens where the level of complexity of work is so high that measurement is problematic (Alvesson and Lindkvist, 1993; Edelenbos and Eshuis, 2009).

But who are the professionals we refer to, and how are they either 'trusted' or 'controlled' by the government? In the policy area analysed here, professionals are those delivering policy outcomes for children and young people—namely, social workers, police constables, health professionals, teachers, and educationalists, as well as people from newer occupations coming from various combinations of these professional backgrounds (such as youth offending officers). We will often refer to them collectively as 'welfare professionals' or 'children's services professionals'. Professionals base their work on competing formal knowledge foundations (Hallett and Stevenson, 1980)—for example, social forms of knowledge for social workers or biological knowledge for medical staff—while tackling the same overall social problems, albeit from different directions. Responsibility for the work they do is carried partly by themselves and the professional bodies to which they belong and report and partly by the government, which is accountable to the public for the ways in which these social problems are tackled. In terms of their professional freedom, Freidson (1984) sustains that the more accessible their skill and knowledge (the less technical, that is) is by laypeople, the less autonomy professionals will enjoy and the more challenged they will be by government regulations (usually as a response to cases of malpractice as well as to growth of the organizations where these professionals work). This is very relevant in the case of children's services professionals that have endured in the last nearly four decades various waves of regulatory challenges to their professional autonomy (e.g. Parton 2004, 2009).

TRUST AND CONTROL AS CONTROL SYSTEMS

If the concepts of trust and control are opposite in meaning yet overlapping in practice, the only way to operationalize them in a study of organizations is to assume that control can be exercised in a number of ways, with some more conducive to trust than others. We build this argument with reference to the management-control theory of 'feedback' and 'feed-forward' systems of control (Kloot, 1997).

Feedback systems of control are based on the cybernetic model: strategic objectives are identified and translated into measurable key performance indicators (KPIs); performance is measured against the targets set for these KPIs; the diagnosis imposes either rewards for achievement, or corrective actions to enforce desired behaviour (Emmanuel et al., 1990). Information-flow feedback loops ensure the continuous adjustment of the system and its viability within the given environmental conditions (Anthony and Young,

2003). The basic design of feedback control systems is seen to rest upon four fundamental assumptions—that the objectives of the controlled process can be specified clearly, that the results of the process can be measured accurately, that the predictive model underlying the process specifies clearly both the critical factors that determine the achievement of objectives and the cause–effect relationships among them and, finally, that there is capability for and freedom to take corrective action so that deviations from objectives can be reduced (Otley and Berry, 1980). In effect, feedback control systems assume a relatively complete understanding of the environment within which the organization operates and of the critical performance variables which determine its survival and success in it. It is on the basis of these four assumptions, implying an accurate predictive model (Tocher, 1976), that top management opt for an emphasis on centralized, top-down control.

In contrast to feedback systems, where control takes place after the event, in a feed-forward system the process of organizational information-seeking, -gathering and analysis occurs before the event. In advance of the actual process taking place, predicted outputs (rather than the actual outputs of the feedback model) are compared to the planned outputs (Kloot, 1997). Any deviation between planned and predicted outputs results then in corrective action being undertaken in advance of the actual event (Emmanuel et al., 1990). In this way, expected environmental changes can be anticipated and allowed for in the planning stage if the predicted outputs do not match the planned outputs. The design of any feed-forward system of control is essentially based on two implicit assumptions. One is that all organizations operate within more or less changing environments, which create ever-new uncertainties and contingencies that threaten to invalidate the organization's current strategy. The second assumption is that the predictive model at the disposal of the people responsible for the strategic planning at the centre of the organization is less complete than that in the hands of those charged with the day-to-day running of the various operations at the periphery of the organization. The latter group, being closer to and in constant interaction with the everyday realities of the organization's external environment and the changes that it undergoes, possess more detailed, up-to-date and relevant models of the specific activities for which they are responsible. Hence, this type of control offers more discretion to front-line professionals than the feedback type does.

In practice, feed-forward systems of control can take the form of frequent, interactive face-to-face meetings among managers from different parts of the organization, to review strategic performance measurement reports on constantly changing information that top management considers to be of strategic importance, or wider forums for interhierarchical discussion, within which the dynamics of a constantly changing environment are discussed and alternative action plans are considered (Kloot, 1997).

The distinction between feedback and feed-forward systems of control reflects that between control and trust. Analysing changes in children's services professionals' work, Parton (2004) asserts that the introduction of systems and procedures aimed at achieving more predictable outputs, whilst simultaneously serving the purpose of a more transparent and accountable system to the public, also had the unintended consequence of undermining the trust in the professionals (see also Parton, 2009). This in turn had an impact upon their morale and mutual confidence. Others (e.g. Cooper, 2005; Harlow and Shardlow, 2006) supported this thesis of undermined professional autonomy and authority leading to professionals' work being reduced to executing primary, mechanical tasks while being devoid of the time and space to engage in 'thoughtful processes' (Reder and Duncan, 2004). As a remedy to this trend towards 'deprofessionalization' (e.g. Freidson, 1984), various authors advise on the necessity to allow the professionals the time to reflect and offer their professionally trained 'situated judgement' (Parton, 1998) on the cases needing intervention. This can be interpreted as a call to revert to a situation of trust in professionals, trust that they would use their professional knowledge to improve the lives of their clients (service users). The ways in which government regulations can embrace this philosophy of trust is through another type of control than that used within the 'audit explosion'; we argue it is a case of interactive, feed-forward type of control.

A CONTINGENCY THEORY PERSPECTIVE: THE ROLE OF UNCERTAINTY

Both the management-control and the organizational-behaviour literature utilize contingency theory to make sense of how strategies can be translated into desired outcomes in various circumstances. Simpson (1985) uses the theory to argue that the external environment can determine how bureaucratic, in the Weberian sense, organizations can be. As Weber's (1971) theory of bureaucracy emphasizes the idea of hierarchical control and rational organization of work, Simpson's argument can be interpreted to mean that the external environment can determine the use of more or less rigid systems of control by organizations. This inference takes us to the theory of 'fit', put forward by management-control theorists, that external circumstances dictate the effectiveness of control design (Emmanuel et al., 1990). In particular, uncertainty in the environment dictates the need to balance traditional 'feedback' with more interactive 'feed-forward' systems of control (Simons, 1995).

At the conceptual level, Perrow's (1967) definition of uncertainty provides a two-dimensional view of internal environmental uncertainty, capturing in particular task variability (or number of exceptions) and task analysability. Perrow describes the variability dimension in terms of the frequency with which unexpected and novel events occur in the process of performing one's tasks, whereas the task analysability dimension refers to the extent to which work can be reduced to programmable, mechanical steps. In environments characterized by low levels of uncertainty, the main key variables can be more precisely identified; means–end relationships are well understood;

the results of managerial action can be more accurately predicted; decision-making and action-taking are largely programmable; the information asymmetry between top- and middle-level management is comparatively low; and the generation and use of data for planning and control purposes is relatively straightforward, in that managerial behaviour is easier to predict, observe and measure. In these conditions, front-line professionals are typically expected to execute centrally decided, largely programmed decisions about mainly static, more or less well-defined, independent, structured and repetitive tasks. Under such conditions, systems of carefully selected performance indicators, preset targets and related incentives (or penalties) may be an effective means of control (Emmanuel et al., 1990).

At the other extreme, in conditions of high uncertainty, the critical success factors are, by definition, difficult to identify and are constantly changing; the means–end relationships are underspecified, that is, they are less clear and definite; the understanding of cause–effect relationships is incomplete; the incidence of unexpected and novel events is high; the nonprogrammed decision-making and action-taking is much more frequent and largely unavoidable; the level of task interdependency is substantially higher; the information asymmetry between top- and middle-level management about the means (i.e. the managerial actions) necessary to achieve the—anyway unclear—organizational ends (purposes) is high; and the ability of the organization to specify and document in advance, either procedures and desirable behaviours for its middle-level managers, or their exact domain of authority and responsibility, is necessarily limited (Emmanuel et al., 1990). Under these circumstances, front-line professionals have to contend with an increasing number of unexpected and novel events, which force them to engage, on a daily basis, in nonprogrammed decision-making about largely interdependent and overlapping tasks and activities. These tasks and activities may be difficult and impractical to specify and document in advance of their execution (Waterhouse and Tiessen, 1978). Under these conditions, devising control systems that are reliant on full knowledge and understanding of the environment is problematic, if not unrealistic, and is more likely to instigate a range of negative psychological and behavioural consequences (e.g. Hirst, 1983; Merchant, 1990; Simons, 1995).

The recognition of uncertainty as an integral part of the environment necessitates the delegation of decision-making authority from the central administration to front-line personnel, together with the resources necessary to achieve agreed goals. Under uncertain conditions, as Otley (1994) points out, the vital responsibility for the mechanisms of organizational adaptation cannot be left to a small team of senior managers at the top of the organizational hierarchy; rather, the 'management of change' increasingly requires the active involvement of front-line managers and professionals, who are trusted to possess more detailed and up-to-date predictive models of the external environment and, furthermore, to be able and ready to use their experience, intuition and judgement to provide solutions to largely unique problems (Emmanuel et al., 1990). In this context, the involvement of and dialogue between different parts of the organization for the examination of the assumptions underlying current strategies is vital. It is in this context that feed-forward systems of control have a critical role to play.

The environment in which the children's services operate is characterized by high uncertainty associated with the high level of risk when dealing with a vulnerable population. Because service users are exposed to a large number of risk factors (e.g. deprivation, substance abuse, domestic violence—see Parton, 2004) that are ever changing, policy makers as well as managers and professionals face high levels of uncertainty about what might make their interventions effective. The uncertainty in their work is revealed repeatedly by the unforeseen circumstances which lead to the policies becoming ineffective and which come to surface through the course of the investigation following adverse events in children's services (Parton 2004).

ILLUSTRATIONS FROM THE FIELD: TRUST AND CONTROL IN CHILDREN'S SERVICES IN ENGLAND

These theoretical assertions find application in the policy area of children and families in England. This policy area is infamous for numerous cases of children falling through the welfare net including the high-profile cases of Maria Colwell (1974) and Victoria Climbié (2001). Maria Colwell was beaten to death by her stepfather in 1973 after a long struggle to resist the ill-informed social services' decision to return her to her natural mother after five years of living with her uncle and aunt. Nearly three decades later, the eight-year-old Victoria Climbié died of malnutrition after a series of incidents involving her great-aunt, who passed for her mother in the eyes of the authorities and who used the loops in the system to hide her neglect of Victoria. The policy developments that followed attempted to address the failings by either strengthening or loosening control, and often both strategies were followed at the same time.

By way of history, many of the policy developments in this area were prompted by the public's reaction to the news of children falling through the welfare net. The reports of inquiry following each of these notorious cases reveal consistently poor communication between the various elements of the systems (e.g. agencies, professions). More important, however, the secondary data presented in these reports also reveal, we argue, how the design of the system supposed to protect children simply did not keep up with the dynamism of change in the policy domain. More to the point, in attempting to measure and control for contingencies, certain societal developments were unaccounted for and ultimately turned out to incubate risk which eventually developed into full-blown crises. Thus, in the process of making sense of the uncertainty of the many different individual cases, labels were attached to the various categories of vulnerable children—for example, 'children in need', 'children at risk' or 'significant harm'—and different procedures were designed to fit each of these labels. However, inquiry reports (DHSS, 1974; Laming, 2009) showed how some children fell between these categories. In the case of Victoria Climbié, every time a label was attached to her situation, she was effectively denied a service that she needed (Laming, 2003; Parton, 2004). The very assumptions on which the control systems were built were proven to be misconstrued, hence our argument about the unsettling terrain of uncertainty.

Munro, in her recently published review of child protection, states:

> Uncertainty pervades the work of child protection and trying to manage that uncertainty is central to the way the system has evolved since the 1970s. . . . The big problem for society (and consequently for professionals) is working out a realistic expectation of professionals' ability to predict the future and manage risk of harm to children and young people. (2011, para. 1.38)

Munro seems to have added very little to Olive Stevenson's assertion in her minority report thirty-seven years before (DHSS, 1974): 'Those who worked in child care social work have learnt of the impossibility to predict the future' (para. 2.62). Thus, working with uncertainty appears to be a constant for children's services professionals, although policies in place to regulate their work tend to overlook this important aspect by advancing often very detailed procedures for cases which, in reality, are very difficult to categorize (e.g. risk of significant harm).

The Every Child Matters (ECM) policy is a landmark in the history of child protection in England, as it marks a shift from overreliance on control in the design of regulations for children's services professionals towards trust-based systems. Whereas both trust and control represent strategies of dealing with uncertainty and are used often simultaneously in the public sector (Edelenbos and Eshuis, 2009), we argue, in line with the extant literature on management control, that excessive dependence on the latter at the expense of the former leads to a mis-fit between the nature of the environment and the control systems in place. This is similar with how overreliance on the feedback type of control in an uncertain environment can lead to crises (e.g. Merchant, 1990). In the policy area of our interest, this mis-fit incubated crises such as the deaths of Maria Colwell and Victoria Climbié. The control systems in place before and after the introduction of ECM will be used to illustrate these claims.

Control Systems before ECM: Controlling for Uncertainty

The inquiry report into the death of Maria Colwell (DHSS, 1974) and the subsequent Children's Act 1975 mark the emergence of the modern child-protection system in England (Parton, 2004; Hudson, 2005). What that essentially entailed was detailed procedures to reduce the variety of potential cases of vulnerable children to categories of 'need' that would make these cases 'manageable'. Subsequently, procedures were established to guide professionals through what needed to be done with each of these 'need categories'. The system introduced was therefore rational and based on a top-down implementation model, and hence posed a very high degree of control over professionals' work (Hudson, 2005). Some authors (e.g. Parton, 2004) trailed the loss of professional autonomy in welfare back to this very moment, acknowledging how it was accompanied by a sense of mistrust.

This phenomenon developed even further under the New Right government in the 1980s and early 1990s. Indeed, subsequent policy developments strengthened the role of control in dealing with the complexity of the policy domain (Edelenbos and Eshuis, 2009). Through its radical series of reforms, the New Public Management (NPM) paradigm gave way to an audit explosion (Power, 1994), through which the principle of accountability in public sector work enhanced its measurable properties through strict performance regimes. Hence, in terms of trust and control, we witnessed a decisive step towards strengthened control at the expense of trust in professionals, with the introduction of a mass of standardized procedures in the 1970s which were refined and intensified in the 1980s.

Part of this rational process through which government attempted to control professionals, by reducing the complexity level in the policy domain, relied on clear causal relationships between risks to children's development and well-being and measures that should be monitored to mitigate these risks. A number of government-led and government-commissioned studies (e.g. DoH, 1995; Children and Young People's Unit, 2002) identified a series of risk factors to children (such as poor parenting or poor schooling) leading to poor outcomes in later life. On the basis of these links, a number of KPIs were designed by the government and implemented to monitor professional work undertaken to mitigate these alleged risk predictors. They were introduced to and used by different relevant government departments, such as the Department for Education and Skills, the Department of Health or the Home Office, to establish policy aims and to measure the achievement of these aims by welfare professionals. Although these KPIs referred mainly to the social services—traditionally, the lead local agency for child protection (Sanders, 1999), they gradually came to apply to a number of other agencies, which were responsible for some of the risks identified to children's development and who therefore had to cooperate, to a greater or lesser degree, with the social services. Examples of these agencies include the increasing involvement of the police authority in child-protection work and health professionals as the first point of contact in the diagnosis of children's health problems where there is suspicion of non-accidental injuries (Sanders, 1999).

Prior to the implementation of ECM in 2005 (Department for Education and Skills [DfES], 2004), the dominant paradigm in the policy area of children and families in England was of 'child protection'. What that meant was a deterministic and fire-fighting approach to risk mitigation by government agencies. Control played a significant role in the implementation of this paradigm, by intending to offer the government a way to manage the complexity of the policy domain essentially by standardizing procedures. The paradigm, however, changed in the aftermath of Victoria Climbié's death, which had revealed serious systemic problems in harmonizing quite inflexible control systems existent in different government departments and therefore in different local agencies, who nevertheless provided services to the same service users.

Control Systems under ECM: An Issue of Trust?

ECM came about at a time of high uncertainty and an unprecedented strong perception by the public of the existence of a 'risk society' (Beck, 1992). At the same time as this diffuse perception of uncertainty in the environment came an ever-wider acknowledgement that the object of public agencies' work ('crime reduction', 'regeneration', 'child protection', etc.) cannot be clearly delineated and therefore falls under the jurisdiction of inter-organizational and interprofessional alliances rather than of a single public agency. Prompted by the ECM policy programme (DfES, 2004), the Children Act (2004) made statutory the partnership between local agencies with stakes in safeguarding children in an attempt to foster creative solutions to complex problems. The role of such partnerships—the Local Safeguarding Children's Boards (LSCBs)—was to 'challenge' current professional and organizational practices (HM Government, 2006) by being 'the key statutory mechanism for agreeing how the relevant organisations in each local area will cooperate to safeguard and promote the welfare of children in that locality, and for ensuring the effectiveness of what they do' (HM Government, 2006, para. 3.2).

In practice, LSCBs provide the structure within which member agencies meet regularly (at least six times a year) to discuss their strategies and actions to promote the welfare of the children in the local area, potential threats and opportunities and any other issues relevant to the safeguarding children policy aims. LSCBs comprise representatives of the five key professions that interact in the area of child protection—social carers, teachers, nurses, doctors and police officers. Professionals of the statutory partners essentially share these five occupational fields (or, in some cases, a mix of these), with some exceptions represented by more generalist professions, such as administrators. Regular meetings are therefore typically attended by professionals from social services, education, health authorities, the Connexions Service (local providers of information and advice for young people), Child and Family Court Advisory Support Services, local probation boards, youth offending teams, local prisons and the police and, occasionally, when required by the agenda, by representatives of local voluntary and community-sector organizations. LSCB meeting agendas at 'Brempton' (anonymized name) typically include issues such as the pooled budget (mainly involving debates as to the individual contributions from the partners), initiatives for policies and guidance arising from local practice, reactions to national policies or guidance, news of relevant research being undertaken, sharing experiences and lessons from practice, training needs and, finally, organizational issues about the partnership itself (such as deciding on business plans, sharing protocols and performance indicators). The assumption is that issues from the ground are brought to the attention of the partnership by middle managers who act as organizational representatives expected to speak on behalf of their 'parent' agencies. These managers have the authority to commit organizational resources where appropriate, disseminate information back to their parent organizations and take action consistent with the decisions taken at the LSCB meeting.

Thus LSCBs represent feed-forward systems of control that appear to have been devised to tackle uncertainty at its grass roots. Indeed, LSCBs enable bottom-up strategy to emerge via intelligence gathering about the client group by those who are closest to it: local agencies. Examples of strategies emerging from the work of LSCB observed in this study included the following areas: anti-bullying, handling and restraint in schools, the children of prisoners and handling photographs of children in schools. These don't strike us as being 'key' strategies for children and families but rather as strategies aimed at certain categories of children for whom national legislation may have been deemed insufficient at the local level. Another LSCB role that is consistent with a feed-forward system of control is that, given their statutory role to monitor the activity of member agencies, LSCBs can 'predict' potential outputs of the work done for children and families at the local level and compare those with planned ones both locally and nationally. Corrective action can therefore be taken before any deviation occurs.

The presence of such a formal yet flexible organizational structure is quite an innovation in the public sector, as is the decentralization of significant levels of decision-making authority from the government to LSCBs. Such delegation of authority even extends to issues such as finance, membership and strategic planning. To illustrate, LSCBs rely on a pooled budget from all their members. The contribution made by each agency is determined by the local agencies themselves, as part of a negotiating process, taking into account factors such as the degree of involvement in children's matters and their priority in relation to the overall aims of the organization. Similarly, membership to the LSCB is left at the discretion of the board. LSCBs have a statutory duty to involve everyone in the local authority area with a stake in promoting children's welfare in the region, and whereas some partners are statutory, others are not; in such cases, the final decision about the inclusion of an agency in the LSCB is usually a matter of debate among board members. Strategic decisions in relation to the mission of the board or the range of issues that it is to tackle are also decided at the board level, in accordance with what is perceived to be needed in each local authority area. We argue that this type of formal yet dynamic partnership arrangement is not accidental. It is intended to encourage leadership and bottom-up decision-making in a context of recognized high uncertainty about societal problems and the ways to resolve them. This dynamism seems to be further encouraged by what Vancil and Buddrus (1979) have termed 'ambiguity by design', which is introduced in the process by an inherently 'blurred' legislative framework. It is within this framework that board members are allowed to make— presumably timelier and better informed—decisions outside the boundaries of traditional organizational hierarchy (see Dudau, 2009).

At its core, ECM argues for a more universal approach to children's needs than taken before in social policy: that is, away from targeted problems and towards early prevention and intervention (Williams, 2004). Underlying this more universal, preventative approach is the recognition of the increased uncertainty in this policy area and the difficulty to predict where the dangers may lie for this client group. Structured upon this fundamental premise, the principal change ECM brings is the redefinition of the problem and a shift from a mindset geared towards 'protecting' children to one focused on 'safeguarding'. 'Safeguarding children' is, in fact, a term gaining centrality in this policy field. It refers not only to critical cases (like 'child protection' does), but also to longer-term strategic preventive measures to protect children's safety (HM Government, 2006). The new terminology signals a paradigm change at the level of core organizational values (from *reacting* to *acting whilst preventing*) that, in turn, has triggered some significant practical implications—the overarching one being that, when prevention is at stake, more stakeholders can be identified than when the goal is just protection. Hence, the number of agencies involved in 'safeguarding children' is raised significantly in comparison to those involved in 'child protection'.

Since 2005, control of government over children's services professionals has not disappeared but rather it was complemented by trust-nurturing policy initiatives, including the use of partnerships as interactive, feed-forward systems of control and of 'grey' areas in legislation (such as the lack of detailed procedures regarding the pooled LSCB budget) that are left to the professionals to interpret. Thus, there appears to be a shift towards entrusting front-line professionals with more responsibility than ever before, as a result of repeated evidence to the complexity in the environment which has been found to be inaccurately captured by people who are remote from service provision.

CONCLUSION: TRUST AND CONTROL IN CHILDREN'S SERVICES

We have argued in this chapter that the pattern of change in the regulatory (control) systems in the past four decades in children's services closely follows change patterns in the policy environment. In the light of the evidence presented, we suggest that despite traditional overreliance on feedback systems of control in the public sector, a shift towards trusting professionals has become apparent. What has also been observed is that there is an ever-growing perception of uncertainty in the policy domain, given largely by inquiry reports with national resonance. We see these phenomena as being related and that the latter triggers the former. From a contingency theory perspective, the alleged shift of governance mode from an emphasis on control to one on trust is interpreted as an attempt to readdress the 'fit' between the uncertain environment (proved to be uncertain mainly by the findings of the inquiry reports) and the control system in place to facilitate decision-making.

Edelenbos and Eshuis (2009) claim that trust and control are two strategies for coping with complexity, one by reducing uncertainty to programmable tasks and the other by leaving discretion to front-line workers. Our findings support this and add empirical illustrations of how this occurs in practice—before 2005, we witness an excessive focus on control, with the balance being readdressed with the ECM implementation. We have also argued, in the light of the management-control literature, that the shift towards a trust-based mode of governance in the public sector is necessary. Failure to do so can result in a lack of fit between the assumption that the external environment is predictable and the reality that it is not. Ultimately this could lead to organizational crises, as raised by management-control theorists such as Merchant (1990) and exemplified in inquiry reports such as DHSS (1974) and Laming (2003).

While it may pose some issues to fundamental features of the public-sector ethos (such as accountability, legality and due processes), embracing uncertainty through trusting front-line managers and professionals to exercise some discretion in their work is shown to be the last resort in trying to prevent institutional inadequacies that allow for crises with child victims, as the opposite strategy of control appears to have failed repeatedly. The latest reports into the state of the field in children's services in England (Local Government Association, 2009; Laming, 2009; Munro, 2011), while part of an ongoing process, appear to support our findings when they tackle the issue of trust in professionals and the importance of not treating front-line professionals in children's services as administrators who execute tasks but rather as decision-makers who go around the daily challenge of managing uncertainty.

REFERENCES

Alvesson, M. and Lindkvist, L. (1993) Transaction Costs, Clans and Corporate Culture. *Journal of Management Studies*, 30, pp. 427–452.

Anthony, R. N. and Young, D. W. (2003) *Management Control in Non-Profit Organizations*. 7th ed. New York: McGraw-Hill/Irwin.

Beck, U. (1992) *Risk Society: Towards a New Modernity*. London: Sage.

Bijlsma-Frankema, K. and Costa, A. C. (2005) Understanding the Trust-Control Nexus. *International Sociology*, 20(3), pp. 259–282.

Children Act 1989. London: The Stationery Office.

Children Act 2004. London: The Stationery Office.

Children and Young People's Unit (2002) *Local Preventative Strategy: Interim Guidance for Local Authorities and Other Local Agencies (Statutory and Non-Statutory)*

Providing Services to Children and Young People. Available at: http://www.cypu. gov.uk/corporate/services/preventative.cfm.

Costa, A. C. and Bijlsma-Frankema, K. (2007) Trust and Control Inter-Relations: New Perspectives on the Trust-Control Nexus. *Group and Organization Management,* 32(4), pp. 392–406.

Department for Education and Skills (2004) *Every Child Matters: Next Steps.* London: HMSO.

Department of Health (1991) *Child Abuse: A Study of Inquiry Reports 1980–1989.* London: HMSO.

Department of Health (1995) *Child Protection: Messages from Research.* London: HMSO.

Department of Health and Social Security (1974) *Report of the Committee of Inquiry into the Care and Supervision Provided in Relation to Maria Colwell.* London: HMSO.

Dudau, A. (2009) Leadership in Public Sector Partnerships: A Case Study of Local Safe-guarding Children Boards. *Public Policy and Administration,* 24(4), pp. 399–415.

Edelenbos, J. and Eshuis, J. (2009) Dealing with Complexity through Trust and Control. In: Teisman, G. et al., eds. *Managing Complex Governance Systems: Dynamics, Self-Organisation and Coevolution in Public Investments.* London: Routledge, pp. 193–204.

Edwards, R. (1979). *Contested Terrain: The Transformation of the Workplace in the Twentieth Century.* New York: Basic Books.

Emmanuel, C. R., Otley, D. and Merchant, K. (1990) *Accounting for Management Control.* 2nd ed. London: International Thomson Business Press.

Freidson, E. (1984) The Changing Nature of Professional Control. *Annual Review of Sociology,* 10, pp. 1–20.

Hallett, C. and Stevenson, O. (1980) *Child Abuse: Aspects of Interprofessional Co-Operation.* London: George Allen and Unwin.

Harlow, E. and Shardlow, S. M. (2006) Safeguarding Children: Challenges to the Effective Operation of Core Groups. *Child and Family Social Work,* 11, pp. 65–72.

Hirst, M. K. (1983) Reliance on Accounting Performance Measures, Task Uncer-tainty, and Dysfunctional Behaviour: Some Extensions. *Journal of Accounting Research,* 21, pp. 596–605.

HM Government (2006) *Working Together to Safeguard Children: A Guide to Inter-Agency Working to Safeguard and Promote the Welfare of Children.* London: The Stationery Office.

HM Government (2010) *The Government's Response to Lord Laming: One Year On.* London: The Stationery Office.

Hood, C., James, O. and Scott, C. (2000) Regulation of Government: Has It Increased, Is It Increasing, Should It Be Diminished? *Public Administration,* 78(2), pp. 283–304.

Hudson, B. (2005) Information Sharing and Children's Services Reform in England: Can Legislation Change Practice? *Journal of Interprofessional Care,* 19(6), pp. 537–546.

Kloot, L. (1997) Organizational Learning and Management Control Systems: Respond-ing to Environmental Change. *Management Accounting Research,* 8, pp. 47–73.

Laming, Lord (2003) *The Victoria Climbié Inquiry: Report of an Inquiry by Lord Laming (Chairman) January 2003.* London: The Stationery Office.

——— (2009) *The Protection of Children in England: A Progress Report.* London: The Stationery Office.

Local Government Association (2009). *Respect and Protect: Respect, Recruitment and Retention in Children's Social Work.* London: LGA.

Merchant, K. A. (1990) The Effects of Financial Controls on Data Manipulation and Management Myopia. *Accounting, Organizations and Society,* 15, pp. 297–313.

Munro, E. (2011) *The Munro Review of Child Protection.* London: The Stationery Office.

Murray, M. A. (1975) Comparing Public and Private Management—an Exploratory Essay. *Public Administration Review*, 35, pp. 364–371.

Otley, D. T. (1994) Management Control in Contemporary Organizations: Towards a Wider Framework. *Management Accounting Research*, 5, pp. 289–299.

Otley, D. T. and Berry, A. J. (1980) Control, Organization and Accounting. *Accounting, Organizations and Society*, 5, pp. 231–244.

Parton, N. (1998) Risk, Advanced Liberalism and Child Welfare: The Need to Rediscover Uncertainty and Ambiguity. *British Journal of Social Work*, 28(1), pp. 5–27.

——— (2004) From Maria Colwell to Victoria Climbie: Reflections on Public Inquiries into Child Abuse a Generation Apart. *Child Abuse Review*, 13(2), pp. 80–94.

——— (2009) From Seebohm to *Think Family*: Reflections on 40 Years of Policy Change of Statutory Children's Social Work in England. *Child and Family Social Work*, 14(1), pp. 68–78.

Perrow, C. (1967) A Framework for Comparative Organisational Analysis. *American Sociological Review*, 32, pp. 194–208.

Power, M. (1994) *The Audit Explosion*. London: Demos.

Reder, P. and Duncan, S. (2004) Making the Most of the Victoria Climbie Inquiry Report. *Child Abuse Review*, 13(2), pp. 95–114.

Sanders, R. (1999) *The Management of Child Protection Services: Context and Change*. Aldershot: Ashgate Arena.

Simons, R. (1995) *Levers of Control: How Managers Use Innovative Control Systems to Drive Strategic Renewal*. Boston, MA: Harvard Business School Press.

Simpson, R. L. (1985) Social Control of Occupations and Work. *Annual Review of Sociology*, 11, pp. 415–436.

Smith, D. (1990) Beyond Contingency Planning: Towards a Model of Crisis Management. *Industrial Crisis Quarterly*, 4(4), pp. 263–275.

Tocher, K. (1976) Notes for Discussion on 'Control'. *Operational Research Quarterly*, 27(1), pp. 231–239.

Vancil, R. F. and Buddrus, L. E. (1979) *Decentralization, Managerial Ambiguity by Design: A Research Study and Report*. Homewood, IL: Dow Jones-Irwin.

Waterhouse, J. H. and Tiessen, P. (1978) A Contingency Framework for Management Accounting Systems Research. *Accounting, Organisations and Society*, 3, pp. 65–76.

Weber, M. (1971). Legitimate Authority and Bureaucracy. In Pugh, D. S., ed. *Organisation Theory: Selected Readings*. Harmondsworth: Penguin, pp. 3–15.

Weibel, A. (2007) Formal Control and Trustworthiness: Shall the Twain Never Meet? *Group and Organization Management*, 32(4), pp. 500–517.

Williams, F. (2004) What Matters Is What Works: Why Every Child Matters to New Labour. Commentary on the DfES Green Paper Every Child Matters. *Critical Social Policy*, 24(3), pp. 406–427.

13 Public Trust in Policing

Stephen Brookes and Peter Fahy

If 'policing' is a public good (Loader and Walker, 2001) and policing—as a public good—has public value (Moore, 1995), can we determine this value by reference to the levels of trust and confidence expressed by 'the community' in the police? This is the key question that this chapter seeks to explore. From earliest times, policing has been critical to communitarianism in balancing individual rights with social responsibilities and by shaping groups of individuals by aligning the values and culture of communities. In what was called the 'hue and cry', medieval communities had a joint responsibility to catch those who committed crimes against pain of sanction if they failed to do so. Modern-day community responsibilities are not so draconian but still favour neighbourhood-based policing and the balancing of individual and community responsibilities, which rely on trust and confidence in legitimizing policing. At the time of writing, the Policing and Social Responsibility Bill is making its way through Parliament, incorporating a number of changes that the government describes as 'a radical shift in power and control away from government back to people and communities' (Home Office, 2010, p. 2).

The chapter will briefly consider the meaning of trust and its correlates. It also explores the changing context of trust in policing, including trends and perceptions. We raise a number of definitional and fundamental questions: what is trust and what is confidence? Are they the same, similar or distinct? Is trust an innate personal perception based on an individual's propensity to give responsibility to another under conditions of consent or indeed coercion, based on the 'trustworthiness' of 'the other' whereas confidence is an institutional outcome of a range of trustworthy behaviours from those who represent the institution? And, finally, is legitimacy the instrumental conception of trust at the macro (governmental or national) level?

Policing has become more complex in the last two decades and, indeed, represents a very fast-moving context of reform post-2010. During these two decades, governments have introduced what is now commonly referred to as New Public Management (NPM), which includes a focus on objectives and targets with a consequential and relentless focus on a culture of compliance with procedures as opposed to the quality of policing services. Under both previous Conservative and Labour administrations, policing plans and objectives were put at the heart of the policing style with a focus on 'counting what can be *counted*' rather than 'counting what *counts*' (Albert Einstein), thus favouring NPM measures rather than public value. Mark Moore (1995) tells us that public value comprises the social goals of the public, the extent to which public-service institutions have the capacity and capability to deliver these social goals and whether these can be delivered in a way that secures trust and legitimacy. Public value should not be construed as representing the rather naïve view that it is simply about delivering what the public most values, but rather it is more about acknowledging what adds most value to the public sphere (Benington and Moore, 2010) from the perspective of many stakeholders.

Government in more recent years encouraged the creation of neighbourhood policing teams in all areas of England and Wales, aiming to close what was perceived to be a gap between the police and the public. Interestingly, the government police reform white paper argues, 'The police have become disconnected from the public they serve' (Home Office, 2010, p. 2). Although some staff associations disagree with this (Police Superintendents' Association of England and Wales [PSAEW], 2010), this may be part of the reason why trust in policing has been declining. Experience suggests that the focus still remained very much with the performance matrices rather than social goals. After much criticism, the previous Labour administration replaced a plethora of policing targets by a 'single measure' of trust and confidence in policing. This was supported by a policing pledge that outlined complex standards and targets. However, in the first few weeks of the Conservative–Liberal Democratic coalition government, even this single measure was swept aside, not without some criticism from policing practitioners.

The chapter considers the importance of trust and confidence in policing, the extent to which the policing style reflects public-value aims and measures and aligns these to the practice of policing. This section will be supported by a brief analysis of empirical research in a large police force that sought to identify the extent to which public value as an outcome was perceived as a legitimate aim of policing and the extent to which trust and confidence support or negate this.

The chapter concludes by looking to the future. The police service faces perhaps its greatest challenges in seeking to build the confidence of the public whilst facing very severe cuts. The rhetoric of public sector reform at the time of writing suggests that the aim is to remove inefficiencies and 'red tape' whilst prioritizing the front line; moving beyond rhetoric has real challenges, and the announced cuts to policing—equating to a quarter of the entire budget over four years—have the potential to strike at the very heart of trust and confidence. In addition to this, more recent announcements by the prime minister seek to 'open up' police leadership arguing that there 'are too few—and arguably too similar—candidates for the top jobs' (BBC, 2011b). More recently, the publication of the report of the Independent

Panel (Hillsborough Independent Panel, 2012) to the Hillsborough disaster in April 1989—in which ninety-six Liverpool supporters lost their lives—identified a number of serious failings in both the police response at the time and subsequent actions in relation to the evidence presented to previous inquiries and the media. This has called into question the role of trust and confidence in policing.

We will explore the challenges of maintaining and building trust and confidence in an age of austerity and consider whether this crisis can lead to opportunities.

THE IMPORTANCE OF TRUST AND CONFIDENCE IN POLICING

In this section, we examine both the meaning and importance of trust and confidence in policing, previous and current trends and the levels at which trust operates and in what ways. We also briefly consider the barriers and opportunities that either inhibit or support trust- and confidence-building on the arguments outlined in chapter one.

Trust sits at the heart of public value and mediates the relationships between citizens and public services; it is deeply embedded in our social relationships (Tilly, 2005). We will explore some of the characteristics of trust and confidence within the context of public value and the diverse stakeholders upon whom public value depends. Grimsley et al. (2006) have shown that there is a distinction to be made between trust in government and community institutions, so-called 'vertical trust', and trust in family, friends and neighbours, so-called 'horizontal trust' (Braithwaite and Levi, 1998).

Why are trust and confidence important? We distinguish the two terms and indeed consider confidence as the institutional reflection of innate trust at the individual level and trustworthiness at the level of interaction. Equally, we view legitimacy as the cumulative outcome of trusting relationships ranging from the individual through to the institutional level. Legitimacy thus defines and regulates policing as a public good (which was our original starting point) from the various viewpoints of the public-value stakeholders. This supports the contention that trust and confidence in the police is important—not only in and of itself but because higher levels of trust are linked to positive outcomes in terms of cooperation, respect and even compliance with the law (Hough et al., 2010; Tyler, 1990; Tyler and Huo, 2002). Tyler (2004) suggests that the degree to which people view the police as legitimate influences whether they comply with police orders or requests. People accept police decisions when they believe the police have acted fairly and openly with them (Tyler and Huo, 2002). At the other end of the scale, Jackson and Bradford (2010) argue that by demonstrating their trustworthiness to the public, the police can strengthen their social connection with citizens and thus encourage more active civic engagement in the domains of security and policing.

Given the current financial crisis, we could ask to what extent a dystopian approach to trust and confidence is taken; that is, where everything to do with policing is imagined to be as bad as it could be. Alternatively, we could ask whether utopian views are perceived: for example, against a depressing economic (or 'cold'[1]) climate, trust and confidence in public services, such as policing, will, at best, improve or remain unaffected or, at worst, be only marginally affected. In reality, the answer is likely to rest between these two extremes, but both trust and confidence are very sensitive to change.

Recent research suggests that trust and confidence in policing—whilst relatively high in comparison to other agencies within the criminal justice system (Roberts and Hough, 2005)—is less well perceived when compared with other public services (Fitzgerald et al., 2002) and is declining. More recently, the home secretary has stated that 'only just over half the public have confidence that the issues that matter locally are being dealt with' (Home Office, 2010, p. 2), although even this single measure of confidence was considered by some to be unreliable and has since been abandoned.

Governments instigate change through reform programmes, and the history of police reform is replete with statements that infer that the trust and confidence of the public in its police service is at its heart. In 1962, the Royal Commission on the Police reported a high level of trust when 'no less that 83 per cent of those interviewed professed great respect for the police' (HMSO, 1962, p. 103). The commission sought to continue these high levels in their recommendations for policing, which led to the structure of policing that remains today.

It seems that trust and confidence appears to have been declining since the 1960s and that this trend has been more marked since the 1980s (Hough, 2007), although others argue that the long-term decline has been apparent since its heyday in the 1950s—often referred to as the 'golden age of policing' (Reiner, 2000, p. 48). During this halcyon period, the 'police stood almost unchallenged as protectors of law and order and as moral representatives of both community and nation' (Bradford, 2011, p. 179).

From the 1970s onwards, the police became far more visible and political in the public eye, and there was an increasing level of debate and criticism around police activity and policies. The 1980s bore witness to public disorder not previously seen in modern times, and discussion in relation to alienation between the police and the socially marginalized or excluded became common. During this period, positive opinions of the police declined among the general population (Jansson, 2008). A number of reasons are offered for the apparent decline: growing antagonism between the police and marginal or excluded groups (Reiner, 2000); society was becoming more diverse, less deferent and the political environment was changing (Loader and Mulcahy, 2003). As Newburn (2003) argued, the police had been 'knocked off' their pedestal! However, although policing had to adapt to changes, Loader and Mulcahy (2003) argued that the changes triggered growing, or at least sustained, identification with the police, particularly among those who see it as a symbol of stability (as much as law and order) in an increasingly disorientating and apparently threatening world. Opinions differed, but the majority of commentators refer to a decline in confidence; indeed, some describe a serious decline in the legitimacy of the police (Jackson and Bradford, 2010). We define legitimacy—in the context of trust and confidence—as the instrumental form of trust but would not go as far as suggesting that legitimacy per se is compromised.

The current reform proposals appear to place strong emphasis on trust and confidence; they aim to transfer responsibility away from government through ensuring that frontline staff will be trusted to use their professionalism to get on with their jobs. It is driven by a new form of political accountability through the election of police and crime commissioners as a means of improving the legitimacy between the police and the citizens. It calls for:

> a strengthened bond between the police and local people . . . We want the public to be safe and feel safe, have a real say in how their streets are policed and be able to hold the police to account locally, having more opportunity to shape their own lives. We want them to trust the police and know that they will be there for them when they need them and to have confidence that the criminal justice system has ethics. (Home Office, 2010, p. 20)

Public cooperation, and not just passive consent, is also advocated with a recognition that dedicated officers will assist in building the trust of communities which will then encourage members of communities 'to come forward and help the police detect and enforce crimes, often very serious ones' (Home Office, 2010, p. 36).

In summary, trust can be viewed as a multifaceted concept ranging from individual to instrumental perceptions of trust in policing (resulting in legitimacy), and these appear to be declining. Determinants of trust in relation to policing have been the subject of wide-ranging research internationally and are related to socio-economic factors, experience of encounters and police procedures and processes in addition to public experience which do not involve direct encounters (Jackson and Sunshine, 2007). There have also been perceptions of corruption which can undermine the moral standing of the police, although some have argued that corruption does not always undermine perceptions (Tankebe, 2010). We have argued that trust is of critical importance to policing and is a major factor in shaping the desired policing style.

A QUESTION OF STYLE?

The police role differs from many other public services by the very nature of the risks, harms and threats that fall to our police service. Health services and local authorities, for example, manage risk, but the distinction for policing is by virtue of the authority and coercion that accompanies the role and the types of risks encountered. In relation to policing, there is a significant challenge in that policing is primarily a monopoly; one cannot opt out of public policing and into private policing as one could with education or health. It is thus a 'public good' without choice and therefore understanding levels of trust of the people, the community and the nation is essential, and creating and demonstrating public value in a way that secures trust and legitimacy must surely lie at the heart of government intentions for policing as a public good? 'We trust the police to do their job' was the statement of Teresa May, Home Secretary, on 9 May 2011 (BBC, 2011a).

Managing risk, harm and threats to society is a core element of policing. How this is led, managed and delivered may reflect determinants of trust briefly discussed in the earlier section. This applies whether it relates to tackling terrorism and serious and organized crime, the 'wicked issues' (Rittel and Webber, 1973) that blight local communities or individual encounters such as that between a patrolling officer and a passing member of the public. How the police respond to these risks, harms and threats will both shape and define the policing style, which, in turn, will help in determining levels of trust and confidence and, ultimately, legitimacy.

Trust exists at both the individual and collective level, and thus the importance of developing relationships based on trust cannot be ignored. Interpersonal behaviour is important to perceptions of trust at the individual level and particularly between those who deliver and receive the service (e.g. the police constable and a member of the public and their various interactions). In relation to police encounters, it is traditionally thought that those who have good experiences will feel positive about trust and confidence in policing, whereas those who have a bad experience will not. As Hilliard (2003) (quoted in Skogan, 2006) suggests, a person can have ten positive encounters with the police and that's good; but one negative encounter, and all the positives disappear. Skogan's research was interesting, if somewhat alarming, in exploring police-initiated and citizen-initiated contacts with police in Chicago. The findings indicated that the impact of having a bad experience is four to fourteen times greater than that of having a positive experience. Perceptions associated with having a good experience included being treated fairly and politely and receiving service that was prompt and helpful. Good service may therefore have little impact in improving trust and confidence, but poor experiences could be significantly detrimental. McCluskey (2003) found that people who were being asked to comply with instructions differed in their response; those who were observed receiving respectful treatment were twice as likely to comply, and those receiving disrespectful treatment were nearly twice as likely to rebel. Skogan's (2006, p. 119) somewhat worrying conclusion is that 'you can't win, you can just cut your losses. No matter what you do, it only counts when it goes against you.'

Other factors include 'well functioning public services' (Kaariainen, 2008, p. 157) in relation to the Finnish police and differences in ethnic background and police procedures. Tyler (2005) argues that public trust and confidence in the police is generally low, with minority-group members especially mistrustful of the police. His study used a sample of New Yorkers to examine, first, whether trust is related to public willingness to cooperate with the police. The results suggested that it is. In relation to police policies and practices, trust is most strongly influenced by public judgements about the fairness of the procedures that the police follow when exercising their authority. These process-based judgements appeared to be more influential than assessments of the effectiveness of police crime-control activities or judgements about the fairness of the police distribution of services.

Developing trust is not just important externally; it is equally important to develop trust within police organizations, which includes the practice of policing. The use of discretion is a reflection of internal trust. For example, the police are trusted and granted a great deal of discretion in identifying and interrogating suspects (Cihan and Wells, 2010, p. 349). However, some authors view discretion as a reflection of how officers view their own source of legitimation (i.e. the sense of legitimacy through power) (Tankebe, 2010), which determines why they follow their own internal rules (Tyler et al., 2007). More recently, some commentators suggest that discretion has been limited. Neyroud in giving evidence to the HASC (Home Affairs Select Committee [HASC], 2011, response to question 5) argued that officers need to be able to exhibit more discretion in the way that they carry out their duties.'

An interesting argument is suggested by Gilmour (2010, p. 1):

> If the police service is to be successful in offering trust, it may have to begin by democratizing trust—to include its own members in the pact that it seeks to create with the public it serves. This is perhaps the intense simplicity of trust; it begins in your own backyard.

In our discussion on the challenges facing police leaders, it was noted that at these times of financial instability, where front-line officers will be more prone to a lack of motivation, declining discretion is viewed as a lack of trust in individual officers. As we argue below, this was a strong feature in our research. Discretion can improve effectiveness, and, indeed, one could argue that by giving more discretion to front-line officers 'more with less' could be achieved, as the service can no longer afford to slavishly follow overbureaucratic procedures. Internal trust has other dimensions; for example, Nyhan (2000) argues that increasing interpersonal trust between managers and staff can increase productivity through improved participation in decision-making, feedback from and to employees and empowerment of employees. The same applies in relation to partnership-working leading to mutual trust and understanding (Wildridge et al., 2004).

At the collective level, collaboration through partnerships—an important element of public service delivery—is reliant on trust between collaborating organizations and the individual collaborating members (Huxham and

Vangen, 2005). This would include, for example, working with health authorities, local authorities and schools in tackling wider social problems. Both in individual and collective encounters, trust can be enhanced by sharing information, displaying and applying competence and demonstrating commitment and a willingness to act in a way that is expected by the truster of the trustee and in providing feedback; conversely, failure to display these trustworthy behaviours can so easily undermine trust. This is also important in new relationships or partnerships (at an individual or collective level) as shared networks on their own do not generate trust (Arino and de la Torre, 1998). Public value is just as much about working with other partners as it is in relation to working with government, and the inability to fulfil commitments will seriously impede trust. If partnerships are not able to secure agreements on public-service delivery and share information and knowledge openly and transparently, partners become critical and less trusting. Archer and Cameron (2008), in discussing the importance of collaborative leadership, suggest that there is a need to share control and trust a partner to deliver.

Collaboration has become an important element of policing during the period under review. This is premised on the view that policing is just too important to be left to the police; crime and disorder reduction partnerships and similar collaborations have become part of the fabric of policing, specifically, and community safety, more generally. As Bryson et al. (2006, p. 44) argue, 'Cross-sector collaboration is increasingly assumed to be both necessary and desirable as a strategy for addressing many of society's most difficult public challenges,' later stating that 'the role of prior relationships or existing networks is important because it is often through these networks that partners judge the trustworthiness of other partners and the legitimacy of key stakeholders' (p. 46). As argued in chapter one, this begins to distinguish between trust and trustworthiness

The leadership role is critical in setting the culture in 'doing the right things' (Brookes, 2010), and this applies to leadership at all levels. A good example of this is illustrated in Greater Manchester, where 'doing the right thing' is promoted as the way in which Greater Manchester Police (GMP) will meet increasing demands on policing, despite a landscape of fewer resources. Officers at all levels are encouraged to take a 'common-sense' approach to everyday problems and to challenge established policies where they have hindered rather than improved the service to the public (GMP, 2011). What people read or hear may be just as powerful as what they experience. There has been much debate on the impact of severe cuts, not just to policing, but also to all aspects of public services. In relation to policing, media attention—as is so often the case—has focused on what government describes as 'scaremongering' by police staff associations in painting dramatic pictures of what the impact of such cuts will have on day-to-day policing, generally, and in encouraging civil disorder and disobedience, more specifically; questions of trust and confidence will clearly be affected. The riots in English cities in 2011 perhaps suggest that this was more professional prediction rather than 'scaremongering', although one may also argue that the public saw that the police did not have capacity, and a small minority decided to capitalize on this.

In more recent years, the question of trust and confidence in policing, it is suggested, has become central to policy debates in policing (Bradford, 2011). Unsurprisingly, at a time when the perceptions of the public of its police are being rehearsed in the media almost on a routine basis, trust, confidence and legitimacy featured strongly during a high-level debate between police chiefs of the United States (US) and the United Kingdom (UK) in relation to leadership challenges at a police executive research forum in Philadelphia in the spring of 2011.[2]

Performance management clearly relies on data. O'Neill (2002) has much to say in this respect and suggests that government sets detailed performance targets for public bodies but are complacent about the perverse incentives they create.

The reform proposals suggest that data need to be recorded in a consistent way so that 'the public can have trust in statistics' (Home Office 2010, p. 3) and with information provided by the force. There is some recognition from the current government that previous governments' performance management regimes have had a detrimental impact on trust and confidence in policing by encouraging a target regime that overshadowed the real needs of policing and shifted the focus to outputs rather than to socially desirable outcomes (Heifetz, 1994).

PUBLIC VALUE AND POLICING

Given the fact that the government spends some £11 billion on policing each year, it would be rather naïve to suggest that the government should not seek to determine how the public receives a return on its investment in policing. This is particularly pertinent given that policing is the strongest example of a public good in which the consumer cannot be excluded from its influence, whether they pay for it or not through taxation, where there are no competitive rivals for its consumption and where policing as a public good cannot be rejected. Added to this is the almost exclusive call upon coercive powers, which draws into the debate the question of legitimacy.

The most recent attempt at measuring confidence in policing was incorporated within the British Crime Survey (BCS) but within an all-encompassing question that sought to measure public confidence in agencies' efforts to reduce crime and anti-social behaviour (ASB). The question 'How much would you agree or disagree that the police and local council are dealing with the anti-social behaviour and crime issues that matter in this area' was introduced as one of the national public-service-agreement shared targets.

A more qualitative approach to police performance management may be needed. In our section on the future of performance management, we suggest a more qualitative approach. This will encompass conversation or narratives, which are often missing in such performance regimes, particularly in relation to understanding the context of performance.

Having set the context of trust and confidence, we now briefly draw on research conducted within the GMP, a large metropolitan force. The aim of the field research was to identify the impact that performance regimes were having on the delivery of policing and to what extent respondents believed that a wider public-value focus (including trust and confidence) was either being delivered or was capable of being delivered and measured.

We explored the perceptions of police officers and support staff (at all levels) and voluntary and community groups in relation to the dichotomy in pursing the NPM-inspired performance regimes compared to a public-value strategic approach. The latter focuses on trust and confidence with the satisfaction of the service user at its heart. Indeed, given the earlier arguments, one could suggest that the more crucial indicator is the level of dissatisfaction with policing services.

The overall view was that there was a much stronger focus on 'performance' rather than 'public value' (Brookes, 2009). In terms of 'trust', it was suggested that there was a perceived loss of discretion as a direct result of the emphasis on targets with an accompanying lowering of empowerment in enabling the delivery of policing services in accord with local expectations in favour of a single-minded focus on what can be counted. In exploring trust further, the community expressed more trust in individual operational officers than in the institutional elements of policing. A number of public-value-related questions were included in one of the bimonthly surveys routinely undertaken as part of GMP's process of customer surveys. This was specifically included as part of this research project. The public was strongly of the view that police officers and Police Community Support Officers (PCSO) would treat the public with respect if you had to contact them for any reason, and the majority considered that the police would treat everyone fairly. 'Visibility' was clearly important, but fewer respondents expressed positive views that the police would be there when they were needed. Further questions were asked in relation to the reputation of the police and levels of confidence at different levels. The public considered that the force had a strong reputation in dealing with more serious issues and honesty but that a stronger reputation was needed in relation to involving and informing the public and taking action on publicly expressed needs. The public had more confidence in the individual officers in the local area more generally but was least confident in policing nationally or at the force level.

Similar views were expressed by chief officers when considering their own ability to deliver policing against a local mandate or strategy when faced with the centrally determined performance management regimes (PMRs).

In exploring trust-enhancing and trust-reducing behaviours, the 'enhancers' were seen to be associated with openness, transparency, visibility and responsiveness in the local delivery of policing. For example, 'while community representatives understand the real challenges that GMP officers face in relation to more serious and organized crime and counter terrorism their perception is more likely to be shaped through the agency of individual officers in terms of interest shown, feedback provided, accessibility and visibility and the ability to address local issues without constraint' (Brookes, 2009, p. 12). Understandably, the behaviours that tended to reduce trust were the opposite, with a strong sense of centralism rather than localism being viewed as a major factor.

THE FUTURE OF POLICING

The future of policing is about creating the right conditions in which trust and legitimacy can grow: 'Trust is a fragile plant. In the wrong growing conditions it will wither' (Murphy, 2001, p. 132).

In relation to these conditions, there is an emerging reality that the police will have fewer staff whilst facing the same or increased demand. Crucially, it is clearly the case that the present government does not view the police as a special case, as previous governments have. Whilst there have been some notable successes in building the trust and confidence of specific local communities through a long-term investment in neighbourhood policing, perceptions generally are declining, and there is an increasing sense of alienation. The notion of charters and targets has played its part in creating this alienation and has misled the public in relation to what can be realistically achieved.

If trust and confidence is to be at least maintained during this difficult time there will be a need to incentivize staff to produce higher quality (Dodd and Travis, 2011) whilst potentially receiving less money. This is a substantial leadership challenge and one that applies in both the UK and the US.[3] It is also about levering in greater public cooperation and encouraging citizens to look after themselves more rather than be viewed as passive receivers of policing services; with rights come responsibilities, and perhaps government should be 'nudging' citizens in this way.

In the UK, police budgets are facing a cut of over one-fifth over four years: this will impact the services' ability to increase trust in three ways; first, attempts at reform often focus on bureaucracy and efficiency. As O'Neill (2002, p. viii) argues, this can result in perverse incentives: 'we try to micromanage complex institutions from the centre, and wonder why we get over complex and inadequate rather than good and effective governance.'

Second, policing is about relationships, and these can be unpredictable and reliant on police encounters that may involve an element of coercion and may also differ between age groups or ethnicity. As Skogan (2006) described earlier, good service has little impact, but poor service has a significant impact on trust and confidence. Some have argued that the financial crisis itself may well lead to the type of civil disorder that led to an erosion of trust in the early 1980s (PSAEW, 2010) and add to, rather than reduce, alienation between the police and the public; and third, a change of policing style has to deal with the prevailing culture which can take a considerable amount of time to change, particularly when officers and staff are feeling vulnerable. A long-term investment in neighbourhood policing will counter this and may well rescue the declining levels of trust and confidence.

We have chosen to adopt Mark Moore's public value framework to assist us in exploring the context for improving trust and confidence in policing. In particular, we focus on Moore's elements of:

- the authorizing environment (as represented by central government reform)
- the public who receive policing services (represented by relationships)
- police staff who deliver the services (represented by the policing style)

This will allow us to consider the appropriate balance between the needs of government and the wider social goals expressed by the public and the capability and capacity of the police service and its partners to deliver services that maintain and build trust and legitimacy.

In terms of legitimacy, the authorizing environment refers to all the sources of authority with which the authorizers (regulators) act, which can be either formal or informal sources. Central government epitomizes the former and authorizes policing on the basis of laws and regulations, which establish the powers of the regulators who act on behalf of government. Informal sources of authority are wider influences, which shape the formal regulator's capacity to exercise power; interest groups, the media and political leaders at all levels and the public themselves.

The community is also an important stakeholder. Skolnick (1977) points to community-based policing as resting upon the cultivation of community trust and cooperation and describes this as the distinguishing feature of a new professionalization of policing. Within the current context of reform, the views and needs of local policing should be the driving force, rather than government priorities, and these local views need to count for more.

We build on the definition of public value described in the introduction by combining views in relation to leadership considered within the question of a policing style. Brookes and Grint (2010) argue that public value should represent the outcome of effective public leadership. We offer a critique of the extent to which policing is currently driven by public value (as opposed to performance management regimes) and the potential that exists to shift the focus of policing to public value and relate this to the most recent government reforms, including the recent election of Police and Crime Commissioners (PCCs). This is likely to represent a significant challenge, given the emerging financial climate, which is inevitably going to lead to less capacity. However, trust and confidence is at real risk in what is universally considered to be a major economic and resource crisis; but every crisis has the potential to lead to opportunities. We briefly consider the role of community and political leadership as well as the traditional approaches to both individual and organizational leadership (Brookes and Grint, 2010). In relation to community leadership, as Penny[4] argued, the public have a stake in what is going on with their police department, have a key role to play in relation to inputs and outputs of policing and to play a part in reversing the alienation that had occurred.

In looking to the future, we ask whether the police service needs to take more responsibility in how public value is understood, created and demonstrated. First, we agree with Myhill et al. (2011, p. 121), who state that single indicator measures can summarize global attitudes to an extent, but that 'they will always be somewhat crude and reductive.' The authors suggest that aggregated measures (i.e. scales or indices), which are constructed from multiple questions and include both instrumental and normative assessments of the police provide a more nuanced and accurate assessment of public trust in the police. This is also true but as we suggest earlier, there is a key role for more qualitatively based narrative assessments, which provide more contexts and will help in ensuring that responses are not subject to bias. Although much more difficult (and time consuming) to collect, the information that it provides would be much more meaningful to improvement processes and may assist in defining a role for the newly elected PCCs.

Traditionally, there has been a strong argument that the police service and the police authorities, which, hitherto, formed two parts of the tripartite structure of accountability for policing with the home secretary, was not effective, although Mawby and Wright (2005, p. 2) argue that these issues have lost some of their controversy in recent years as discussion surrounding accountability has shifted to a focus on performance and effectiveness. There is an interesting analogy between accountability and trust with the medical profession; from 1858 trust was placed in the medical profession to protect the public and to maintain quality (Salter, 1999) through a tripartite trust relationship between the public (civil society), the government (state) and the medical profession. As we know, policing has similarly been a party to a tripartite trust relationship between the public (through the police authority), the government (Home Office) and the police service, but it has been on a much less professional foundation. Failure in any area of the triangle has implications for all members and potential loss of political power and leverage. Smith (2005) argues that the medical professions systems of self-regulation are reliant on trust; however if a gap grows between the regulators and the public the whole triangle could collapse

The proposal of the coalition government to create elected police and crime commissioners has been described as a unique and bold move that will introduce democratic involvement in the leadership of policing. Gibbs argues that 'this distinctive British model will make police chiefs truly accountable for the first time and the public will notice the difference' (Gibbs, 2010). The Home Office describes this as a radical new programme of reform that will 'strengthen the bond between the police and the public' (Home Office, 2010,

p. 2). There is no doubt that the PCCs can play a key role in taking responsibility for assessing trust and confidence as a key indicator of both policing style and leadership (with both self-informing the other). However, the elections took place on 15 November 2012, and, as widely predicted, it was a record low turnout. The Electoral Commission launched an inquiry into the organization of the election and said that the poor turnout was a 'concern for everyone who cares about democracy' (Telegraph Newspapers 2012).

A question mark therefore hangs over the democratic mandate of the newly elected commissioners given that the turnout rate was between 10% and 20%. They can, however, play a key role in raising trust and confidence; the commissioners and the chief constables have the opportunity to develop a public-value approach to policing that is driven by trust and confidence as both quantitative and qualitative outcomes of policing and thus ensuring the legitimacy of policing. Public-value policing would thus define and prioritize the preferred policing style, influence the values and behaviours that are important in ensuring trust and provide the impetus for continuous improvement based on leadership at all levels, with public value as the outcome of effective and collective leadership. Further discussion in relation to the development of a public-value model is beyond the scope of this chapter, but we hope that we have sewn the seeds for a move in this direction.

Finally, police leaders (at all levels) should play the key role in shaping future policing policy and be held accountable for this, both to the authorizing environment but also within the service. Is there, as Neyroud (HASC, 2011) argues, a compelling case for policing to follow a self-regulated approach in a similar way to the General Medical Council in relation to medicine? If there is a compelling case, how important is trust and confidence to its purpose, and, in contrast, how will trust and confidence be enhanced? These are all important questions to raise and, as reform continues, to respond to.

CONCLUSION

This chapter has considered public trust in policing against a background of severe and unprecedented financial cuts, an apparent decline of trust and confidence in policing and more recent events such as the publication of the independent panel report on the Hillsborough disaster. It has given due consideration to those factors that are thought to either enhance or diminish trust. Based on international research that suggests that poor service or behaviour is significantly more likely to impact trust and confidence at, respectively, both individual and institutional levels, we suggest that the main emphasis should be given to the encouragement of a policing style that focuses on public-value outcomes rather than traditional performance measures and to reinstate discretion as a means of building trust internally and improving the motivation of officers.

Specific research within the police has illustrated that the police service has 'lost the art of discretion' due, primarily, to a single-minded focus on quantitative performance measures and an over-reliance on processes rather than quality of service. Reform of policing should take heed of Munro's report in relation to the reform of child protection services when she said, 'The problem is that previous reforms have not led to the expected improvements in frontline practice. Moreover, there is a substantial body of evidence indicating that past reforms are creating new, unforeseen complications' (Munro, 2010, p. 7). Part of this problem is a reactive rather than a proactive approach to reform and responding often to single critical incidents.

Against the context of a crisis in relation to the economic position and an apparent long-term decline in trust in the police, the chapter argues for an approach that seeks to identify and respond to opportunities and build on the current reform process that seeks to close the gap between the police and the public it serves. There is an opportunity for the newly elected police and crime commissioners to help in bridging this gap, although they face a significant challenge in relation to their electoral mandate given the very low turnout. We argue that improving active engagement between the police and the public can only be achieved if a public-value policing strategy which balances stakeholder needs and expectations with internal capacity and capability is adopted with measures of trust and confidence at its heart. Such a strategy should be developed through an increased level of professionalism, in which government places trust in the service in securing policing legitimacy as a public good and where its leaders at all levels both shape and deliver a policing style that is clearly driven by collective values and behaviours.

Trust and confidence may well remain a single measure of police legitimacy but only as a reflection of a policing culture that seeks to continuously improve the quality of service while significantly reducing or eliminating poor service or activity in the eyes of a more discerning public.

NOTES

1. A term originally used by Hutton (1992), in which national economic competition was perceived as likely to be intense, and in which the old props of inward investment and short-term capital flows were likely to grow less rapidly and be harder to attract; now a reality at the time of writing!
2. Leadership in Action: Police Executive Research Forum, held in May 2011, Philadelphia (attended by police chiefs in the US, including those from New Orleans, San Francisco and Philadelphia and the chief constable of Greater Manchester Police, UK).
3. The authors were present at a Police Executive Forum in Philadelphia attended by police chiefs from the US. Chiefs described how they were having to shed a third of their staff and, in some cases, that those who delivered police services at the front line were paid more than those who supervised them.
4. Police Executive Leadership Workshop, Philadelphia (see above).

REFERENCES

Archer, D. and Cameron, A. (2008) *Collaborative Leadership: How to Succeed in an Interconnected World*. Oxford: Butterworth Heinemann.

Arino, A. and de la Torre, J. (1998) Learning from Failure: Towards an Evolutionary Model of Collaborative Ventures. *Organization Science*, 9, pp. 306–325.

BBC (2011a) Police Reform, Interview of Teresa May, Home Secretary. BBC News, 9 May, 13.00.

——— (2011b) Police Chiefs in Job Recruitment Warning. BBC News, 21 July. Available at: http://www.bbc.co.uk/news/uk.

Benington, J. and Moore, M. (2010) *Public Value: Theory and Practice*. Basingstoke: Palgrave Macmillan.

Bradford, B. (2011) Convergence, Not Divergence? Trends and Trajectories in Public Contact and Confidence in the Police. *British Journal of Criminology*, 51, pp. 179–200.

Braithwaite, V. and Levi, M., eds. (1998) *Trust and Governance*. New York: Russell Sage Foundation.

Brookes, S. (2009) *Policing and Public Confidence: A Question of Trust*. Paper presented at the British Society of Criminology Conference, Cardiff, Wales, 29 June–1 July. Available at: http://manchester.academia.edu/StephenBrookes/Papers/1829413/Policing_and_public_confidence_A_question_of_trust.

——— (2010) Community Leadership: Telling the Story of Place. In: Brookes, S. and Grint, K., eds. *The New Public Leadership Challenge*. London: Palgrave Macmillan, pp. 150–165.

Brookes, S. and Grint, K., eds. (2010) *The New Public Leadership Challenge*. London: Palgrave Macmillan.

Bryson, J. M., Crosby, B. C. and Middleton Stone, M. (2006) The Design and Implementation of Cross-Sector Collaborations: Propositions from the Literature. *Public Administration Review*, 66(s1), pp. 44–55.

Cihan, A. and Wells, W. (2010) Citizen's Opinions about Police Discretion in Criminal Investigations. *Policing: An International Journal of Police Strategies & Management*, 34(2), pp. 347–362.

Dodd, V. and Travis, A. (2011) Police Chiefs: We Will Lose 28,000 Staff. *Guardian*, 7 March. Available at: Guardian.co.uk.

Fitzgerald, M. et al. (2002). *Policing for London*. Cullompton: Willan.

Gibbs, G. (2010) The Welcome Arrival of Elected Police and Crime Commissioners. *The Spectator*, 1 December. Available at: http://www.spectator.co.uk/coffeehouse/6508433/the-welcome-arrival-of-elected-police-and-crime-commissioners.thtml.

Gilmour, S (2010) The Confident Constable: A Search for the Intense Simplicity of Trust? *Policing*, 4(3), pp. 218–222.

Greater Manchester Police (2011) Doing the Right Thing. *Brief*, April. Available at: http://www.gmp.police.uk/mainsite/0/F672B63C8A4F3A848025788E004B817A/$file/Brief%20April%202011.pdf.

Grimsley, M., Meehan, A. and Gupta, K. (2006) *Evaluative Design of E-Government Projects: A Public Value Perspective*. In: Proceedings of the Twelfth Americas Conference on Information Systems, Acapulco, Mexico, 4–6 August.

Heifetz, R. (1994) *Leadership without Easy Answers*. Cambridge, MA: Harvard University Press.

Hilliard, T. (2003) Comments Delivered at the Third National Symposium on Racial Profiling, Center for Public Safety, Northwestern University, Evanston, IL, November.

Hillsborough Independent Panel (2012) Hillsborough: The Report of the Hillsborough Independent Panel, Return to an Address of the Honourable the House of Commons, 12 September.

HMSO (1962) Report on the Royal Commission on the Police, Cmnd 1728.

Home Affairs Select Committee (2011) *The New Landscape of Policing: Uncorrected Transcript of Oral Evidence*. To be published as HC 939-I House of Commons Oral Evidence Taken before the Home Affairs Committee, Tuesday, 26 April. Available at: http://www.publications.parliament.uk/pa/cm201011/cmselect/cmhaff/uc939-i/uc93901.htm.

Home Office (2010) *Policing in the 21st Century: Reconnecting Police and the People*. Cm. 7925. Norwich: The Stationery Office.

Hough, M. (2007) Policing, New Public Management and Legitimacy in Britain. In: Fagan, J. and Tyler, T., eds. *Legitimacy, Criminal Justice and the Law*. New York: Russell Sage Foundation, pp. 63–83.

Hough, M. et al. (2010) Procedural Justice, Trust and Institutional Legitimacy. *Policing: A Journal of Policy and Practice*, 4, pp. 203–210.

Hutton, W. (1992) Britain in a Cold Climate: The Economic Aims of Foreign Policy in the 1990s. *International Affairs*, 68(4), pp. 619–632.

Huxham, C. and Vangen, S. (2005) *Managing to Collaborate: The Theory and Practice of Collaborative Advantage*. Abingdon, UK: Routledge.

Jackson, J. and Bradford, B. (2010) What Is Trust and Confidence in the Police? *Policing*, 4(3), pp. 241–248.

Jackson, J. and Sunshine, J. (2007) Public Confidence in Policing: A Neo-Durkheim Perspective. *British Journal of Criminology*, 47, pp. 214–233.

Jansson, K. (2008) *British Crime Survey: Measuring Crime over 25 Years*. London: Home Office.

Kaariainen, J. (2008) Why Do the Finns Trust the Police? *Journal of Scandinavian Studies in Criminology and Crime Prevention*, 9, pp. 141–159.

Loader, I. and Mulcahy, A. (2003) *Policing and the Condition of England*. Oxford: Oxford University Press.

Loader, I. and Walker, N. (2001) Policing as a Public Good: Reconstituting the Connections between Policing and the State. *Theoretical Criminology*, 5(9) No. 1, pp. 9–35.

Mawby, R. and Wright, A. (2005) *Police Accountability in the United Kingdom*. Written for the Commonwealth Human Rights Initiative, January. Available at: http://www.humanrightsinitiative.org/programs/aj/police/res_mat/police_accountability_in_uk.pdf.

McCluskey, J. (2003) *Police Requests for Compliance: Coercive and Procedurally Just Tactics*. New York: LFB Scholarly.

Moore, M. (1995) *Creating Public Value: Strategic Management in Government*. Cambridge, MA: Harvard University Press.

Murphy, J. (2001) *The Lifebelt: The Definitive Guide to Managing Customer Reputation*. Sussex: Wiley.

Myhill, A. et al. (2011) It Depends What You Mean by 'Confident': Operationalizing Measures of Public Confidence and the Role of Performance Indicators. *Policing*, 5(2), pp. 114–124.

Newburn, T. (2003) Policing since 1945. In: Newburn, T., ed., *Handbook of Policing*. Cullompton: Willan, pp. 84–105.

Nyhan, R. (2000) Changing the Paradigm: Trust and Its Role in Public Sector Organisations. *American Review of Public Administration*, 30(1), pp. 87–109.

O'Neill, O. (2002) *A Question of Trust: The BBC Reith Lectures*. Cambridge: Cambridge University Press.

Police Superintendents' Association of England and Wales (PSAEW) (2010) Response of the PSAEW to the *Policing in the 21st Century: Reconnecting Police and the People, Home Office Consultation Paper*. Pangbourne: PSAEW.

Reiner, R. (2000) *The Politics of the Police*. 3rd ed. Oxford: Oxford University Press.

Rittel, H. and Webber, M. (1973) Dilemmas in a General Theory of Planning. *Policy Sciences*, 4, pp. 155–169.

Roberts, J. and Hough, M. (2005) *Understanding Public Attitudes to Criminal Justice.* Maidenhead: Open University Press.

Salter, B. (1999) Change in the Governance of Medicine: The Politics of Self-Regulation. *Policy and Politics*, 27(2), pp. 144–157.

Skogan, W. (2006) Asymmetry in the Impact of Encounters with Police. *Policing & Society*, 16(2), pp. 99–126

Skolnick, J. (1977) *Justice without Trial: Law Enforcement in a Democratic Society.* 2nd ed. New York: John Wiley & Sons.

Smith, P. (2005) Performance Measurement in Health Care: History, Challenges and Prospects. *Public Money and Management*, 25(4), pp. 213–220.

Tankebe, J. (2010) Public Confidence in the Police: Testing the Effects of Public Experiences of Police Corruption in Ghana. *British Journal of Criminology*, 50(2), pp. 296–319.

Telegraph Newspapers (2012) Electoral Commission to Investigate 'Comedy of Errors' PCC Vote, *The Telegraph*, 16 November. Available at: http://www.telegraph.co.uk/news/uknews/law-and-order/9683851/Electoral-Commission-to-investigate-comedy-of-errors-PCC-vote.html.

Tilly, C. (2005) *Trust and Rule.* New York: Cambridge University Press.

Tyler, T. (1990) *Why People Obey the Law.* New Haven, CT: Yale University Press.

Tyler, T. R. (2004) Enhancing Police Legitimacy. *Annals of the American Academy of Political & Social Science*, 593, pp. 84–99.

Tyler, T. R. (2005) Policing in Black and White: Ethnic Group Differences in Trust and Confidence in the Police. *Police Quarterly*, 8(3), pp. 322–334.

Tyler, T. R., Callahan, P. and Frost, J. (2007) Armed, and Dangerous(?): Can Self-Regulatory Approaches Shape Rule Adherence among Agents of Social Control. *Law and Society Review*, 41(2), pp. 457–492.

Tyler, T. R. and Huo, Y. J. (2002) *Trust in the Law.* New York: Russell Sage Foundation.

Wildridge, V. et al. (2004) How to Create Successful Partnerships—A Review of the Literature. *Health Information and Libraries Journal*, 21, pp. 3–19.

Part IV

Conclusion

14 Trust and Confidence in Government and Public Services

Emergent Themes

Stephen Brookes, Ann Mahon and Sue Llewellyn

This edited volume focuses on trust and confidence in government and public services. In this final chapter, we review some of the key themes emerging from the authors' contributions against three of the questions posed in the introduction. First, we asked, 'What is trust in government and public services?' which leads us to a series of related questions, such as: How is trust defined in the context of government and public services? When we speak of trust and trustworthiness, does this imply a relationship between individuals, institutions or both? Trust and confidence in government and public services are often used interchangeably, but is trust different from confidence and, if so, how?

'In what ways does trust matter for the business of government and the delivery of public services?' was our second question. Our evidence is that trust does matter, but in what ways is trust important? Trust and confidence are often associated with legitimacy, but what is the nature of the relationship between them in government and public services? Does trust confer legitimacy on government and public services?

Our third and final question was 'Do accountability, performance information and leadership influence trust and confidence in government and public services?' This question brings us into the domain of broader questions about how management systems and leadership behaviours might influence trust.

It was never our intention to limit our contributors to the questions posed. Indeed, we welcome the diversity of contributions, in both style and content, to this volume. Inevitably, therefore, some chapters have focused more on these questions than on others; some have explored them directly and systematically, others in a more emergent and discursive form. In returning to the questions posed, we seek here not to offer definitive answers or full, systematic coverage of the contributions to his book but rather to extract some of the key points, findings and debates made by our contributors using the three questions as a guide.

WHAT IS TRUST IN GOVERNMENT AND PUBLIC SERVICES?

Sonnenberg (1994, p. 14) argues that '"trust"—or a lack of it—is inherent in every action that we take and affects everything we do.' In this sense, trust is ubiquitous and underpinned by a belief that others will act beneficially rather than maliciously (Gambetta, 2000). For Newton, trust is 'the belief that others will not deliberately or knowingly do us harm, if they can avoid it, and will look after our interests, if this is possible' (Newton, 2007, p. 343). Klijn and Eshuis (this volume) express trust as a belief that others will refrain from opportunistic behaviour. Trust makes individuals vulnerable. Drawing on Rousseau's work, Dunn (this volume) defines trust as 'a psychological state comprising the intention to accept vulnerability based on positive expectations of the intentions or behaviours of another,' whilst Lynn (this volume) contends that 'others' can be individuals, organizations or institutions, and trust reflects the perceived reliability, legitimacy and honesty of any of these 'others'.

Manning and Guerrero (this volume) offer a specific definition. For them, trust in government implies that government and public officials are responsive, honest and competent, 'even in the absence of constant scrutiny' (Miller and Listhaug, 1990, p. 358). Lynn (this volume) argues that a breach of trust is a perceived failure by the object of trust to live up to or to fulfil expectations to which they have been assumed to be unconditionally committed. Trust in government and public services assumes both commitment to such principles as honesty and reliability and certain levels of competence. Trust also implies that constant scrutiny of competence and commitment is unwarranted or even redundant.

Trust does not exist in a vacuum. Expectations of trust depend on context and time. Giddens (2005) argues that in today's society the notion of trust has changed from 'passive trust' to 'active trust', where the latter is more systemic in continuously working at gaining trust rather than the former, which relied more upon traditional sources of belief. Here our contributors offered some interesting perspectives. Gunter and Hall (this volume) refer to O'Neill (2002, p. 76) in this context; she argues that well-placed trust is generated by active inquiry, such as asking questions, not blind acceptance of the status quo. Klijn and Eshuis (this volume) also depict trust as an active and dynamic process in the sense that trust is built through planned and unplanned interactions between various and, often, diverse actors in order to achieve minimum coordination. The active nature of trust can be compared to a living function; trust grows over time as interactions become more intense and enduring (Klijn and Eshuis). In his exploration of trust, Dunn (this volume) employs two lenses—the psychological contract and the trinitarian model, whereby the former implies a more passive role for individuals, the latter a more active and dynamic role for the institutions and entities involved in creating and sustaining or, indeed, diminishing trust in the military. Mahon (this volume) discusses the transitional nature of trust in healthcare relationships, where traditional passive and almost unquestioning trust in healthcare professionals is giving way to the development of more complex and dynamic trusting relationships between patients and professionals.

In recent times, trust has become inextricably linked to the notion of social capital. Putnam (2000, p. 19) says that social capital refers to 'connections among individuals—social networks and the norms of reciprocity and trustworthiness that arise from them.' Social capital is active in the sense that shared values, norms and expectations are generated through making these social connections. Newton (2007, p. 342) argues:

> There has been an explosion of interest in the concept [trust], partly because of evidence of its decline in western society, and partly because of the intense interest in theories of social capital. Social capital . . . has important implications for a large number of diverse phenomena important to government—from economic efficiency, educational attainment, and crime to longevity, good health, stable democracy and life satisfaction . . . and trust is the central core of social capital and the best single empirical indicator of it.

The question of who can garner most social capital is central to Dyke and Clifford's analysis (this volume) of the changing relationship between the United Kingdom's government and the BBC after the weapons of mass destruction issue. Murdock (this volume) claims that the third sector has greater social capital than the public sector, indicating that in public endeavours the third sector may sometimes be able to succeed where the public sector has failed. Trust across the interface between the public and third sectors may sometimes be confounded by a lack of shared values. Some common values are embedded in both sectors; others, Murdock argues, are more embedded in the third sector culture—sociability and loyalty are examples, whilst some actions consistent with charitable values may be at odds with public-service values.

The connections between trust, social capital and values raise the issue of 'trustworthiness'. Hardin (2006) points out that much of the contemporary debate about the value of trust would be better framed within the concept of 'trustworthiness'. How can trustworthiness and social capital be created? Pollitt and Chambers (this volume) argue that the creation of trust is a gradual process, where indications of trustworthiness are a foundation for trust-building. They draw on Lewicki and Bunker's (1996) three-fold classification of trust: calculus-based trust, where a conscious calculation takes place of the rewards and penalties of trusting or not trusting; knowledge-based trust, which is based on the provision of information and confidence in the reliability of that information; and identification-based trust, which rests on an assumption of shared goals or values. Gunter and Hall (this volume) take a similar approach, using Bottery's (2003, p. 249) four forms of trust hierarchy: calculative, i.e. whether someone can be trusted is a risk calculation; practice, i.e. 'repeated encounters' improve the calculation as people become better known to each other; role, i.e. the existence of professional occupations can speed up and enable the calculation because of expectations and knowledge about ethics and practices; and identificatory, i.e. when people work together over time then they become known to each other and so feel that they can trust.

Trust flourishes where there are shared values on honesty and competence supported by mutual knowledge gained through shared experiences (Barber, 1983; Coleman, 1988; Gillespie and Mann, 2004; Jones and George, 1998). Intuitively, it makes sense to speak of trust forming between people who know each other. However, it is also meaningful to speak of trust in institutions and organizations; for example, trust between clients and service providers can be established on the basis of expectations about roles, organizational ethics and known practices, particularly in the context of repeated encounters (Bottery, 2003).

The distinction between thick (or particularized) trust in individuals on the one hand and thin (or generalized) abstract trust in social groups and situations on the other is useful (Newton, 2007). He comments:

> I trust (or distrust) the people I know because I know them, and I trust (or distrust) my fellow countrymen not because I know them personally, but because I have first-hand knowledge of how society generally works: it is safe to walk this street, not that one; it is safe to walk through the park during the day, but not at night; it is safe to trust registered taxi drivers but not the pirate cabs. (2007, p. 344)

Delhey and Newton (2003, p. 94) sum up on such views: they say that understanding trust requires not only the study of individuals but also a 'top-down approach that focuses on the systemic or emergent properties of societies and their central institutions.'

Klijn and Eshuis point out that institutional rules can play a key, 'top-down' role in building trust because the rules that govern institutions structure the behaviour of the individuals within them. This, in turn, enhances the continuity and the predictability of behaviour, which can augment trust. Dyke and Clifford discuss how trust forms on the basis of institutional identity; for example, people may define themselves as 'Radio 4 listeners'. Such self-definitions may be an aspect of people's resistance to shifts in institutional identity. Murdock's perspective on the somewhat different institutional values inherent in the third and public sectors also emphasizes that values can be shared (or not) at the institutional as well as the individual level. Mahon's adoption of the social-ecology model suggests that trust in health practitioners and associated institutions can produce a generalized trust at the societal level, beyond the health system itself, in the form of social capital (Mahon, this volume).

Manning and Guerrero (this volume) argue that, in the absence of repeated interactions with a specific individual within an organization, trust in organizations and institutions seems to be more a question of expectations regarding honest and responsive behaviour than an assessment about the current objective level of service delivery. This may be because many of the complex issues facing public officials today are 'wicked problems' which lie, at least in the short term, beyond the competence of organizations, as opposed to 'tame' or 'critical' problems which can be solved (Grint, 2005).

The terms 'trust' and 'confidence' are sometimes conflated and often seen as interrelated. Dyke and Clifford state that trust forms the basis of confidence, so that to be confident in the media, we need to trust it. Yet trust and confidence can be distinct: 'Trust presupposes awareness of circumstances of risk, whereas confidence does not' (Giddens, 1990, p. 31). Quoting Luhmann, he continues, 'Confidence refers to a more or less taken-for-granted attitude that things will remain stable.' Therefore, a distinguishing feature between trust and confidence is that trust continues under circumstances of risk and uncertainty, whereas confidence may not. Concomitantly, Manning and Guerrero (this volume) describe trust as enabling individuals to take risks in their dealings with others. For Klijn and Eshuis also, trust is inextricably related to risk. Mahon (this volume) refers to Gilson's (2006) distinction between trust and confidence in healthcare relationships: whereas judgements about trust are associated with risk, vulnerability and uncertainty, judgements about confidence imply a situation where there is a degree of certainty and predictability. Adopting this distinction, it can be seen that, over time, trust may grow through demonstrations of trustworthiness, which in turn may provide the conditions for confidence. Such an argument is both consistent with Dyke and Clifford's assumption that trust forms the basis for confidence and also Manning and Guerrero's association of risk with trust and confidence with predictability. Another distinction that is sometimes drawn is that trust is more driven by perceptions of public integrity and shared values whilst confidence is engendered by good performances (Hardin, 2006, p. 69). These distinctions imply that the evidence required for forming judgements about trust and confidence may also be different, with trust drawing more on intuitive sources of information and confidence more on data and evidence.

In what ways does trust matter for the business of government and the delivery of public services?

> When Confucius was asked about government by his disciple, Tzu-kung, more than 2000 years ago, he said that three things are needed for government: weapons, food and trust. If a ruler can't hold on to all three, he should give up the weapons first and the food next. Trust should be guarded to the end: without trust we cannot stand. (Analects 12, p. 7, quoted in Tao, 2008, p. 83)

This wisdom from Confucius brings us to the notion of legitimacy and its reliance on trust. In its broadest sense, something is legitimate if it, in accord with norms, values, beliefs, practices and procedures, is deemed to be acceptable by a group (Zelditch, 1998). Conceptually, it is close to the concepts of trust and, particularly, confidence, discussed earlier. Both Warren (1999) and Evans (1996) suggest that institutional confidence comes close to the concept of legitimation. To function effectively, a government and public services must be perceived to be legitimate; they need to be regarded as keeping to the expectations and values of the society they serve. Seligman (1997, p. 14) argues that 'the very "legitimation" of modern societies is founded on the "trust" of authority and of governments as generalizations of trust on the primary interpersonal level.'

A key element of Lynn's argument (this volume) is that sustained low trust ultimately challenges government legitimacy. Lynn draws together work on the impact of distrust on the business of government. For example, without trust, governments may not be able 'to make binding decisions, commit resources to attain societal goals, and secure citizen compliance without coercion' (Chanley et al., 2000, p. 240). Yang and Holzer (2006, p. 114) add, 'Without trust, citizens are less likely to pay taxes and invest in the work of government.' In accordance with these observations, Pollitt and Chambers (this volume) suggest that trust and, therefore, legitimacy are not just outcomes of government actions but simultaneously inputs to what governments can hope to accomplish.

Klijn and Eshuis (this volume) point to several further reasons why trust is important for the business of government and the delivery of public services. First, trust can reduce transaction costs; trust might also cut the costs associated with contracts by reducing the level of detail and specification required. Second, trust may increase the probability that actors will invest financial and human resources in mutual relationships, creating an even stronger basis for cooperation. Third, trust stimulates learning and the exchange of knowledge and information. A fourth argument is that trust has the ability to stimulate innovation. The outcome of innovation processes is usually uncertain, and thus, to secure investment, trust is crucial.

Given that trust does matter to governments, what do they have to do to maintain it? Lynn draws attention to three clusters of factors that matter: first, the performance of the national economy; second, rising crime, infant mortality, divorce rates and other socio-cultural indicators; and, third, citizens' evaluations of political actors and institutions. Manning and Guerrero (this volume) conclude that government performance matters in policy areas that citizens view as important, and, therefore, the public's trust in government can be augmented, at least in the short term, by focusing on areas with the largest trust pay-off.

In terms of maintaining trust in public services, there are several contributions. For the police, Brookes and Fahy (this volume) argue that determinants of trust are: socio-economic factors, personal experience of encounters and police procedures; and public experiences which do not involve direct encounters. They also describe how perceptions of corruption undermine the moral standing of the police and, by implication, the police's role in public order. Public trust matters for policing, particularly for community policing and civic engagement. They cite research that shows trust is linked to cooperation with the police, respect for the police and, even, observation of the law.

In the context of healthcare relationships trust matters intrinsically and instrumentally (Mahon, this volume). Trust is intrinsically important in itself, for example, in terms of the ethical basis of relationships between patients and practitioners. Trust between different stakeholders in the health system is also instrumentally important in terms of the impact it might have on health outcomes, both directly and indirectly. A trusting relationship between doctors and managers may produce in more effective systems of performance management. A trusting relationship between doctors and patients may contribute to greater compliance, satisfaction and continuity of care.

DO ACCOUNTABILITY, PERFORMANCE INFORMATION AND LEADERSHIP INFLUENCE TRUST AND CONFIDENCE IN GOVERNMENT AND PUBLIC SERVICES?

Lynn (this volume) explicates Keele's theory of the links between government performance and public trust. Keele (2007) argues that these links are based on the idea of democratic representation, where citizens delegate the power to act in their name to elected officials in the expectation of certain levels of competence in key areas, such as the economy, the maintenance of peace, the control of crime and the avoidance of scandal. The implication is that if the government does not perform well in these crucial areas, trust is eroded.

Manning and Guerrero (this volume) make a similar point, concluding that performance matters in policy areas that citizens view as important and that trust can be improved in the short term by focusing on areas with the largest trust pay-off. They also investigated whether trust in government as a whole is an aggregative process of trust in government institutions weighted by the importance that citizens attribute to the role of these institutions and their actual visibility (i.e. the knowledge that citizens can have about their existence and performance). The authors empirically test a model of the determinants of trust in government;, determinants include previous levels of trust, perceived performance in recent times, visibility of the institution, homogeneous delivery and fair, nondiscriminatory service provision.

At the macro level, Lynn argues, performance-based trust will take time to emerge and could be misplaced if there are errors of perception concerning government performance. This raises the issue of the extent to which government and public services should strive to produce reliable performance information.

In the delivery of public services contributors were less convinced about the links between performance, accountability and trust. This is partly because they focus on the production of performance information and accountability mechanisms, although, as argued earlier, trust is defined by the absence of constant scrutiny. So the very presence of accountability mechanisms and the production of performance information could seem to imply low trust. The empirical basis of conclusions relating to performance, accountability and trust is, however, weak.

Gunter and Hall (this volume) think that the external regulation of schools through accountability and transparency can result in perverse outcomes, such as a 'league table' mentality that has little to do with actual pedagogic outcomes. Brookes and Fahy (this volume) make a similar point in relation to policing; they contend that accountability should focus on what counts for public value rather than what can easily be counted. Gunter and Hall draw on O'Neill (2002, p. 58) to argue that trust in the presence of accountability mechanisms can only be reconciled if the schools work towards a form of 'intelligent accountability'. With this form of accountability, Gunter and Hall consider that teachers' accounts should not be so much about achieving targets but should consist of narratives on pedagogic successes or failures which should be delivered to others who have the time and experience to assess these narratives and report on them.

Greasley (this volume) addresses the puzzle of how political-citizens, who rarely collect performance information and who generally have little interaction with local officials, form views about local government performance and trustworthiness. His empirical data show an association between performance and perceived council trustworthiness. Greasley supports the following: 'To restore public trust, public administrators must improve their performance and communicate it to citizens' (Yang and Holzer, 2006, p. 116). He suggests, however, that performance information should be simple and thus easily interpreted to enable citizens to form views. Pollitt and Chambers (this volume) make a sustained argument that the conditions under which performance information can be employed to increase trust are constrained by a range of factors, so that the relationship between the availability of performance data and judgements about trust are not straightforward. In healthcare, although there has been an emphasis on the publication of different performance indicators of individual and organizational performance within healthcare systems, there is little evidence about what impact specific performance indicators have on trust and confidence (Mahon, this volume).

Kezar (2004) argues that leadership, relationships and trust are more significant to good governance than structures and processes of accountability. This raises the issue of whether and how leadership can build trust in individuals and organizations, and is worthy of some further scrutiny here. Transformational leadership and shared values are thought to be the 'building blocks' of trust (Gillespie and Mann, 2004). Allert and Chatterjee (1997) contend that trust is built largely through organizational leaders who implement a 'culture of communication'. Rebuilding trust with effective communication is considered one of the five key leadership skills in turnaround strategies (O'Callaghan, 2010). Manning and Guerrero (this volume) pinpoint the leadership role of the mayor in implementing a comprehensive program which broke up clientelistic political cliques, raised tax revenues and improved basic public services; these reforms were accompanied by high-profile communication events to build citizens' trust so that the turnaround strategy could continue. The contributors on public services focused on relationships between trust and leadership, both within and between organizations and institutions. Brookes and Fahy (this volume) refer to the lack of trust that current politicians have in police leadership, as demonstrated by a government move to 'open up' entry to the top policing jobs. In contrast, Dudau and Kominis (this volume) present an increasing body of evidence suggesting a shift from government control towards greater trust in leadership strategies and partnerships between the several professional groups involved in delivering children's services. Klijn and Eshuis (this volume) suggest that partnerships encourage both leadership and bottom-up decision-making. They further argue that both are necessary in the context of the high uncertainty that characterizes many societal problems and the ways to resolve them. Gunter and Hall (this volume) provide a very different example of how 'leadership' and trust can interact. They draw attention to deceptions being enacted in schools. One concerns the motif of 'dispersed leadership'. They argue that this is largely illusory and, therefore, the rhetoric around 'dispersed leadership' is eroding trust between teachers and senior management in schools. Finally, Mahon (this volume) offers examples of how organizational systems and processes are not only shaped by external factors but may well, in turn, help to shape trust in healthcare institutions as well as in individual practitioners.

CONCLUDING COMMENTS

Attempts to define trust, drawing on the respective contributions to this volume, demonstrate that trust is a contested concept. It is of interest and importance to academics, practitioners, politicians and managers from diverse disciplines of inquiry and practice. Trust is a social construct, emerging and transforming in time and context. Trust is also an important mediating variable in terms of its role in enhancing or diminishing social value and social capital at a societal level and in conferring legitimacy both in government and in public services at an institutional level. In reviewing the contributions to this volume, we suggest that it is meaningful to distinguish between trust at different levels, individual, organizational and societal, and that a more generalized trust in institutions is as important as particularized trust in individuals. Given our contemporary reliance on organizations to meet our needs, generalized organizational and institutional trustworthiness can be regarded as equally, if not more, significant than specific interpersonal trust.

Trust matters for the business of government and the delivery of public services. It drives legitimacy, has intrinsic value and is instrumentally important. Distrust matters too. Lynn (this volume) is concerned about the detrimental effect of distrust on legitimacy at governmental level. Mahon's consideration of trust in healthcare relationships suggests that a level of distrust in individuals and in institutions may be both necessary and functional within a system. In this sense distrust also matters and not just because of the dysfunctional consequences for legitimacy. Given the association between risk and trust, it follows that a degree of distrust is a rational judgement. Placing trust where it is not warranted is risky. The dangers of being too trusting or not sufficiently distrusting can be seen in the wake of public inquiries and reports such as House of Commons (2012) and the Shipman Inquiry (2005). Government, politicians and public sector workers all do important work. At times, things go wrong. This may be due to systemic or individual failings and wrongdoings, or both. Writing in the *Independent* newspaper in the wake of the 2012 Hillsborough report, the barrister John Cooper notes the place of distrust in contemporary society: 'Hillsborough, Bloody Sunday and other disgraces would have been exposed far sooner had we shown a more mature capacity for disrespect and doubt,' and he concludes, 'It is time for Britain to be disrespectful, to put away our cosy 1950s subservience and trust for our "betters"' (Cooper, 2012).

Whilst, intuitively, trends towards greater accountability and transparency would seem to enhance trust and confidence, the arguments proposed in this volume—and the available empirical evidence—suggest a complex picture. The performance of government and public services is important, but how performance is assessed and judged is problematic. The unintended consequences of policy, perverse incentives and the absence of conditions required to meaningfully use performance data to make decisions sometimes confound a direct relationship between performance data and trust.

In the process of editing this volume, we have the opportunity to reflect on the contributions and to identify some emerging ideas to provide focus for future work on trust and confidence in government and public services. There are complex and reinforcing relationships relating to trust and confidence in government and public services. The potential to explore and to test these relationships empirically is enormous but underexploited. Furthermore, a wide range of disciplines, methods, perspectives and contexts have been covered in this volume. Again, the potential for empirical investigation across different settings and, indeed, different countries, employing methods that allow meaningful comparison over time, would offer a valuable contribution to the knowledge base. Finally, there are practical implications relating to the behaviours of politicians, local officials, professionals and managers and their values. There are also practical questions for management systems and processes, such as the nature and availability of performance data and how it is used by the public to make judgements. But, ultimately, developing, challenging and sustaining trust and confidence in government and public services is everyone's business—and everyone's responsibility.

REFERENCES

Allert, J. R. and Chatterjee, S. R. (1997) Corporate Communication and Trust in Leadership. *Corporate Communications: An International Journal*, 2(1), pp. 14–21.
Barber, B. (1983) *The Logic and Limits of Trust*. New Brunswick, NJ: Rutgers University Press.

Bottery, M. (2003) The Management and Mis-Management of Trust. *Educational Management and Administration*, 31(3), pp. 245–261.

Chanley, V. A., Rudolph, T. J. and Rahn, W. M. (2000) The Origins and Consequences of Public Trust in Government: A Time Series Analysis. *Public Opinion Quarterly*, 64(3), pp. 239–256.

Coleman, J. S. (1988) Social Capital in the Creation of Human Capital. *American Journal of Sociology*, 94, pp. 95–120.

Cooper, J. (2012) The Outcry over Hillsborough Won't Stop This Happening Again. *Independent*, 13 September. Available at: http://www.independent.co.uk/voices/comment/the-outcry-over-hillsborough-wont-stop-this-happening-again-8135657.html.

Delhey, J. and Newton, K. (2003) Who Trusts? The Origins of Social Trust in Seven Countries. *European Societies*, 5, pp. 93–137.

Evans, P. (1996) Government Action, Social Capital and Development: Reviewing the Evidence on Synergy. *World Development*, 24(6), pp. 1119–1132.

Gambetta, D. (2000) Mafia: The Price of Distrust. In: Gambetta, D., ed. *Trust: Making and Breaking Cooperative Relations*. Oxford: Department of Sociology, University of Oxford, pp. 158–175.

Giddens, A. (1990) *The Consequences of Modernity*. Cambridge: Polity Press.

——— (2005) *Modernity and Self Identity Revisited*. Paper presented at the ESRC Identities and Social Action Programme Launch, 14 April, Royal Society of Arts, London.

Gillespie, N. A. and Mann, L. (2004) Transformational Leadership and Shared Values: The Building Blocks of Trust. *Journal of Managerial Psychology*, 19(6), pp. 588–607.

Gilson, L. (2006) Trust in Health Care: Theoretical Perspectives and Research Needs. *Journal of Health Organization and Management*, 20(5), pp. 359–375.

Grint, K. (2005) Problems, Problems, Problems: The Social Construction of Leadership. *Human Relations*, 58(11), pp. 1467–1494.

Hardin, R. (2006) *Trust*. Cambridge: Polity Press.

House of Commons (2012) *Hillsborough: The Report of the Hillsborough Independent Panel*. HC 581. London: The Stationery Office. Available at: http://hillsborough.independent.gov.uk/repository/report/HIP_report.pdf.

Jones, G. R. and George, J. M. (1998) The Experience and Evolution of Trust: Implications for Cooperation and Teamwork. *Academy of Management Review*, 23(30), pp. 531–546.

Keele, L. (2007) Social Capital and the Dynamics of Trust in Government. *American Journal of Political Science*, 51(2), pp. 241–254.

Kezar, A. (2004) What Is More Important to Effective Governance: Relationships, Trust and Leadership, or Structures and Formal Processes? *New Directions for Higher Education*, 127, pp. 35–46.

Lewicki, R. and Bunker, B. (1996) Developing and Maintaining Trust in Work Relationships. In: Kramer, R. and Tyler, T., eds. *Trust in Organizations: Frontiers of Theory and Research*. Thousand Oaks, CA: Sage, pp. 114–139.

Miller, A. H. and Listhaug, O. (1990) Political Parties and Confidence in Government: A Comparison of Norway, Sweden and the United States. *British Journal of Political Science*, 20, pp. 357–386.

Newton, K. (2007) Social and Political Trust. In: Dalton, R. J. and Klingerman, H. D. *The Oxford Handbook of Political Behaviour*. Oxford: Oxford University Press, pp. 342–361.

O'Callaghan, S. (2010) *Turnaround Leadership: Making Decisions Rebuilding Trust and Delivering Results after a Crisis*. London: Kogan Page.

O'Neill, O. (2002) *A Question of Trust: The BBC Reith Lectures 2002*. Cambridge: Cambridge University Press.

Putnam, R. D. (2000) *Bowling Alone: The Collapse and Revival of American Community.* New York: Simon and Schuster.

Seligman, A. (1997) *The Problem of Trust.* Princeton, NJ: Princeton University Press.

Shipman Inquiry (2005) *Shipman: The Final Report.* Report of an independent private enquiry. Available at: http://www.shipman-inquiry.org.uk/reports.asp.

Sonnenberg, F. (1994) Ethics: Trust Me . . . Trust Me Not. *Journal of Business Strategy*, 15(1), pp. 14–17.

Tao, J. (2008) Confucian Trust, Market and Health Care Reforms. In: China: Bioethics, Trust, and the Challenge of the Market. Special issue, *Philosophy and Medicine*, 96, pp. 75–87.

Warren, M. E. (1999) Democratic Theory and Trust. In: Warren, M. E., ed. *Democracy and Trust.* Cambridge: Cambridge University Press, pp. 310–345.

Yang, K. and Holzer, M. (2006) The Performance-Trust Link: Implications for Performance Measurement. *Public Administration Review*, 66(1), pp. 114–126.

Zelditch, M. (1998) Theories of Legitimacy. In: Lost, J. T. and Major, B., eds. *The Psychology of Legitimacy.* Cambridge: Cambridge University Press, pp. 33–53.

Contributors

Naomi Chambers joined the University of Manchester in 1999 as senior fellow in healthcare management and was promoted to professor in 2008. Her teaching and research interests are diverse and include leadership in healthcare, doctors in management, primary care, commissioning practice, board governance, action learning for personal development and organizational change, and international comparisons in healthcare. In 2006–2007 she was appointed as director of executive education at Manchester Business School and was elected president for 2007–2010 of the European Health Management Association, which is based in Brussels and represents over 200 academic and service delivery bodies across thirty-five countries.

Nick Clifford is a senior fellow in public policy and management at Manchester Business School (MBS). He has previous experience in community work, local government and academic executive education. He currently directs MBS programmes for UK and international clients. His research interest is in managing and understanding public service organizational development and change.

Adina Dudau is lecturer in management at the University of Glasgow Adam Smith Business School. Her research focus is on public sector management, including crisis management, leadership, diversity and management control, mainly in the context of welfare partnerships. She published in international journals including *Management Accounting Research*, *Public Management Review* and *Public Policy and Administration*.

Mike Dunn is a senior lecturer in Cranfield University's School of Defence and Security, based at the Defence Academy of the UK. He lectures and researches within the broad field of defence and security sector management. He previously worked in the telecoms industry and was a senior manager at British Telecom (BT) before moving to Cranfield University to bring a managerial perspective to the study of the UK's defence sector. His primary research interest is the impact of New Public Management

(NPM) on the defence and security sectors. In addition, he is currently adjunct professor to the Baltic Defence College at Tarttu, Estonia.

Greg Dyke is a British media executive, journalist and broadcaster. His career in the media began in print journalism but led on to creative programme production, and he quickly rose to prominence at TV-am. He was subsequently chief executive at London Weekend Television and Pearson Television and chairman of Channel 5. He was appointed director-general of the BBC in 2000 but resigned four years later after the publication of the Hutton Inquiry into the death of David Kelly, which criticised the BBC. He has a wide range of business interests including television, theatre, hotels and football (he was formally a director at Manchester United and is currently chair of Brentford Football Club); he is chair of the British Film Institute, and he is also chancellor of the University of York and has been awarded a number of honorary doctorates from British universities.

Jasper Eshuis is an assistant professor in public administration at Erasmus University Rotterdam. His research interests include co-production between governmental organizations, citizens and private parties. His current research focuses on branding and marketing in the public sector. He has published in journals such as *Administration and Society*, *Public Management Review* and *Urban Studies*. Recently he wrote together with Erik Hans Klijn the book *Branding in Governance and Public Management* (Routledge).

Peter Fahy has been chief constable of Greater Manchester since September 2008. He previously served in four other forces and was chief constable of Cheshire for five years. He holds national responsibility within the Association of Chief Police Officers for workforce development and is director of the Strategic Command Course at the National Police Leadership College Bramshill. He is a strong promoter of police and wider public sector reform and has been a school governor for twenty-five years. He grew up in the East End of London and holds a degree in French and Spanish from Hull University and a master's from the University of East Anglia. He was awarded the Queen's Police Medal in 2004 and received a Knighthood in the Queen's Birthday Honours 2012. He is married with four children.

Stephen Greasley is a lecturer in comparative public policy at the University of East Anglia. His research focuses on political leadership in local government, outsourcing of public services and management functions and the operation of arm's-length bodies.

Alejandro Guerrero is an evaluation specialist at the Office of Evaluation and Oversight, Inter-American Development Bank. He is a political economy researcher whose work has focused upon public management, institutional performance and trust, and the political economy of policy reform. His research has been supported by organizations including the Juan March Institute for Social Research, Yale University and the World Bank. Previous to the Inter-American Development Bank, he served for five years at the World Bank, as public sector management specialist, contributing to strengthen government performance in Latin America and the Caribbean.

Helen Gunter is professor of educational policy and director of research in the School of Education, University of Manchester, UK, and is an academician of the Academy of Social Sciences. She co-edits the *Journal of Educational Administration and History*. Her work focuses on education policy and knowledge production in the field of school leadership, where she has used Bourdieu's thinking tools to explain the configuration and development of the field. Her most recent book is *Leadership and the Reform of Education*, published by Policy Press (2012).

David Hall is a senior lecturer in education at the School of Education, University of Manchester. He is an education policy researcher whose work has focused upon professional identities, leadership and educational disadvantage. His research has been funded by organizations including the Joseph Rowntree Foundation, the Department for Education, the Training and Development Agency for Schools and the Department for International Development. He has recently completed, as principal researcher, a programme of research funded by the Economic and Social Research Council (ESRC). He has published in a range of journals, including the *Journal of Education Policy*, *Oxford Review of Education* and *Educational Review*.

Erik Hans Klijn is professor at the Department of Public Administration at Erasmus University Rotterdam. His research and teaching activities focus on complex decision-making and management in networks, institutional design and public-private partnerships. He is president of the International Research Society for Public Management (IRSPM). He has published extensively in international journals like *JPART*, *Administration and Society*, *Public Administration*, *PAR* and *PMR*. Recently, he wrote, together with Jasper Eshuis, the book *Branding in Governance and Public Management* (Routledge, 2012).

Georgios Kominis is lecturer in management accounting and control at the University of Glasgow Adam Smith Business School. He has a particular interest in the way control systems and personal values interact to determine human behaviour in organizations. His research focus is on the design of incentive schemes and reward systems for middle managers. His recent publications include articles in *Management Accounting Research* and *Qualitative Research in Accounting and Management*. He is a member of the Management Control Association.

Laurence E. Lynn, Jr. is Sid Richardson Research Professor at the Lyndon B. Johnson School of Public Affairs at the University of Texas at Austin, and the Sydney Stein Jr. Professor of Public Management Emeritus at the University of Chicago. His previous faculty affiliations have included the John F. Kennedy School of Government at Harvard University, the Irving B. Harris School Graduate School of Public Policy Studies at the University of Chicago, the Manchester (UK) Business School, the George Bush School of Government and Public Affairs at Texas A&M University and the Graduate School of Business at Stanford University. He spent nearly a decade in senior policy-making positions in the US federal government. His most recent books are *Public Management: Old and New, Madison's Managers: Public Administration and the Constitution* (with Anthony M. Bertelli) and a textbook, *Public Management: A Three Dimensional Approach* (with Carolyn J. Hill.)

Nick Manning is one of the leaders of the Public Sector Performance Global Expert Team of the World Bank and an adviser in the Public Sector and Governance Group. He was previously sector manager for the Public Sector and Governance Unit in the World Bank for the Latin American and Caribbean Region; head of the Public Sector Management and Performance Division at the OECD; and lead public sector management specialist for South Asia in the World Bank. He has also held positions as adviser on public management to the Commonwealth Secretariat and senior technical adviser to UNDP in Lebanon.

Nick began his public sector career in local government in the UK and, before moving to international advisory work, was head of strategic planning for an inner London borough. He is also a visiting professor at the Herbert Simon Institute for Public Policy, Administration and Management, adviser to the Commonwealth Association for Public Administration and Management and member of the editorial board of the *Public Management Review*.

Alex Murdock is professor of not for profit management and leadership and head of the Centre for Government and Charity Management at London South Bank University. He is interested in the intersection of the public, private and third sectors. He has published on stakeholders, partnerships, public management and managerial effectiveness (including two books). His recent research has focused on aspects of trust and solidarity in social enterprise and the implications of public service delivery by the third sector.

Christopher Pollitt is emeritus professor at the Public Management Institute, Katholieke Universiteit Leuven (formerly research professor, 2006–2011).

Previously he held professorships at Erasmus University Rotterdam and Brunel (UK). He is the author of more than a dozen scholarly books and over sixty articles in refereed scientific journals. He has undertaken advisory work for, inter alia, the OECD, the World Bank, the European Commission and five national governments. In 2004 he won the Hans Sigrist Stiftung international prize for 'outstanding scientific research in the field of public governance'.

Index

Printed in the United States
by Baker & Taylor Publisher Services